# ASIA-PACIFIC TRADE AND INVESTMENT REPORT 2015

## *Supporting Participation in Value Chains*

UNITED NATIONS
ESCAP
Economic and Social Commission for Asia and the Pacific

# ASIA-PACIFIC TRADE AND INVESTMENT REPORT 2015

## *Supporting Participation in Value Chains*

United Nations publication
Sales No. E.15.II.F.15


ISBN: 978-92-1-120701-9
e-ISBN: 978-92-1-057632-1
ISSN 2221-500X
ST/ESCAP/2731

Reference to dollars ($) are to United States dollars unless otherwise stated.

A space is used to distinguish thousands and millions.

The designations employed and the presentation of the material in this publication do not imply the expression of any opinion whatsoever on the part of the Secretariat of the United Nations concerning the legal status of any country, territory, city or area, or of its authorities, or concerning the delimitation of its frontiers or boundaries.

Where the designation "country or area" appears, it covers countries, territories, cities or areas.

Bibliographical and other references have, wherever possible, been verified. The United Nations bears no responsibility for the availability or functioning of URLs.

The views expressed in this publication are those of the authors or case study contributors and do not necessarily reflect the views of the United Nations.

The opinions, figures and estimates set forth in this publication are the responsibility of the authors and contributors, and should not necessarily be considered as reflecting the views or carrying the endorsement of the United Nations. Any errors are the responsibility of the authors.

Mention of firm names and commercial products does not imply the endorsement of the United Nations.

The Asia-Pacific Trade and Investment Report and supporting online documents are the sole responsibility of the ESCAP secretariat. Any opinions or estimates reflected herein do not necessarily reflect the opinions or views of Members and Associate Members of the Economic and Social Commission for Asia and the Pacific.

# FOREWORD

This year's Asia-Pacific Trade and Investment Report highlights the importance of reviving trade and investment flows at a time when the United Nations Member States have just endorsed the centrality of trade and investment as critical means of implementation for the new Sustainable Development Goals (SDGs) and the related historic, universal and people-centric agenda. Advancing the diagnostics and analyses of trade and investment trends, the report offers perspectives on the challenges and opportunities facing trade and investment flows in Asia and the Pacific against the backdrop of the lingering effects of the 2008 global crisis.

The Asia-Pacific region stands out for its significant and sustained achievements in leveraging trade and investment flows – the region still accounts for 40 per cent of global exports and imports. Of concern, however, is the slowdown and volatility of these flows since 2008, which does not augur well as we embark on the process of implementing the SDGs, which call for strong, diversified and well-balanced growth propelled by both external and domestic demand. Although Asia and the Pacific exports grew by 1.6 per cent in 2014 – better than global trade figures – they remain well below pre-crisis levels and have been primarily driven by China, which is now also exporting and importing less within the region. Given the integration of regional economies, the slowdown in China and its commodity demand has caused a ripple effect, although the rebalancing of its growth now offers new opportunities for the country as well as the wider region.

Weak external demand, particularly in the economies of the European Union (the region's chief external trade partner), as well as low commodity demand, continues to have negative consequences for merchandise trade growth. The outlook for the services sectors linked to trade in goods is also grim, but prospects are better for other services sectors, such as tourism, where growth remains strong. The Asia-Pacific region also remains relatively attractive as a destination for foreign direct investment (FDI): China surpassed the United States in 2014 to become the single largest FDI recipient globally.

The changing dynamics in the global economy call for a renewed effort to enhance the prospects of export-led growth, both of merchandise trade and in commercial services. Looking ahead, to mitigate the consequences of considerable uncertainty as the global economy undergoes a series of adjustments, a more aggressive and holistic strategy is needed to regain at least the pre-crisis momentum in the region.

The rise of global value chains (GVCs) as major vehicles for trade offers new opportunities for the region if effectively exploited. Harnessing GVCs depends, however, on how closely and well the region can work with the private sector to tap financial systems, government services and logistics, flows of knowledge and skills development. Together these form the complex adaptive systems which facilitate trade by transcending geographical and legal jurisdictions. In many respects, GVC-based trade requires shifts in the economic, political and social relationships between nations, along with changes in existing paradigms. This report analyses the options for developing countries in the Asia-Pacific region to better integrate into GVCs, with supportive structural changes in the context of stagnant growth in global and regional trade and investment flows.

The report also highlights the policies and measures that developing countries can adopt to support direct entry into – or indirect linkages to – GVCs and to ensure that participation in GVCs contributes beneficially to sustainable development. These include measures to facilitate upgrading within GVCs to allow for a move away from an exclusive focus on "low-skilled, low-cost" to high-value production. The report shows that GVCs are often strongly regional in nature, which, for the countries of Asia and the Pacific, offers opportunities for deeper integration within the region by connecting producers in the developed and developing economies. There is still no clear evidence, however, regarding the role of preferential trade agreements in the expansion of GVCs. A number of regional value chains have evolved between economies with no trade agreements. However, empirical and anecdotal evidence confirms the utility of agreements if they include deep and comprehensive liberalization and facilitation policies.

Particular groups of countries face common challenges. For instance, many low-income countries are effectively excluded from GVCs: 90 per cent of GVC trade occurs in just 10 regional economies. The report estimates the strength of various policy variables with bearing on the ability of countries to enter and prosper in GVCs. This analysis confirms that the liberalization of trade policies allows more efficient sourcing of inputs, for both goods and services, and is a precondition for GVC participation. Likewise, country openness to FDI, which is dependent on the investment climate and the ability of business to acquire and diffuse technologies, is critical. There are also other paths, beyond FDI, which facilitate the transfer of technology necessary for both participation in GVCs and upgrading, including the licensing and direct purchase of technology. This reflects the importance of import and intellectual property regimes.

GVC participation also entails a number of potential downsides, which require careful attention, including greater dependence on external economies and associated vulnerability to shocks. Governments need to be mindful of these risks, in order to ensure that GVC participation is accompanied by policies for managing exposure to external shocks and preventing exacerbated inequalities or environmental degradation.

It is good news that the ratification of the World Trade Organization (WTO) Trade Facilitation Agreement is proceeding well, and more than 50 members have now formally accepted the Agreement. Moreover, many countries in the Asia-Pacific region are moving ahead with implementation of trade facilitation measures even before ratification. These changes will help to reduce regional trade costs, but much more still needs to be done, especially in landlocked countries. A regional agreement on paperless trade would represent a substantial breakthrough.

The positive impacts from trade facilitation agreements are, however, being partially offset by additional obstacles to market access. Non-tariff measures (NTMs) are often less visible than tariffs, but their effects on trade can be equally detrimental. Of greater concern, least developed countries often face significant NTMs on their export products. This needs to be addressed if we are to reach the goal of doubling the least developed countries' share of global exports by 2020.

Significant pessimism surrounds the ability of multilateral trade liberalization through the WTO Doha round to tackle the remaining barriers. Thus businesses and policymakers have been anxiously awaiting the outcomes of progress in several major trade negotiations, including the "mega-regionals" such as the Trans-Pacific Partnership Agreement (TPP), the Regional Comprehensive Economic Partnership (RCEP) and the Eurasian Economic Union. In early October, a deal was clinched on the TPP with 12 economies finally reaching an agreement on several "next generation" issues (including competition, investment and dispute settlement), but also on some old issues (such as tariffs on car parts or dairy products). Similarly, the establishment of the ASEAN Economic Community and the completion of the RCEP negotiations will add more opportunities, which, if seized, can help drive the next stage of regional economic integration. The ESCAP secretariat is helping member States to pursue alternative paths towards deeper Asia-Pacific integration by utilizing current trade and investment agreements. With the region's trade in a period of flux, it is our hope that this report will lessen the likelihood of neglect of key issues by raising awareness and deepening understanding. Trade and investment have been identified as key channels for achieving the 2030 Agenda for Sustainable Development. Thus, keeping these essential elements moving forward is a priority regional objective.

**Shamshad Akhtar**
Under-Secretary-General of the United Nations and
Executive Secretary, United Nations Economic and
Social Commission for Asia and the Pacific

November 2015

# ACKNOWLEDGEMENTS

The Asia-Pacific Trade and Investment Report (APTIR) 2015 was prepared under the substantive direction and guidance of Susan F. Stone, Director, Trade and Investment Division (TID) of the Economic and Social Commission for Asia and the Pacific (ESCAP). The core team of authors led by Mia Mikić, who was also the substantive editor, comprised TID staff (in alphabetical order) Maame Agyeben (chapter 4), Witada Anukoonwattaka (chapters 1, 2 ,7 and 8), Yann Duval (chapter 4), Adam Heal (chapter 5), Soo Hyun Kim (chapter 3), Marc Proksch (chapter 3) and Rajan Sudesh Ratna (chapter 6), research assistants and consultants, Fiona Jing Huang, Aman Saggu, Marco Scagliusi, Ben Shepherd and Chorthip Utoktham who contributed towards chapters 1, 6, 7, 8 and 9. Many researchers, research assistants from the Asia-Pacific Research and Training Network on Trade (ARTNeT) as well as ESCAP interns contributed to the report through the compilation and tabulation of statistical data, the preparation of country and subregional trade briefs as well as undertaking background research and referencing. These were (also in alphabetical order): Noelan Arbis, Khanindra Ch. Das, Pietro Guzzetti, Uijin Im, Miso Kim, Giulia Olivero, Giovanni Palmioli, Luca Parisotto, Niccoló Patrone, Mari Tomova, Pooja Tripathi, Yuexi Wang, Kefang Yao and Yifan Ye.

Eric Hermouet and Krisana Boonpriroje of the ESCAP Statistics Division and Panjai Limchupong of TID collaborated on the preparation of the trade performance indicator tables available on the ESCAP online statistical database. Giovanni Palmioli, guided by Masato Abe, designed and implemented a survey of firms in the region related to their participation in trade. The findings of the survey are available on a dedicated APTIR webpage. Aman Saggu, Luca Parisotto and Chorthip Utoktham, guided by Witada Anukoonwattaka and Adam Heal, produced the country trade factsheets.

A number of collaborators and researchers from ARTNeT institutional members as well as interns assisted in translating the country briefs into various languages for more effective dissemination. They included Sven Callebaut, Rina Oktaviani, Miso Kim, Phouphet Kyophilavong, Puspa Sharma, Enkhbold Voroshilov, Vu Hoang Dat, Jeevika Weerahewa and Mohammad Yunus. Special thanks go to Anna Ivanova and Kefang Yao for translating the executive summary of APTIR into the Russian and Chinese languages, respectively.

Valuable comments and suggestions that helped shape the report were received from Ravi Ratnayake, former Director of TID, and the participants of the Expert Group Meeting on "Global Value Chains, Regional Integration and Sustainable Development: Asia-Pacific Perspectives" held on 12 December 2014, with special thanks to Javier Lopez Gonzales (OECD), Christian Henn (WTO), Amita Batra (JNU, New Delhi) and Julia Tijaja (ASEAN Secretariat). Special acknowledgement and appreciation is extended to the following peer reviewers from ESCAP and other institutions (in alphabetical order) for their efforts to ensure the quality and relevance of APTIR: Shuvojit Banerjee, Sudip Basu and Marko Javorsek (ESCAP); Florian Alburo (CATIF and University of the Philippines); Tom Butterly (ECE); Daniel Cracau (ECLAC); Jose Duran (ECLAC); Elena Egorova (UNCTAD); Simon Evenett (St. Gallen University); Alina Rodriguez (UNCTAD); Mario Saeteros (ECLAC); and Martin Wermelinger (OECD). Special thanks also to ARTNeT adviser Alan Deardorff, for suggestions to the glossary entries.

Robert Oliver provided copy editing of the report, while Witada Anukoonwattaka, Adam Heal and Charuwan Chongsathien of TID performed final checks. The graphic concept, design and layout was carried out by 105 Digital Printing Co., Ltd. The Strategic Communications and Advocacy Section provided support in disseminating and communicating APTIR's findings through media outlets, while Martin Dressart helped with arrangements for timely online publication and making sure APTIR 2015 is accessible by readers worldwide.

# CONTENTS

Foreword iii

Acknowledgements v

Abbreviations xv

Glossary xviii

Executive summary xx

## PART I RECENT TRENDS AND DEVELOPMENTS

### Chapter 1 Is merchandise trade in trouble?

A. Slowing external and regional demand drag on trade growth 1

B. Subregional performance: Asia-Pacific trade is still driven by East and North-East Asia 3

C. External conditions open the door to even stronger intraregional trade 5

D. China's transition to a new normal and its implications for Asia-Pacific trade 6

E. Near-term prospects and conclusion 11

References 15

### Chapter 2 Commercial services trade on the mend?

A. Asia-Pacific commercial services exports outperform merchandise 17

B. Commercial services trade remains geographically concentrated 20

C. Other commercial and travel services gaining importance 22

D. International tourism in Asia and the Pacific is slowing 25

E. Conclusion 30

References 32

Annex 33

## Chapter 3 Structural shifts in regional foreign direct investment flow

A. Recent trends in foreign direct investment 35

B. Asia-Pacific subregional trends 41

C. Highlights for selected economies 44

D. Conclusion 48

References 50

## Chapter 4 Trends and developments in trade facilitation

A. Taking stock of trade costs reduction and trade facilitation implementation 53

B. Fostering regional cooperation on cross-border paperless trade 62

C. Towards seamless supply chains: international connectivity 63

D. Conclusion 66

References 67

## Chapter 5 Opening doors or building fences? Regional trends in trade policy

A. Recent trade policy developments 69

B. Shifting sands: changes in the relative importance of tariff and non-tariff measures 74

C. Towards trade policies that benefit Asia-Pacific least developed countries 79

D. Conclusion 84

References 85

## Chapter 6 Preferential trade policies and agreements

A. Trends in preferential trade agreements: selected features and stylized facts 88

B. Trade with preferential trade agreement partners 95

C. Transparency and preferential trade agreements: the record of Asia-Pacific economies 97

D. Conclusion 98

References 100

Annex 101

# PART II SUPPORTING PARTICIPATION IN VALUE CHAINS

## Chapter 7 Global value chains and interconnectedness of Asia-Pacific economies

A. Concepts and development benefits of global value chains 104

B. Global value chains and Asia-Pacific countries: stylized facts 111

C. Determinants of global value chain-related exports: evidence and implications for trade-related policies 117

D. Conclusion 127

References 130

Annexes 133

## Chapter 8 Services in industrial value chains

A. Contribution of services in Asia-Pacific industrial exports 139

B. Key services for export competitiveness of Asia-Pacific industries 141

C. Intraregionally traded services in industrial exports from Asia-Pacific economies 144

D. Conclusion 145

References 146

## Chapter 9 Global value chains, technology transfers and innovation

A. Global value chains and technology transfer: direct and indirect channels 149

B. The development context 157

C. Policy implications and conclusion 159

References 160

## Chapter 10 Policies for supporting participation in value chains

A. Securing entry 164

B. Expanding participation 165

C. Upgrading 165

D. Looking forward 166

Annex 167

LIST OF BOXES


1.1 China's economic slowdown and commodity trade of Asia-Pacific countries

2.1. Royalties and license fee payments still on a rise

2.2. Tourism statistics: Flows between China, Hong Kong, China and Macao, China

2.3. The increasing role played by China's outbound tourism

4.1 Identifying synergies between regional, subregional and bilateral initiatives for cross-border paperless trade

5.1. Has the balance swung away from protectionism in the G-20?

5.2. Export subsidies: China-United States dispute highlights use of trade distorting measures

5.3. India's duty-free scheme for least developed countries: Are benefits limited by non-tariff measures?

6.1 Trans-Pacific Partnership finally arrives

7.1. Outward FDI, trade cost and India's participation in GVCs

7.2. Augmented gravity model of GVC-related exports by Asia-Pacific economies

7.3. How to interpret figures 7.11 and 7.12

9.1. Technology transfer through GVCs in Thailand

9.2. Technology upgrading in China's photovoltaic cell industry


LIST OF FIGURES


1.1. Growth of merchandise trade across Asian and Pacific developing economies, 2007-2014

1.2. Monthly trade growth in selected developing Asia-Pacific economies, 2010-2015

1.3. Asia-Pacific shares in world merchandise trade, by subregion, 2006-2014

1.4. Destinations of merchandise exports from Asia and the Pacific, 2002-2014

1.5. Sources of Asia-Pacific merchandise imports, 2002-2014

1.6. Growth of Chinese exports and GDP, 1998-2020

1.7. Industry contributions to employment and GDP in China, 1980-2014

1.8. Primary (including fuels), intermediate and final goods exports to China across selected economies, 2014

2.1. Growth in commercial services trade in Asia-Pacific economies and the world

2.2. Share of commercial services exports and imports in Asia-Pacific economies, 2014

2.3. Growth of services exports and imports, by Asia-Pacific economy, 2014

2.4. Commercial services trade, by subregion

2.5. Exports of Asia-Pacific commercial services, by sector, 2005-2014

2.6. Average export-growth rate, by subsector, during 2005-2014 – Asia-Pacific region compared with the rest of the world

2.7. Growth of international tourist arrivals

2.8. Growth of tourist arrivals, by Asia-Pacific subregion and selected economy, 2014

3.1. FDI inflows to developed and developing economies, 1995-2014

3.2. FDI outflows from developed and developing economies, 1995-2014

3.3. FDI inflows to the Asia-Pacific region and their share in the global FDI inflows, 2009-2014

3.4. FDI outflows from the Asia-Pacific region and their share in the global FDI outflows, 2009-2014

3.5. FDI flows through mergers and acquisitions in the Asia-Pacific region, 2009-2014

3.6. Greenfield FDI flows in the Asia-Pacific region, 2009-2014

3.7. Intraregional greenfield FDI inflows in the Asia-Pacific region and their share in total greenfield FDI inflows to the region, 2005-2014

3.8. Destinations of intraregional FDI flows, 2009-2014

3.9. Intraregional greenfield FDI flows between selected countries, and total inflows and outflows to and from those countries, 2012-2014

3.10. Greenfield FDI inflows to the Asia-Pacific region, by sector, 2009-2014

3.11. FDI inflows to the Asia-Pacific developing subregions and developed economies, 2012-2014

3.12. Greenfield FDI inflows to South-East Asia, by sector, 2009-2014

3.13. Greenfield FDI inflows to South and South-West Asia, by sector, 2009-2014

3.14. FDI outflows from the Asia-Pacific developing subregions and developed countries, 2012-2014

3.15. FDI flows in China, 2009-2014

3.16. Greenfield FDI inflows to China, by sector, 2009-2014

3.17. FDI flows in India, 2009-2014

3.18. FDI inflows to Asia-Pacific least developed countries and their share in global FDI inflows, 2005-2014

3.19. FDI inflows to Asia-Pacific least developed countries, by sector, 2005-2014

4.1. Trade costs of Asia-Pacific subregions with developed economies, 1996 to 2012

4.2. Trade facilitation implementation and trade costs of Asia-Pacific economies

4.3. Trade facilitation implementation around the world (excluding cross-border paperless trade measures), 2015

4.4. Overall implementation of trade facilitation measures in 44 Asia-Pacific economies, 2015

4.5. Trade facilitation implementation of individual economies in Asia-Pacific subregions and in countries with special needs, 2015

4.6. Implementation of different groups of trade facilitation measures: Asia-Pacific average, 2015

4.7. Implementation of WTO TFA-related measures in Asia-Pacific, 2015

4.8. Moving up the trade facilitation ladder towards seamless international supply chains, 2015

4.9. Contribution of export, import and liner shipping connectivity performance to international supply chain connectivity, 2015

4.10. Evolution of performance by economies in International Supply Chain Connectivity Index, 2009-2015

5.1. Sectoral composition of new restrictions, including less-transparent measures (share of total), mid-November 2013 to mid-May 2015

5.2. Bound and applied MFN tariff rates in selected Asia-Pacific economies (all products, simple averages)

5.3. Growing initiations of TBT and SPS measures in the Asia-Pacific region

5.4. Estimated exposure of least developed countries' exports to non-tariff measures

6.1. Cumulative number of PTAs (notified and non-notified to WTO) enacted by Asia-Pacific economies, 1971-June 2015

6.2. Number of PTAs among economies of subregions and their import intensity

6.3. Asia-Pacific "noodle bowl"

6.4. Breakdown of trade agreements, by their type and number of partners

6.5. Share of tariff lines with zero duty on total non-agriculture merchandise imports, by Asia-Pacific economy

6.6. Areas of liberalization pursued by Asia-Pacific PTAs

6.7. Share of trade with PTA partners, 2011-2013

6.8. Preferential trade agreements with WTO notification, June 2015

7.1. A simplified value chain

7.2. Simplified illustration of sourcing strategies in GVCs

7.3. Main factors behind GVCs

7.4. Contribution of various policy-related factors to changes in trade costs

7.5. Major exporters and importers of GVC-final products, 2013

7.6. Major exporters and importers of GVC-intermediate products, 2013

7.7. Shares of Asia-Pacific economies by income groups in GVC-export sectors, 2013

7.8. Shares of Asia and the Pacific in global trade of GVC-final products, before and after the 2008-2009 global economic crisis

7.9. Structure of intermediate trade by Asia-Pacific countries, 1995-2013

7.10. Shares of intraregional trade, 1995-2013

7.11. Impacts of trade policy factors on exports in GVCs (estimated coefficients)

7.12. Impacts of trade facilitation factors on exports in GVCs (estimated coefficients)

8.1. Services content in gross exports of Asia-Pacific economies, by industrial sector, 2009

8.2. Changes in the shares of services value-added in gross industrial exports by Asia-Pacific economies 1995-2009

8.3. Services inputs to gross industrial exports by Asia-Pacific economies, 2009

8.4. Changes in services value-added in gross industrial exports by Asia-Pacific economies, by source, 1995-2009

8.5. Services inputs to gross industrial exports by Asia-Pacific economies, by the industrial sector, 2009

8.6. Intraregional imports of services inputs in industrial exports of Asia and the Pacific, by source, 2000 and 2009

9.1. GVC transmission channels

9.2. GVC participation versus export sophistication, 2009

9.3. Productivity differential between domestic and foreign-owned firms

9.4. Conceptual framework for understanding FDI spillovers in developing countries

9.5. Productivity differential between firms in cities with FDI and those without FDI

9.6. Productivity differential between firms that only use domestic technology and those that license foreign technology

9.7. Productivity differential between firms that only use domestic inputs and those that use imported inputs

9.8. From technology diffusion to national upgrading – the role of absorptive capacity

10.1. Key policy priority areas for supporting participation in value chains

LIST OF TABLES

1.1. Shares in Asia-Pacific total trade, by subregion, 2014

1.2. Intraregional merchandise imports, by Asia-Pacific subregion, 2014

1.3. Prospects for real merchandise trade growth for selected Asia-Pacific economies, 2015-2016

2.1. Other commercial services exports breakdown – comparison between 2005 and 2014

2.2. Major tourist destinations in the Asia-Pacific region

3.1. FDI inflows to South-East Asia, totals for 2009-2011 and 2012-2014

3.2. The top 10 destinations for greenfield FDI from China, 2012-2014

4.1. Intra- and extraregional comprehensive trade costs in the Asia-Pacific region (excluding tariff costs)

4.2. Performance rankings according to ISCCI, TAB and LSCI, 2015

5.1. New trade and trade-related restrictive measures, mid-November 2013 to mid-May 2015

5.2. New trade liberalizing measures, mid-November 2013 to mid-May 2015

5.3. Trade remedy measures, mid-November 2013 to mid-May 2015

5.4. Ranking of Asia-Pacific countries according to the overall number of red measures implemented, 2012-2015

5.5. Top 10 targeted jurisdictions in the Asia-Pacific region, 2012-2015

5.6. Non-tariff measures ad-valorem equivalents by HS Section and NTM Chapter

5.7. Duty-Free Quota-Free schemes for least developed countries in selected major markets, 2014

5.8. Top five export sectors in Asian and Pacific least developed countries

7.1 Intraregional exports of GVC products, by income group, 2013 and changes from 1995

7.2. Estimated RTA coefficients from the gravity models, by group of exports and importers

7.3. Estimated coefficients of policy variables from the gravity models of GVC-related exports, by low-income Asia-Pacific exporters

7.4. Estimated coefficients of policy variables from the gravity models of GVC-related exports, by lower-middle income Asia-Pacific exporters

7.5. Estimated coefficients of policy variables from the gravity models of GVC-related exports, by upper-middle income Asia-Pacific exporters

# ABBREVIATIONS

| | |
|---|---|
| ACIA | ASEAN Comprehensive Investment Agreement |
| ADB | Asian Development Bank |
| AEC | ASEAN Economic Community |
| AFTA | ASEAN Free Trade Area |
| APTIAD | Asia-Pacific Trade and Investment Agreements Database |
| APTIR | Asia-Pacific Trade and Investment Report |
| ASEAN | Association of Southeast Asian Nations |
| ASW | ASEAN Single Window |
| AVE | ad valorem (tariff) equivalents |
| BEC | Broad Economic Categories |
| BIMSTEC | Bay of Bengal Initiative for Multi-Sectoral Technical and Economic Cooperation |
| BRICS | Brazil, Russian Federation, India, China and South Africa |
| CISFTA | Commonwealth of Independent States Free Trade Area |
| Comtrade | United Nations Commodity Trade Statistics Database |
| CU | custom union |
| CVD | countervailing duties |
| DFQF | duty-free quota-free |
| DFTP | Duty-Free Tariff Preference |
| EAEU | Eurasian Economic Union |
| ECLAC | Economic Commission for Latin America and the Caribbean |
| EFTA | European Free Trade Association |
| EIA | economic integration agreement |
| EIU | Economist Intelligence Unit |
| ENEA | East and North-East Asia |

| | |
|---|---|
| EU | European Union |
| FDI | foreign direct investment |
| FSSA | Food Safety and Standards Act |
| FTA | free trade agreement |
| GATS | General Agreement on Trade in Services |
| GATT | General Agreement on Tariffs and Trade |
| GCC | Gulf Cooperation Council |
| GDP | gross domestic product |
| GSP | Generalized System of Preferences |
| GSTP | Global System of Trade Preferences among Developing Countries |
| GTA | Global Trade Alert |
| GVCs | global value chains |
| HS | Harmonized Commodity Description and Coding System |
| ICT | information and communications technology |
| IMF | International Monetary Fund |
| ISCCI | International Supply Chain Connectivity Index |
| LSCI | Liner Shipping Connectivity Index |
| M&A | mergers and acquisitions |
| MFN | most-favoured-nation |
| MNCs | multinational corporations |
| MNEs | multinational enterprises |
| NAFTA | North American Free Trade Area |
| NCA | North and Central Asia |
| NSW | National Single Window |
| NTBs | non-tariff barriers |
| NTMs | non-tariff measures |

| | |
|---|---|
| OECD | Organisation for Economic Co-operation and Development |
| PACER | Pacific Agreement on Closer Economic Relations |
| PTA | preferential trade agreement |
| R&D | research and development |
| RCEP | Regional Comprehensive Economic Partnership |
| RTA | regional trade agreement |
| RoO | rules of origin |
| SAARC | South Asian Association for Regional Cooperation |
| SAFTA | Agreement on South Asian Free Trade |
| SAPTA | SAARC Preferential Trading Agreement |
| SEA | South-East Asia |
| SMEs | small and medium-sized enterprises |
| SPS | sanitary and phytosanitary |
| SSWA | South and South-West Asia |
| TAB | trading across border |
| TBT | technical barriers to trade |
| TFA | Trade Facilitation Agreement |
| TiVa | trade in value added |
| TPP | Trans-Pacific Partnership |
| UNCTAD | United Nations Conference on Trade and Development |
| UNIDO | United Nations Industrial Development Organization |
| UNNExT | United Nations Network of Experts on Paperless Trade and Transport for Asia and the Pacific |
| UNWTO | United Nations World Tourism Organization |
| WITS | World Integrated Trade Solution |
| WTO | World Trade Organization |

# GLOSSARY [1]

**Cumulation:** In the context of rules of origin, the concept of "cumulation" allows countries which are part of a preferential trade agreement to share production and jointly comply with the relevant rules of origin provisions, i.e. a producer of one contracting party of a free trade zone is allowed to use input materials from another contracting party without losing the originating status of that input for the purpose of the applicable rules of origin.

**Densification:** (of global value chains) refers to the process of growing integration between domestic firms and international production networks. In practice it can involve foreign direct investment, both Greenfield and mergers and acquisitions, or domestic firms supplying inputs (or acquiring them) to (and from) foreign firms.

**EXPY index of export sophistication**: The index aims to capture the productivity level associated with a country's export basket.[2] It is calculated by summing the share-weighted PRODY of a country's exports, where PRODY is calculated as the average GDP per capita of the countries exporting this product weighted by their respective revealed comparative advantage in exporting it. A country that mainly exports products that other rich countries export will therefore have a high EXPY measure, for example, China has a high EXPY relative to its income level given the high technological content of its exports.

**Factory Asia:** A model which seeks to explain the remarkable growth of East Asian production networks in recent years. It highlights the connection between factories in Asian economies through regional value chains, where components are manufactured and assembled in different countries with the final goods being exported, mainly to developed countries' markets.

**Fragmentation:** The splitting of production processes into separate parts that can be done in different locations. The term "international product fragmentation" is often used when describing the split of the production process across national borders. There are also other terms used interchangeably in economic literature. Some of them include "disintegration of process", and "international unbundling of production".

**Global value chains:** The concept of a "value chain" implies a full range of functions (or activities) undertaken to bring a product from its conception to its end use and beyond. Typically, a value chain includes activities in the value-adding process from designing, production, marketing, distribution to supporting the final consumer. The fact that these activities are increasingly spread over several countries explains why value chains have come to be regarded more and more as "global". The term "international supply chain" is also used interchangeably in economic literature. Also, the term "network" is often used instead of "chain" when highlighting the complexity of the interactions among global producers which is more complicated than a simple circuit or a linear flow.

**New normal:** This term is used in this report in the context of China. It refers to an expectation of moderate economic growth in the medium to long term.

**Non-tariff measures (NTMs):** Non-tariff measures are generally defined as policy measures other than ordinary customs duties that can potentially have an economic effect on international trade in goods, changing quantities traded, or prices or both.

**Offshoring:** It refers to the relocation of part of the production process by the lead firm to a foreign country. The term "offshore production" is also used. The offshoring activities are conducted via vertical foreign direct investment, and trade within a respective GVC are considered to be an intra-firm trade.

**Outsourcing:** The term "outsourcing" is often used to highlight that activities within a respective GVC are subcontracted to independent contractors and suppliers. Trade between an outsourcing firm and its independent supplier is described as an "arm's length transaction".

**Sanitary and phytosanitary standards (SPS):** Sanitary (human and animal health) and phytosanitary (plant health) measures apply to domestically produced food or local animal and plant diseases, as well as to products coming from other countries. They can take many forms, such as requiring products to come from a disease-free area, inspection of products, specific treatment or processing of products, setting of allowable maximum levels of pesticide residues or permitted use of only certain additives in food.

**Servicification:** The phenomena of increasing value created, directly or indirectly, by services in the process of manufacturing, distribution and marketing of goods.

**Technical barriers to trade:** Technical barriers to trade (TBTs), a category of nontariff barriers to trade, are the widely divergent measures that countries use to regulate markets, protect their consumers, or preserve their natural resources (among other objectives), but they also can be used (or he perceived by foreign countries) to discriminate against imported products.

**Trade in tasks:** A task refers to a unit of specialisation based on specific workers' activities of a firm. The term is close to the "business functions" described in the GVC literature. "Trade in tasks" refers to the part of activities that can be outsourced and offshoring. Instead of referring to trade as being an exchange of goods, using the term "task" is highlighting that trade increasingly involves bits of value being added in many different locations.[3]

**Trade in value added:** Value-added refers to the amount by which the value of a product or service is increased at each stage of its production, excluding initial costs. An index of trade in value added tells us how much of a country's export value is accounted for by its domestic value-added.

**Trade intensity index:** Tells us if a country exports more – as a percentage – to a given destination than the world does on average. It is calculated as the ratio of two export shares: the numerator is the share of a destination country in the exports of a region, and the denominator is the share of the destination country in the exports of the world.

**Vertical FDI**: Foreign direct investment made by a firm to locate different stages of production in different countries. It has been distinguished from horizontal FDI, where multi-plant firms duplicate roughly the same activities in multiple countries.

## ENDNOTES

[1] This glossary includes some specific terms used in this report and provides interpretations in a context of the report. Glossary of trade terms compiled by Alan Deardorff provided useful starting point and we acknowledge additional suggestions received from Prof. Deardorff. Luca Parisotto, Aman Saggu and Witada Anukoonwattaka were the core team tasked with putting this Glossary together.

[2] Ricardo Hausmann, Jason Hwang and Dani Rodrik, "What you export matters", *Journal of Economic Growth*, vol. 12, pp. 1-25 (2007).

[3] Gene M. Grossman and Esteban Rossi-Hansberg, "Task trade between similar countries", NBER Working Paper No. 14554 (Cambridge, M.A.: National Bureau of Economic Research, 2008).

# EXECUTIVE SUMMARY

The idea of an interconnected world economy is nothing new. Writing about the situation prior to the outbreak of the First World War, economist John Maynard Keynes described the ease with which an inhabitant of London might, while sipping his morning tea in bed, order by telephone the "various products of the whole earth, in such quantity as he might see fit, and reasonably expect their early delivery upon his doorstep." Keynes went on to note how the same gentleman, from the comfort of his home, could also choose to invest his wealth in the "natural resources and new enterprises of any quarter of the world" or, if he were feeling adventurous, he might even go forth himself "by cheap and comfortable means of transit to any country or climate without passport or other formality" (Keynes, 1919, p. 9).

While we have yet to achieve the ease of movement envisioned by Keynes, global commerce today touches the lives of more people than ever before. Indeed, the internationalization of the global economy has intensified significantly during recent decades. Many services – once thought to require physical interaction and hence essentially non-tradable – can now be exchanged anywhere in the world using information and communications technologies. The share of cross-border capital flows in global GDP has surged. Manufactured goods today are made using parts sourced from across the world and the assembly of products can be fragmented and dispersed among a range of locations.

In many ways, the developing countries in the Asia-Pacific region have been the most successful at leveraging these trends and integrating themselves into global and regional value chains. This integration has contributed to making Asia and the Pacific the single largest trading region in the world, and biggest recipient of global inward foreign direct investment (FDI). The expansion of trade and investment in the region has directly contributed to the substantial gains witnessed in poverty reduction and improved welfare.

Since the financial crisis of 2008, however, both global and regional growth in trade and investment has slowed significantly. As the global economy continues to face headwinds posed by one challenge after another, trade and investment flows have remained volatile and have yet to return to the pre-crisis pattern of sustained expansion. The period 2014-2015 has, thus far, exhibited a continued lacklustre performance. Volumes of merchandise trade, FDI and, to a certain degree, trade in commercial services were all essentially flat. Looking forward, considerable uncertainty remains as the global economy undergoes a series of adjustments, not least from slackening growth in China.

A failure to return to patterns of strong trade and investment growth is of particular concern for the region's developing economies – especially those in the low-income category. Following trade-led strategies for inclusive and sustainable development will be particularly difficult in a weakened external environment. Indeed, we may be observing a "new normal" in which changing dynamics in global supply chains see trade growing at only the same rate, or more slowly than, global growth in GDP – a reversal of the pre-crisis trend. To devise an effective response to these conditions, it is imperative to more fully understand the dynamics behind the region's recent trade and investment performance. This involves disentangling the cyclical features from the structural aspects. Such an exercise will provide better informed expectations of the medium-term outlook as well as offer policy makers a solid basis for formulating appropriate trade policy and development strategy responses.

The Economic and Social Commission for Asia and the Pacific (ESCAP) has dedicated the *Asia-Pacific Trade and Investment Report 2015* to discussing this disentanglement. The report is divided into two parts. Part I assesses trends and developments in regional trade and investment flows and policies in an attempt to provide the insights and information necessary to separate the cyclical from the structural aspects. Part II analyses the participation of Asia-Pacific economies in global and regional value chains and discusses the degree to which the so-called "new normal" can be traced to their maturation. By observing how Asia-Pacific economies at different levels of development have integrated into supply chains at different speeds and to varying extents, we can also cast light on those policies that influence and shape value chain participation, and hence influence future patterns of trade and investment. The particular features of participation in value chains also have an impact on the ability of countries to access foreign technology and build innovative capacity, which in turn influences structural change and future development options. The main findings of the report are summarized below.

# PART I: RECENT TRENDS AND DEVELOPMENTS

## A MERCHANDISE TRADE: ADJUSTING TO SLOWER GROWTH IN CHINA

Driven by progressively weaker global demand, the growth of world exports slowed substantially from 2.3% in 2013 to 0.6% in 2014. The Asia-Pacific region performed better than the global average with growth in merchandise exports standing at 1.6% in 2014. However, when excluding China from the regional total, exports from the Asia-Pacific region registered a decline of 0.4%.

Since the 2008-2009 trade collapse, Asia-Pacific economies have been reacting to the changed environment in global demand by adjusting their reliance on trade. Figure 1 depicts trade dependence – measured by a ratio of exports or imports to gross domestic product (GDP) – as falling for developing and developed economies alike in the region after reaching a peak just around the start of the finanical crisis. Declining trade dependence ratios in developing economies can be attributed to both cyclical and structural factors.

**Figure 1. Trade dependence of developing and developed economies in Asia and the Pacific**

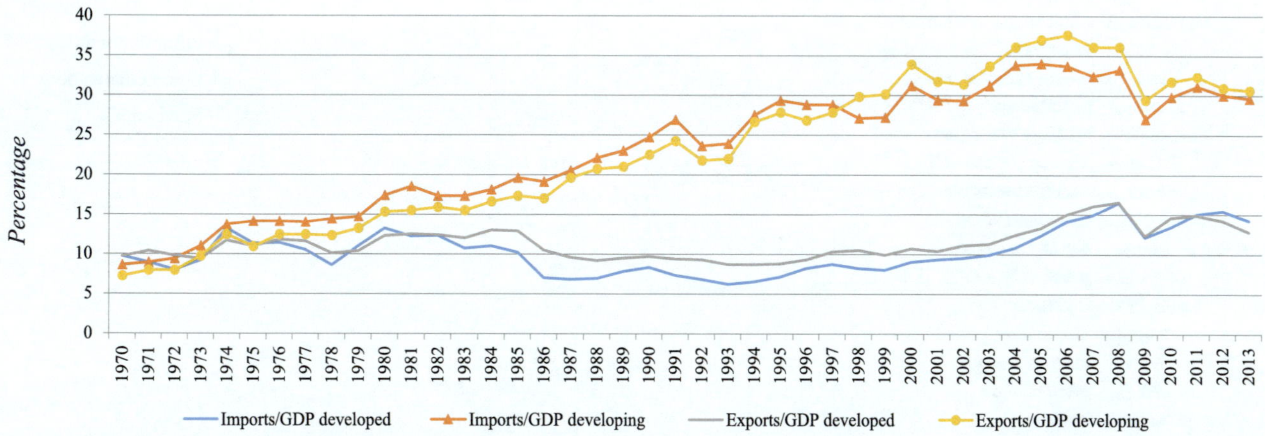


*Source:* ESCAP Statistics Online Database (accessed September 2015).

Weak external demand, particularly in the economies of the European Union – the region's chief external trade partner – continues to have negative consequences for trade growth. Within the region, continued economic stagnation in Japan is further dampening regional trade figures. While the relatively strong performance of the Indian economy is encouraging, it is unlikely to compensate for sluggish performances elsewhere given that India's market remains only weakly and selectively integrated with the Asia-Pacific region overall.

The most notable challenge to regional trade growth, however, are the structural changes affecting the Chinese economy. China is the dominant economic force in the region. In 2007, China overtook the United States as the largest individual trading partner for regional economies – a position it has maintained ever since. By 2014, China was sourcing 41% of its imports from other Asia-Pacific countries, while other Asian and Pacific countries were exporting 19% of their goods to China.

While the region has become accustomed to year-on-year double-digit economic expansion in China, recent trends have prompted international organizations, including ESCAP, to anticipate that the annual GDP growth in China will be below the official target of 7%. The recent stock market turmoil in Shanghai has heightened anxiety among policymakers and analysts. Slowing investment in China is having a direct impact on demand (and hence prices) for global commodities.

Economies that export to China are seeing declines across primary commodities such as coal, copper, iron ore and palm oil as well as inputs such as steel. In particular, countries with special needs [1] and whose economies are highly reliant on commodity exports to China – such as Kazakhstan, the Lao People's Democratic Republic, Mongolia, the Solomon Islands and Turkmenistan – are especially vulnerable to further declines in exports in the short to medium term (figure 2).

The downward pressure is not limited to commodities. Manufacturing exporters such as the Philippines and Thailand are also in an export recession because of the drop in China's processing exports. This, in turn, has led to falling demand for intermediate inputs across the board.

**Figure 2. Primary, intermediate and final goods exports to China across selected economies, 2014**

*(Percentage)*

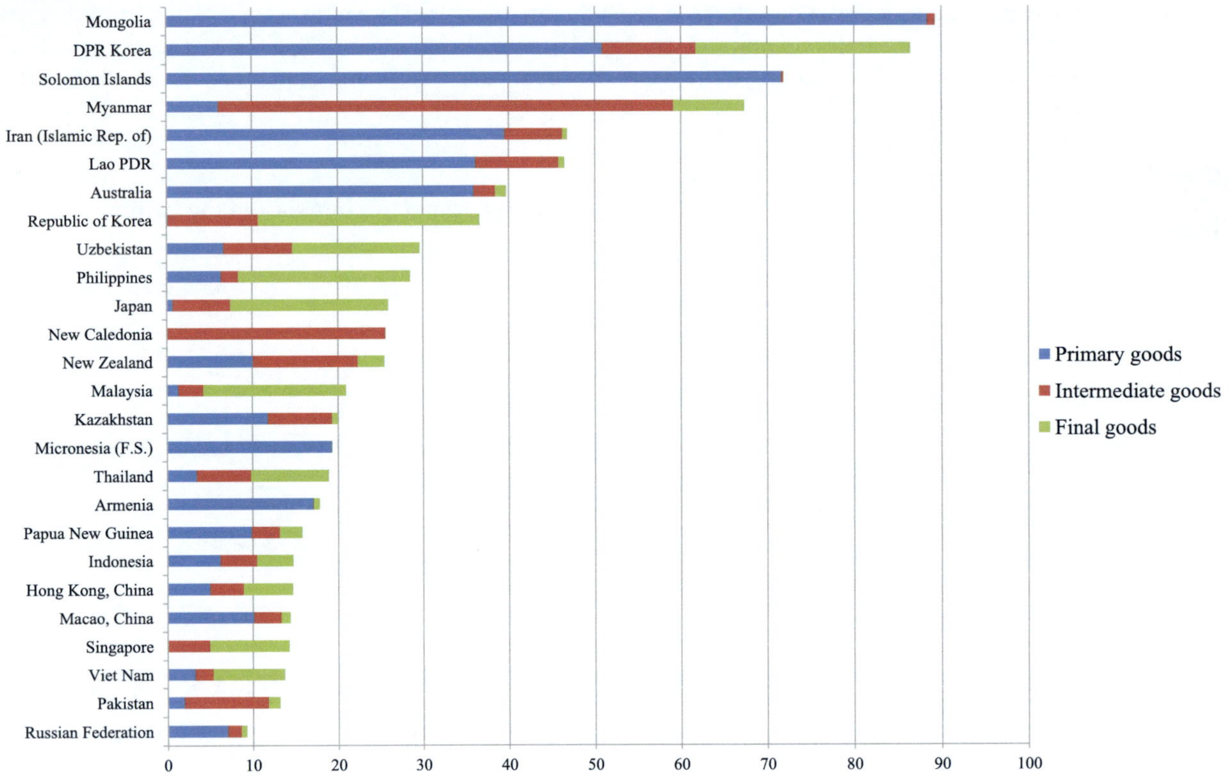


*Source:* Chapter 1 in this report.

While the current slowdown in China is posing challenges to some regional exporters, structural reforms in the country are likely to create new opportunities for others. At present, the Chinese authorities are trying to bring about dual structural shifts in the economy: (a) towards consumption at the expense of investment; and (b) away from manufacturing and towards services. Some success has been observed to date. The share of manufacturing in total output began to decline in 2010 with the share of services overtaking manufacturing in 2012. For countries exporting final goods – especially high-tech and branded consumer goods – rising purchasing power among Chinese consumers offers new prospects. Countries best positioned to benefit include Japan, Malaysia, the Philippines, the Republic of Korea and Singapore. The only real roadblock could be the temptation to implement import-substituting incentives to manage domestic demand. Thus a careful balancing act is needed in order not to stifle these additional opportunities through trade, for both the region and the broader Chinese economy.

For other emerging market economies, rising wages in China and that country's move toward higher-end goods and services presents an opportunity to compete with, and potentially replace China as a hub for low-cost manufacturing. Countries that have competitive labour markets and good access to natural resources will be well placed in this regard. However, the ability to enter global value chains (GVCs) also depends upon other factors, such as the availability and efficiency of trade-related infrastructure, the quality of services such as communications, transportation and logistical networks, access to financing, and the ability to access imports (through minimal restrictions on trade) and capital (FDI).

Despite the lowering of trade growth prospects, it is likely that the Asia-Pacific region will hold on to its position as the largest trading region in the world. In 2014, the region accounted for almost 40% of global exports and imports, while the share of intraregional trade has remained fairly high and stable over the past decade. Intraregional imports remained at slightly more than 50% of the total in 2014, while the intraregional export share increased gradually to 54%.

While these intraregional shares remain high, over half of the intraregional imports in each of Asia and the Pacific's subregions are sourced from East and North-East Asia, and 50% of these are sourced specifically from China. This leaves significant unexploited potential for greater South-South cooperation within Asia and the Pacific. Boosting trade connections between and among other subregions will require improvement in trade infrastructure as well as the development of institutions to support such trade.

Taking the above challenges into account, ESCAP anticipates that the growth prospects of merchandise exports by Asia-Pacific economies will continue to soften throughout 2015 before stabilising in 2016. Across the region, the volume of merchandise exports in 2015 is projected to grow by 2.3% while imports will contract by 2.4%. The contraction of imports is a reflection of the substantial drop of imports by the Russian Federation (-30.4%) and other large declines in imports by the Republic of Korea (-10.8%), Bangladesh (-8.3%), Indonesia (-4.8%) and China (-4.2%). This is likely evidence of the so-called "bullwhip effect" where the demand for intermediate goods is much more sensitive to changes in income than in the demand for final goods.

In 2016, trade performances are expected to vary widely across countries, depending on the regional intensity of their trade. Countries such as India and Viet Nam are expected to do relatively well because their exports are largely directed to advanced economies in Europe and North America that are expected to expand in 2016, while those countries with a heavy reliance on the Chinese market will likely continue their pattern of slow growth.

## B COMMERCIAL SERVICES TRADE: ON THE MEND?

Global exports of commercial services – which can be grouped into the four broad categories covering travel, transport, other commercial services,[2] and goods-related services[3] – grew by 4.9% in 2014, slightly slower than the 5.4% growth registered in 2013. Despite the moderation in growth, services trade increased substantially and more rapidly than merchandise trade. Further, even with the global slowdown, Asia-Pacific exports of services increased at a slightly faster rate at 5.1%, compared with 4% in the previous year. Import growth, at 6.1%, was also slightly higher than in 2013. The region remains a net importer of commercial services, accounting for 28% of world exports and 33% of world imports.

Exports of travel and other commercial services were especially strong. Expanding intraregional demand for travel by China has been a key factor in this growth. As a result, the region captured an increased share of the global exports of travel services, reaching 34% in 2014 (up from 24% in 2005). Similarly, the region accounted for an increased share of global exports of other commercial services, growing from 19% to 24% during the same period. Export growth for transport- and goods-related services was 6%, almost on a par with the world average.

Charges related to use of intellectual property – a subsector in other commercial services – is often linked to a country's capacity to absorb technology and engage in innovative activities. The region runs a deficit associated with the payment of royalties and license fees, with the notable exception of Japan, indicating that the region is still largely paying for innovation and creativity that is registered, if not necessarily sourced, abroad. As 39 regional economies had royalty and license fee-related exports worth $5 million or less, there is a clear need for further encouragement of innovation and, perhaps even more importantly, better intellectual property protection in the Asia-Pacific economies.

A small number of regional economies in recent years dominate Asia-Pacific trade in commercial services; China, Japan, India and Singapore alone represent more than half of the region's total trade (figure 3). Nevertheless, during the past decade, developing economies have been recording growing shares of total regional services exporters, especially China and India. From 2005 to 2014, China's exports increased from 15% to 17% of the region's total exports while India's share grew from 9% to 11%.

## Figure 3. Commercial services export and import share of Asia-Pacific economies

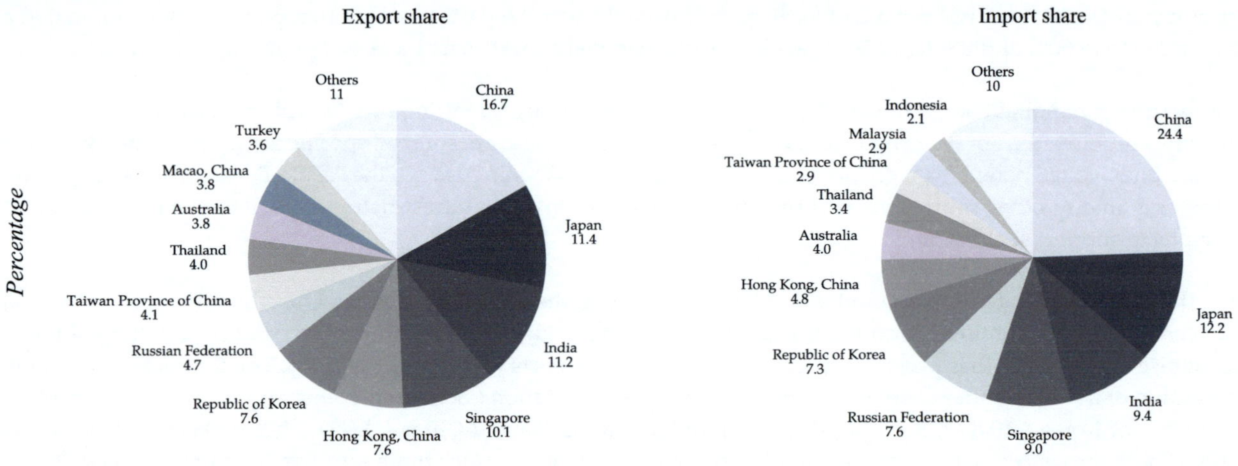


*Source:* Chapter 2 in this report.

Services trade performance in the rest of the Asia-Pacific region has varied widely. Some countries enjoyed dynamic growth – both in exports and in imports – in 2014, while others experienced sharp declines. Armenia, Cambodia, China, the Islamic Republic of Iran and Japan are among those in the former group, having experienced double-digit growth, both in exports and imports. Meanwhile, Malaysia, Mongolia, Papua New Guinea, the Russian Federation, Thailand, Tonga and Macao, China recorded falls.

Future prospects, as in the case of merchandise exports, hinge on China's economic performance. A continued slowdown is likely to have a negative impact on regional trade. China has become an important importer of services, especially travel services. In tourism, it is estimated that Chinese tourists represent more than 15% of the total arrivals to Asia-Pacific destinations. Countries that attract large numbers of Chinese tourists, such as the Republic of Korea and Thailand, are therefore at risk of a drop in Chinese consumer spending if China's economic growth slows more sharply.

# C ASIA-PACIFIC MAINTAINS ITS LEADING ROLE IN GLOBAL FOREIGN DIRECT INVESTMENT

Fragility in the global economy, creating an atmosphere of policy uncertainty, together with heightened geopolitical risks combined to lower global FDI flows in 2014. Total inflows were worth $1.23 trillion, a 16% fall from 2013. While developing countries still received the bulk of funds, in 2014 their total amount of FDI ($730 billion) decreased 5%. However, this decline was still much smaller than 28% drop (to $499 billion) in FDI inflows to developed economies.

The Asia-Pacific region remains a major destination for FDI, receiving 43% of total global inflows ($533 billion) in 2014 (figure 4). While this amount represented an absolute decline of 1.5% from the preceding year, the region continued to outperform the global average. The region is also continuing to gain prominence as a major outward investor. In 2014, outflows from developing Asian economies reached $450 billion, a 20% increase compared with 2013, compared with a 15% decline in outflows from regional developed economies.

**Figure 4. FDI inflows to the Asia-Pacific region and its share in the global FDI inflows, 2009-2014**

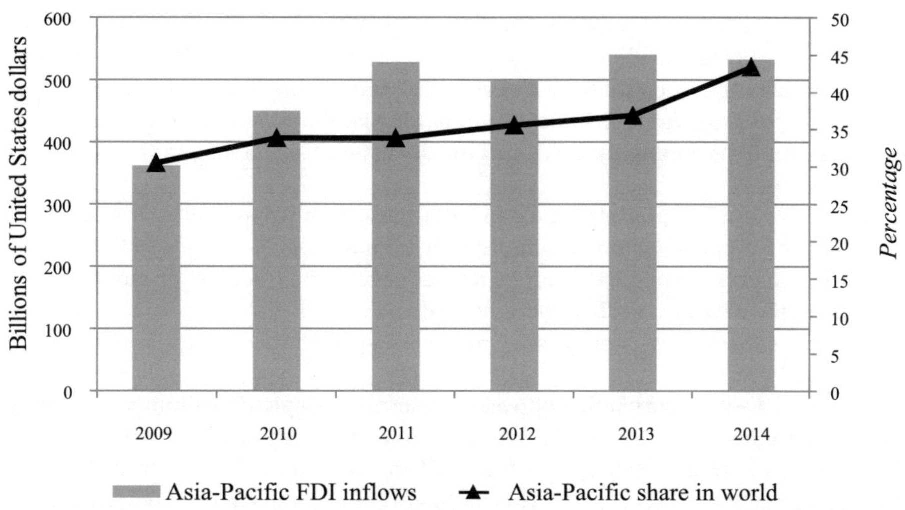


*Source:* Chapter 3 in this report.

In recent years Asia-Pacific economies have experienced a structural shift in investment inflows. While manufacturing still attracts the greatest inflows – especially in South-East Asian economies that are benefiting from China's rising labour costs – the overall gap with services has narrowed since 2009. Service activities that received the largest FDI inflows include real estate, communications, warehousing and storage, and leisure and entertainment.

Changes can also be observed in the preferred mode of investment. In Asia and the Pacific, mergers and acquisitions (M&A) surged to $123 billion in 2014, an increase of 137% over 2013. This follows several years of steady growth in M&A activity in the region. Greenfield FDI flows, in comparison, rose a more modest 17% (to $279 billion). This trend may be a reflection of the uncertain global economic environment leading companies to prefer the relatively less risky route of acquiring existing entities. But it also raises the question as to the extent this M&A activity results in a consolidation of productive activity in the region and reduces competition.

Among the Asia-Pacific subregions, developing East and North-East Asia as well as South-East Asia recorded higher FDI inflows and outflows than the other subregions. China became the single largest recipient of FDI globally - surpassing the United States - with $129 billion in 2014, an increase of 3.7% over 2013. While this can be taken as evidence of increasing Chinese openness, the slow pace of import growth indicates continuing room for improvement.

In terms of the region's least developed countries, FDI inflows have been rising continuously, albeit modestly, during the past decade, reaching $5.1 billion in 2014. While this figure is nearly three times higher than the 2005 total, it still accounts for less than 1% of total FDI to the overall region. Least developed countries have continued to take steps to strengthen their investment environments, addressing liberalization and facilitation bottlenecks. Notably, Bangladesh has had considerable success in attracting steady inflows of FDI for several decades, on account of its liberal investment policy and incentive regimes. Relatedly, Bangladesh also has one of the fastest growing shares of intraregional trade.

Broader efforts to spur regional integration will also be significant for the regional investment environment, and are likely to support both intraregional FDI flows as well as overall FDI flows to and from the region. In particular, South-East Asian countries are moving towards deeper levels of integration with the forthcoming establishment of the ASEAN Economic Community by the end of 2015. Mega-regional trade agreements such as the Regional Comprehensive Economic Partnership, Trans-Pacific Partnership and the Eurasian Economic Union also have the potential to strengthen and harmonise investment regimes.

# D TRADE FACILITATION MEASURES REDUCE TRADE COSTS AND IMPROVE COMPETITIVENESS

Recent global events, such as the successful conclusion of the WTO Trade Facilitation Agreement (TFA) negotiations (December 2013), have brought trade facilitation into sharp focus. It is clear that the WTO TFA implementation will become the new standard for trade facilitation as a means of reducing trade costs. Trade costs play a significant role in shaping regional and global trade patterns and thus in determining the distribution of benefits. Trade costs also shape consumer welfare by acting as a factor determining the price and the diversity of available goods.

Trade costs vary widely across subregions. East Asian countries typically have the lowest trade costs of the region, on a par with those of the large European Union economies. While trade costs of North and Central Asian economies remain about three times higher than those of East Asia, the former have made the most progress since 1996 in reducing these costs. South Asian economies have also made important strides in reducing their trade costs. In contrast, the Pacific islands developing economies have the highest overall costs and have displayed no clear improvement.

ESCAP research has found a strong correlation between the levels of implementation of trade facilitation by Asia-Pacific economies and their international trade costs. The results show that trade facilitation implementation levels explain (a) about 45% of the variations in trade costs, and (b) that a 1% increase in the level of trade facilitation implementation is associated with a decrease in trade costs of 2.3%. This highlights the benefits of pursuing trade facilitation measures with a view to increasing competitiveness and expanding trade opportunities. The Global Survey on Trade Facilitation initiated by United Nations Regional Commissions (UNRCs), shows wide disparities in trade facilitation implementation levels between regions with the highest average levels of implementation recorded in Latin America and the Caribbean and East and North East Asia,[4] while the Pacific region lags significantly behind most others in this area.

In the case of the Asia-Pacific region, the Survey compiled data for 44 economies representing five subregions (figure 5). Overall, the average level of trade facilitation implementation by the 44 Asia-Pacific economies, based on a set of 31 trade facilitation and paperless trade measures, is 46.5%. Within the Asia-Pacific region Australia, the Republic of Korea and Singapore have obtained scores in excess of 85%, while other countries have yet to achieve 15% implementation levels.

**Figure 5. Overall implementation of trade facilitation measures in 44 Asia-Pacific economies**

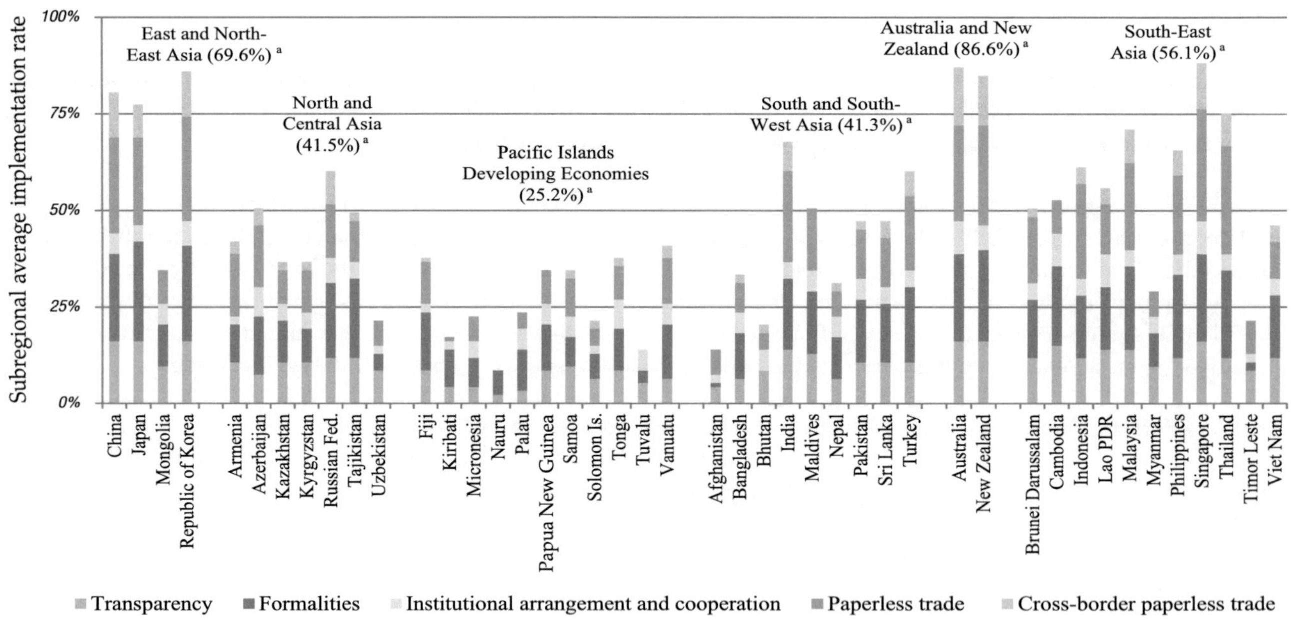


*Source:* Chapter 4 in this report.

The progress of countries in relation to specific trade facilitation measures is also mixed. The trade facilitation measure related to enhancing transparency and the reduction of formalities have the highest levels of implementation, as all countries in the Asia-Pacific region are engaged in the implementation of such measures. Overall, the least implemented measures in the region are those in the cross-border paperless trade category; in fact, the category of measures showing the widest implementation disparities is paperless trade.

As this report shows, ESCAP estimates that full region-wide implementation of cross-border paperless trade can bring about export gains in the order of $257 billion annually. Work being done by ESCAP Member States and Associate Members towards a regional arrangement on cross-border paperless trade furthers the objective of the Asia-Pacific region to achieve more efficient flows in this area as well as building synergies with other ongoing initiatives including the TFA. The negotiations on this regional arrangement present an opportunity for economies to cooperate on cross-border paperless trade implementation in order to promote the seamless exchange of information and documents along international supply chains.

While moving towards more competitive supply chains involves the seamless exchange of data and documents, it also requires the efficient movement of physical goods themselves across borders. Countries in the Asia-Pacific region have been making progress in overall international supply chain connectivity, with countries of East, North-East and South-East Asia remaining regional and global frontrunners. However, the subregion that has shown the greatest progress in international supply chain connectivity between 2009 and mid-2015 has been North and Central Asia.

## E TRADE POLICY: TIPPING THE BALANCE AWAY FROM PROTECTIONISM

The tipping of the balance between liberalizing and trade-restrictive measures away from the latter, should not engender complacency among regional policy makers. While globally, the number of trade liberalizing measures slightly outpaced trade restrictive measures in the most recent reporting period, the same cannot be said for the Asia-Pacific. In the region, 108 new trade-restrictive measures were recorded in the mid-November 2013 to mid-May 2015 period compared with 80 liberalizing measures. This worked out as an average of six new restrictive measures being introduced each month compared with just over four liberalizing measures. Asian and Pacific economies accounted for 40% of all trade-restrictive measures introduced globally – up from 38% in the previous period – but only 27% of liberalizing measures. Indonesia and India were the two economies responsible for the largest number of new trade-restrictive measures, with 28 and 22 measures respectively. The majority of new trade-restrictive measures were tariff increases.

Trade remedy measures give Governments some flexibility in the application of their WTO commitments allowing them to respond to particular situations, typically by imposing temporarily higher tariffs on imports from particular sources. During the reporting period, 263 new trade remedies were initiated, with 97 in the Asia-Pacific region (see table, Trade remedy measures), a modest decrease from the previous period. Both globally and in the Asia-Pacific region, initiations slightly outstripped terminations, leading to a small increase in the overall number of measures restricting trade. By far the most common form of trade remedies remained anti-dumping initiations. India was the top initiator of new trade remedies, introducing 34 during the reporting period.

**Trade remedy measures, mid-November 2013 to mid-May 2015**

| Trade remedies | | World | Asia-Pacific region |
|---|---|---|---|
| **Initiation** | **Total** | **263** | **97** |
| | Anti-dumping | 208 | 78 |
| | Safeguards | 29 | 15 |
| | Countervailing | 26 | 4 |
| **Termination** | **Total** | **243** | **87** |
| | Anti-dumping | 195 | 66 |
| | Safeguards | 27 | 17 |
| | Countervailing | 21 | 4 |

*Source:* Chapter 5 in this report.

The Sustainable Development Goals recognize the importance of trade as an engine of growth and development, and prioritize the expansion of engagement by least developed countries in international trade. If the ambitious goal of doubling the share of global exports from least developed countries is to be met, it will require concerted actions to ensure meaningful market access for least developed country goods and services.

For trade in merchandise goods, non-reciprocal preferences have helped least developed countries to export to developed and some developing economies. These schemes include the Generalized System of Preferences (GSP) and, more recently, Duty-Free Quota-Free (DFQF) programmes. As part of the WTO "Bali package" agreed in 2013, developed countries committed to offering DFQF access to at least 97% of products originating from least developed countries on a tariff line basis (although many were already doing so). At present, all developed economies meet this requirement, with the exception of the United States and the Russian Federation. Many developing countries in the region, including China, India, the Republic of Korea and Thailand are also introducing preferential schemes. For least developed countries to reap the full benefits of available preferences, however, restrictive rules of origin and other non-tariff barriers need to be tackled.

In services trade, there has been some recent progress in implementing the 2011 "Services Waiver", which provides the legal framework for allowing countries to give better-than-MFN treatment for least developed country services and service suppliers. At a meeting of the WTO Services Council in February 2015 more than 25 WTO members provided indications of the preferential access they were prepared to offer and by August 2015, 11 members had submitted official notifications. Early evaluation of these offers, suggests that a majority of the sectors collectively requested by the least developed countries were covered to some extent. However, the limited progress on Mode 4 access (covering the movement of natural persons) – for example, through visa requirement waivers – implies that preferential access will fall short of meeting the full request by least developed countries. Yet, timely progress towards implementation remains important because the life span of the waiver extends only until 2026.

# F TRADE AGREEMENTS: AWAITING THE MEGA-REGIONALS

The slow progress in multilateral trade liberalization through the WTO Doha Round has prompted countries to seek new trade opportunities elsewhere. Many Asia-Pacific economies continue to pursue preferential trade agreements (PTAs) with partners both within and outside the region. Between January 2014 and June 2015 a number of new trade agreements were signed, including deals between Malaysia and Turkey, China and Australia, China and the Republic of Korea as well as Japan and Mongolia. In addition, several previously-signed agreements came into force, including China-Switzerland, Singapore-Taiwan Province of China, China-Iceland, Hong Kong, China-Chile, Republic of Korea-Canada, and Thailand-Peru agreements. At present, there are more than 231 agreements associated with Asian and Pacific economies, of which 155 are in force.

Despite this activity, the pace of concluding new agreements, especially bilateral ones, has slowed somewhat. From 2010 to 2014, an annual average of 6.5 PTAs involving regional economies were brought into force, compared with an average of 9 per year from 2005 to 2009. This slowdown may reflect the fact that the attention of regional policy makers is increasingly being taken up by the negotiation of the so-called "mega-regional" deals – the Regional Comprehensive Economic Partnership (RCEP) and the Trans-Pacific Partnership (TPP) – each of which involves several regional economies.

Existing PTAs in the Asia-Pacific region vary significantly in their scope and coverage. More than half of all agreements brought into force create free trade areas for trade in (merchandise) goods, while a further 39% of agreements allow free trade of both goods and services.

While Asia Pacific economies have undertaken more PTAs than any other region, they remain reluctant to form common customs territories, In fact only one regional customs union, the Eurasian Economic Union (EAEU), exists, apart from the one between Turkey and the European Union. Despite this apparent reluctance for deep integration, countries are going beyond traditional "free trade areas" to create economic or comprehensive partnership agreements. These agreements include commitments to liberalize areas not covered by WTO disciplines at present, such as investment and government procurement. The number of agreements containing these areas of liberalization featuring "next generation" trade issues is still low however (figure 6).

## Figure 6. Areas of liberalization included in PTAs

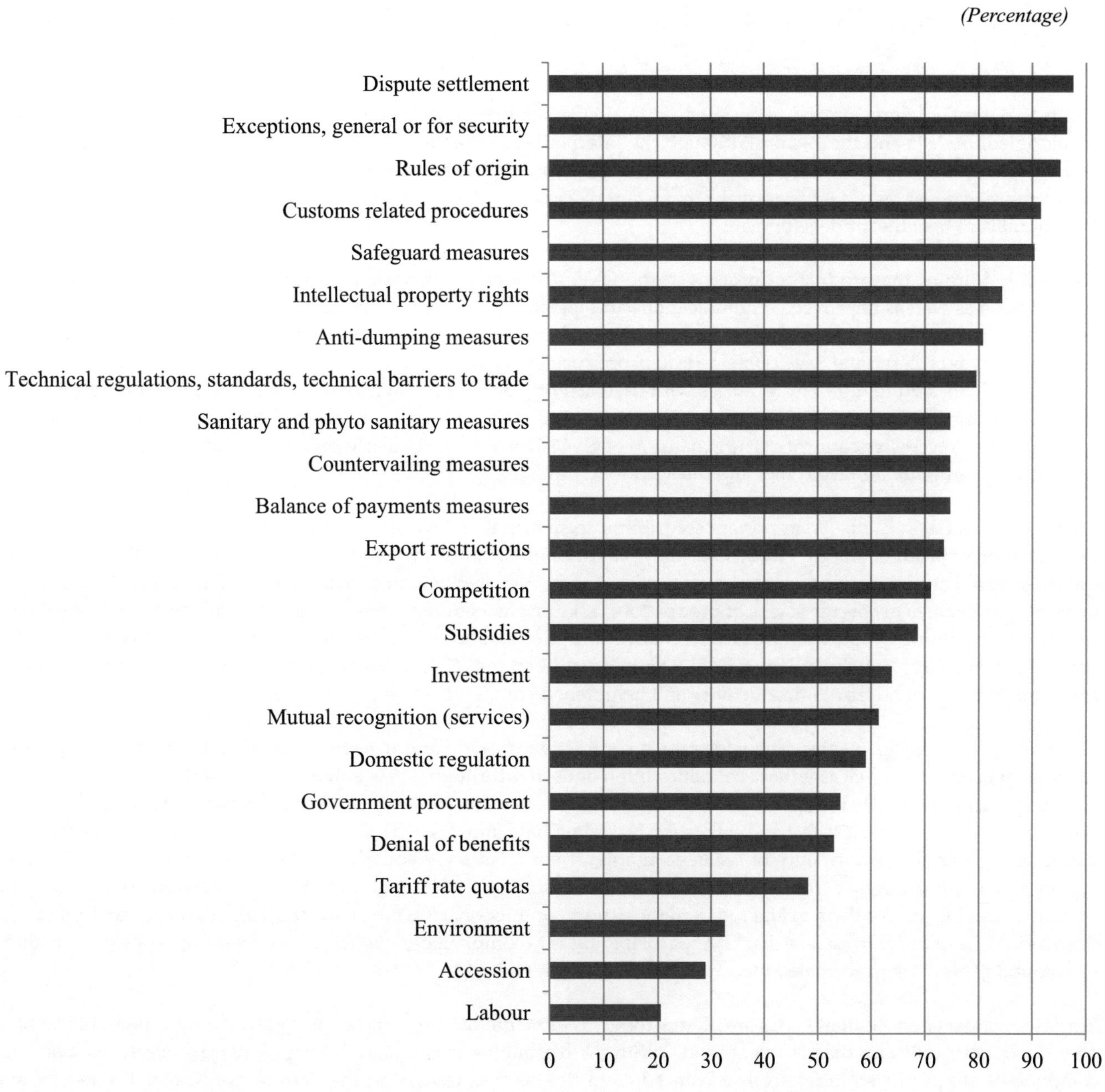


*Source:* Chapter 6 in this report.

The extent to which economies in the Asia-Pacific region trade with their PTA partners varies considerably. Only 35% of exports and 45% of imports are transacted with the PTA partners for all the economies in Asia and the Pacific (as a simple average for 2011-2013). Least developed countries such as Afghanistan (72%), Bhutan (88%), the Lao People's Democratic Republic (86%) and Myanmar (92%) show a very high share of exports with their PTA partners, typically neighbouring nations. At the other end of the spectrum, the Pacific island countries export less than 10% of their total exports to PTA partners and the figure for North and Central Asian economies is only 16%. Import patterns are likewise diverse. Some countries show much higher propensity to import from the PTA partners compared to their export pattern, for example Bangladesh (60%), Cambodia (90%), Sri Lanka (51%), or Macao, China (60%), while some others tend to import much less from the PTA partners than what they export to them (for example in the case of Afghanistan, Bhutan, and some Pacific islands).

# PART II: SUPPORTING PARTICIPATION IN VALUE CHAINS

## A VALUE CHAINS IN TODAY'S ASIA-PACIFIC REGION

The international fragmentation of production in GVCs has been a defining feature of trade and overall economic development in Asia and the Pacific. Although the international exchange of inputs along a value chain is not new, the rapid growth in the scope and complexity of GVCs since the late 1980s is unprecedented. Experience from the region shows that even small developing countries can be important players in GVCs, by specializing in a particular stage of production, with significant benefits for development.

The unbundling of the production process in the GVC phenomenon occurs across both countries and firms. Trade liberalization as well as improved communications and logistics have made it easier than ever to separate the individual functions in a value chain, which can then be located anywhere in the world. Business activities at different stages of value addition, such as research and development, design, production of parts, manufacturing assembly, marketing and branding, are frequently located in different countries with each activity taking place where it can be most efficiently produced or supplied. Although the nature of GVCs may be sector-specific, they all typically involve the movement of intermediate goods through successive countries. The expansion of GVCs has been particularly pronounced in sectors such as apparel and footwear, automobile, electronics and the agro-food industry.

Participation in GVCs can be an important contributor to sustainable development. A greater division of labour and the segmentation of production on a global scale allow larger numbers of countries to benefit from trade. With today's GVCs, countries do not need to develop sophisticated and vertically integrated industries to participate in global trade; it is enough to develop capacities in specific stages of production, tasks or business functions. In other words, even small developing countries with limited capacity now have a chance to undertake tasks that would have previously been executed in developed countries, thereby creating local jobs and value-added. GVC participation also produces wider economic spillovers in terms of improved productivity and heightened competitiveness.

There are, of course, downsides. The widespread contraction in trade and investment in the aftermath of the financial crisis demonstrated very clearly that economies interconnected through GVCs either swim or sink together. Because of efficiency reasons related to the operation of GVCs, these economies have to be open; as a result, the transmission of external shocks is, as seen in 2008-2009, fast and extensive. The immediate impacts of demand shocks in these economies are strong but, judging from the performance of Asian economies, their recovery is equally fast. Participation in GVCs was one of the key factors contributing to the export recovery of those economies; the more diversified and networked the economies were, the easier it was for them to emerge from the export contraction. However, Governments still need to be mindful of downside risks in order to ensure that GVC participation is accompanied by policies for managing exposure to external shocks and preventing exacerbated inequalities or environmental degradation.

Empirical evidence shows that GVCs are often strongly regional in nature. This fact has played out in the Asia-Pacific by opening opportunities for deeper integration within the region. For example, technology-intensive electronic parts and components are produced in relatively advanced countries such as Japan and the Republic of Korea. The assembly of intermediate components into finished products, meanwhile, is typically taking place in emerging economies, such as China and Viet Nam. Intermediate goods trade now accounts for about 22% of total regional trade.[5]

The linkages between regional value chains and preferential trade agreements (PTAs) are complex and not easily generalized. The Asia-Pacific experience shows that regional value chains were established even while the connected economies did not share too many formal PTAs. As GVCs became established in some regional economies, their further expansion needed policies for reducing costs in the operation of GVCs. ESCAP research shows that PTAs alone will have limited benefits unless they are part of more comprehensive liberalization and facilitation policies, including multilateral and unilateral efforts. Results suggest that PTAs may be particularly supportive of GVC-related exports to countries outside the region: having a PTA may increase final exports to the world by 73.9%, while the impact on intraregional export is only 58.6%. A possible explanation could be that formal trade agreements may be not crucial to driving GVC-trade at the intraregional level because Asia-Pacific economies are already connected through the regional production networks established by multinational corporations (MNCs).

In addition, the effectiveness of PTAs in helping GVC-related exports appears to depend on development levels of exporter and importer economies. For example, having a formal trade agreement will significantly help low-income countries to export to high-income countries. The same cannot be said for countries that are not in a group of high-income countries. The result appears to be the opposite when looking at exports from high-income countries, i.e. PTAs do not help exports to countries in the same peer group. In contrast, having a PTA plays a significant role in helping lower-middle income countries increase their exports to intraregional markets, regardless of the level of income.

Although the results are quite mixed, a general conclusion seems to be that having a PTA with high-income import partners might be a useful strategy for Asia-Pacific exporters in both low and middle income groups. Given the fact that high-income countries are likely be the large market for intermediate and final products in GVCs, this finding implies that a PTA strategy that might effectively help GVC-related exports by low and middle income Asia-Pacific countries would be the market-driven PTAs.

Today, the Asia-Pacific region is a major exporter of GVC-produced final products, but not yet a major source of final demand. In 2013, the Asia-Pacific accounted for about 45% of the world's GVC-related exports of final products, with around half coming from China alone. In contrast, the region only accounted for around 26% of final product imports. The United States and countries in the European Union remain the most significant importers of final products. This pattern is gradually shifting though: the region has increased its share of final imports by 7 percentage points between 2007 and 2013.

Intraregional trade, especially South-South trade, is playing an increasing role in GVCs. The share of intraregional exports in total intermediate exports by Asia-Pacific countries grew gradually from 52.6% in 1995 to 58% in 2013. Intraregional imports of intermediate goods are especially important. In 2013, more than 65% of the GVC-intermediate imports of Asia and Pacific countries came from countries within the region. Regional import intensity was particularly high for apparel and footwear and electronics with shares of intraregional intermediate imports as high as 91.5% and 82%, respectively (figure 7).

While GVCs can open up opportunities for nearly all countries, at present GVC-related trade in the Asia-Pacific is highly concentrated in just 10 economies. Indeed, 90% of these trade flows are concentrated in the following: Australia, China, Japan, India, Indonesia, Malaysia, the Republic of Korea, Singapore, Thailand, and Turkey. Low-income countries are thus at present not fully participating in the spread of GVCs across the region. In most sectors, low-income countries represent a negligible share of final exports with the exception of apparel and footwear, mainly from Bangladesh and Cambodia.

**Figure 7. Structure of intermediate trade by Asia-Pacific countries, 1995-2013**

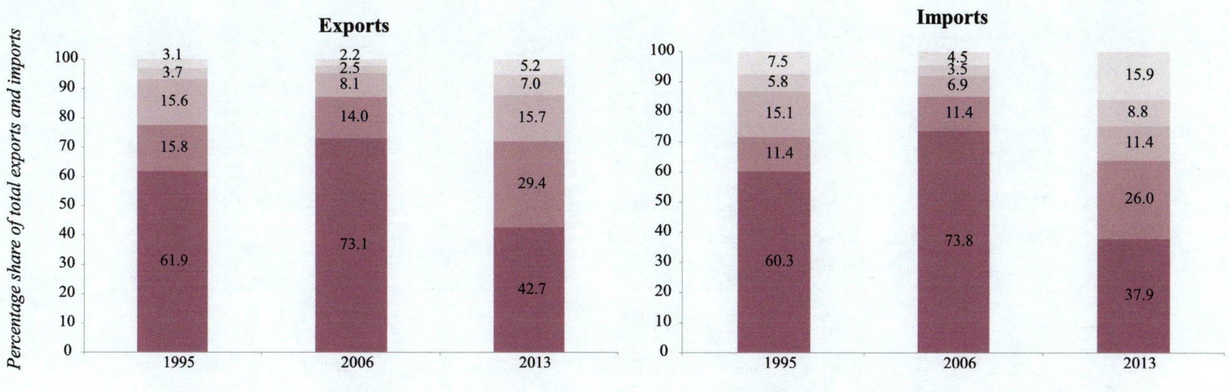


*Source:* Chapter 7 of this report.

# B AVAILABILITY OF SERVICES CRUCIAL FOR GVCS

While GVCs are most clearly observed in manufacturing production, services create a significant proportion of the value in the process of manufacturing, distribution and marketing process of goods in GVCs. The growing recognition of the value created, directly or indirectly, by services in this process has become known as "servicification". Better statistical tracking of trade in value-added has uncovered the extent to which services contributed to trade values. The increased importance, or "servicification", implies that access to services has become a key factor in enhancing the competitiveness of economies, especially those exporting industrial products through GVCs.

In fact, GVC-related production and trade have spread more extensively through the Asia-Pacific region than in the rest of the world implying the high importance of servicification, inter alia, to the development of industrial exports of the region. ESCAP analysis shows that services accounted on average for 29.4% of the total value-added in the industrial exports of Asia and the Pacific in 2009 (Figure 8), which is at par with the world average of 29%, but considerably lower than the EU average of close to 55%. The OECD-WTO TiVA data shows that the spread of GVCs in the region has also resulted in an expansion of servicification across Asia-Pacific developing economies. Indeed, the share of intraregional imports of services has increased, especially in GVC-related industrial exports. The Republic of Korea and China are the economies that benefited the most in terms of intraregional export growth in services. In contrast, Japan has lost market share.

**Figure 8. Services content in gross exports of Asia-Pacific economies, by industrial sector, 2009**

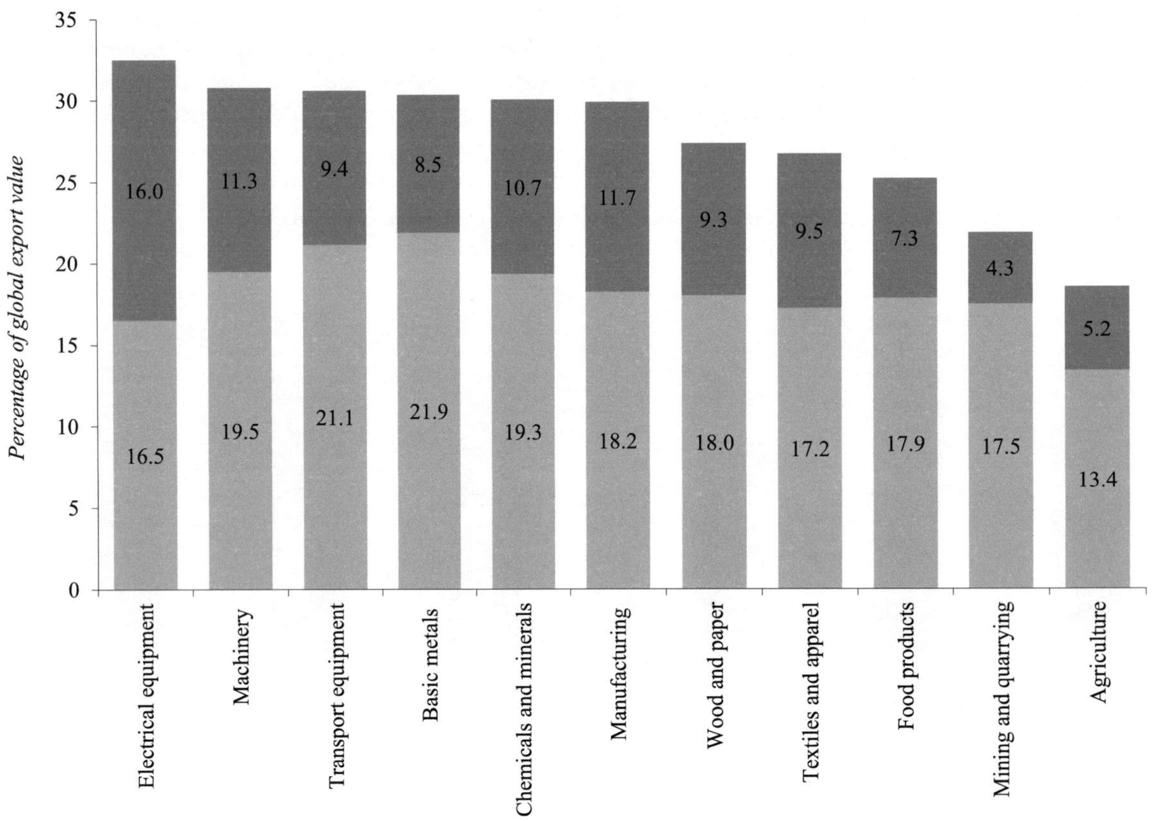


*Source:* Chapter 8 of this report.

Distribution-related services and business services are the major elements of service inputs to industrial exports from Asia and the Pacific. These services accounted for 9% and 7.5%, respectively, of industrial exports from the Asia-Pacific region in 2009. Business services contribute extensively to the exports of electrical equipment, machinery, and transport equipment. These equipment exports happen to be the sectors where MNCs have an intensive presence.

Although domestic sourcing of services remains dominant, especially in the cases of agriculture and mining exports, the contribution of imported services has been rising. The share of imported services in industrial exports increased from 7.6% in 1995 to 11.1% in 2009. The increase in service imports is particularly rapid in the case of business services, but is also important in other subsectors.

Liberalizing services trade would allow more efficient imports of services inputs and facilitate the competitiveness of the Asia-Pacific region's industrial participation in GVCs. Liberalization should not be restricted to regional South-South flows, as developed economies remain the dominant source of imported service inputs.

## C GLOBAL VALUE CHAINS, TECHNOLOGY TRANSFERS AND INNOVATION

From a development standpoint, the early stage in GVC participation typically involves labour-intensive low value-added operations, such as product assembly. However, on reaching higher levels of development there is the possibility for specializing in higher value-added tasks, such as component manufacture, ultimately culminating in research and development (R&D). Higher value-added tasks are often accompanied by positive spillovers in terms of technology, productivity and skills upgrading, and ideally lead to endogenous technology creation. Identifying the policies needed to support "moving up" value chains is therefore important.

When an upwards GVC partner or lead firm (assumed to be located in a developed country) makes a conscious decision to transfer technology downwards to a firm in the supply chain (in a developing country), this is an important vector supporting value chain upgrading. The business case for such a transfer is that it can help the firm in the developing country to produce more efficiently, which in turn has benefits for the entire value chain. Empirical analysis of the relationship between GVCs and technology transfer has found a number of channels through which this can take place.

One common way in which GVC participation can lead to technology transfer and upgrading is FDI . A country's investment climate is therefore an important determinant of a lead firm's appetite to undertake FDI. Empirical evidence bears out the contention that FDI can be a vector of direct technology transfer at the firm level. After controlling for country, time and sector-specific factors foreign-owned firms are, on average, 82% more productive than domestically-owned firms, consistent with foreign-owned firms having access to superior technology.

Another way in which GVCs can facilitate technology transfer is through the licensing of technology by a foreign firm to domestic producers. In this case, the lead firm or technology supplier does not take an equity position in the firm receiving the technology, but instead allows it to use the technology in return for payment of a fixed sum. This can be an importance source of competitive advantage as firms that license foreign technology are, on average, 48% more productive than firms that do not license foreign technology.

It is also possible to gain access to technology within a GVC through transactions in the marketplace. One example is importing appropriate capital goods, such as machines and equipment. Access to world markets for intermediate goods gives firms the ability to use high-quality inputs that may not be available domestically. Imported capital goods can generate spillovers, as workers learn how to use them and can then take that knowledge with them to other firms that can themselves acquire the same technology. Firms that import at least some intermediates are, on average, 38% more productive than firms that use only domestic intermediates.

# D POLICIES FOR SUPPORTING PARTICIPATION IN VALUE CHAINS

Given the benefits from engaging in GVC-related activities, policy makers should consider actions that support entry into value chains, improve competitiveness, facilitate upgrading and support sustainable development more broadly. Empirical analyses undertaken by ESCAP as well as evidence from other studies point to a number of key recommendations.

**1. Securing entry to GVCs**

As many smaller and low-income regional economies are not yet fully integrated into GVCs, the key question for policy makers is how to create an enabling environment for local firms to gain entry into existing networks. In this regard, it has been found that:

- Trade cost reduction is essential for a country to participate more effectively in GVCs and overcome geographical disadvantages. Trade costs comprise one of the key determinants of a country's performance in GVCs. Trade-cost reduction policies include liberalization of trade in goods, services and investment, with a removal or reduction of direct and indirect barriers;

- Trade facilitation, development of ICT infrastructure, improved logistics performance, regulatory transparency and other policies that reduce broader behind-the-border obstacles to trade are necessary conditions for GVC participation;

- Regional economic integration agreements could be a catalyst in enhancing GVC participation of developing Asia-Pacific countries, provided such agreements are deep in commitments and broad in scope and coverage. However, bilateral and regional trade agreements will have little effect without the implementation of necessary domestic trade reforms – in particular, trade facilitation. Furthermore, there is a need to rationalize and consolidate existing preferential trade agreements as their effectiveness may face adverse impacts through the noodle bowl phenomenon;

- Enabling GVC development will increasingly require more international cooperation and coordination among Governments. The need to harmonize regulation and domestic rules and regulation with international standards is particularly strong in Asia and the Pacific, as burdens created by those rules and regulations can be amplified across GVCs and result in damage to region-wide competitiveness;

- There is a need to increase the involvement of low-income countries in GVCs. The dynamic nature of GVCs may offer new opportunities for countries that have, thus far, not been integrated into regional trade. The key to unlocking the potential of low-income countries is infrastructure development, especially in relation to trade facilitation;

- Once a country is significantly integrated into GVCs, Governments should pay attention to the broader policy environment. Domestic policy and regulatory reforms to facilitate trade and business operations help to maintain attractiveness to FDI as well as preserve competitive advantages.

**2. Realizing the potential of services in supporting GVCs**

The importance of servicification requires a comprehensive approach to policy formulation. While liberalizing trade in goods is a starting point for creating new trade opportunities, the value chains of industrial goods also require efficient services. The findings of this report show that:

- Improvements in the performance of the service sector, including through liberalizing services trade, will enhance the competitiveness of manufacturing firms and facilitate their participation in global production networks. Many regional economies maintain highly restrictive services sectors, which could hamper efforts to promote goods exports;

- There is a risk that too much reliance on imported intermediate services and goods may lead to limited development spillovers from GVCs to the rest of the economy. The general direction of service trade policy should then focus on creating competitive market conditions and developing a well-functioning domestic service sector that meets high regulatory standards;

- Measures need to vary from sector to sector. For example, ensuring access to the grid or network for new entrants in the telecommunications or electricity sectors should help in creating a level playing field and result in pro-competitive efficiency gains;

- Openness of financial services with a good regulatory framework could enhance competition and stability in the financial sector and contribute to macro stability. In addition, it is important to have a comprehensive set of policies in place in order to encourage spillovers and technological diffusion from foreign to domestic providers. This may include, for example, public investment to upgrade and improve accessibility to backbone infrastructure such as railways, ports, health and education;

- The provision of education and training (e.g. in IT, languages and professional skills) as well as greater domestic and international labour mobility will enable domestic firms as well as individuals to take advantage of service-export opportunities.

**3. Facilitating technology transfer and moving up the value chain**

Developing country firms and workers can only benefit from new technology through GVC participation if the domestic policy environment is right. Smooth transitions from labour-intensive to skills-intensive segments of GVCs need enabling policies to facilitate the adjustment process through well-designed labour market and social reforms, and investment in education and skills. This requires several actions, including:

- Building institutional capacity – including governance, the rule of law and contract enforcement – and respecting intellectual property rights for securing the benefits of technology transfers. All types of technology transfer within GVCs rely on some type of legal relationship between the source and the recipient;

- Openness to FDI is one of the most vital and beneficial vectors for technology transfer within GVCs. In many countries excessive restrictions remain, particularly in services. Appropriate relaxation of foreign investment rules – which includes limits on foreign ownership and legal forms – can encourage GVC partners and lead foreign firms to strengthen relationships with local firms, including through technology transfers;

- Maintaining an open stance by developing countries in relation to international trade, particularly in the case of intermediate inputs and capital goods. A liberal trade policy stance facilitates movements of goods that bring technology embedded in them;

- Development of human capital to improve the capacity of firms to absorb technology transfer. For technology transfer to be fully effective, the new machines or techniques need to be understood and internalized as well as potentially adapted to domestic conditions, both by workers and by local engineers.

**ENDNOTES**

[1] Comprising least developed countries, landlocked developing counties and small island developing States. A list of these countries in Asia and the Pacific is available at www.unescap.org/our-work/macroeconomic-policy-development/countries-special-needs.

[2] Other commercial services category includes the following subcategories: charges for the use of intellectual property (n.i.e.), computer and information services, construction, financial services, insurance and pension services, other business services, personal, cultural and recreational services, and telecommunications.

[3] Goods-related services is a new aggregate combining two subsectors defined in the BOP6 as: (1) Manufacturing services on physical inputs owned by others cover processing, assembly, labelling, packing, and similar activities undertaken by enterprises that do not own the goods concerned and are paid a fee by the owner. Only the fee charged by the processor, which may cover the cost of materials purchased, is included under this item. Examples include oil refining, liquefaction of natural gas, assembly of clothing and electronics, assembly, labelling, and packing, and (2) Maintenance and repair services n.i.e. cover maintenance and repair work – by residents – on goods that are owned by non-residents (and vice versa). The

repairs may be performed at the site of the repairer or elsewhere. The value recorded for maintenance and repairs is the value of the work done — not the gross value of the goods before and after repairs.

[4] East and North-East and South-East Asia: Brunei Darussalam, Cambodia, China, Indonesia, Lao People's Democratic Republic, Malaysia, Mongolia, Myanmar, Philippines, Republic of Korea, Singapore, Thailand, Timor-Leste, Viet Nam.

[5] A detailed list on intermediate goods included is provided in on line Appendix A.

## REFERENCES

Keynes, John Maynard (1919). *The Economic Consequences of the Peace*. Available from: http://socserv2.socsci.mcmaster.ca/econ/ugcm/3ll3/keynes/pdf%26filename%3Dpeace3.pdf

# PART 1
# RECENT TRENDS AND DEVELOPMENTS

# 1 IS MERCHANDISE TRADE IN TROUBLE ?

Although the Asia-Pacific region as a whole is the largest trading region of the world – having captured almost 40% of global exports and imports – recent figures on the merchandise trade performance of the region's economies fail to inspire much confidence.[1] China faces a sharper than expected slowdown in economic growth, a debt crisis and heightened volatility in financial markets. Coupled with continued economic stagnation in demand markets, there are substantial downside risks for "Factory Asia". The relatively strong performance of the Indian economy is not easing these worries as India's market remains only selectively integrated in to the region. The share of intraregional trade was relatively stable during the past decade, especially on the import side. Intraregional imports by the region as a whole remained just over the 50% mark in 2014. The intraregional export share increased gradually to 54%, helped by relatively faster growth of exports to developing Asia-Pacific economies during that period when there was still no robust recovery of import demand from the eurozone. All these factors indicate the likelihood of global merchandise trade, including Asia and the Pacific, remaining stagnant with the risk of slipping into another crisis episode.

## A SLOWING EXTERNAL AND REGIONAL DEMAND DRAG ON TRADE GROWTH

The slowing growth of the Chinese economy, coupled with the persistent weakness in global demand, has dragged the trade growth of Asia and the Pacific down since 2012, despite a modest improvement in the growth of European economies from zero to 1.4% in 2014 and the robust growth of the United States economy to more than 2% in the same year. The downside risks of growth path conversion to a "new normal" in the large Asia-Pacific economies have become prominent. In 2014, the growth of the Chinese economy slowed further to 7.4%, from 7.7% in the preceding year. It is anticipated that China will register growth of below 7% in 2015, with further deceleration to 6% by 2017 (IMF, 2015a). Economic stagnation in Japan continues to remain an issue – having persisted since the 1990s – and in 2014, its economy again registered negative growth (-0.06%), which has done little to demand for exports from Asia-Pacific developing economies. Furthermore, with their heavy reliance on exports of fuel, metal and mineral commodities, the region's emerging and developing economies have been adversely affected by the double shift – China's slowdown and continued downward trend in world commodity prices.

> *"In 2014, merchandise exports by the Asia-Pacific region were up by 1.6%. However, when excluding China, the region's exports fell by 0.4%."*

Due to continued weakness in global demand, the growth of world exports slowed down substantially from 2.3% in 2013 to 0.6% in 2014. The Asia-Pacific region performed better than the global average with growth in merchandise exports standing at 1.6% in 2014.[2] However, this figure is biased upward due to impact of the 6% growth in exports by China whose exports accounted for more than 30% of the region's total. Excluding China, exports from the Asia-Pacific region registered a decline of 0.4%. This figure is a combined result of export stagnation in other developing Asia-Pacific economies, which grew by only 0.6%, and a 4% decline in exports across Asia-Pacific developed economies that, in 2014, accounted for 13% of total exports by the region (figure 1.1). However disappointing this export performance might appear, it has to be kept in mind that this is mainly due to the deflationary impact of export prices, especially with regard to primary commodities (Saggu and Anukoonwattaka, 2015a).[3]

Exports have been a major engine of economic growth for the Asia-Pacific economies;[4] hence, disappointing export growth has transmitted into weaker final and intermediate demand for domestically-produced goods as well as for imports. It is not surprising that total Asia-Pacific imports declined by 0.9% in 2014. Imports by China grew by only 0.5% in 2014, the lowest rate – excluding the 2009 crisis – since 2000.[5] Import demand by other Asian and Pacific economies has been even weaker – falling by 1.4% across other developing economies and by 1.5% across developed economies in the region.

## Figure 1.1. Growth of merchandise trade across Asian and Pacific developing economies, 2007-2014

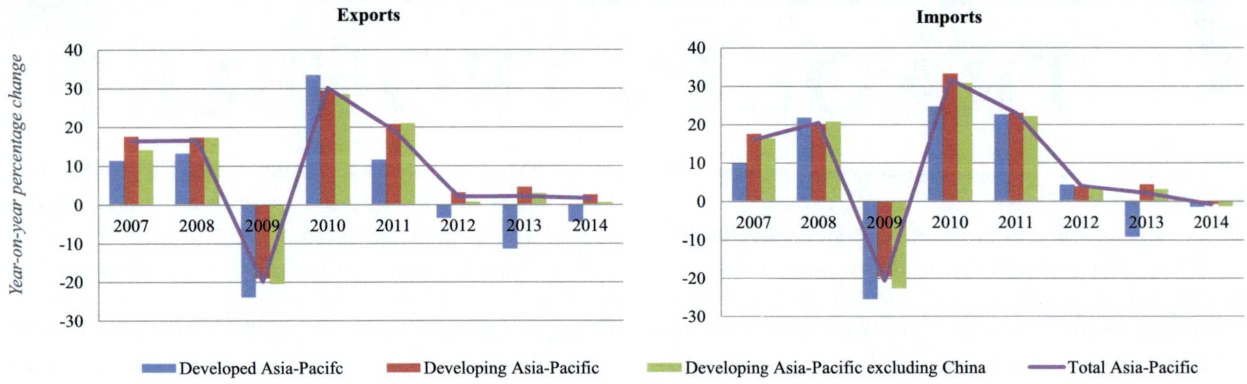


*Source:* ESCAP calculation, based on available data from the World Trade Organization International Trade Statistics Database (accessed September 2015). Data for individual economies are available from the ESCAP online statistical database.

As mentioned above, while the recovery of extraregional demand remains fragile – especially for the European Union economies – intraregional demand has also progressively weakened due to slow demand from China (see section D for more details). Countries that export primary and intermediate goods to China – particularly commodity exports – are facing a decline in export prices. Lower prices of fuel and other commodities are expected to reduce costs of production across commodity-importing economies; however, their ability to boost consumption will also depend on their being able to maintain stable or rising export revenue, a goal that is becoming more uncertain.

> *"Weak external demand and slowing growth are depressing trade prospects in the near future."*

National and international data provide no indication of merchandise trade growth recovery in 2015. The major exporting economies in the region have continued to face a year-on-year decline in export and import activity, especially in 2014-2015 (figure 1.2).[6] Sluggish performance by those economies will trickle down to have a negative impact on growth performance across all developing economies through the trade linkages within global and regional value chains. As trade is an important growth driver for developing Asia-Pacific economies it is not surprising that their growth is projected to dip further in 2015, while advanced economies may expand only modestly (IMF, 2015a). As already noted, China is not expected to regain its impressive double-digit economic growth; instead it is regressing onto a moderate growth path of 6%-7% annually or lower (see section D for more details). China's slowing rate of production has strong implications for global demand for primary commodities and inputs such as coal, copper, iron ore, palm oil and steel.[7] The downward pressure is not limited to primary resources and commodities, as countries dependent on manufacturing exports – such as the Philippines and Thailand – are also in an export recession because the drop in volume of China's processing exports. This, in turn, has led to falling demand for intermediate inputs.

**Figure 1.2. Monthly trade growth in selected developing Asia-Pacific economies, 2010-2015**

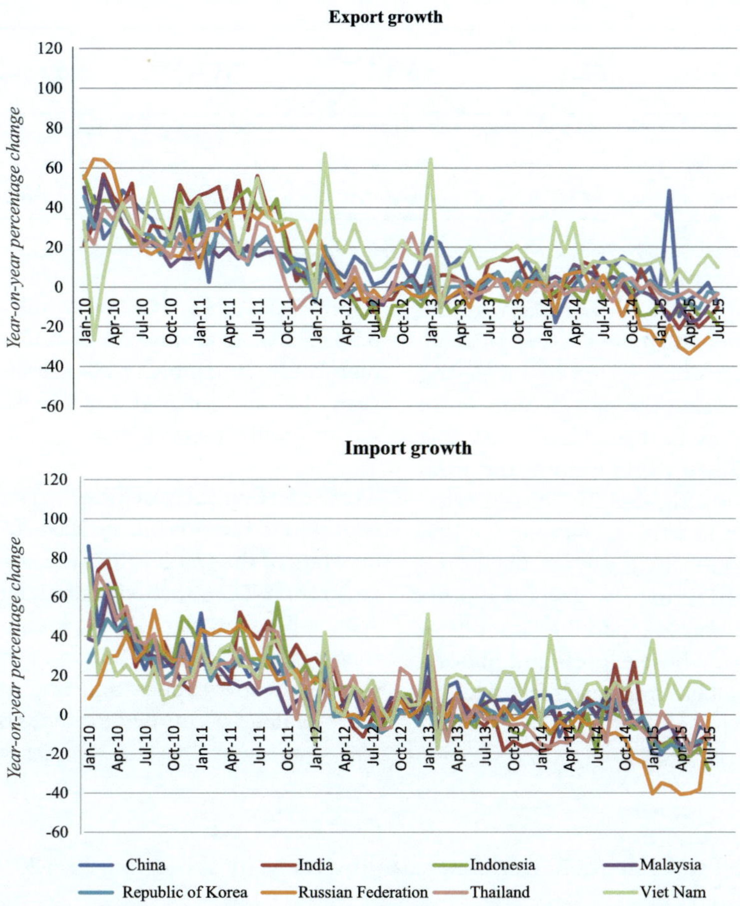


*Source:* ESCAP calculation, based on World Trade Organization online short-term statistics (accessed September 2015).
Note: This is nominal growth rate which indicates the change in export and import value.

# B SUBREGIONAL PERFORMANCE: ASIA-PACIFIC TRADE IS STILL DRIVEN BY EAST AND NORTH-EAST ASIA

*"The Asia-Pacific region as a whole is the largest trading region in the world, with a 39% share of world exports and 37% share of world imports."*

The Asia-Pacific region as a whole is the largest trading region in the world, accounting for a 39% share of world exports and a 37% share of world imports.[8] The region's dominance in world trade has been driven by economies in East and North-East Asia (ENEA), which accounted for just over 60% of total Asia-Pacific trade with the world in 2014 (table 1.1). South-East Asia (SEA) followed with a share of almost 18%. South and South-West Asia (SSWA) played a larger role on the import side (12.6%) than in exports (8.7%). On the other hand, the contribution by North and Central Asia (NCA) to the region's exports in the same year was larger (8.8%) than the share it captured on the import side (5.8%). Pacific economies accounted for only 4.0% of the region's trade.

**Table 1.1. Shares in Asia-Pacific total trade, by subregion, 2014**

*(Percentage)*

| | ENEA | SEA | SSWA | NCA | Pacific | Total Asia-Pacific |
|---|---|---|---|---|---|---|
| Exports | 60.8 | 17.7 | 8.7 | 8.8 | 4.0 | 100 |
| Imports | 59.8 | 17.6 | 12.6 | 5.8 | 4.2 | 100 |

*Source:* ESCAP calculation, based on data from the World Trade Organization International Trade Statistics Database (accessed September 2015).

Although dominated by East and North-East Asia, all the Asia-Pacific subregions have contributed to Asia-Pacific region becoming the largest trading region by increasing their shares in world trade during the past decade. From 2006 to 2014, the contribution by East and North-East Asia increased from 20.6% to 23.5% of world exports and from 17.9% to 22.1% of world imports (figure 1.3). China was the largest merchandise exporter, in 2014, accounting for 12% of exports and 10% of imports globally. Japan was the second largest region's exporter, contributing 4% of world exports and imports; this was slightly higher than the Republic of Korea and Hong Kong, China, whose exports and imports accounted for around 3% of global trade each in 2014.

South-East Asia's share of world exports increased from 6.3% in 2006 to around 7% in 2014 – mainly by five ASEAN members – Singapore (2.2%); Thailand and Malaysia (1.2% each); Indonesia (0.9%); and Viet Nam (0.8%) – with similar shares on the import side.

North and Central Asia increased its shares slightly in world exports and imports during 2006-2014. However, some three quarters of the trade value was attributable to the Russian Federation. The situation is similar to South and South-West Asia, where India accounted for more than 50% of trade by that region. The Pacific subregion represented a negligible share in world exports and imports, while Australia and New Zealand accounted for more than 95% of that trade.

**Figure 1.3. Asia-Pacific shares in world merchandise trade, by subregion, 2006-2014**

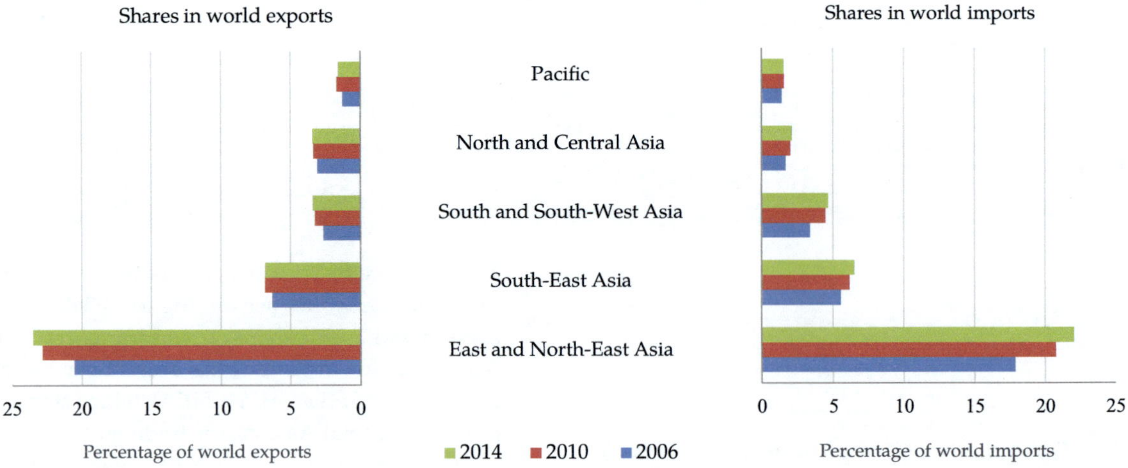


*Source:* ESCAP calculation based on data from the World Trade Organization International Trade Statistics Database (accessed September 2015).

# C EXTERNAL CONDITIONS OPEN THE DOOR TO EVEN STRONGER INTRAREGIONAL TRADE

The share of intraregional exports increased during the past decade from 46% of total Asia-Pacific exports in 2002 to 54% in 2014, while the share of intraregional imports quite stable at above 50% throughout that period (figure 1.4). The increase was driven by exports to China and other developing Asia-Pacific economies; their joint share rose from 36% to 46%, respectively, during the same period. At the same time, the share of exports reaching developed markets – principally the United States, the European Union and developed Asia-Pacific economies – declined from 50% to 37%.

**Figure 1.4. Destinations of merchandise exports from Asia and the Pacific, 2002-2014**

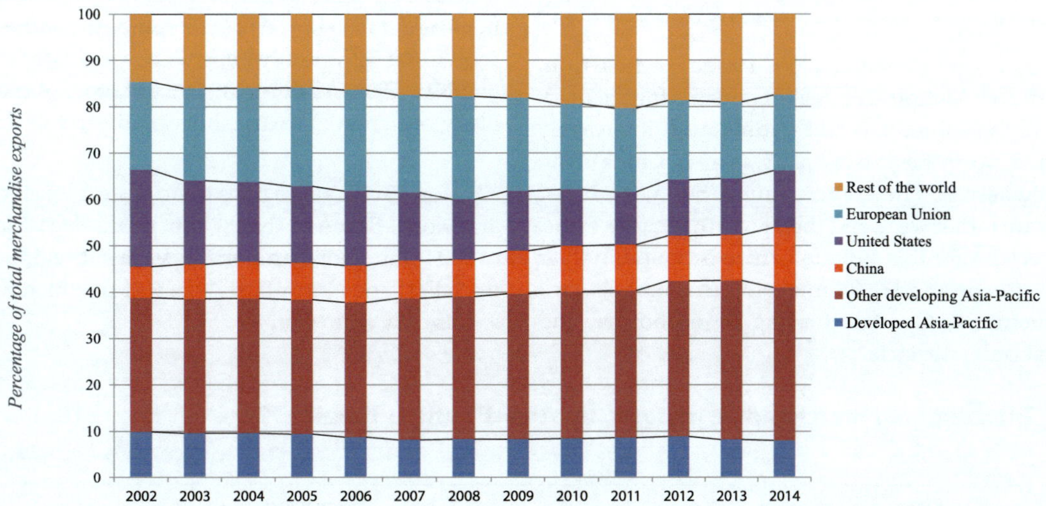


*Source:* ESCAP calculation based on United Nations Comtrade data accessed through the World Bank World Integrated Trade Solution (WITS) Database (accessed September 2015). Data for 2014 were sourced from the IMF DOTS database.

**Figure 1.5. Sources of Asia-Pacific merchandise imports, 2002-2014**

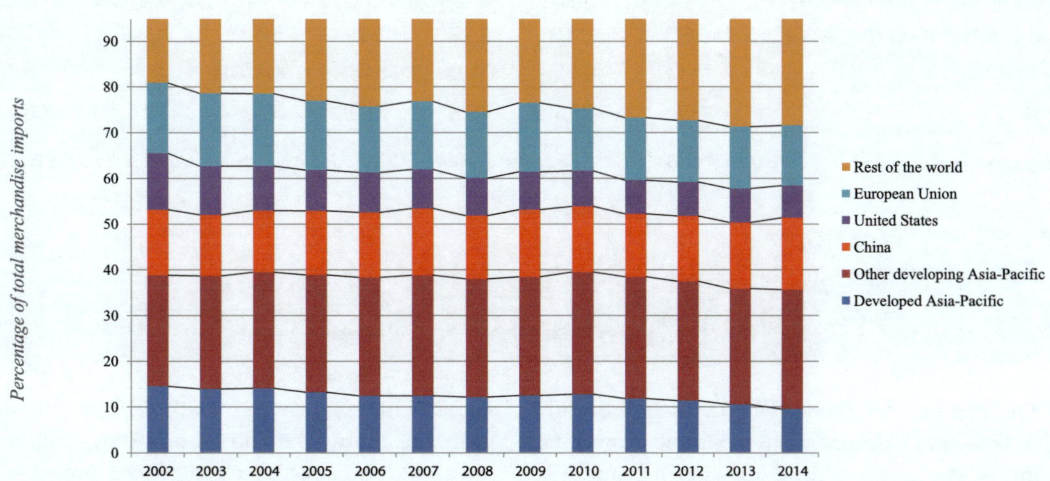


*Source:* ESCAP calculation based on United Nations Comtrade data accessed through the World Bank World Integrated Trade Solution (WITS) Database (accessed September 2015). Data for 2014 were sourced from the IMF DOTS database.

Intraregional imports accounted for slightly more than 50% of total Asia-Pacific imports throughout the 2002-2014 period (figure 1.5). In terms of growth, imports from developing economies outside the region dominated all other sources. As a result the share of import sourcing from developing economies outside the region increased substantially from 19% to 28% of total Asia-Pacific imports, while the share of traditional import sources declined– especially the United States and Japan, whose joint share decreased from 27% to 17%.

> *"More than half of Asia-Pacific total trade is intraregional."*

There remains a significant unexploited trade potential from South-South cooperation. The region remains fragmented, with most of the subregions still trading most intensively with East and North-East Asia (in fact, mainly China) than among themselves. The trade connections with other subregions are rather weak and their growth remains static. The main reasons for this situation are to be found in their production structure and economic complementarities, lack of infrastructure to facilitate trading across border, and behind-the-border obstacles.

> *"All Asia-Pacific subregions trade more intensively with East and North-East Asia than within themselves."*

The intensity of intraregional trade varies across subregions (table 1.2). Intraregional trade linkages are particularly strong in South-East Asia and the Pacific, whose imports are sourced from within the region at substantial levels (64.8% and 59.7% of total imports in 2014, respectively). However, different factors explain the high intraregional trade intensity of South-East Asia and the Pacific. The high intraregional trade intensity of South-East Asian economies reflects their participation in regional value chains (discussed in more detail in part II of this report). In contrast, the Pacific economies show heavy dependency on trade with Australia and New Zealand due to distance to other markets and very likely preferential treatment available in these markets.

All Asia-Pacific subregions trade more intensively with East and North-East Asia than within themselves. More than half of the intraregional imports by each subregion are sourced from East and North-East Asia, 50% of which were sourced specifically from China.

**Table 1.2. Intraregional merchandise imports, by Asia-Pacific subregion, 2014**

*(Percentage of total merchandise imports)*

| Importers | Exporters | | | | | | | |
|---|---|---|---|---|---|---|---|---|
| | Excl. China | China | ENEA | SEA | SSWA | NCA | Pacific | Asia-Pacific |
| East and North-East Asia (ENEA) | 13.7 | 13.9 | 27.6 | 11.7 | 2.4 | 2.8 | 4.7 | 49.1 |
| South-East Asia (SEA) | 16.5 | 19.0 | 35.5 | 22.8 | 2.5 | 1.7 | 2.4 | 64.8 |
| South and South-West Asia (SSWA) | 5.8 | 15.1 | 20.9 | 7.6 | 7.3 | 4.4 | 1.5 | 41.6 |
| North and Central Asia (NCA) | 6.5 | 20.2 | 26.7 | 2.2 | 5.6 | 11.4 | 0.2 | 46.1 |
| Pacific | 11.8 | 19.6 | 31.4 | 18.8 | 1.8 | 0.6 | 7.0 | 59.7 |
| Asia-Pacific | 12.6 | 15.7 | 28.3 | 13.0 | 3.3 | 3.2 | 3.6 | 51.4 |

*Source:* ESCAP calculation, based on IMF Direction of Trade Statistics (accessed September 2015). Country data are available from the ESCAP online statistics database.

## D CHINA'S TRANSITION TO A NEW NORMAL AND ITS IMPLICATIONS FOR ASIA-PACIFIC TRADE[9]

Following the accession of China to WTO in 2001, the world witnessed a decade of extraordinary economic growth for that economy – averaging around 10% per annum. The recovery of global trade following the Global Financial Crisis in 2008-2009 was mostly credited to dynamism of Chinese economy (ESCAP, 2010). This generated the expectation that robust Chinese growth would play a stabilizing role in the global economy. The Chinese economy – together with India – was widely expected to replace or compensate for the loss of consumption growth across many advanced economies, such as those in Europe and North America.[10]

## Figure 1.6. Growth of Chinese exports and GDP, 1998-2020

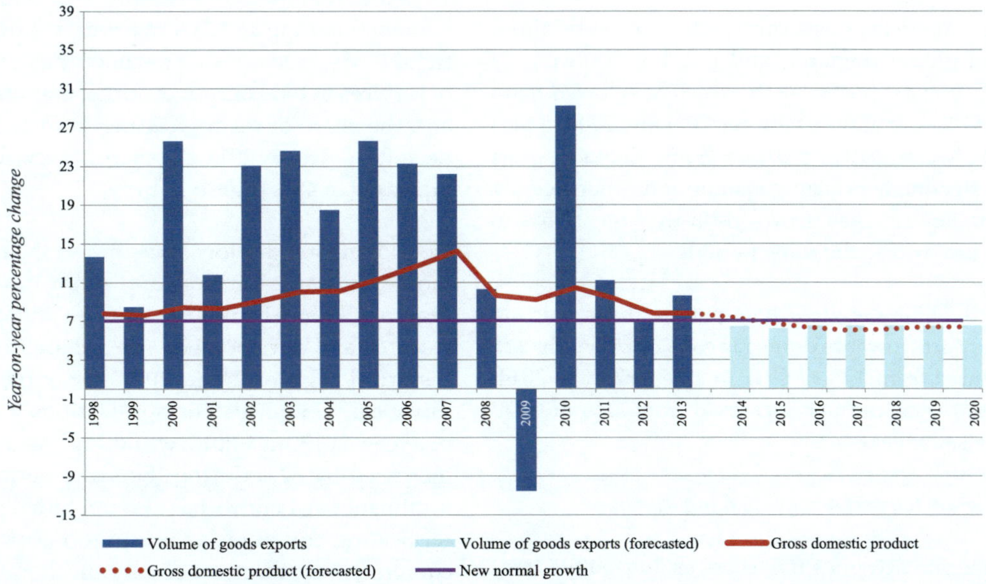


*Source:* ESCAP calculation, based on data from the IMF World Economic Outlook and World Trade Organization International Trade Statistics (accessed June 2015).

However, the expectation that the world economy could be supported by robust Chinese growth has weakened substantially. For the third year in a row (since 2012), China's economy has shown a marked slowdown – with growth rates declining from double-digit levels – before the crisis – to around 7% in 2014 (figure 1.6).[11] A statement by Xi Jinping – President of China – indicated that China was entering a "new normal" for its growth path (Xuequan, 2014).[12] This suggests that the Government of China anticipates moderate economic growth in the medium to long term. Recent estimates indicate that China may register lower growth than currently predicted. For example, the IMF (2015a) has revised its growth forecasts for China, projecting it to steadily decline to 6% by 2017. In addition, the Chinese economy has been in manufacturing recession since March 2015 after the HSBC Purchasing Manager's Index – which measures China's manufacturing activity – indicated contraction for six consecutive months (Waldmeir and Hunter, 2015; and Zhu, 2015).

Structural and cyclical factors explain China's economic slowdown.[13] Structurally, the growth factors of production (labour and capital) in the Chinese economy have peaked in 2012. In addition, China's technological gap with advanced economies has continued to narrow, implying that productivity growth will be lower. More recently, problems from credit bubbles have added to risks of a sharper-than-expected slowdown in the Chinese economy (IMF, 2015b). Indeed, public, private and financial debt increased from 176% of GDP in 2007 to 258% of GDP in mid-2014 (Sterne and Theiss, 2014). Much of the credit flowed to property developers, and resulted in non-performing loans.[14]

The structural rebalancing of China will have important implications for the trade prospects of Asian and Pacific economies as China has been a major export market, absorbing 19% of exports from the rest of the Asia-Pacific region in 2014. Given the persistent weakness in demand across many advanced economies, the growth of China's import demand is of particular importance to both the region and the global economy.[15]

### 1. Implications of China's economic rebalancing for Asia-Pacific trade

The major structural changes in China that may reshape Asia-Pacific trade patterns include the shifting of China towards a domestic consumption-led growth strategy as well as the rising importance of services and innovation in total production.

> *"China's shift towards an economy driven by consumption, services and innovation may reshape Asia-Pacific trade patterns."*

*(a) The shift from export-driven growth to consumption-driven growth*

The 2007-2009 financial crisis contributed to a substantial downturn in global demand, and this has been partly reflected in China's export growth, which has slowed from an average of 24% per annum between 2001 and 2008 to 14% per annum between 2010 and 2014.[16] While China's export growth has declined, private consumption – boosted by domestic retail sales – has grown robustly from 12.5% to 14% per annum during the same periods.

As a result, the Chinese growth engine has been shifting away from exports towards domestic consumption. In fact, exports declined from 35% of GDP in 2007 to 23% in 2014, while domestic consumption increased from 35% of GDP to 41% in the same years.

*(b) The transition towards services and innovation*

Tertiary economic activities (i.e. services and innovation) are playing an increasingly important role in the Chinese economy while the share of primary industry in GDP and employment has continued to decline. In 2011, the share of workers employed in services superseded those in primary industries for the first time (figure 1.7a). Since then, the gap has continued to widen, and by 2013, 38% of employees were found in the services industry, compared to just 30% in manufacturing and 31% in primary industries. A similar trend is observed across the economy as a whole. The share of services in total output overtook manufacturing in 2012, and the share of manufacturing in total output began to decline in 2010. By 2014, the share of services in total output increased to 48% (figure 1.7b).

Development indicators also support the trend in China of moving towards services and innovation activities. For example, World Bank Development Indicators show that research and development – as a share of GDP – rose to a historical high of 2% in 2012, the same level as in the European Union. Patent applications also rose by 11% between 2012 and 2013 while high-technology exports increased by 32% during the same period. The Chinese multinational, Lenovo, has also upgraded its business from replicating computer products to becoming an original equipment manufacturer of computer hardware. It has more recently begun innovating in the field and now owns the patent for clip-on keyboards for tablets (see www.patentbolt.com).[17]

**Figure 1.7. Industry contributions to employment and GDP in China, 1980-2014**

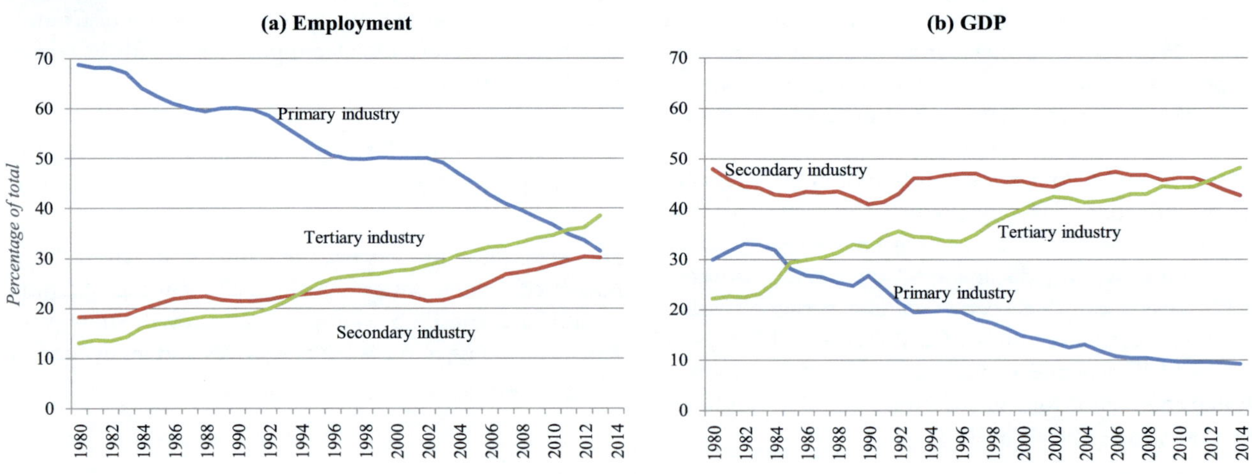


*Source:* ESCAP calculation based on data from the CEIC database (accessed June 2015).

## 2. Trade linkages between China and other Asia-Pacific economies

The structural changes of China, as noted above, will have important implications for other Asia-Pacific economies, particularly those in which exports and production are highly integrated with China through both forward and backward linkages in global value chains (GVCs). Although China is the world's largest exporter, it is also an important export market for producers across Asia and the Pacific. In 2007, China overtook the United States as the largest individual trading partner in the region – a position it has maintained since that year.[18] In 2014, China sourced 41% of its imports from other Asia-Pacific countries, while other Asia-Pacific countries exported 19% of their goods to China.[19]

Raw materials and intermediate inputs now constitute a quarter of China's imports from other Asia-Pacific economies. A part of those intermediate imports are for use in further processing and assembly, and are subsequently re-exported from China to the rest of the world.[20] Using the

OECD-WTO database on trade in value-added (TiVA), imports from Asia-Pacific economies measured in value-added terms are contributing around 16% of exports by China.[21]

A slowdown in Chinese exports and economic growth has reduced demand for imported inputs. This has already been partly reflected in lower prices for energy and other commodities. Several Asia-Pacific economies – particularly those exporting copper, coal, iron ore and steel – have already experienced adverse impacts from the commodity price decline. Countries with special needs[22] whose economies are highly reliant on commodity exports to China – such as Kazakhstan, the Lao People's Democratic Republic, Mongolia, the Solomon Islands and Turkmenistan – are at greatest risk and may experience a further decline in exports in the short to medium term (see box 1.1, China's economic slowdown and commodity trade of Asia-Pacific countries).

**Figure 1.8. Primary (including fuels), intermediate and final goods exports to China across selected economies, 2014**

*(Percentage)*

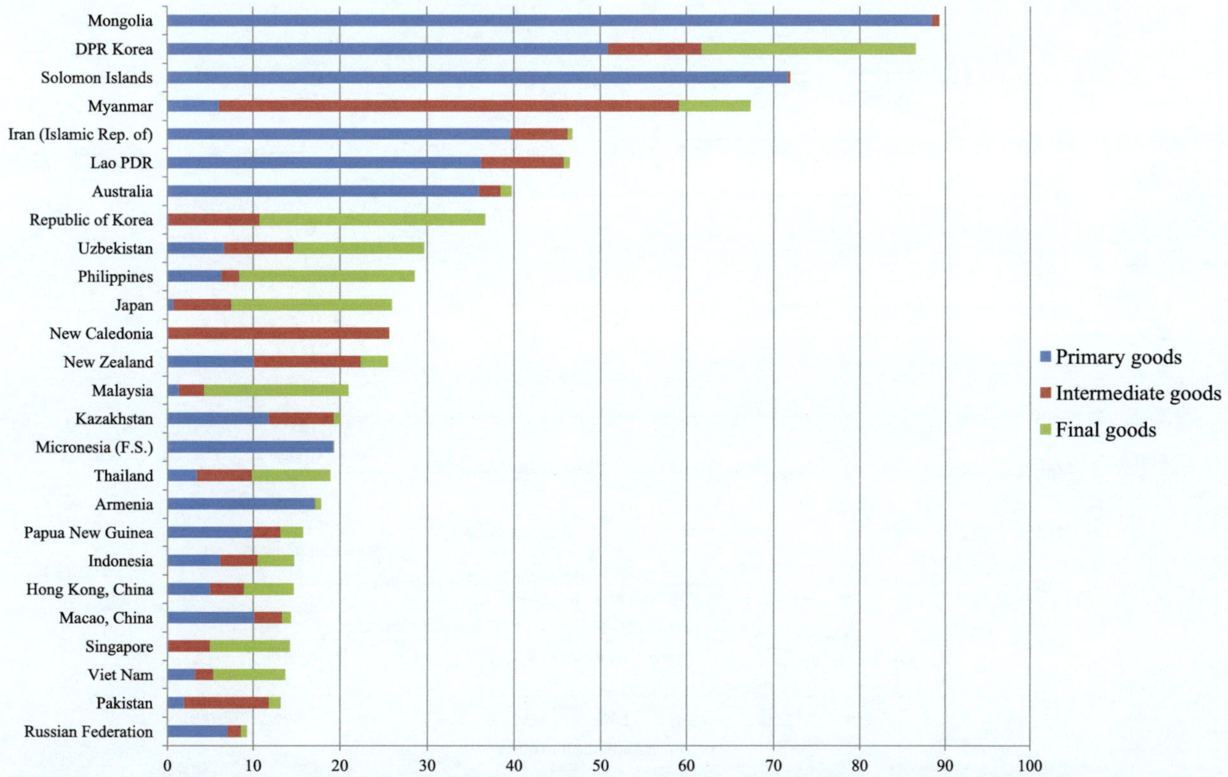


*Source:* ESCAP calculation based on United Nations Comtrade data accessed through WITS (accessed September 2015).
*Notes:* Mirror data are used. The numbers are based on gross value, which may include re-exports. The classification of goods is based on Systems of National Accounts (SNS), which distinguish between primary, intermediate, consumer and capital goods (United Nations Statistics Division, 2011). Final goods are defined as the sum of consumer and capital goods, excluding fuels.

Nevertheless, the structural shift towards a consumption-based economy in China may increase opportunities for countries exporting final goods – especially high-tech and branded consumer goods – as the purchasing power of Chinese consumers gradually increases. The countries that could benefit include Japan, Malaysia, the Philippines, the Republic of Korea, Singapore and Viet Nam (figure 1.8). Japan and the Republic of Korea are the region's largest final goods exporters to China, and opportunities for export to China may increase further given their strength in high-tech consumer goods. There are risks that imports will be partially replaced by domestic production (in view of weakened exports). Competition in the Chinese market for final goods is likely to become stronger and more intensified given the continuing rebalance towards slower growth. While it is reasonable to expect that some import-substituting incentives could be used to manage demand for consumer goods, a careful balancing act is desirable in order not to stifle these additional trade opportunities for the region with too many defensive policies.

The transition of China towards more innovation-based production and services presents an opportunity for emerging market economies to (a) utilize the advantages of having more competitive labour costs and access to natural resources, and (b) replace China in some segments of GVCs.

However, the ability to enter GVCs depends upon many other factors, such as the availability and efficiency of trade-related infrastructure as well as services such as communication, transportation and logistical networks, access to financing, and minimal restrictions on trade and foreign direct investment (discussed more fully in part II of this report).

### Box 1.1 China's economic slowdown and commodity trade of Asia-Pacific countries[23]

The transition of China's economy to more sustainable levels of economic growth contributed to a sharp fall in international commodity prices in the second half of 2014. In particular, copper, coal, iron ore and crude oil prices – traditional yardsticks of China's demand – fell by 6%, 14%, 31% and 58%, respectively (World Bank, 2015). The combination of lower commodity prices and expectations of falling commodity imports by China has important implications for Asia-Pacific economies – which collectively account for a third of global commodity imports and exports.

**Figure A. Economies vulnerable to downturn in Chinese demand and commodity prices, 2014**

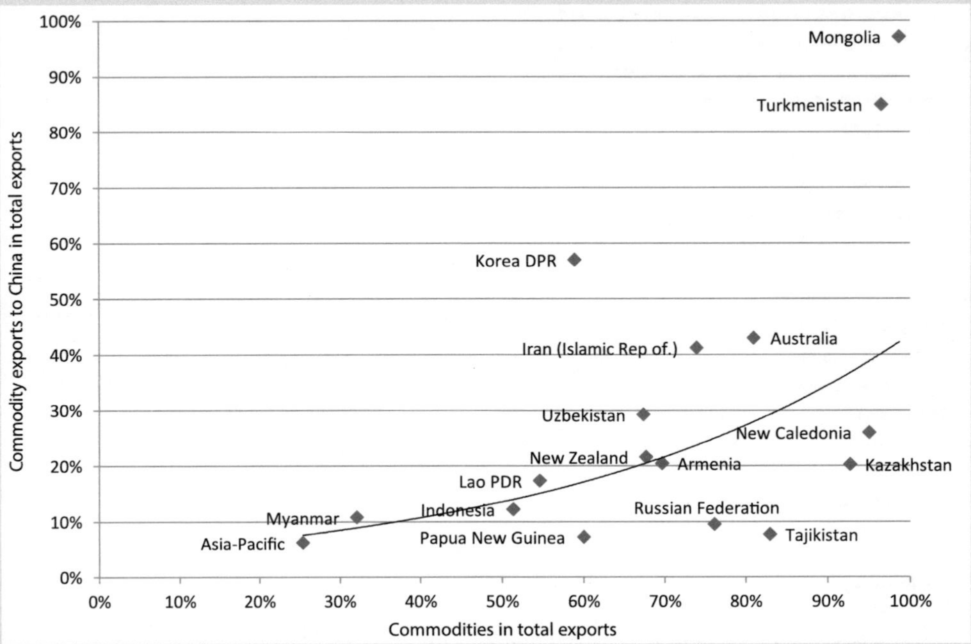


*Source:* ESCAP calculation based on United Nations Comtrade data accessed through WITS (accessed June 2015).
*Notes:* The classification of commodities is based on clusters: 25-26_Minerals, 27-27_Fuels, 72-83_Metals, WTO_H3_Agrri and Total. The fitted line is an exponential trend. Mirror data are used

Exports and economic growth are at significant risk across economies reliant on commodity exports as an engine of growth. The most vulnerable economies are countries with special needs (i.e. least developed countries, landlocked developing countries and small island develping States) and those with high dependence on fuel and mineral exports to China, such as the Democratic People's Republic of Korea, Mongolia and Turkmenistan – where primary commodity exports account for 59%-99% of total exports, and more than 50% of total exports are destined for China (figure A). The decline in China's demand for commodities is also adversely affecting the growth of exports and GDP of large commodity-exporting economies such as Australia (minerals) and the Russian Federation (fuel).

However, lower commodity prices may also be expected to translate into an improvement in the trade balance – through lowering the cost of raw materials and fuels – across commodity importing economies. There are 32 net-commodity importing economies in the Asia-Pacific region. Many are countries with special needs that run current account deficits amounting to around 11% of GDP – partly attributable to commodity import dependency. These countries include Cambodia, Kyrgyzstan, Nepal and other remote island nations – Kiribati, Maldives, Micronesia (F.S), Samoa, Tonga and Tuvalu – which are highly dependent on fuel and agricultural imports (figure B).

**Figure B. Asia-Pacific net commodity importers, 2014**

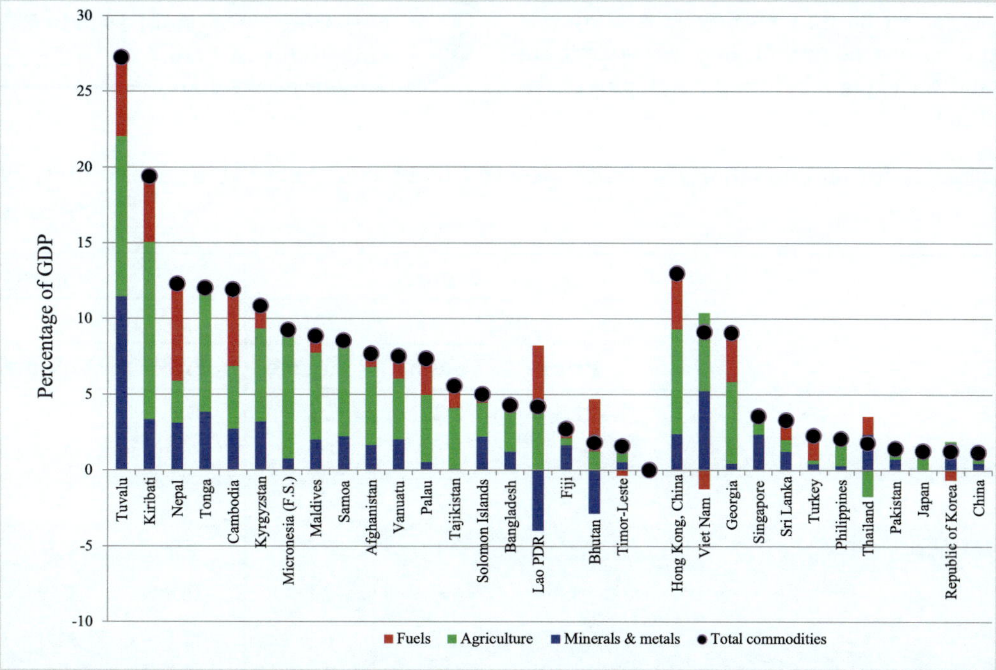


*Source: ESCAP* calculation based on United Nations Comtrade data accessed through WITS (accessed June 2015).
*Notes:* The classification of commodities is based on clusters: 25-26_Minerals, 27-27_Fuels, 72-83_Metals, WTO_H3_Agri and Total. Mirror data are used. GDP data are from the International Monetary Fund's World Economic Outlook Database (April 2015). The following countries are excluded due to insufficient data coverage: American Samoa; Cook Islands; French Polynesia; Guam; Democratic People's Republic of Korea; Macao, China; Nauru; New Caledonia; Niue; and Northern Mariana Islands.

The improved growth momentum of India amidst China's economic slowdown leads to the expectation that India may offer a new hope for regional and global economy. IMF (2015a) expects that India will overtake China as the fastest growing economy in the world in 2015. Although the rapid growth of Indian GDP in recent years may be partly a result of the change in GDP calculation method introduced by Indian in the early 2015,[24] it is expected that the growth momentum of India will be sustained by economic reforms, a consequent pickup in investment and lower oil prices. In addition, population growth adds to India's growth potential. It is expected to have the largest labour force in the world by 2030, with about one billion people of working age (IMF, 2015a). However, India is still not in a position to support global and regional trade and investment flows as China did. The size of Indian economy and GDP per capita, measured in real term, is around 30% of China.[25] India's economy is still domestically driven and the share of the country's industrial sector is still relatively small (Anukoonwattaka and Mikic, 2011). Therefore, India needs to significantly strengthen its manufacturing sector in order to become competitive as a global and regional export hub.

# E NEAR-TERM PROSPECTS AND CONCLUSION

There are substantial downside risks to trade across Asia and the Pacific. Countries that are highly integrated into GVCs and international supply chains cannot ignore these risks; if they do, they will be exposed to pass-through effects from other countries. The expectation that intraregional demand alone – i.e. China's demand – will be sufficient to maintain a healthy level of economic activities without robust demand from the outside the region remains premature.

The near-term prospects for trade by Asia and the Pacific are influenced by the balance between the impacts from intraregional demand and the modest recovery of the United States and Eurozone economies. The economic transition of China presents a major risk to trade as well as an opportunity for exports of final goods to China. Based on economic performance observed so far in 2015, there are worrying concerns that China may not achieve its 7% growth target, and the slowdown may persist in to the medium term. This presents greater concern that the transition of China towards a consumption-driven economy will not generate sufficient external demand for exports by other developing Asia-Pacific economies.

*"Growth prospects of merchandise exports by Asia-Pacific economies will continue softening throughout 2015 before stabilizing in 2016."*

**Table 1.3. Prospects for real merchandise trade growth for selected Asia-Pacific economies, 2015-2016**

*(Annual percentage change)*

| | Exports | | | Imports | | |
|---|---|---|---|---|---|---|
| | 2015[a] | | 2016[a] | 2015[a] | | 2016[a] |
| | Price | Volume | Volume | Price | Volume | Volume |
| Australia | -21.3 | 2.2 | 2.2 | -8.7 | 0.8 | 3 |
| Bangladesh | 0.4 | -3.5 | -0.1 | -7.2 | -8.3 | 0.5 |
| China | -1.8 | 3.7 | 4 | -14.2 | -4.2 | 4.6 |
| Hong Kong, China | -1.7 | 2.1 | 3.7 | -4.0 | 0.9 | 2.8 |
| India | -10.0 | 6.6 | 2.8 | -26.9 | 12.9 | 7.3 |
| Indonesia | -13.9 | -1.2 | 6.3 | -11.5 | -4.8 | 5 |
| Japan | -3.2 | 2.9 | 5 | -19.4 | 0.1 | 4.5 |
| Malaysia | -11.1 | 5.5 | 4.8 | -11.0 | 1.4 | 4.1 |
| New Zealand | -2.4 | 3.3 | -2.4 | -9.1 | 9.5 | 5.1 |
| Pakistan | -4.7 | -1.8 | -2.2 | -16.8 | 6.8 | 3.2 |
| Philippines | -4.7 | 5 | -0.7 | -12.1 | 2.9 | 3.9 |
| Republic of Korea | -4.4 | 0.4 | -3.6 | -20.6 | -10.8 | -4.8 |
| Russian Federation | -33.0 | 0.1 | -0.2 | -2.6 | -30.4 | 9.5 |
| Singapore | -8.0 | -0.7 | -1 | -15.1 | -2.6 | 1.1 |
| Sri Lanka | 6.9 | 2.3 | 3.6 | -13.1 | 3.5 | 3.9 |
| Taiwan Province of China | -2.6 | -0.8 | 1.5 | -7.1 | 0.7 | 2.4 |
| Thailand | -4.2 | -1.5 | 5.4 | -14.5 | -1.1 | 5.6 |
| Turkey | -4.0 | 5.5 | 5.6 | -6.9 | 1.7 | 4.2 |
| Viet Nam | -4.4 | 9.7 | 9.2 | -3.1 | 11.2 | 11.2 |
| Asia and the Pacific[b] | -9.1 | 2.3 | 2.6 | -13.7 | -2.4 | 3.8 |
| Developing Asia-Pacific[b] | -9.2 | 2.3 | 2.3 | -13.1 | -3.1 | 3.7 |

*Source:* ESCAP and ECLAC estimate based on UN Comtrade data from 2014, and evolution of commodity and manufacturing prices on a monthly basis (from 2014 until July 2015) taken from the World Bank, IMF, UNCTAD, United States Bureau of Labour Statistics, among others. For projections until December 2015, an index composed by data from the World Bank, FMI and the Economist Intelligence Unit was applied. Volumes are from the Economist Intelligence Unit, *as of September 2015.*

*Note:* The estimated growth rates are calculated based on constant prices (in 2005 terms) and exchange rates. The selected countries cover 98 per cent of trade across the Asia-Pacific. ESCAP calculation based on United Nations Comtrade data accessed through the World Bank, World Integrated Trade Solution (WITS) Database (accessed August 2015).

[a] Projections.

[b] Regional trade growth is the trade-weighted, time-varying average growth rate.

Taking these challenges into account, ESCAP anticipates that the growth prospects of merchandise exports by Asia-Pacific economies will continue softening throughout 2015 before stabilizing in 2016. Across the Asia-Pacific region, merchandise export volume in 2015 is projected to grow by 2.3% while imports are moving in the opposite direction (table 1.3). However, trade performance will be diverse across countries, depending on the regional intensity of their exports. Countries such as India and Viet Nam will be in a relatively good position since their exports are significantly directed to the United States and advanced European countries. Based on the expectation that the demand recovery from the European Union and the United States will gain some momentum in 2016, trade growth is anticipated to improve modestly to about 2.3% for exports and 3.7% for imports.

It is important to note that the growth prospects indicated above are based on change in trade volume, not nominal value. The downward trend in global commodity and manufacturing prices – especially in 2015 – indicates that the export income of Asia-Pacific economies will shrink. Export and import prices of the Asia-Pacific region as a whole are projected to drop by 9.1% and 13.7%, respectively. However, the impacts on terms of trade differ across Asia-Pacific economies, depending on their trade basket. In terms of export prices, Australia and the Russian Federation are likely to experience the sharpest price declines due to lower commodity prices. Minerals, metals and fuels also account for around half of Australia's exports while the Russian Federation's exports are dominated by fuels – particularly gas exports. Nevertheless, the estimated price development in 2014/2015 may translate into positive shock in terms of trade for the whole Asia-Pacific region and the vast majority of the region's countries. This is mainly due to the fact that many larger economies have strong manufacturing sectors, particularly China, Japan, the Republic of Korea and Singapore.

The slowdown in China and persistent weakness in global demand will inevitably lead to a slowdown in trade across countries that supply goods to China. Those at particular risk include Factory Asia as well as primary commodity and fuel exporters. However, the transition by China may also present several opportunities for other Asia-Pacific economies.

First, the structural shift towards domestic consumption may increase opportunities for countries exporting final goods – especially high-tech and branded products – to China. Second, as China moves away from an intermediate-industry based towards higher value-added production and services activities, this presents an opportunity for emerging economies to fill the gap and replace China in some segments of GVCs. Economies with more competitive labour costs and access to natural resources could potentially fill the void left by China in processing, manufacture, assembly and construction. However, the ability of economies to participate in GVCs cannot be left to the private sector to identify opportunities, but critically depends upon a holistic approach to policy formulation to improve trade and investment environments in the context of long-term sustainable development strategy.

## ENDNOTES

[1] The numbers on merchandise trade were compiled by the ESCAP secretariat, based on data available from WTO and IMF at the time of preparing this report. More recent revisions of trade data by those data sources may result in different trade balance values. The numbers include trade data of Taiwan Province of China, which is not an ESCAP member, but represents sheer size of merchandise trade in the Asia-Pacific region. The use of other sources of trade data may produce different estimates. Individual economy data for ESCAP member States are available from the ESCAP online statistical database.

[2] These numbers are estimates by the ESCAP secretariat, based on WTO data at the time of preparing this report. More recent revisions of trade data by WTO may result in different trade balance values.

[3] According the estimation by WTO secretariat, export price of Asia declined by 2.1% in 2014 while export volume increased by 4.7%.

[4] Systematic evidence on the growth experience during the past 40 years offers an overwhelming support to the hypothesis that trade is a necessary condition for economic growth. No country in past decades has sustained high levels of economic growth and reduced poverty significantly without greatly expanding its imports and exports. A large majority of the empirical studies on the linkages between trade openness and economic growth have confirmed that positive association between trade openness and economic growth. Some of the commonly quoted studies based on cross-country evidence are Dollar (1992), Edwards (1998), Frankel and Romer (1999), Harrison (1996), and Sachs and Warner (1995). In addition, there is now highly consistent and largely uncontested evidence that firms in more open sectors tend to be more productive, and experience faster productivity growth – see, for example, Pavcnik (2002), Ruiz and Utar (2009) and Trefler (2004). Following the financial crisis of 2008-2009, the questions of the merits of export-led growth strategies for developing countries arise – see for example, Harrison and Rodriguez-Clare (2009), Rodrik (2009) and UNCTAD (2010). Nonetheless, the IMF Managing Director noted that "Reinvigorating trade is not just a 'nice-to-have'. It is an 'essential-to-have' – to help prevent what I have called the new mediocre of low growth over a long period" (Lagarde, 2015). The estimates made by Xing and

Pradhananga (2013) show that the impressive recovery of the Chinese economy in the post-crisis period owed at least 53% of its growth to exports and foreign direct investment.

[5] Imports by China account for 29% of total merchandise imports of Asia and the Pacific.

[6] In February 2015, there was a 48% surge in exports. GDP and exports in China decline every year in January because of a post-Christmas drop in orders from developed countries' markets combined with a week-long holiday for the Chinese New Year, which leads to a sharp decline in production. In 2015, the holiday period fell in February; hence, the month-to-month change in February 2014 is affected.

[7] Based on monthly data from January 2000 through September 2011, Roache (2012) found that China's demand shocks explained about 7% of the price variation in the global market for crude oil and copper.

[8] This includes both intraregional trade flows and flows with the rest of the world.

[9] This section is drawn from Saggu and Anukoonwattaka (2015c).

[10] It has been argued that the high rates of consumption across many advanced economies in Europe and North America during the 1990s was made possible through a series of financial bubbles – most notably in housing – which enabled consumers to draw upon the wealth from appreciating values of real estate, thereby diminishing their need for savings (see Farooki and Kaplinsky, 2013). This structural weakness contributed to a rise in the balance of payments across many advanced economies.

[11] The slowdown of growth in China could be seen as being symptomatic of a general decline in the rate of growth of the ratio of global trade to GDP following the 2007-2009 financial crisis.

[12] The term "new normal" was initially popularised by the investment management company PIMCO to describe economic growth in China following the 2007-2009 financial crisis (Roberts, 2014).

[13] Hoekman, ed., (2015) argued that the lack of trade dynamism in the global economy in recent years stemmed primarily from cyclical factors such as weakness in aggregate demand from the Eurozone and, more recently, from China. He also suggested that the slowdown in China could be a reflection of non-cyclical factors such as the end of an integration process of China and central and eastern Europe, explaining that higher growth rates in the past might simply have been a transitional phenomenon. Alternatively, the slowdown could represent the limits having being achieved on the ability of companies to engage in international fragmentation of production networks through GVCs.

[14] The property and construction industry has borrowed heavily from domestic and international lenders. State-owned enterprises are among the most indebted companies because they have easier access to credit (Magnier, Wei and Evans, 2015). The downside risks for Chinese construction have also become more apparent as the country recently experienced its first corporate bond default.

[15] ESCAP's calculation, using IMF Direction of Trade Statistics (accessed June 2015).

[16] Calculation based on geometric mean of the growth rates during the indicated period.

[17] See www.patentlymobile.com/2012/05/lenovo-invents-handgrip-keyboards-for-tablet-computers.html.

[18] Calculated using data from United Nations Comtrade accessed through WITS (June 2015).

[19] Calculated using data from IMF Direction of Trade Statistics (accessed June 2015).

[20] See Chapter 1 of the Asia-Pacific Investment Report (ESCAP, 2012 and 2013) for more details.

[21] Calculation based on data in 2009, which are the latest available data in the OECD-WTO Trade in Value-Added database.

[22] Comprising least developed countries, landlocked developing counties and small island developing States. A list of these countries in Asia and the Pacific is available at www.unescap.org/our-work/macroeconomic-policy-development/countries-special-needs.

[23] More details are available in Saggu and Anukoonwattaka (2015a and 2015b).

[24] Since January 2015, India has announced GDP figures based on the new measures that calculate GDP by market prices instead of factor costs, and shifted the base year from 2005 to 2012. The revised calculation also incorporates more comprehensive data on corporate activity as well as newer surveys of spending by households and informal businesses. In principle, the new method is more in line with global practices and gives a better picture of economic activity. However, shifting the GDP calculation method requires caution when comparing the economic performance of India during the recent period with historical ones. For example, under the old method, the economic growth of India hit a decade low at 4.5% in 2013, and then increased slightly to

4.7% in 2014. Using the new methodology, the GDP growth rate for 2013 became 5.1% and accelerated to 6.9% in 2014.

[25] See country data in ESCAP online database for details.

## REFERENCES


Anukoonwattaka, Witada, and Mia Mikic, eds. (2011). *India: A New Player in Asian Production Networks?* Studies in Trade and Investment No. 75. ST/ESCAP/2624. Available from www.unescap.org/resources/india-new-player-asian-production-networks-studies-trade-and-investment-no-75.

Dollar, David (1992). Outward-oriented developing economies really do grow more rapidly: evidence from 95 LDCs, 1976-1985. *Economic Development and Cultural Change*, vol. 40, No. 3, pp. 523- 544.

Edwards, Sebastian (1998). Openness, productivity and growth: what do we really know? *Economic Journal*, vol. 108, No. 447, pp. 383-398.

Farooki, Masuma, and Raphael Kaplinsky (2013). *The Impact of China on Global Commodity Prices: the Global Reshaping of the Resource Sector.* London and New York: Routledge.

Frankel, Jeffrey A., and David H. Romer (1999). Does trade cause growth? *American Economic Review*, vol. 89, No. 3, pp. 379-399.

Harrison, Ann (1996). Openness and growth: a time-series, cross-country analysis for developing countries. *Journal of Development Economics*, vol. 48, No. 2, pp. 419-447.

Harrison, Ann, and Andrés Rodriguez-Clare (2009). Trade, foreign investment, and industrial policy for developing countries. Working Paper No. 15261. Cambridge, M.A.: National Bureau of Economic Research.

Hoekman, Bernard, ed. (2015). *The Global Trade Slowdown: A New Normal?* London: CEPR Press. Available as the VoxEU.org eBook from www.voxeu.org/sites/default/files/file/Global%20Trade%20Slowdown_nocover.pdf.

International Monetary Fund (2015a). *World Economic Outlook: April 2015.* Washington, D.C. Available from www.imf.org/external/pubs/ft/weo/2015/update/02/pdf/0714.pdf.

____ (2015b). Global Prospects and Policy Challenges. Report prepared for G-20 Finance Ministers and Central Bank Governors Meeting, 4-5 September, Ankara, Turkey. Washington, D.C. Available from www.imf.org/external/np/g20/pdf/2015/090415.pdf

Lagarde, Christine (2015). Reinvigorate trade to boost global economic growth. Speech Address at the U.S. Ex-Im Bank Conference, Washington, D.C., 23 April. Available from www.imf.org/external/np/speeches/2015/042315.htm

Magnier, Mark, Lingling Wei and Peter Evans (2015). China confronts 'new normal' of slower growth. Wall Street Journal Website. Available from www.wsj.com/articles/china-confronts-new-normal-of-slower-growth-1421767359

Melitz, Marc (2003). The impact of trade on intra-industry reallocations and aggregate industry productivity. *Econometrica*, vol. 71, pp.1695–1725.

Pavcnik, Nina (2002) Trade liberalization, exit, and productivity improvements: evidence from Chilean plants. *Review of Economic Studies*, vol. 69, No. 1, pp. 245-276.

Roache, Shaun K. (2012). China's impact on world commodity markets. IMF Working Paper No. 12/115. Washington, D.C.: International Monetary Fund. Available from www.imf.org/external/pubs/ft/wp/2012/wp12115.pdf.

Roberts, Dexter (2014). What is Xi's 'new normal' Chinese economy? Bloomberg Website. Available from www.bloomberg.com/bw/articles/2014-12-12/china-has-a-new-normal-too.

Rodrik, Dani (2009). Growth after the crisis. Discussion Paper No. 7480. London: Centre for Economic Policy Research.

Ruiz, Luis Bernardo Torres, and Hâle Utar (2009). The impact of Chinese competition on Mexican maquiladoras: evidence from plant-level panel data. Working Paper. Colorado: University of Colorado.

Sachs, Jeffrey D., and Andrew Warner (1995). Economic reform and the process of global integration. *Brookings Papers on Economic Activity*, vol. 26, No. 1, pp. 1-118.

Saggu, Aman, and Witada Anukoonwattaka (2015a). Global commodity price falls: a transitory boost to economic growth in Asia-Pacific countries with special needs. Trade Insights, No. 8. Bangkok: ESCAP. Available from www.unescap.org/resources/global-commodity-price-falls-transitory-boost-economic-growth-asia-pacific-countries

____ (2015b). Commodity price crash: risks to exports and economic growth in Asia-Pacific LDCs and LLDCs. Trade Insights, No. 6. Bangkok: ESCAP. Available from. www.unescap.org/resources/commodity-price-crash-risks-exports-and-economic-growth-asia-pacific-ldcs-and-lldcs-trade

_____ (2015c). China's 'new normal': challenges ahead for Asia-Pacific trade. Trade Insights, No. 11. Bangkok: ESCAP. Available from www.unescap.org/resources/chinas-new-normal-challenges-ahead-asia-pacific-trade-trade-insights-issue-no-11

Sterne, Gabriel, and Alessandro Theiss (2014). China's debt time bomb – the fall out, Financial Times Website, Available from blogs.ft.com/beyond-brics/2014/12/02/guest-post-chinas-debt-time-bomb-the-fall-out/

Trefler, Daniel (2004). The long and short of the Canada-U.S. free trade agreement. *American Economic Review,* vol. 94, No. 4, pp. 870-895.

United Nations Conference on Trade and Development (2010). *Trade and Development Report 2010.* Sales No. E.10.II.D.3. Available form unctad.org/en/docs/tdr2010_en.pdf

United Nations, Department of Economic and Social Affairs (2011). Revision of the Classification by Broad Economic Categories (BEC). Available from unstats.un.org/unsd/class/intercop/expertgroup/2011/AC234-25.PDF.

United Nations, Economic and Social Commission for Asia and the Pacific (2010). *Economic and Social Survey of Asia and the Pacific 2010.* Sales No. E.10.II.F.2. Available from www.unescap.org/sites/default/files/01-Cover-Survey2010.pdf

_____ (2012). *Asia-Pacific Trade and Investment Report 2012 : Recent Trends and Developments.* ST/ESCAP/2650. 2012 Available from www.unescap.org/resources/asia-pacific-trade-and-investment-report-2012-recent-trends-and-developments

_____ (2013). *Asia-Pacific Trade and Investment Report 2013: Turning the Tide – Towards Inclusive Trade and Investment.* Sales No. E.14.II.F.2. Available from www.unescap.org/resources/asia-pacifictrade-and-investment-report-2013-turning-tidetowards-inclusive-trade-and

Waldmeir, Patti, and Michael Hunter (2015). Global stocks hit by China manufacturing. Financial Times Website. Available from www.ft.com/intl/cms/s/0/ 47b76b70-505c-11e5-8642-453585f2cfcd.html#axzz3l2NdMaYC.

World Bank (2015). *Commodity Markets Outlook.* July. Washington D.C. Available from http://siteresources.worldbank.org/INTPROSPECTS/Resources/334934-1304428586133/GEP2015c_commodity_Jul2015.pdf.

Xing, Yuqing, and Manisha Pradhananga (2013). How important are exports and foreign direct investment for economic growth in the People's Republic of China? ADBI Working Paper No. 427. Tokyo: Asian Development Bank Institute. Available from www.adb.org/sites/default/files/publication/156282/adbi-wp427.pdf.

Xuequan, Mu (2014). China should adapt to new norm of growth: Xi. Xinhuanet News Website. Available from news.xinhuanet.com/english/china/2014-05 / 10/c_126484869.htm.

Zhu, Grace (2015). China HSBC PMI contracts for third month in May. Marketwatch Website. Available from www.marketwatch.com/story/china-hsbc-pmi-contracts-for-third-month-in-may-2015-05-31.

## ONLINE DATABASES

Economist Intelligence Unit. EIU database. Available from www.eiu.com/

International Monetary Fund. World Economic Outlook database. Available from www.imf.org/external/pubs/ft/weo/2015/01/weodata/index.aspx.

Direction of Trade Statistics (DOTS) database. Available from data.imf.org/?sk=9d6028d4-f14a-464c-a2f2-59b2cd424b85

United Nations, Economic and Social Commission for Asia and the Pacific. ESCAP online statistical database. Available from www.unescap.org/stat/data/statdb/DataExplorer.aspx.

World Bank. World Integrated Trade Solution (WITS) database. Available from wits.worldbank.org/wits/.

# 2 COMMERCIAL SERVICES TRADE ON THE MEND?

## A ASIA-PACIFIC EXPORTS OF SERVICES RECORD SLIGHTLY BETTER PERFORMANCE THAN GLOBAL FIGURES

Global commercial services trade outperformed merchandise trade in 2014, despite slow growth.[1] The global export services growth rate decreased slightly from 5.4% to 4.9% compared with the 2013 level; similarly, on the import side, growth weakened from 5.9% to 5.2%.[2] In contrast, the Asia-Pacific commercial services trade growth improved in 2014, from 4% to 5.1% for exports and from 5.7% to 6.1% for imports (figure 2.1). Nevertheless, it remained consistently lower than its 2012 level of 8.2%.

*"Moving against the global trend, the growth of commercial services trade in Asia and the Pacific improved in 2014."*

**Figure 2.1. Growth in commercial services trade in Asia-Pacific economics and the world**

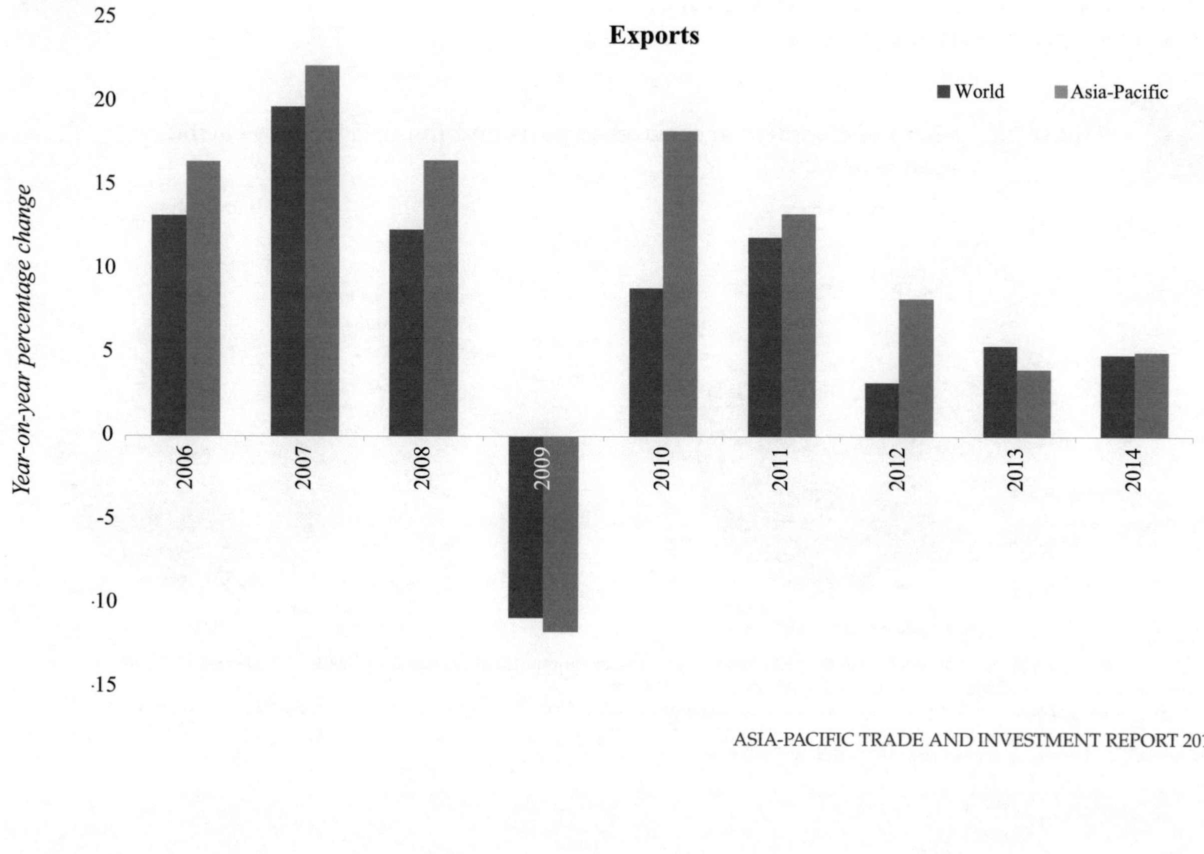


CHAPTER 2

## Figure 2.1. (Continued)

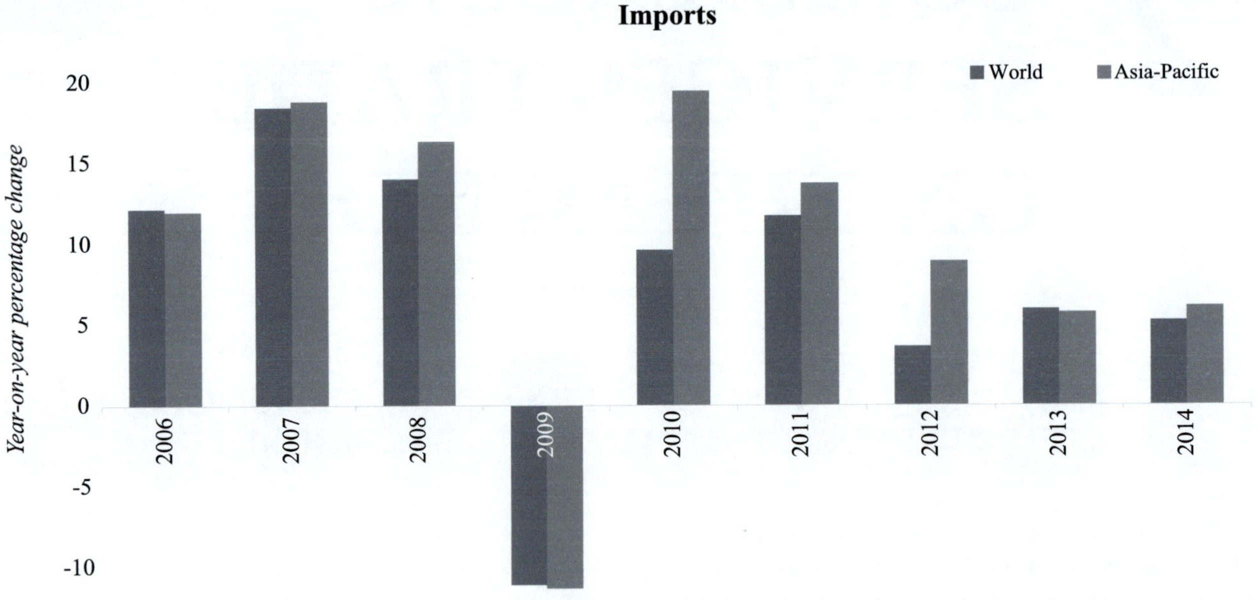


*Source:* ESCAP calculation based on the WTO International Trade Statistics Database.

The share of world trade captured by the Asia-Pacific area remained at almost the same level as in the previous year. The region as a whole has apparently not yet become a premier provider and exporter of services. The region remains a net importer of commercial services, accounting for 28% of world exports and 32.6% of world imports. Exports from China, India, Japan and Singapore represent about a half of the region's total exports (figure 2.2). As far as imports are concerned, China alone represents more than a quarter of the region's total imports.

> *"The region is a net importer of commercial services providing 28% of world exports and purchasing 32.6% of world imports."*

## Figure 2.2. Share of commercial services exports and imports in Asia-Pacific economies, 2014

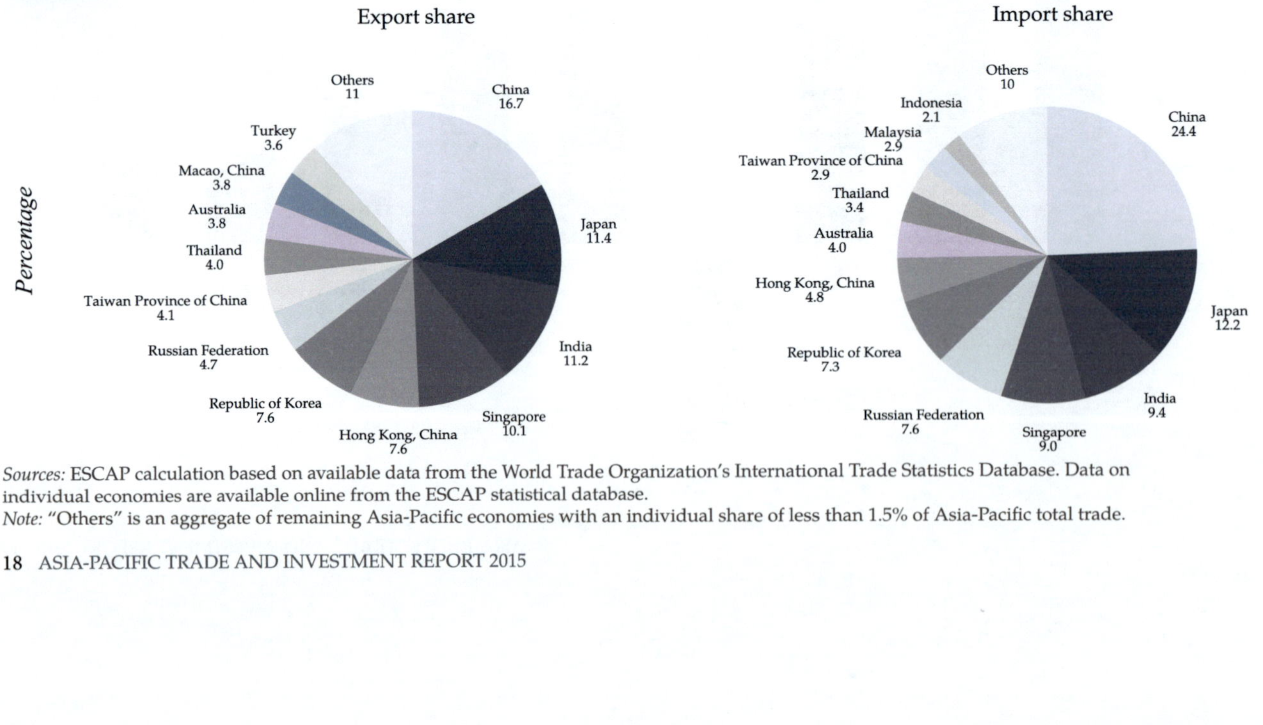


*Sources:* ESCAP calculation based on available data from the World Trade Organization's International Trade Statistics Database. Data on individual economies are available online from the ESCAP statistical database.

*Note:* "Others" is an aggregate of remaining Asia-Pacific economies with an individual share of less than 1.5% of Asia-Pacific total trade.

Trade performance at the country level presents a mixed picture. Some countries in the Asia-Pacific region enjoyed dynamic growth of both exports and imports in 2014 (Armenia, Cambodia, China, Islamic Republic of Iran and Japan, which recorded double-digit growth), while others experienced sharp export and import declines (Malaysia, Mongolia, Papua New Guinea, the Russian Federation, Thailand, Tonga and Macao, China).

On the export side, Japan stood out among the major exporters for its remarkable export growth, which reached 19% in 2014. High export growth performance was also achieved by economies that are only starting to exploit advantages from their commercial services sectors, mainly in travel services. For example, double-digit export growth in 2014 was registered by Armenia (49.8%), Cambodia (17%), Kazakhstan (24%), Maldives (14.7%), Sri Lanka (19.7%), and Timor-Leste (11.5%), (figure 2.3). However, some relatively important exporters suffered declines in their export levels, including the Russian Federation (-6.1%), Thailand (-5.7%), and Macao, China (-1%). A combination between political and economic factors explains the decline.[3]

> *"2014 sees even more variation in services trade performance across the region."*

As far as imports are concerned, China and Japan represent the major importers that are continuing to maintain high levels of growth (15.5% and 12.3%, respectively). Several small economies also recorded consistently high growth, such as Armenia (44%), Azerbaijan (24.6%), Bangladesh (18.1%), Bhutan (20%), Cambodia (14.9%), Maldives (11.7%), the Philippines (22.6%) and Viet Nam (4.9%). Conversely, some relatively large importers experienced a decline in their services imports, including Australia (-7%), the Russian Federation (-5.4%) and Thailand (-3.13%).

**Figure 2.3. Growth of services exports and imports, by Asia-Pacific economy, 2014**

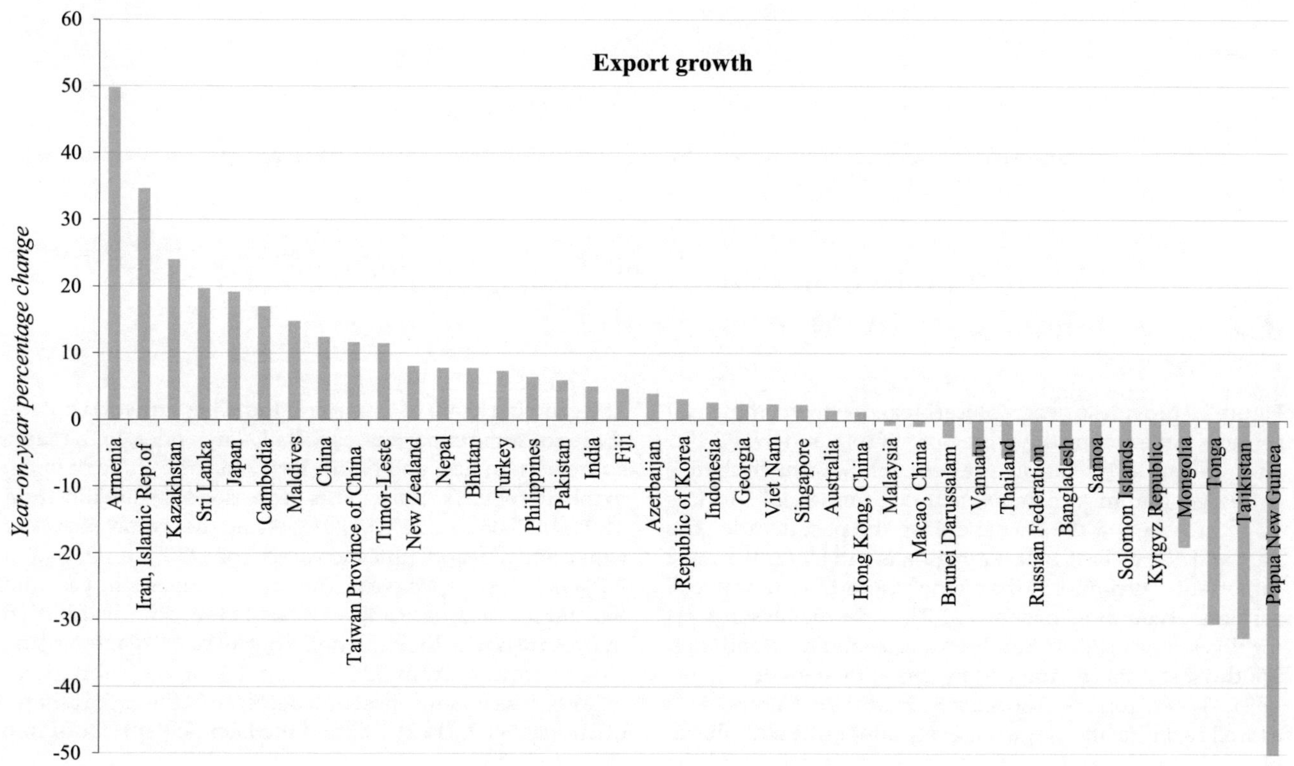


CHAPTER 2

## Figure 2.3. (Continued)

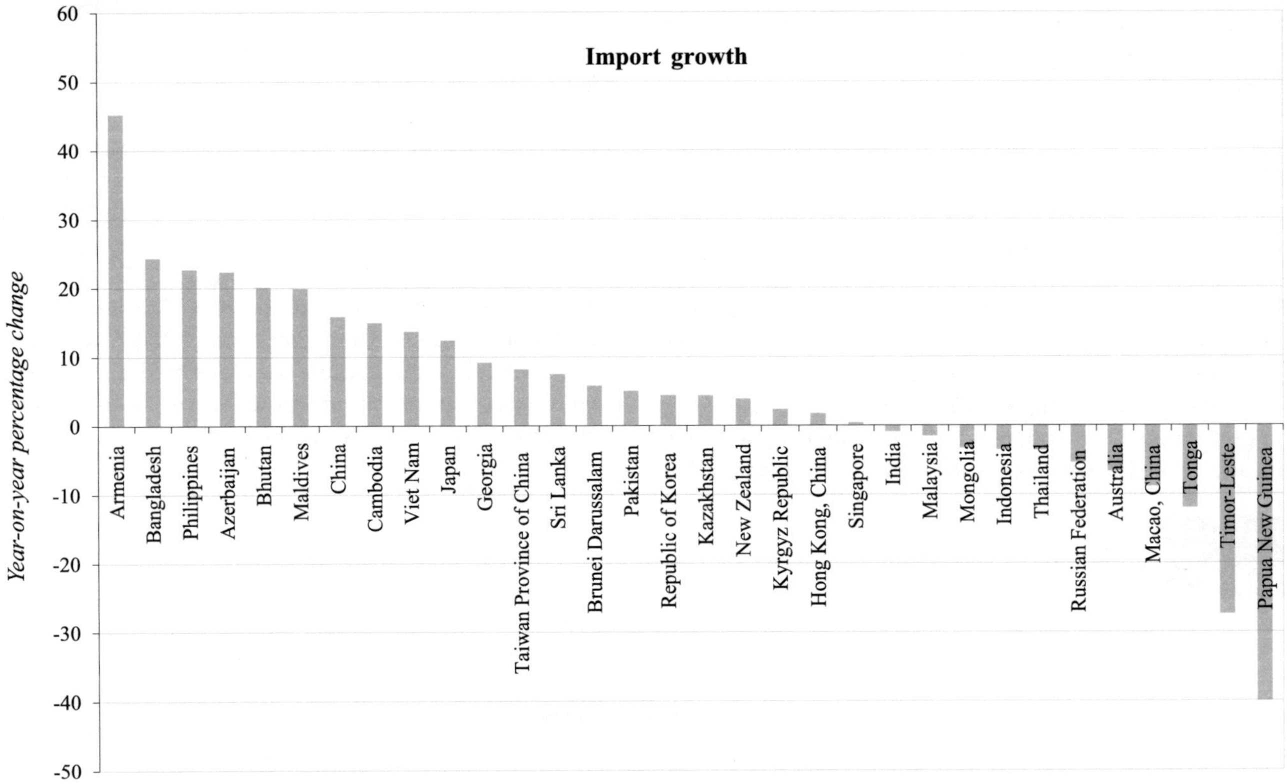


*Source:* ESCAP calculation based on available data from the World Trade Organization's International Trade Statistics Database. Data on individual economies are available online from the ESCAP statistical database.

# B COMMERCIAL SERVICES TRADE CONTINUES ITS GEOGRAPHICAL ADJUSTMENT

Figure 2.4 provides a geographical breakdown of commercial services trade among the subregions of Asia and the Pacific. At aggregate levels, the picture does not show much change in the geographical composition of commercial services trade in Asia and the Pacific during the past decade. The East and North-East Asia subregion is still by far the most important contributor to the region's exports in commercial services, accounting for nearly 51.3% of the region's exports for this sector in 2014. South-East Asia and the South and South-West Asia (dominated by India) follow with shares of 21.4% and 16.45%, respectively. North and Central Asia as well as the Pacific play a relatively minor role with shares of 5.85% and 5% of the region's exports, respectively. The subregional distribution of imports is similar.

However, repositioning occurs at the country level. During the past decade, the importance of services exports for developing Asia-Pacific countries, especially China and India, has been growing. From 2005 to 2014, the share of China's exports increased from 14.8% to 16.7% of the region's total exports while India's share grew from 8.6% to 11.2%. The growing share of China and India has crowded out the shares of some exporters, especially large ones, in the same subregion. In East and North-East Asia, the share of Japan in the subregion's total exports decreased substantially from 31.2% in 2005 to 22.2% in 2014, while the export shares of China and Macao, China increased from 27.7% to 32.6% and 2.7% to 7.5%, respectively. The other countries in East and North-East Asia, basically maintained the same distribution of export shares. In South and South-West Asia, the rising share of India, from 58.2% to 68.1% of the subregion's exports, was mainly offset by a decrease in the export shares of Turkey (30.9% to 21.7%) and the Islamic Republic of Iran (5.5% to 3.7%).

What is also important to note is the high country concentration in services trade in most of the Asia-Pacific subregions. For example, in 2014, Australia and New Zealand accounted for nearly 97% of the total exports and imports of the Pacific's commercial services trade. India represented 68% of South and South-West Asia's exports while the Russian Federation's share was 79.8% of the exports by North and Central Asia. The remaining two subregions, South-East Asia, and East and North-East Asia, have a more even distribution among their economies. In South-East Asia, the largest contributor of the subregion's exports of services was Singapore (47.1%) while China accounted 32.6% of East and North-East Asian services exports.

### Figure 2.4. Commercial services trade, by subregion

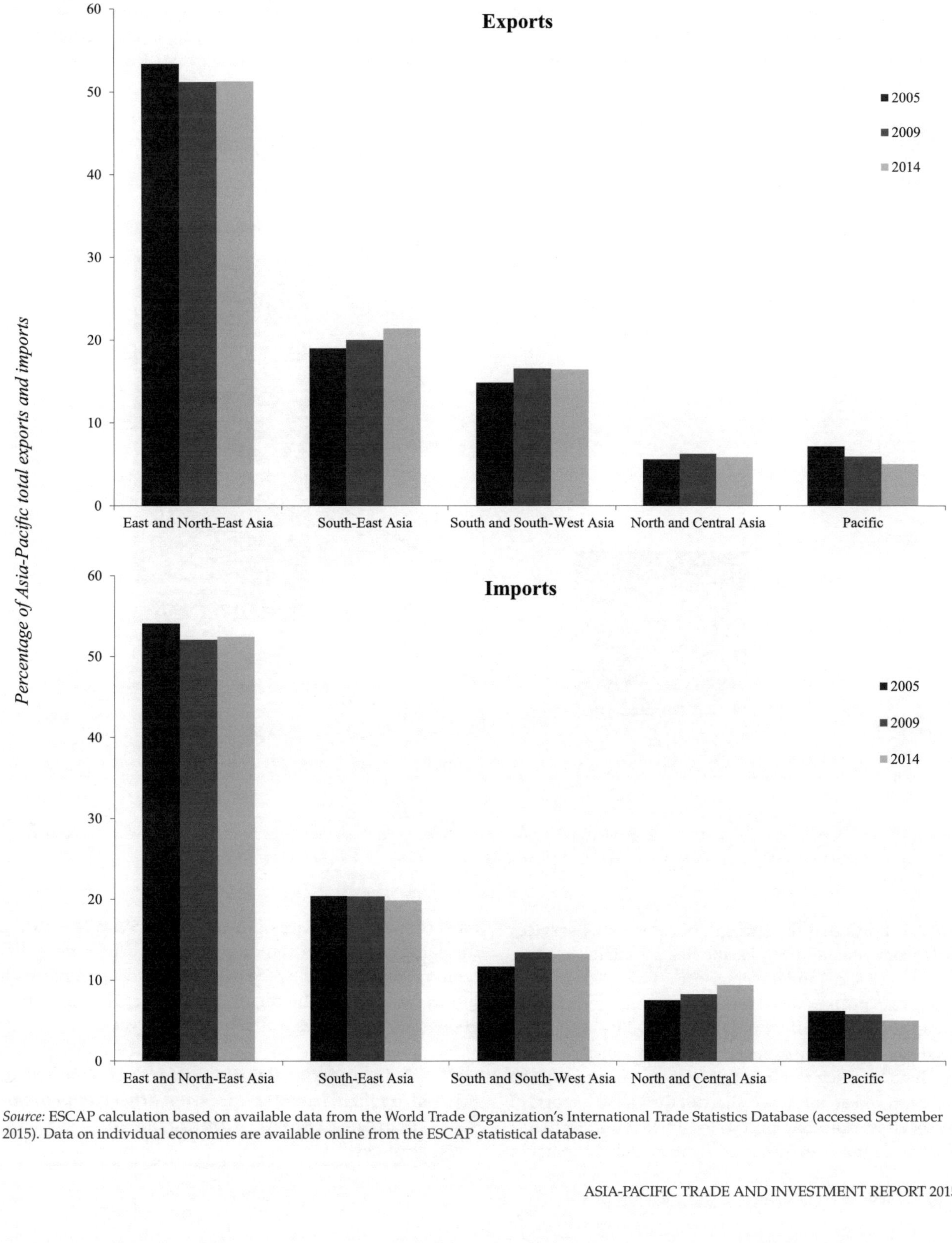


*Source:* ESCAP calculation based on available data from the World Trade Organization's International Trade Statistics Database (accessed September 2015). Data on individual economies are available online from the ESCAP statistical database.

# C SECTORAL BREAKDOWN SHOWS THAT OTHER COMMERCIAL AND TRAVEL SERVICES ARE GAINING IMPORTANCE

Between 2005 and 2014, the region's exports of commercial services increased more than twofold (figure 2.5). Commercial services exports can be divided into four broad categories: (a) transport, (b) travel, (c) other commercial services[4] and (d) goods-related services.[5] Other commercial services and travel services have been a relatively fast-growing component. The share of other commercial services, dominated by business services, in total exports increased from 38% to 45% between 2005 and 2014 while the share of travel services grew from 28% to 30.5%. Due to the much faster export growth of travel and other commercial services, it is not surprising that there was a significant reduction in the export share of transport services from 29% to 21% during the same period.

**Figure 2.5. Exports of Asia-Pacific commercial services, by sector, 2005-2014**

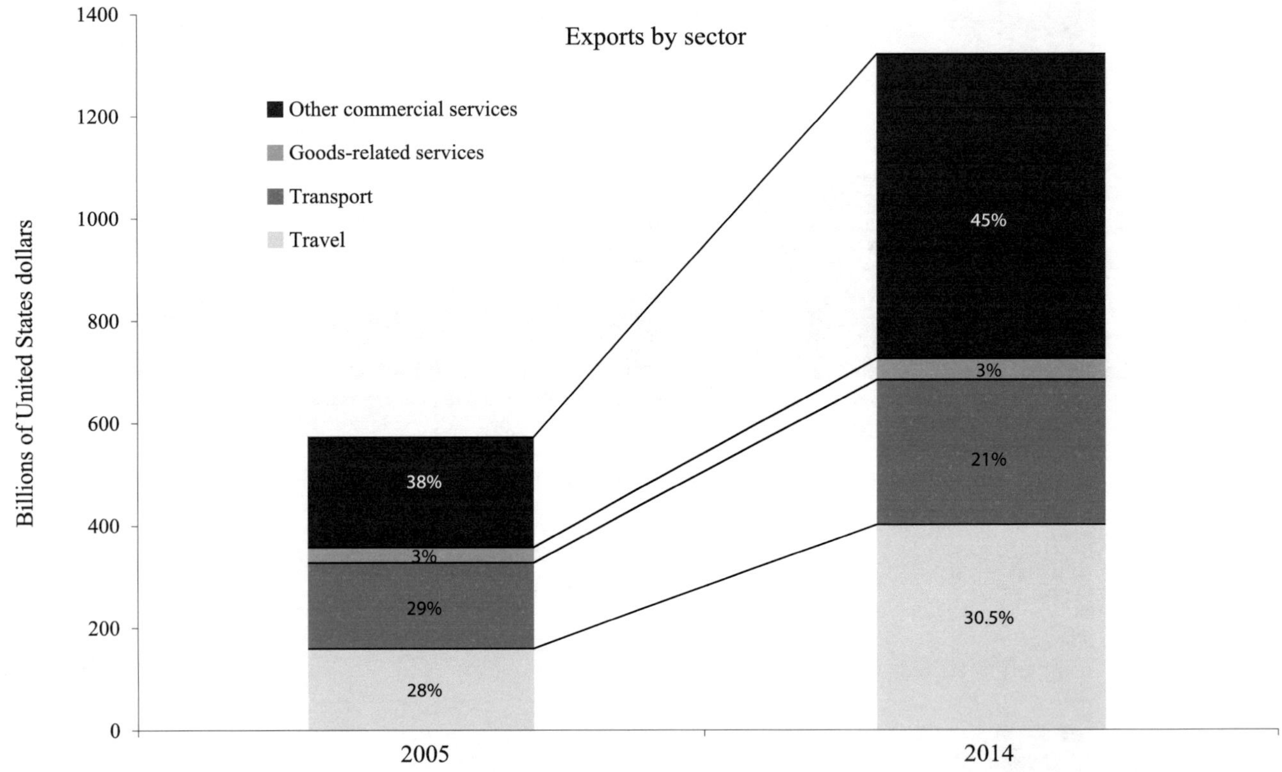


*Source:* ESCAP calculation based on available data from the World Trade Organization's International Trade Statistics Database (accessed September 2015). Data on individual economies are available online from the ESCAP statistical database.

Figure 2.6 shows that the strength of commercial services exports from Asia and the Pacific lies especially in other commercial services and travel services. From 2005 to 2014, the region's exports of travel services and other commercial services grew annually, on average, by 11% and 12%, respectively. The strong expansion of intraregional demand from China is a key factor in this growth. As a result, the region captured an increased share of the global exports of travel services, from 24% in 2005 to 34% in 2014. Similarly, the region captured an increased share of global exports of other commercial services, growing from 19% to 24% during the same period. In the case of transport services, the region's exports grew by 6% per year, almost on a par with the world average. The region's average export growth of goods-related services was about 5% per year.

> *"Asia and the Pacific performed especially strongly in travel services and other commercial services exports, dominated by business services."*

## Figure 2.6. Average export-growth rate, by subsector, during 2005-2014 – Asia-Pacific region compared with the rest of the world

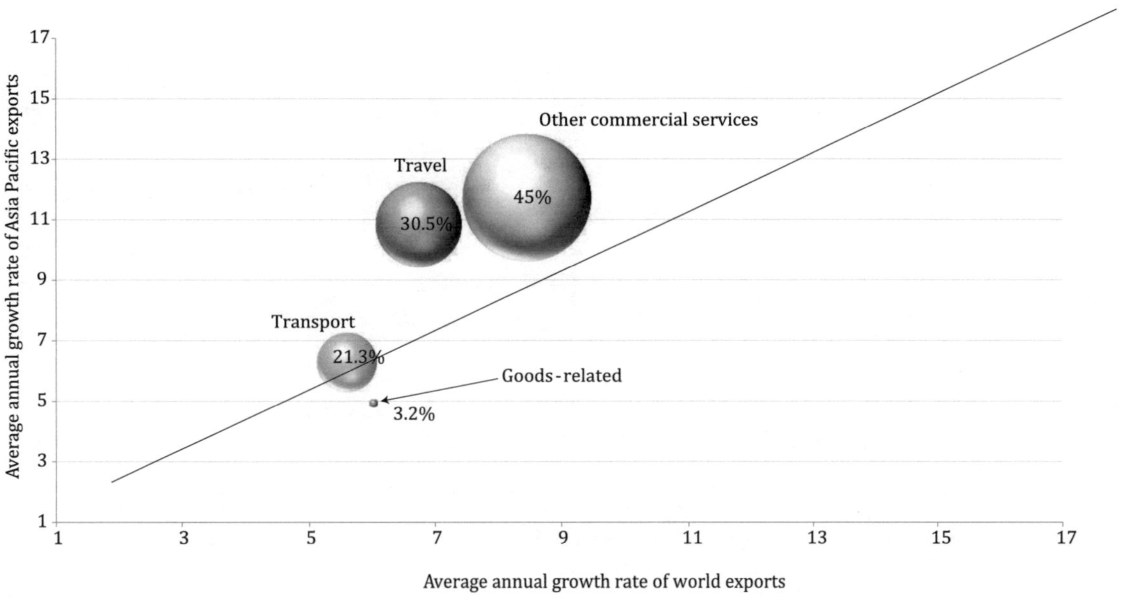


*Source:* ESCAP calculation based on available data from the World Trade Organization's International Trade Statistics Database. Data on individual economies are available online from the ESCAP statistical database.
*Note:* A geometric average is used. The size of the bubbles represents the share of the respective service sector in Asia-Pacific total exports of commercial services in 2014 (as indicated in the bubble).The equal growth rate between exports by the world and Asia-Pacific region is represented by points on the diagonal line, while points above the diagonal line implies that export growth of the Asia-Pacific region is higher than that of the world.

### Other commercial services trade performance

The breakdown of the exports of other commercial services into its seven subcategories is shown in table 2.1. From 2005 to 2014, exports of this sector increased by more than twofold from $235 billion to $630 billion. Asia-Pacific increased its share in global exports of all other commercial services from 18.9% to 24.3%. In terms of subsectors, it still claims half of all global construction services exports. However, that is not the largest or the most dynamic sector when it comes to importance to the region's exports. Other business services, while growing slowly in terms of value, still make up almost one half of the Asia-Pacific region exports of other commercial services. Telecommunications, computer and information services are among the most dynamic export sectors. The rapidly growing exports of these services have resulted in the Asia-Pacific region gaining a significantly increased share of global exports, which jumped from 16.1% in 2005 to 24% in 2014.

The rising market share of Asia and the Pacific in the world exports of services related to finance, insurance and pensions indicate that there has been a significant improvement in the region's export competitiveness in these service subsectors. The Asia-Pacific region's share in global exports of those categories increased by almost 5 percentage points to reach 15.7% and 14.4% in 2014, respectively. At the same time, there has been a significant improvement in the region's export performance in services related to "creative economies" and other activities linked to the use of intellectual property rights (box 2.1). Export income from royalties and licence charges for the use of intellectual property doubled, which translates into an increase by 3 percentage points of the Asia-Pacific share in global exports. On the other hand, the region continues to underperform in terms of exports of personal, cultural and recreational services.[6] The export value remains small, and furthermore the region suffered a small decline from 19.7% to 18.1% in its share of global exports.

**Table 2.1. Other commercial services exports breakdown – comparison between 2005 and 2014**

| | Export value ($) | | Share in Asia-Pacific exports (%) | | Asia-Pacific shares in world exports (%) | |
|---|---|---|---|---|---|---|
| | 2005 | 2014 | 2005 | 2014 | 2005 | 2014 |
| Other commercial services (total) | 235 | 630 | 100 | 100 | 18.9 | 24.3 |
| Other business services | 123 | 299 | 52.2 | 47.4 | 23.4 | 26.7 |
| Telecommunications, computer and information services | 32 | 110 | 13.7 | 17.4 | 16.1 | 24.0 |
| Financial services | 23 | 65 | 9.8 | 10.4 | 10.5 | 15.7 |
| Charges for the use of intellectual property n.i.e. | 22 | 50 | 9.5 | 7.9 | 13.5 | 16.6 |
| Construction | 23 | 57 | 9.9 | 9.1 | 48.8 | 53.0 |
| Insurance and pension services | 6 | 19 | 2.8 | 3.0 | 9.8 | 14.4 |
| Personal, cultural, and recreational services | 5 | 8 | 2.0 | 1.3 | 19.7 | 18.1 |

*Source:* ESCAP calculation based on the World Trade Organization's International Trade Statistics Database.

## Box 2.1. Royalties and license fee payments still on a rise

Royalties and license fees refer to transactions made in connection with the use of intangible proprietary rights such as patents, copyrights, trademarks, industrial designs and so forth. Such transactions touch upon trade in goods and services alike and cover a vast range of activities, from the production of patented pharmaceuticals to the use of franchise logos and trademarks. Because exports of royalties and license fees reflect the cross-border sale of intellectual property they are often considered to be an important indicator of the state of so-called "creative economies". Likewise, the import of royalties and license fees by a developing economy can indicate technology transfer. However, this can overlook the vast majority of developing countries' technological upgrading that occurs through the introduction of new technologies – including organizational and management systems – that are unpatented or which may not be a product of the latest technology available (UNCTAD, 2010).

During the past decade, the world's receipts of royalties and license fees have grown steadily and proved to be more resilient to the adverse effects of the 2008-2009 economic crisis than other commercial services. In the Asia-Pacific region, despite a drop during the crisis, receipts and payments for royalties and fees (i.e. exports and imports) during 2005-2014 grew faster than in the rest of the world, at an average annual growth rate of about 9.6% and 9.8%, respectively, compared with 6.5% for the rest of the world.

The Asia-Pacific region held about a 17% share of the global exports of royalties and license fees in 2014, with Japan ranked as the second largest global exporter. The Republic of Korea was ranked ninth, while Singapore claimed thirteenth place. By more than quadrupling its export value during 2005-2014, China climbed to the position of twentieth largest exporter of royalties and license fees in 2014. However, its share in the region's exports remains at the 1.4% mark. In contrast, China's payments on royalties and license fees grew at more than twice the rate of the rest of Asia-Pacific during 2005-2014, to reach 21% of the region's global imports in 2014.

Almost all of the Asian and Pacific countries for which data are available are net importers of royalties and license fees, with the notable exception of Japan, meaning that they are dependent on innovation and creativity that is sourced – and paid for – abroad (figure). Globally, net exporters of royalties and license fees are mostly located in the European Union and North America. Within Asia-Pacific region, only Japan, the Republic of Korea and Singapore have been able to develop a meaningful export share with a combined $45 billion in 2014, of which Japan constitutes the large majority. The fact that 39 countries in the region exported zero (less than $5 million) reinforces the notion of diversity within the region with regard to innovative and creative capacity and the need for policy action to encourage innovation.

**Balance of payment for royalties and license fees, by selected Asia-Pacific economy, 2014**

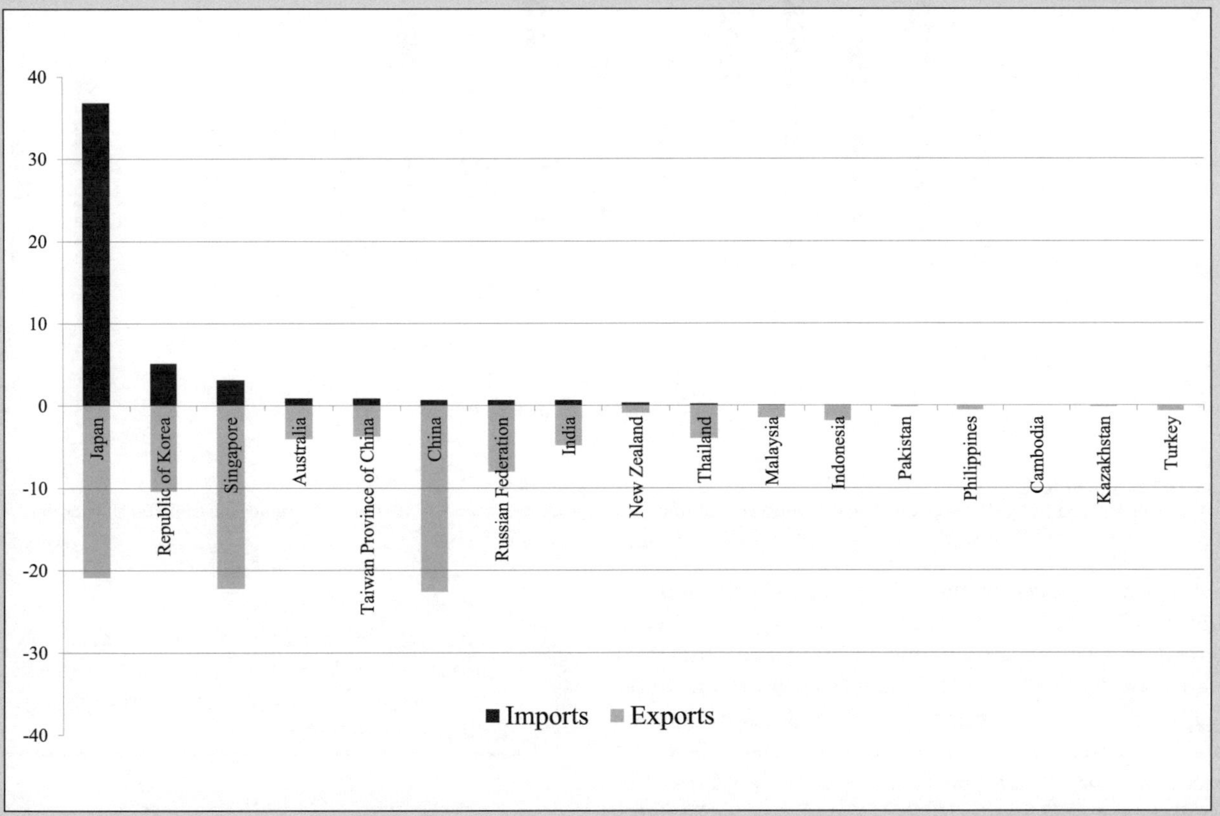


*Source:* ESCAP calculation based on the World Trade Organization's International Trade Statistics Database.

# D INTERNATIONAL TOURISM IN ASIA AND THE PACIFIC IS SLOWING

Since the last quarter of 2013, international tourist arrivals in Asia-Pacific region have decreased from 6.8% in 2013 to 5.4% in 2014 and 4.2% in the first four months of 2015 (figure 2.7).[7] Risks of a further slowdown will persist throughout the rest of 2015. The economic slowdown in China and the Russian Federation, which are among the main determinants of this phenomenon, will probably soften the supply of outbound tourism flows from those two countries.

CHAPTER 2

## Figure 2.7. Growth of international tourist arrivals

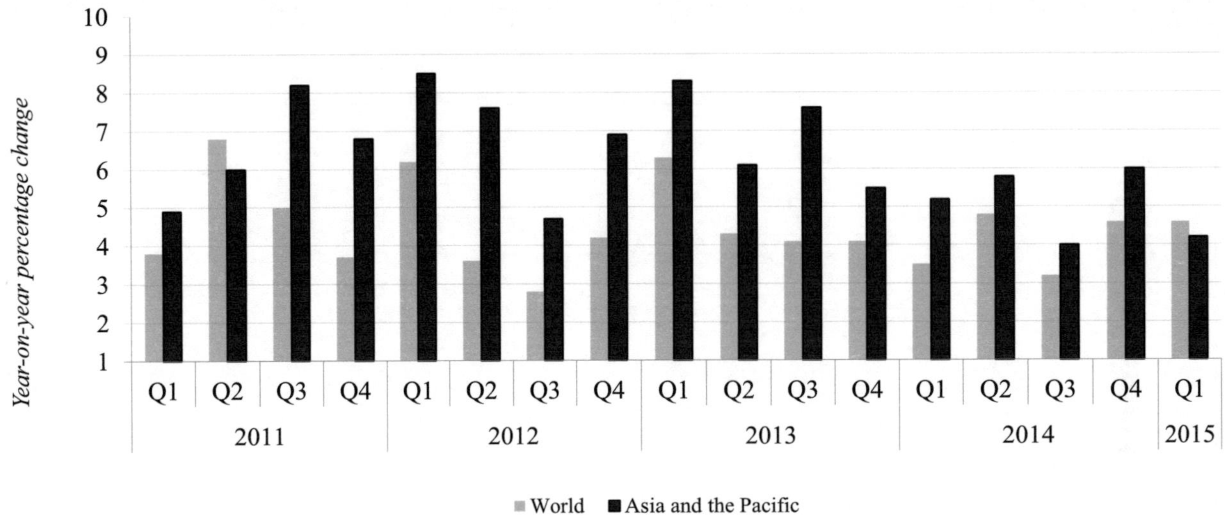


*Source:* UNWTO, 2015.
*Note:* Number estimated by UNWTO. Countries in North and Central Asia are excluded from Asia-Pacific region under the UNWTO classification.

Using country data from the United Nations World Tourism Organization (UNWTO) to estimate the number of tourist arrivals to Asia-Pacific economies in 2014, reveals that there were some 263 million international tourist arrivals to the region as a whole.[8] Among the subregions, the highest number of arrivals was in East and North-East Asia, which accounted for 12% of global arrivals in 2014, followed by South-East Asia (8.5%), North and Central Asia (3.8%), South and South-West Asia (1.5%)[9] and the Pacific (1.2%).

China remained the most popular tourist destination in Asia and the Pacific, accounting for 15% of international tourists arrivals in the region in 2014 (table 2.2). Other major tourist destinations in 2014 included Macao, China (13.5%), and Thailand and Hong Kong, China (10% each). However, before the 2008-2009 crisis, China attracted a much higher share of tourists; for example, in 2007 tourist arrivals in China totaled almost 20% (table 2.2). This could be a reflection of a shift in China's role, from being a major destination to becoming an important source of tourists. In contrast, Macao, China and Hong Kong, China experienced the most significant increase in share, gaining respectively 6.2 and 2.8 percentage points from 2007 to 2014 (box 2.2).

> ***"The rate of growth of tourist arrivals to Asia and the Pacific fell from 6.8% in 2013 to 5.4% in 2014 and 4.2% % in the first four months of 2015."***

**Table 2.2. Major tourist destinations in the Asia-Pacific region**

*(Percentage of tourist arrivals in the Asia-Pacific region)*

| | 2007 | 2008 | 2009 | 2010 | 2011 | 2012 | 2013 | 2014 |
|---|---|---|---|---|---|---|---|---|
| China | 19.9 | 19.8 | 19.4 | 17.9 | 16.5 | 15.2 | 14.3 | 15.1 |
| Macao, China | 7.3 | 6.5 | 8.9 | 10.9 | 13.1 | 13.3 | 14.4 | 13.5 |
| Thailand | 8.9 | 8.8 | 7.9 | 7.9 | 9.3 | 10.3 | 11.6 | 10.2 |
| Hong Kong, China | 7.4 | 7.4 | 8.0 | 8.7 | 9.4 | 10.0 | 10.8 | 10.2 |
| Malaysia | 7.5 | 7.4 | 7.6 | 7.1 | 6.7 | 6.1 | 6.0 | 5.8 |
| Singapore | 4.9 | 5.1 | 4.6 | 5.5 | 6.1 | 5.8 | 5.4 | 5.1 |
| Japan | 5.0 | 5.2 | 5.0 | 5.2 | 3.7 | 4.4 | 4.2 | 5.0 |
| Republic of Korea | 3.3 | 4.4 | 4.8 | 4.0 | 4.2 | 4.1 | 4.1 | 4.8 |
| Taiwan Province of China | 2.8 | 2.9 | 3.3 | 3.4 | 3.8 | 3.6 | 3.4 | 3.9 |
| Russian Federation | 5.1 | 5.8 | 4.6 | 3.5 | 3.9 | 3.3 | 3.3 | 3.1 |
| Others Asia-Pacific economies | 27.8 | 26.8 | 25.8 | 26.0 | 23.2 | 23.9 | 22.6 | 23.3 |

*Source:* ESCAP's estimation based on data from UNWTO database, 2015.

### Box 2.2 Tourism statistics: Flows between China, Hong Kong, China and Macao, China

When making use of tourism statistics, a distinction should be made between net visitor flows and strictly defined "tourism". The UNWTO definition of international tourism arrivals and departures excludes same-day visits or those made by "excursionists". However, these figures are not excluded from other UNWTO aggregated data and are presented in certain country-specific tourism datasets. In particular, outbound tourism statistics for the region typically do not make a distinction between same-day and overnight travel.

For most countries, excursionist travel is relatively small in volume compared with travel that involves overnight stays. However, regions with daily, cross-border commuting may report substantially higher same-day flows than tourism flows in the strictest sense. This is the case with reports of tourism flows between China, Hong Kong, China and Macao, China. The borders between the three economies are treated as national borders, and tourism statistics are independently reported.

The effect of these tourism flows is highly significant with regard to Hong Kong, China and Macao, China. In both cases, the destination of more than 90% of outbound visits is reported to be China (figure), and they also play a major role in total tourism outflows from China. As of 2013, 30.5% of China's total outbound visits were reported to be to Macao, China while 11.3% were reported to be to Hong Kong, China.

**Breakdown of outbound visits between China, Hong Kong, China and Macao, China, 2013**

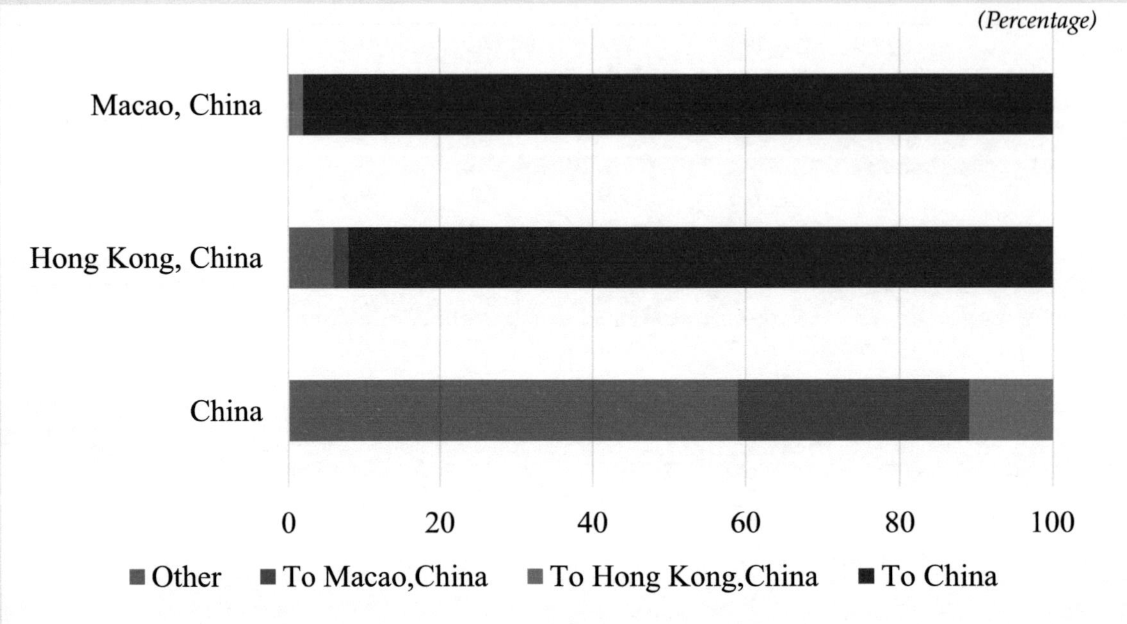


*Source:* ESCAP calculation based on UNWTO database, 2015.

A closer look at the statistics suggests that much of the outbound visits are in fact daily commutes of individuals who work in Hong Kong, China or Macao, China, but who live in China. Approximately 52% of all inbound visits to Hong Kong, China and 57% of all inbound visits to China in 2013 were same-day visits. Aggregated outbound travel statistics that include China and Hong Kong, China or Macao, China appear to be significantly inflated. It is impossible to analyse the data accurately, unless same-day travel figures can be approximated. If possible, analytical work using inbound visit statistics should contain overnight travel data instead of net visit figures for these three destinations.

Despite the fact that foreign tourist arrivals grew in 2014 by only 0.3% in China, East and North-East Asia still led other subregions in terms of inbound tourism, with growth of 7.3%. The depreciation of the Japanese currency and the relaxation of visa requirements turned out to be positive factors for the dynamic growth of tourist arrivals to Japan in 2014. The growth in visits to Japan (29.4%) was followed by Taiwan Province of China (23.6%) and the Republic of Korea (16.6%) (figure 2.8). In contrast, the growth of tourist arrivals to South-East Asia reached a five-year-record low of 2.7% in 2014, mainly driven by a 6.7% drop of tourist arrivals in Thailand, which represents 25.6% of total arrivals in South-East Asia. In contrast, other South-East Asian destinations still showed robust growth in tourist arrivals such as Myanmar (50.7%), Cambodia (7%) and Indonesia (7.2%).

Tourist arrivals are often highly concentrated in one destination in each of the respective subregions. In South and South-West Asia, India attracted 43.6% tourists travelling to the subregion. In North and Central Asia, the Russian Federation was a dominant destination with a share of approximately 59% of the total arrivals in the subregion. Similarly, 71.8% of the tourist arrivals in the Pacific went to Australia and New Zealand. However, several small destinations within those subregions registered relatively dynamic growth of tourism in 2014. For example, in South and South-West Asia, Sri Lanka recorded impressive growth of tourist arrivals (19.8%). In North and Central Asia, Armenia, led with growth of 11%. In the Pacific, Palau registered the highest growth of some 34%.

## Figure 2.8. Growth of tourist arrivals. by Asia-Pacific subregion and selected economy, 2014

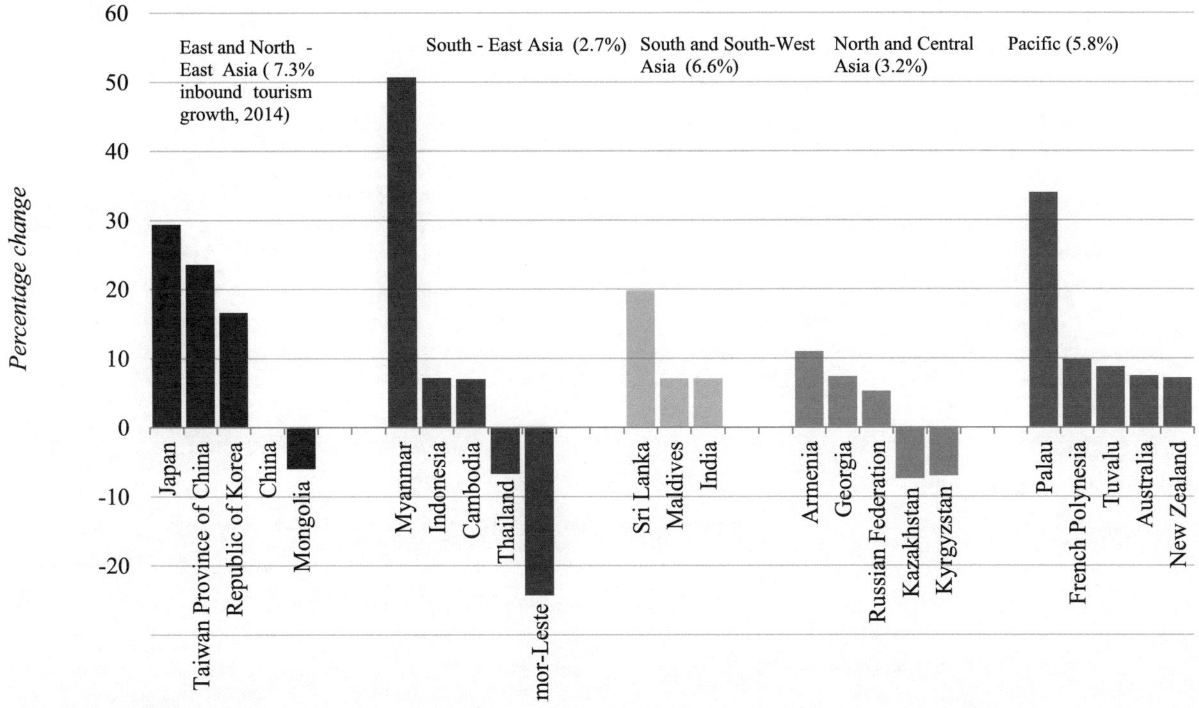


*Source:* UNWTO, 2015.

For the remainder of 2015 and in 2016, UNWTO projections for tourist arrivals at Asia-Pacific destinations are not particularly encouraging. A trend is the softening of intraregional demand of outbound tourists from China, which has become a major source of tourism income for many Asia-Pacific economies, especially since the 2008-2009 global economic crisis (box 2.3).

### Box 2.3. The increasing role played by China's outbound tourism

Asia-Pacific countries have increasingly relied on China for their tourism income. The share of Chinese arrivals in total inbound tourism in the region increased from 11.9% in 2009 to 15.2% in 2013. Based on National Bureau of Statistics of China database (2015), China has rapidly increased its share of outbound tourism since the 2008-2009 economic crisis. Chinese outbound tourism experienced outstanding growth from 8.4 million in 1998 to 116.6 million in 2014. The growth rate of outbound tourism, which was 18.2% per year, outpaced the 5.5% growth of tourist arrivals from 1999 to 2014. Asia-Pacific countries are the major destination of Chinese tourists. From 1999 to 2011, about 89.2% of the outbound tourists from China travelled to Asia-Pacific destinations.

As highlighted in chapter 1 of this report, Asia-Pacific merchandise exports to China are suffering from the country's economic slowdown. Exports of travel services to China are no exception. Those countries relying heavily on tourists coming from China are highly vulnerable; for example, in Mongolia, the Republic of Korea and Hong Kong, China, Chinese tourists accounted for more than 30% of total arrivals in 2013 (table). Likewise, Viet Nam and Macao, China are at significant risk, as they have each been relying on China for more than 20% of total tourism arrivals. However, reductions in fuel prices are expected to be an encouraging factor for travel and tourism, which are fuel-intensive sectors. Taking into account the impacts of these factors, UNWTO estimates that tourist arrivals in the Asia-Pacific region will grow by between 4% and 5%, which is slightly below the growth recorded in 2014.

**Importance of China's outbound tourism to Asia-Pacific destinations, 2009-2013**

*(Percentage of total inbound tourists)*

| Destination | 2009 | 2010 | 2011 | 2012 | 2013 |
|---|---|---|---|---|---|
| Australia | 6.5 | 7.7 | 9.2 | 10.3 | 11.1 |
| Azerbaijan | 0.3 | 0.3 | 0.3 | 0.2 | 0.3 |
| French Polynesia | 0.3 | 0.6 | 0.5 | 0.6 | 0.9 |
| Georgia | 0.1 | 0.0 | 0.1 | 0.1 | 0.1 |
| Hong Kong, China | 32.7 | 32.4 | 32.4 | 31.1 | 31.5 |
| Iran, Islamic Republic of | 0.2 | 0.3 | 0.7 | 0.7 | 0.7 |
| Japan | 14.8 | 16.4 | 16.8 | 17.1 | 12.7 |
| Kazakhstan | 3.6 | 2.7 | 2.3 | 2.5 | 3.0 |
| Republic of Korea | 17.2 | 21.3 | 22.7 | 25.5 | 35.5 |
| Kyrgyzstan | 1.6 | 2.2 | 1.1 | 1.0 | 1.0 |
| Lao People's Democratic Republic | 6.4 | 6.4 | 5.5 | 6.0 | 6.5 |
| Macao, China | 15.1 | 16.1 | 16.8 | 19.1 | 21.5 |
| Mongolia | 39.0 | 34.9 | 31.9 | 36.6 | 34.6 |
| New Caledonia | 0.1 | 0.2 | 0.2 | 0.2 | 0.1 |
| New Zealand | 4.1 | 4.9 | 5.6 | 7.7 | 8.3 |
| Russian Federation | 3.4 | 3.4 | 3.4 | 3.5 | 3.5 |
| Samoa | 0.9 | 1.0 | 1.2 | 1.2 | 1.2 |
| Singapore | 9.7 | 10.1 | 12.0 | 14.0 | 14.6 |
| Sri Lanka | 1.6 | 1.4 | 1.7 | 2.3 | 3.8 |
| Tajikistan | 1.2 | 1.7 | 2.1 | 1.7 | 0.5 |
| Tonga | 1.1 | 1.3 | 1.0 | 1.0 | 1.0 |
| Turkey | 0.2 | 0.2 | 0.3 | 0.3 | 0.3 |
| Viet Nam | 13.8 | 17.9 | 23.6 | 20.9 | 25.2 |
| **Total** | **11.9** | **13.1** | **13.6** | **14.2** | **15.2** |

*Source:* ESCAP calculation based on UNWTO database, 2015.

# E CONCLUSION

The performance of the Asia-Pacific region's commercial services sector performance has slightly improved in 2014 compared with the previous year. Export growth improved from 4% in 2013 to 5.1% in 2014, while import growth improved from 5.7% to 6.1% during the same period. The Asia-Pacific region basically maintained its share of global exports and imports (28% and 32.6%, respectively). Trade in Asia and the Pacific commercial services has been dominated by a small number of countries, especially China, Japan, India and Singapore which represented more than half of the region's trade.. Specifically, business and travel services together accounted for about 75% of total commercial services exports.

However, as discussed in chapter 1, the evidence from trade in commercial services confirms that China's economic slowdown is likely to have a negative impact on the overall trade performance of the region in 2015 and beyond. China has not only been an important Asia-Pacific exporter, but is also becoming an important importer of services, especially travel services. China actually accounts for more than a quarter of the total services imports by the Asia-Pacific region. With regard to tourism, available data show that Chinese tourists represent more than 15% of the total arrivals at Asia-Pacific destinations.

## ENDNOTES

[1] The commercial services category in this report is defined as being equal to services minus government services, n.i.e. The commercial services category is further subdivided into goods-related services, transport, travel and other commercial services. The commercial services and their subcategories in this report are based on the newly available classification in the sixth edition of the Balance of Payments and International Investment Position Manual (BPM6), published by IMF (Please see annex for details). Due to different editions of BPM being used, the numbers presented in the Asia-Pacific Trade and Investment Report 2015 may differ from those presented in the previous volumes of APTIR. In order to deal with the lack of data on trade in commercial services for many economies in Asia and the Pacific, the analysis in this chapter uses data compiled from different sources, including mirror data. However, even with this approach, it is not possible to provide an up-to-date and detailed account of intraregional services trade flows. Data presented in this chapter mainly come from data most recently released by the WTO database on International Trade Statistics during the preparation of this report.

[2] The data related to Asia and the Pacific in this chapter include Asia-Pacific members of ESCAP as well as Taiwan Province of China, which is not a member of United Nations and ESCAP. Taiwan Province of China has been allocated to the East and North-East Asia subregion.

[3] A major factor for the reduction of foreign tourists in the Russian Federation might be related to the country's involvement in the Ukraine crisis (Smith, 2014; and Kuzmin, 2014). A combination between political tension and sluggish demand explains the decline in Thailand's tourism (Kositchotetahna, 2015). While the numbers of European tourists has been falling since the 2009 economic crisis, a drop in both the numbers and the expenditures of tourists from the Russian Federation has hit Thailand's travel exports hard during recent years (Pattaya Today, 2015). A decline in casino visitors from China has affected the numbers of tourist arrivals in Macao, China (Wong, 2015; and Wong and Chan, 2015).

[4] Other commercial services comprise the following subcategories: construction, insurance and pension services, financial services, charges for the use of intellectual property n.i.e., telecommunications, computer and information services, other business services, and personal, cultural and recreational services (see also annex).

[5] Goods-related services include manufacturing services using physical inputs owned by others and maintenance and repair services that are not included elsewhere.

[6] According to the IMF definition, personal, cultural, and recreational services involving transactions between residents and non-residents are subdivided into two categories: (a) audiovisual and related services; and (b) other cultural and recreational services. The first category comprises services and associated fees related to the production of motion pictures (film or video tape), radio and television programmes (live or on tape), and musical recordings. Included are: receipts or payments for rentals; fees received by resident actors, directors, producers etc. (or by non-residents in the compiling economy) for productions abroad; and fees for distribution rights sold to the media for a limited number of showings in specified areas. Fees to actors, producers etc. involved with theatrical and musical productions, sporting events, circuses etc. and fees for distribution rights (for television, radio etc.) for these activities are included. The second category comprises other personal, cultural, and recreational services such as those associated with museums, libraries, archives, and other cultural, sporting and recreational activities. Also included are fees for services, including provision of correspondence courses, rendered abroad by teachers or doctors.

[7] According to the UNWTO's classification, Asia and the Pacific includees four subregions: (a) North-East Asia (China; Japan; the Republic of Korea; Mongolia; Hong Kong, China; Macao, China; and Taiwan Province of China); (b) South-East Asia (Brunei Darussalam, Cambodia, Indonesia, the Lao People's Democratic Republic; Malaysia; Myanmar; the Philippines; Singapore; Thailand; Timor-Leste; and Viet Nam); (c) Oceania (Australia; Fiji; French Polynesia; Guam; Kiribati; Marshall Islands; Federated States of Micronesia; New Zealand; Niue; Palau; Papua New Guinea; Samoa; Solomon Islands; Tonga; Tuvalu; Vanuatu; American Samoa; Cook Islands; New Caledonia; and the Northern Mariana Islands); and (d) South Asia (Bangladesh; Bhutan; India; and the Islamic Republic of Iran).

[8] This is estimated by using country data and shares of country groups if country data are not available. The estimated tourist arrivals in the Asia-Pacific region include tourist arrivals in North and Central Asian countries. However, the number excludes tourist arrivals in Turkey to avoid double counting.

[9] The number does not include tourist arrivals in Turkey, which is defined as a European country by UNWTO.

## REFERENCES

Kositchotetahna, Boonsong (2015). Thailand drops in global tourism rankings. *Bangkok Post*, 22 April. Available from www.bangkokpost.com/news/general/536583/thailand-drops-in-global-tourism-rankings.

Kuzmin, Viktor (2014). Concern in Russia as foreign tourist numbers slump. *Russia Beyond the Headline*, 3 July. Available from http://asia.rbth.com/business/2014/07/03/concern_in_russia_as_foreign_tourist_numbers_slump_37899.html.

*Pattaya Today* (2015). Thai tourism drop, 6 May. Available from http://pattayatoday.net/news/latest-edition/thai-tourism-drops/

Smith, Oliver (2014). Russian aggression deters tourists. *Telegraph*, 2 September. Available from www.telegraph.co.uk/travel/destinations/europe/russia/11069901/Russian-aggression-deters-tourists.html.

United Nations Conference on Trade and Development (2010). Foreign direct investment, the transfer and diffusion of technology, and sustainable development. Note by the UNCTAD Secretariat, 8 December. TD/B/C.II/EM.2/2. Available from http://unctad.org/en/Docs/ciiem2d2_en.pdf.

United Nations World Tourism Organization (2015). *World Tourism Barometer*, vol. 13. Madrid. Available from www.e-unwto.org/loi/wtobarometereng.

Wong, Stephanie (2015). Macau's empty tables are a sign of a radically changing tourism market. Bloomberg, 3 February. Available from http://skift.com/2015/02/03/macaus-empty-tables-are-a-sign-of-a-radically-changing-tourism-market/

Wong, Stephanie, and Billy Chan (2015). Macau tourism declines as china cuts down on corruption. Bloomberg, 2 January. Available from http://skift.com/2015/01/02/macau-tourism-declines-as-china-cuts-down-on-corruption/

## ONLINE DATABASES

United Nations, Economic and Social Commission for Asia and the Pacific. ESCAP online statistical database. Available from www.unescap.org/stat/data/statdb/DataExplorer.aspx.

World Trade Organization. International Trade Statistics Database. Available from http://stat.wto.org/Home/WSDBHome.aspx?Language=

World Tourism Organization. UNWTO database. Available from www2.unwto.org/content/data-0

# Annex

## Statistics on trade in commercial services – ongoing changes in methodology

The new methodology followed in the datasets of WTO and other international organizations is based on the sixth edition of the IMF Balance of Payments and International Investment Position Manual (BPM6) as well as the 2010 edition of the Manual on Statistics of International Trade in Services (MSITS 2010).

The new methodology clarifies the coverage of several service items and eliminates all exceptions to the change of ownership principle. There are some added service categories, while the coverage of others has been modified and some renamed to reflect new ways of measuring the services trade. As a result, there are 12 standard services components in BPM6, but they could be grouped in four major categories as presented in the chart below (full details on all the component definitions and measurements are available at http://webservices.wto.org/resources/meta/def_method_e.pdf.

While several economies worldwide have fully implemented BPM6 for the recording of their Balance of Payments services transactions, others are still compiling their statistics according to the BPM5 methodology. Therefore, comparability and coverage of data may not always be complete. It should be noted in particular that global and regional estimates of trade in new services items such as manufacturing services on physical inputs owned by others, and maintenance and repair services n.i.e. may be underestimated, as some economies do not report these items yet.

| | | |
|---|---|---|
| **Goods-related services** | Manufacturing services on physical inputs owned by others | Processing, assembly, labelling, packing and similar activities |
| | Maintenance and repair, n.i.e. | Maintenance and repair work by residents on goods that are owned by non-residents (and vice-versa). |
| **Transport** | | Can be classified by mode of transport (sea, air or other) and by what is carried – passengers or freight. Also included are postal and courier services. |
| **Travel** | | Lodging, food and beverages, entertainment and transportation (within the economy visited), gifts and souvenirs. Travel is further subdivided into: (a) personal travel and (b) business travel. |
| **Other commercial services** | Construction | Creation, renovation, repair or extension of fixed assets in the form of buildings, land improvements of an engineering nature, and other similar engineering constructions such as roads, bridges, dams and so forth. Construction also covers the acquisition of goods and services by the enterprises undertaking construction work from the economy of location of the construction work. Construction can be divided into (a) construction abroad and (b) construction in the compiling economy. |
| | Insurance and pension services | Services providing life insurance and annuities, non-life insurance, reinsurance, freight insurance, pensions, standardized guarantees, and auxiliary services to insurance, pension schemes, and standardized guarantee schemes. |
| | Financial services | Financial intermediary and auxiliary services, except insurance and pension fund services, provided by banks and other financial corporations. |

| | | |
|---|---|---|
| | Charges for use of intellectual property n.i.e. | Charges for the use of proprietary rights (such as patents, trademarks, copyrights, industrial processes and designs including trade secrets, franchises); charges for licences to reproduce or distribute (or both) intellectual property embodied in produced originals or prototypes (such as copyrights on books and manuscripts, computer software, cinematographic works and sound recordings) and related rights (such as for live performances and television, cable or satellite broadcast). |
| | Telecommunication computer and information services | Telecommunications services encompassing the broadcasting or transmission of sound, images, data, or other information by telephone, telex, telegram, radio and television cable transmission, radio and television satellite, electronic mail, facsimile and so forth, including business network services, teleconferencing, and support services; computer services consisting of hardware- and software-related services and data-processing services; information services including news agency services, such as the provision of news, photographs and feature articles to the media as well as database services. |
| | Other business services | Research and development services, professional and management consulting services and technical, trade-related and other business services. |
| | Personal cultural and recreational services | Audio-visual and related services and other personal, cultural and recreational services. |
| | Government goods and services n.i.e. | Goods and services supplied by, and to enclaves, such as embassies, military bases and international organizations; goods and services acquired from the host economy by diplomats, consular staff and military personnel located abroad as well as their dependents; services supplied by, and to Governments, and not included in other categories of services. |

*Source:* WTO Statistics – Trade in Commercial Services. Available from http://webservices.wto.org/resources/meta/def_method_e.pdf.

# 3 STRUCTURAL SHIFTS IN REGIONAL FOREIGN DIRECT INVESTMENT FLOW

## A RECENT TRENDS IN FOREIGN DIRECT INVESTMENT

### 1. General global and regional trends

By the end of 2015 global foreign direct investment (FDI) inflows are expected to move closer to their 2013 level, followed by a mild but stable climb in 2016 and 2017 (UNCTAD, 2015).[1] The main drivers of this upward trend are found in improved growth prospects in the United States, the demand-stimulating effects of lower oil prices, accommodating monetary policy, and continued investment liberalization and promotion measures. However in 2014 these factors were not strong enough to prevent the FDI inflow falling by 16% to $1.23 trillion (figure 3.1). The fragile global economy, an uncertain policy environment and elevated geopolitical risks were the primary causes of the decline (UNCTAD, 2015).

Figure 3.1. FDI inflows to developed and developing economies, 1995-2014

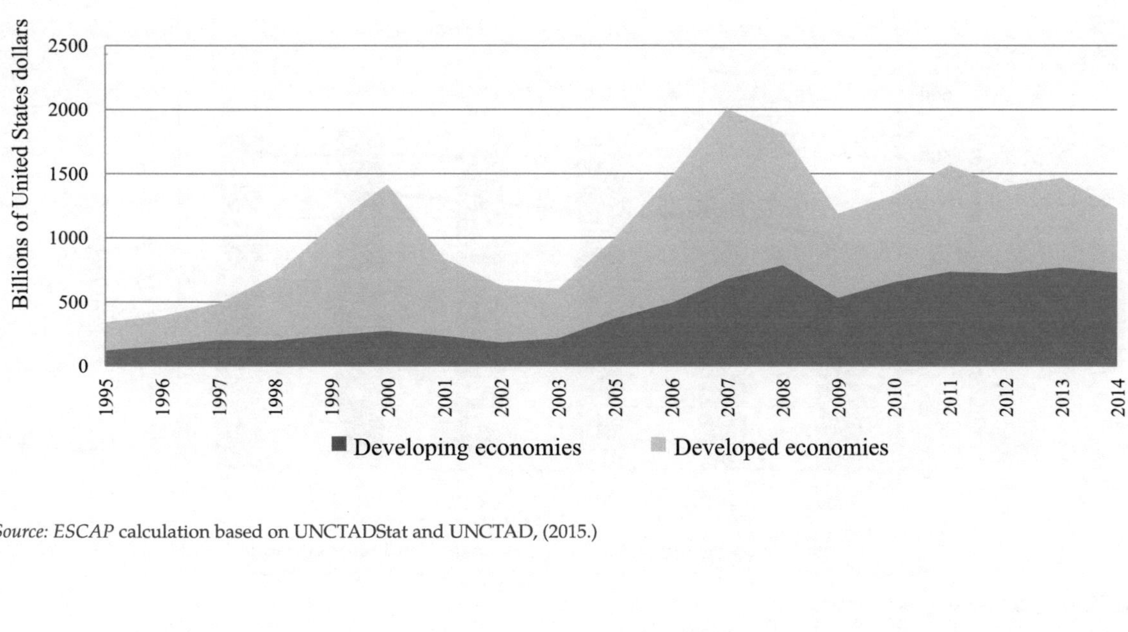


*Source: ESCAP* calculation based on UNCTADStat and UNCTAD, (2015.)

CHAPTER 3

Developing economies have been less affected by the global financial crisis and they have also recovered faster than developed economies. Since 2012, the share of developing economies' in global FDI inflows has surpassed that of developed economies.

In 2014, developing economies received $730 billion in FDI, a decrease of 5% from the previous year; however, this was inconsequential compared to the 28% drop in FDI inflows to developed economies in the same year. Global FDI outflows in 2014 also showed an increasing share of developing economies. Although FDI outflows from developed economies still dominate at $823 billion they dipped by 1% in 2014, while outflows from developing economies grew by 12% to reach $531 billion (figure 3.2).

Figure 3.2. FDI outflows from developed and developing economies, 1995-2014

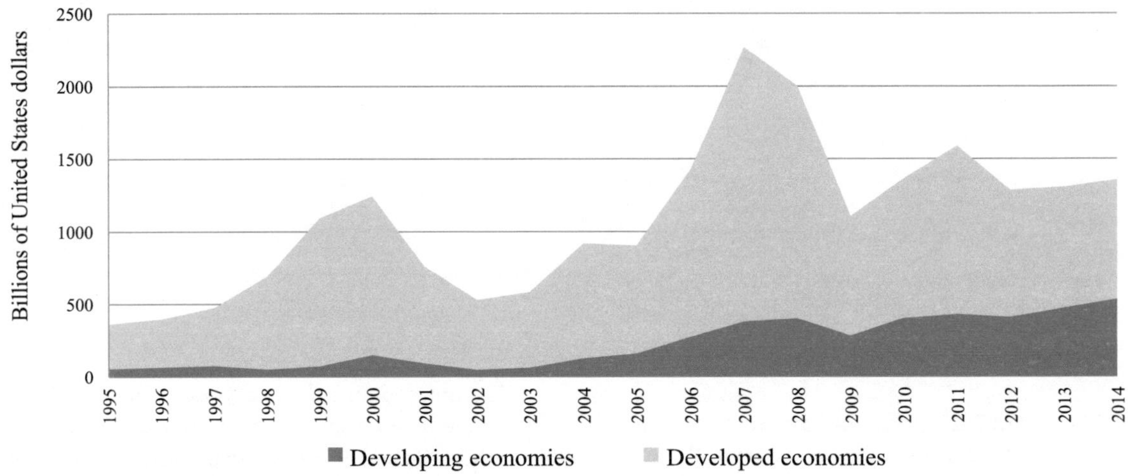


*Source:* ESCAP calculation based on UNCTADStat and UNCTAD, 2015.

Asia and the Pacific as a whole received a significant FDI inflow totalling $533 billion in 2014, which boosted its share of global FDI inflow to 43%, up from 38.7% in 2013 (figure 3.3). Although the amount of FDI inflow into the Asia-Pacific region declined by 1.5% the region's share increased because the global decline was 10 times greater.

*"The Asia-Pacific region has firmly established its leading position as the investment destination and also continued to grow as a major outward investor."*

Figure 3.3. FDI inflows to the Asia-Pacific region and their share in global FDI inflows, 2009-2014

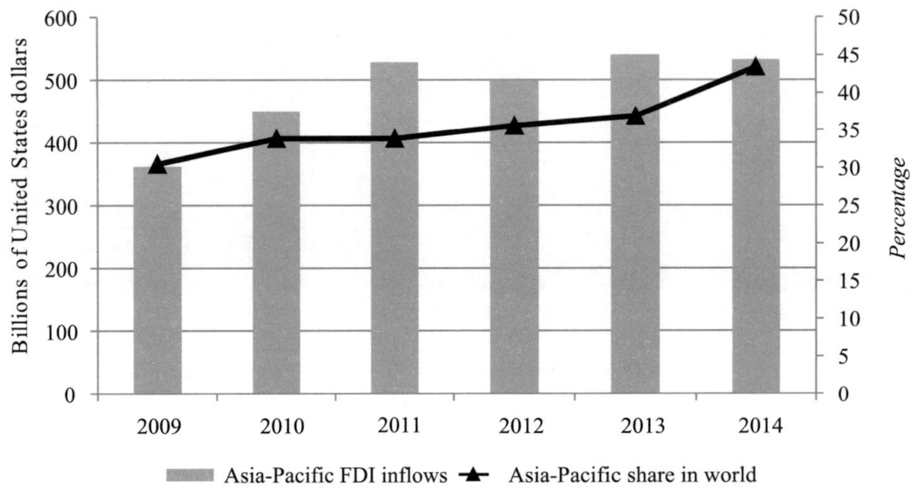


*Source:* ESCAP calculation based on UNCTAD, (2015).

The Asia-Pacific region has not only emerged as the leading investment destination; it has also continued to grow as a major outward investor, continuously increasing its share of global FDI outflow since 2010, with total FDI from the region reaching $563 billion in 2014, representing 41.6% of total global FDI outflow. Developing Asia-Pacific invested $450 billion abroad in 2014 – a 20% increase compared with 2013 – with 6 of the 20 largest outwardly investing economies located in the region. On the other hand, investment from three developed economies in Asia and the Pacific recorded a 15% decrease in 2014 compared with the previous year, pulled down by Japan's decline of 16% (figure 3.4).

Figure 3.4. FDI outflows from the Asia-Pacific region and their share in the global FDI outflows, 2009-2014

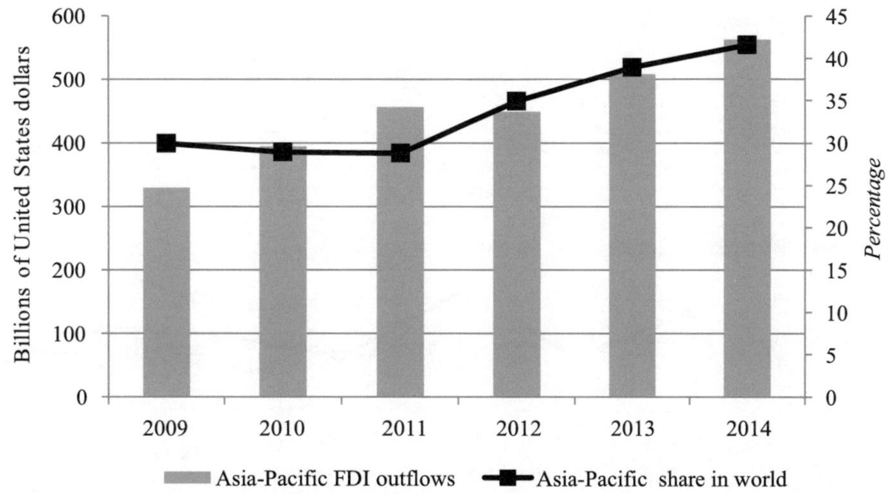


*Source:* ESCAP calculation based on UNCTAD (2015).

## 2. Trends in mergers and acquisitions and greenfield FDI flows[2]

Globally, FDI reached $399 billion in 2014 through mergers and acquisitions (M&A), which represented a 28% increase from the previous year. Multinational enterprises (MNEs) regained confidence in resuming acquisitions but continued to follow a more conservative approach in managing their significant cash reserves; instead of greenfield investment they opted more for cross-border acquisitions. In the Asia-Pacific region, FDI inflows through M&A surged to $123 billion in 2014, an increase of 137% compared with 2013 (figure 3.5). A number of large deals, including MNEs from China, Singapore and Hong Kong, China, contributed to the increase (UNCTAD, 2015).

> *"Cross-border M&A have been increasing with MNEs regaining their confidence and managing their cash reserves with lesser risk."*

Figure 3.5. FDI flows through mergers and acquisitions in the Asia-Pacific region, 2009-2014

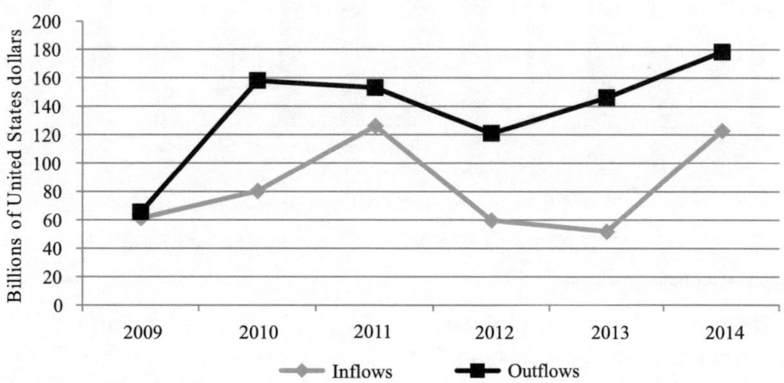


*Source:* ESCAP calculation based on UNCTAD (2015).

The growth in greenfield FDI inflows in Asia and the Pacific was less pronounced, totaling $279 billion in 2014, which was a 17% increase from the previous year (figure 3.6). This increase is significant in the context of the 2% decline in greenfield investment at the global level, amounting to $696 billion. Despite increasing importance of cross-border M&As in the Asia-Pacific region, greenfield FDI still accounts for the majority of FDI.

Whether this change in the composition of FDI shares of greenfield and M&A will have impact on the region's growth is uncertain. First, the decision as to the mode of investment depends on several factors, such as the financial position of the firms involved as well as country and industry characteristics. Moreover, there is often a lack of distinction between greenfield and M&A in reporting statistics; this could be the reason that most of the empirical and theoretical literature has not distinguished between these two modes of FDI (Calderon, Loayza and Serven, 2004; and Nocke and Yeaple, 2007).

Figure 3.6 Greenfield FDI flows in the Asia-Pacific region, 2009-2014

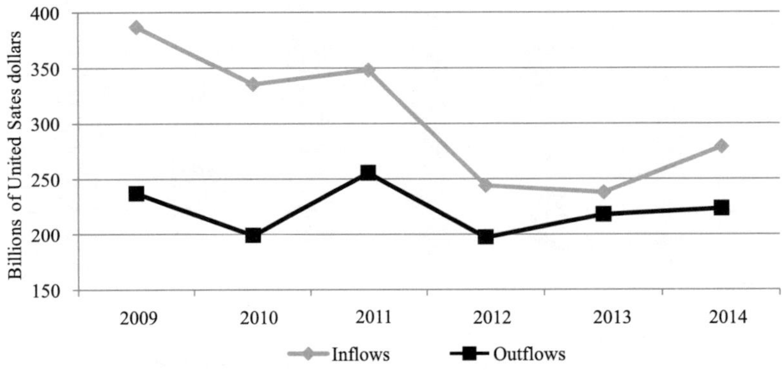


*Source:* ESCAP calculation based on fDi Intelligence data, 2015.

### 3. Intraregional greenfield FDI trends[4]

Intraregional greenfield FDI flows have fluctuated for the past decade, but their share in total greenfield FDI has remained at a stable level. Intraregional investment is replacing investment from the developed economies, which have traditionally supplied the bulk of FDI in the Asia-Pacific region. Reflecting the decrease in total greenfield FDI into the region, intraregional greenfield FDI has also been declining in recent years. However, in 2014, intraregional greenfield FDI flows reached $279 billion, which is a 95% increase compared with the amount in 2005, and accounting for 48% of total regional greenfield FDI inflows (figure 3.7).

Figure 3.7. Intraregional greenfield FDI inflows in the Asia-Pacific region and their share in total greenfield FDI inflows to the region, 2005-2014

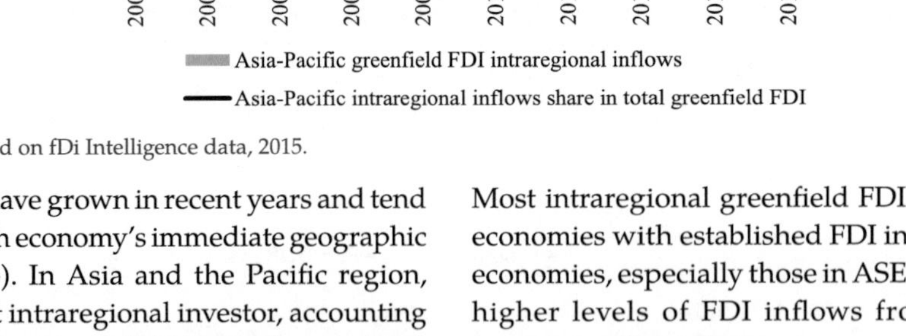


*Source:* ESCAP calculation based on fDi Intelligence data, 2015.

South-South FDI flows have grown in recent years and tend to occur more within each economy's immediate geographic region (UNCTAD, 2015). In Asia and the Pacific region, China is now the biggest intraregional investor, accounting for 21% of total intraregional greenfield FDI inflows in 2014.

Most intraregional greenfield FDI has targeted the bigger economies with established FDI inflows. However, smaller economies, especially those in ASEAN, increasingly receive higher levels of FDI inflows from other Asian-Pacific economies (figure 3.8).

Figure 3.8. Destinations of intraregional FDI flows, 2009-2014

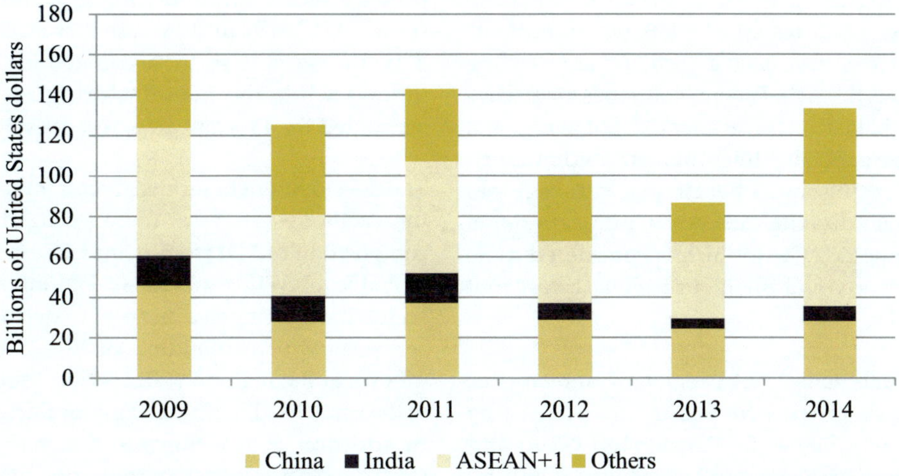


*Source:* ESCAP calculation based on fDi Intelligence data, 2015.

The importance of intraregional FDI is more evident when outflows are considered. Of the total $222 billion in greenfield investment from the Asia-Pacific region, $133 billion (60%) went to other economies in the region. In particular, China, Japan and the Republic of Korea have continued to be major investors in the Asia-Pacific region, with China and ASEAN members continuing to be the most attractive destinations (figure 3.9).

*"Intraregional greenfield FDI flows were on the increase – of the total $222 billion in greenfield investment from the Asia-Pacific region, $133 billion (60%) targeted other economies in the region."*

Figure 3.9. Intraregional greenfield FDI flows between selected economies, and total inflows and outflows to and from those economies, 2012-2014

*(Billions of United States dollars)*

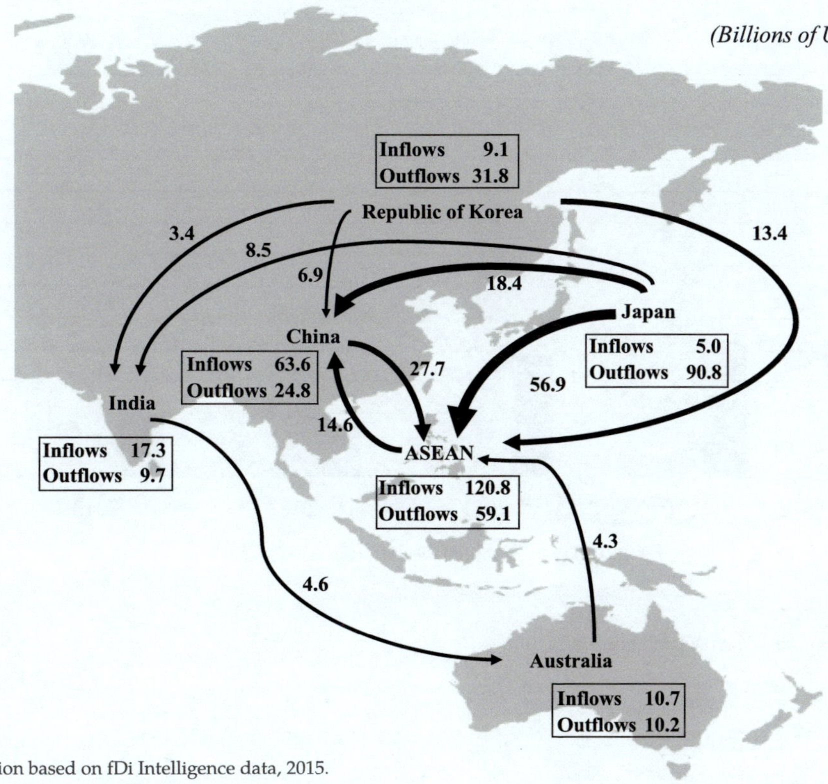


*Source:* ESCAP calculation based on fDi Intelligence data, 2015.

CHAPTER 3

Intraregional investment is further promoted and encouraged with bilateral and multilateral investment agreements. In the Asia-Pacific region, growth of preferential trade agreements has been rapid, resulting in 168 such agreements that are now in force or have been signed and are pending ratification. Of these, the Asia-Pacific economies are parties to 43 agreements that cover "investment".[5] Some regional and subregional trade and investment agreements have been instrumental in easing and liberalizing intraregional investment, especially the ASEAN Comprehensive Investment Agreement (ACIA) which is considered to be one of the most advanced and ambitious regional investment tools (ESCAP, 2011).

Currently, some ambitious "mega-regional" agreements, which include investment provisions, are also being discussed, i.e. the Trans-Pacific Partnership (TPP) and Regional Comprehensive Economic Partnership (RCEP). By pursuing these mega-regional agreements, and by consolidating and advancing current regional and subregional agreements, it is hoped that some complexities resulting from the current interwoven bilateral trade and investment agreements will be tackled, thereby advancing the intraregional investment agenda in Asia and the Pacific.

### 4. FDI in services sectors almost fully recovered after the crisis[6]

At the global level, services have progressively claimed increasing importance in the international investment landscape. In 2012, the year for which the latest UNCTAD sectoral data are available, the services sector accounted for 63% of global FDI stock, while manufacturing and the primary sector accounted for 26% and 10%, respectively (UNCTAD, 2015). In 2014, based on available greenfield FDI data, the services sector accounted for 39% of global FDI inflows while the manufacturing and primary sectors accounted for 43% and 18%, respectively.

The development in services sector investments in Asia and the Pacific results from the ongoing shift in the sectoral composition of FDI from manufacturing to services at the global level. While greenfield FDI inflows to the primary sector have witnessed a notable decline, FDI inflows to services – which accounted for 40% of total greenfield FDI inflows in the region in 2014 – have remained more or less at the same level, with some minor fluctuations, since 2009. In addition, FDI inflows to the manufacturing sector, strategically important for the region, started to grow again after a sharp decline in 2012; however, they have yet to reach the 2009 level (figure 3.10).

*"In the Asia-Pacific region, FDI inflows to services have remained at a stable level, accounting for 40% of total greenfield FDI inflows to the region."*

Figure 3.10. Greenfield FDI inflows to the Asia-Pacific region, by sector, 2009-2014

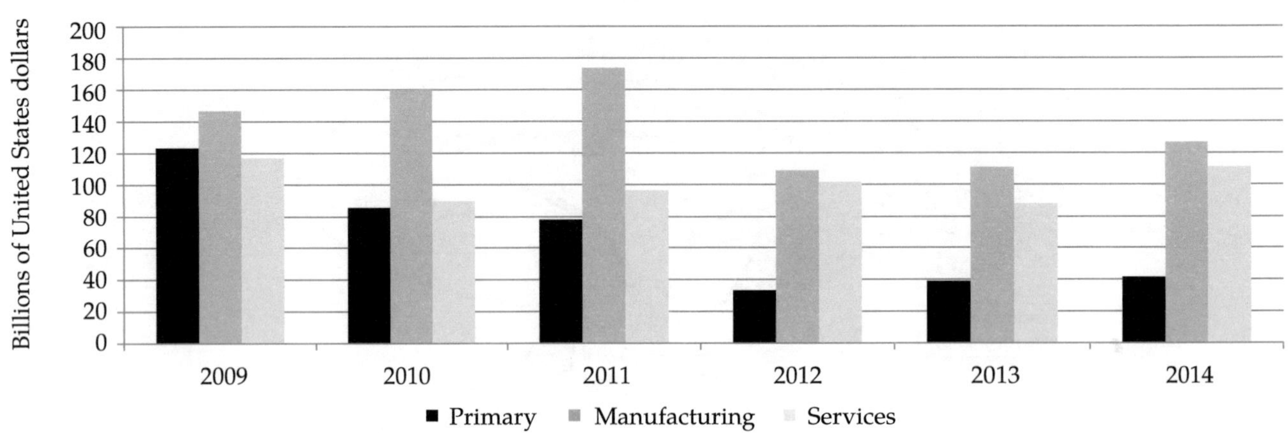


*Source:* ESCAP calculation based on fDi Intelligence data, 2015.

# B ASIA-PACIFIC SUBREGIONAL TRENDS[7]

## 1. FDI inflows

Within the Asia-Pacific region, FDI inflows varied among the subregions and economies (figure 3.11). Developing East and North-East Asia and South-East Asia showed significant increases in the level of FDI inflows. These subregions received $245 billion and $133 billion in 2014, respectively. China became the main global investment destination and received the largest FDI inflow in the world, surpassing the United States, with $129 billion in 2014, an increase of 3.7% from the previous year. Hong Kong, China received $103 billion in FDI inflow in 2014, second to China, with a 39% increase from the previous year.

Figure 3.11. FDI inflows to the Asia-Pacific developing subregions and developed economies, 2012-2014

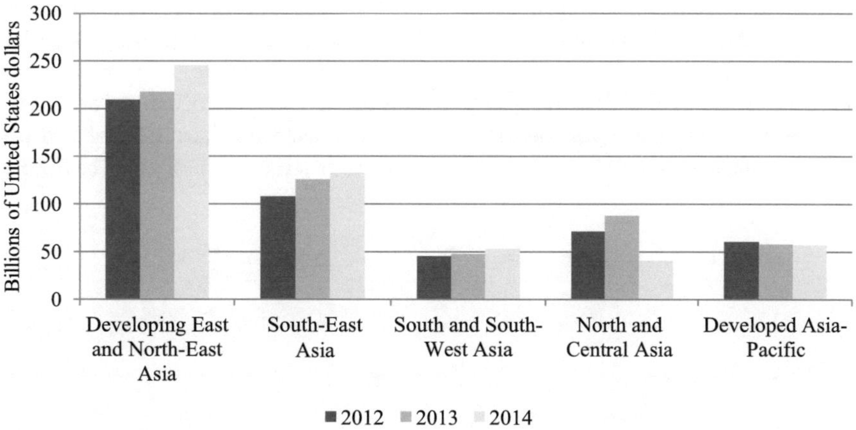


*Source:* ESCAP calculation based on UNCTAD, 2015.

In South-East Asia, which comprises the 10 ASEAN members and Timor-Leste (which applied for ASEAN membership in 2011), FDI inflows amounted to $133 billion in 2014, a 5.4% increase from 2013. Compared with 2009-2011, total FDI inflows during 2012-2014 increased for all South-East Asian countries except Myanmar and Timor-Leste. FDI inflows to the Philippines and Thailand showed remarkable growth, with FDI inflows more than doubling in 2012-2014 compared with 2009-2011 (table 3.1).

Table 3.1. FDI inflows to South-East Asia, totals for 2009-2011 and 2012-2014[a]

*(Millions of United States dollars)*

| Countries ranked by size of FDI inflows | 2009-2011 | 2012-2014 | Percentage change |
|---|---|---|---|
| Singapore | 126 899 | 188 975 | 49 |
| Indonesia | 37 889 | 60 535 | 60 |
| Thailand | 15 196 | 35 750 | 135 |
| Malaysia | 22 711 | 32 153 | 42 |
| Viet Nam | 23 119 | 26 468 | 14 |
| Philippines | 5 113 | 11 971 | 134 |
| Cambodia | 3 642 | 5 437 | 49 |
| Brunei Darussalam | 1 542 | 2 209 | 43 |
| Myanmar | 7 814 | 2 027 | -74 |
| Lao People's Democratic Republic | 770 | 1 442 | 87 |
| Timor-Leste | 126 | 123 | -2% |

*Source: ESCAP* calculation based on UNCTAD, 2015.

[a] In order to even out the volatile annual FDI flows, the total invested FDI flow during 2009-2009 and 2012-2014 is used instead of annual flows.

CHAPTER 3

Since all but one of the countries in the South-East Asia subregion are members of ASEAN, their performance in terms of trade and investment should be examined in the context of their joint efforts towards the establishment of the ASEAN Economic Community (AEC) and associated investment regime adopted under the ASEAN Comprehensive Investment Agreement (ACIA).

ACIA is among the most progressive regional investment agreements between developing economies (ESCAP, 2011). Despite the slow progress towards the AEC,[8] South-East Asian countries have benefited from ongoing concerted efforts towards increasing stability and predictability of growth prospects in the subregion, which has been instrumental in attracting increased FDI inflows. These efforts have included improving the ease of conducting business, increasing infrastructure investment and providing investment incentives. In addition, South-East Asian countries have implemented measures to promote, liberalize and facilitate investment. In terms of the Ease of Doing Business Index, 7 out of 10 South-East Asian countries have improved their rankings or at least remained the same.[9]

*"Progressive regional investment agreements such as ACIA, and ongoing concerted efforts towards AEC, are instrumental in attracting increased FDI inflows."*

South-East Asian countries receive significant amounts of FDI from within the subregion; intraregional investment within ASEAN accounted for 17.4% of total FDI inflows to the region (ASEAN, 2014). The subregion receives significant flows from East and North-East Asia, which provides an even stronger base for the future growth of economic cooperation among RCEP economies (Economist Intelligence Unit, 2014c).

The manufacturing sector in South-East Asia has received the bulk of FDI inflows due to the relocation of businesses from areas experiencing increasing labour costs, such as China, and to anticipating utilization of the benefits that will occur with the formation of RCEP. The services sector also increased its share in total FDI inflows to South-East Asia, to reach $35 billion in 2014 (figure 3.12).

Figure 3.12. Greenfield FDI inflows to South-East Asia, by sector, 2009-2014

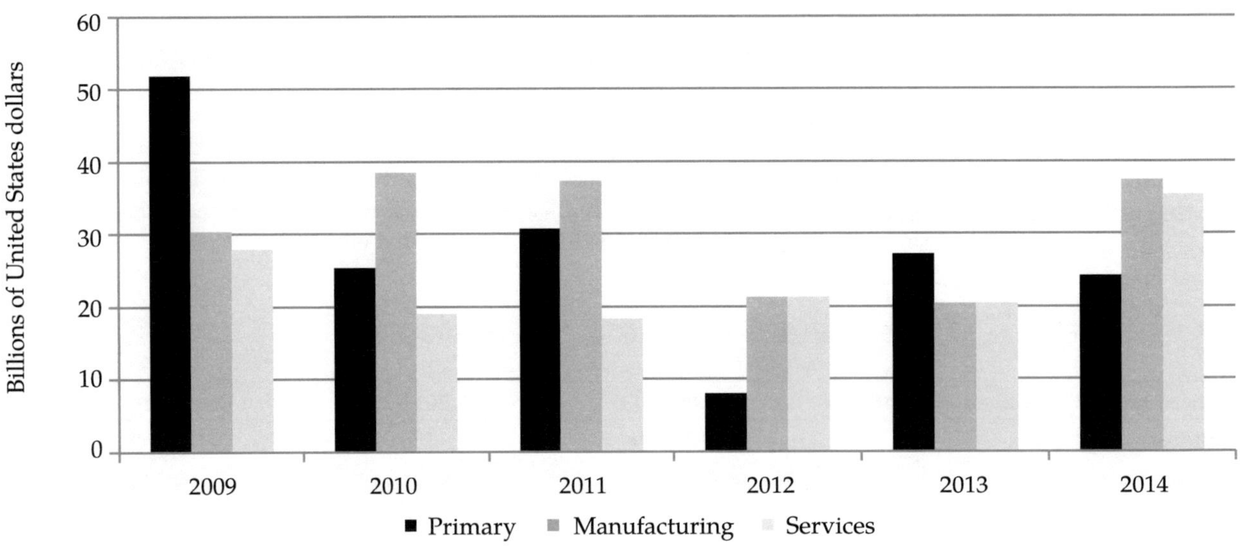


*Source:* ESCAP calculation based on fDi Intelligence data, 2015.

The South and South-West Asia subregion has witnessed slow but steady growth of FDI inflows during the past three years, and in 2014, the subregion recorded a $53 billion FDI inflow. This improvement was mainly due to the increase of FDI inflows to India and Pakistan, by 21.1% and 31.1%, respectively. These increases were due to improved performance by the Indian economy, the recovery of investors' confidence and the rise of Chinese FDI flows to Pakistan. In terms of greenfield FDI, the subregion saw a recovery in primary sector investment in 2014 (figure 3.13).

Figure 3.13. Greenfield FDI inflows to South and South-West Asia, by sector, 2009-2014

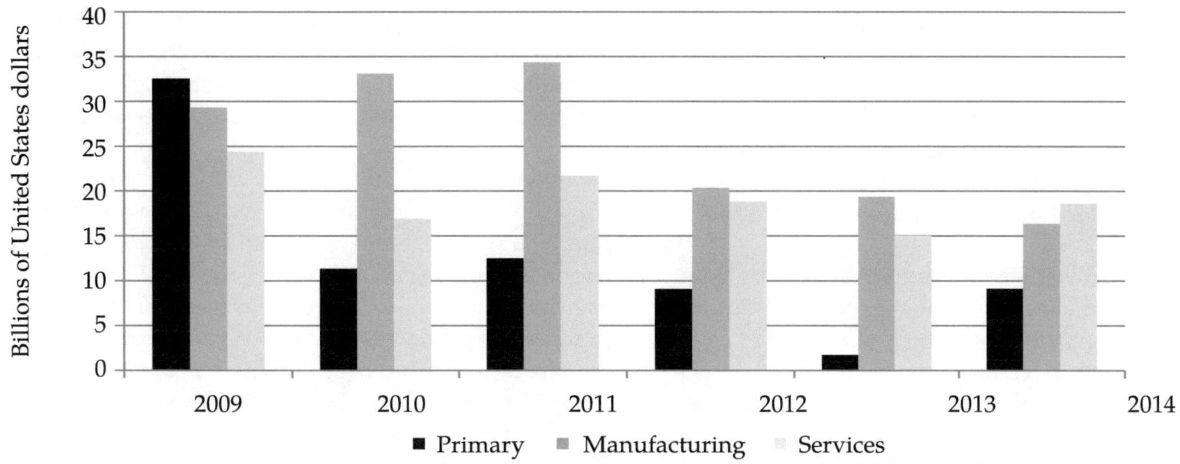


*Source:* ESCAP calculation based on fDi Intelligence data, 2015.

North and Central Asia experienced a pronounced drop of 53.3% in FDI inflows, receiving only $41 billion in 2014, compared with $88 billion in the previous year. This was mainly due to a virtual halt in FDI flows to the Russian Federation, which in 2014 fell by almost 70%. This drop can be explained by the international sanctions placed on the country, which have severely affected the economy in various ways; it has led to increased volatility in the Russian foreign exchange market and a significant depreciation of the rouble. The sanctions include restrictions on access to international financial markets, and have undermined domestic business and consumer confidence by depressing consumption and investment (World Bank, 2015). Also, an adjustment is due to the exceptional level of inflows reached in 2013 (UNCTAD, 2015).

The developed economies in Asia and the Pacific recovered from a big drop in FDI inflows in 2009 and 2010, but are still struggling to reach the pre-crisis level. The year 2014 did not bring much reprieve in this regard, as FDI inflows of $57 billion to developed economies were actually 1.4% less than in the previous year.

## 2. FDI outflows

In 2014, the FDI outflow from the Asia-Pacific region totalled $563 billion, an 11% increase from 2013 (figure 3.14). Unsurprisingly, East and North-East Asia as well as South-East Asia contributed to the increase of FDI outflows. China invested $116 billion in 2014, an increase of 15% from the

Figure 3.14. FDI outflows from the Asia-Pacific developing subregions and developed economies, 2012-2014[a]

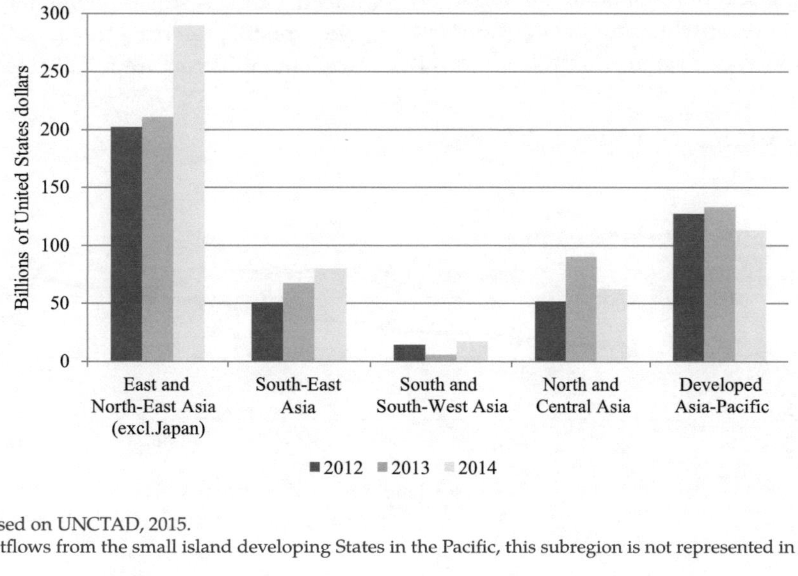


Source: ESCAP calculation based on UNCTAD, 2015.

[a] Due to the small share of outflows from the small island developing States in the Pacific, this subregion is not represented in figure 3.14

previous year, while Hong Kong, China invested $143 billion, registering an exceptionally high increase of 77%. China has been a major regional player in the growth of developing economies' outward FDI; this is discussed in more detail in the following section.

In South-East Asia, which witnessed a 19% increase in FDI outflows amounting to $80 billion in 2014, the Philippines almost doubled its outward FDI at $7 billion, while Singapore invested $41 billion abroad, an increase of 41%.

South and South-West Asia invested $17 billion abroad in 2014, which is a 206% increase from the previous year. The high increase is partly a statistical effect due to the exceptionally low investment level in 2013, which was prompted by the huge decline that India experienced (ESCAP, 2014). FDI outflows were particularly high in India and the Islamic Republic of Iran in 2014, which recorded 487% and 314% increases in FDI outflows, respectively.

North and Central Asia showed a significant decrease in outward FDI, investing $62 billion in 2014, which was a 31% decrease compared with the previous year. As in the case of FDI inflows the drop was heavily dominated by the Russian Federation, which recorded a 35% decrease to $54 billion in outward investment in 2014. This drop is large but when compared with previous years, given the exceptionally high outflows in 2013 that were driven mainly by a single transaction, the FDI outflows have not changed much.

Developed economies in the region not only received less inward investment, as noted above, they also showed sluggish outward investment. FDI outflows from developed economies in the region fell by 15%, to just $113 billion in 2014, which put an end to the steady increase of FDI outflows from developed economies in the Asia-Pacific region since 2009. Japan, which has been driving the outcome of the developed economies in the Asia-Pacific region for past years, was behind the steady increase. Thus, when in 2014 FDI outflows from Japan declined by 16%, it pulled down the performance of the group.

## C HIGHLIGHTS FOR SELECTED ECONOMIES

### 1. China

In 2014, China became the main investment destination, surpassing the United States in total FDI inflows. China received $129 billion in 2014, an increase of 3.7% from the previous year (figure 3.15). However, the growth in FDI inflow is slowing due to rising labour costs and input prices, discouraging FDI in manufacturing (China Today, 2014). Many companies have moved their production base to other economies in the region, mainly to nearby low-wage economies such as Bangladesh, Cambodia, Indonesia, Sri Lanka and Viet Nam. However, while the ongoing economic reform and anti-corruption campaign will probably result in structural changes in China's overseas investment, they are unlikely to alter its broader growth trend and, thus, the attraction as a destination for overseas investment flows (Economist Intelligence Unit, 2014b).

> *"China became the main investment destination and received the largest FDI inflow in the world, surpassing the United States of America.*

Indeed, China is still attracting large amounts of FDI; with investors still preferring to stay in the country because of its excellent infrastructure and effective participation in global

Figure 3.15. FDI flows in China, 2009-2014

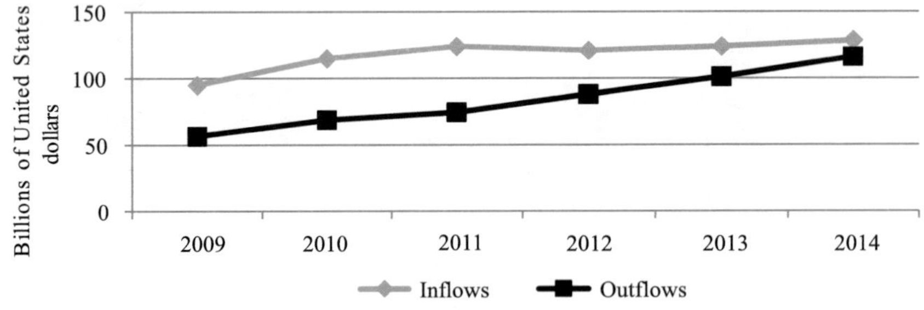


*Source:* ESCAP calculation based on UNCTAD, 2015.

China is likely to continue receiving significant amounts of FDI inflows (Economist Intelligence Unit, 2014a).

Greenfield FDI inflows in the manufacturing sector in China witnessed a sharp drop from 2011 to 2012; however, since then they have been increasing gradually. Greenfield FDI in other sectors has witnessed small declines in recent years, but still accounts for a significant portion of total greenfield FDI inflows (figure 3.16).

In contrast to inflows, FDI outflows from China have continued to rise rapidly (figure 3.15). During the past five years, FDI from China almost doubled and now accounts for 9% of total global FDI outflows. Initiatives by the Government, such as the "going global" strategy[11] and the "One Belt One Road" initiative[12] provide incentives for Chinese investment abroad. China has continued to invest in other BRICS economies as well as developed markets, becoming the largest investor in the United States in 2014. However, it is also increasingly investing in smaller economies in the Asia-Pacific region and is establishing long-term partnerships, especially with new development finance institutions such as the Asian Infrastructure Investment Bank and the Silk Road Infrastructure Fund of China (ESCAP, 2015a). Of the top 10 destinations for Chinese outward greenfield FDI, six were in the Asia-Pacific region (table 3.2).

Figure 3.16. Greenfield FDI inflows to China, by sector, 2009-2014

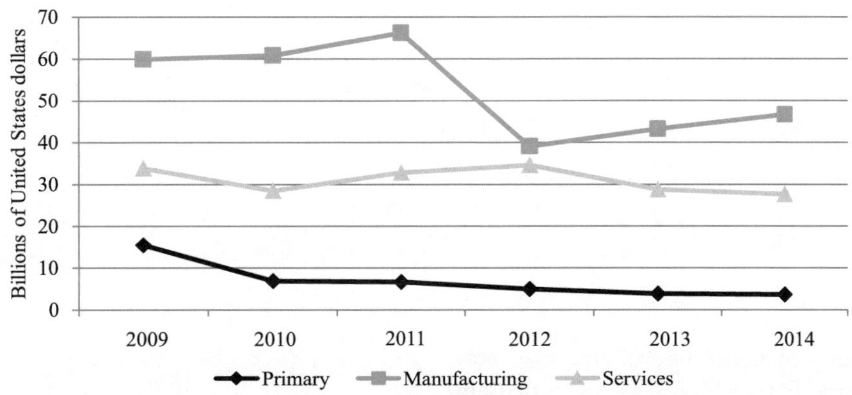


*Source:* ESCAP calculation based on UNCTAD, 2015.

Table 3.2. The top 10 destinations for greenfield FDI from China, 2012-2014[a]

*(Millions of United States dollars and percentage)*

| Destination country | Total invested in 2012-2014 | Share in total |
|---|---|---|
| United States | 19 950.2 | 19 |
| United Kingdom | 13 000.4 | 12 |
| Russian Federation | 12 738.7 | 12 |
| Malaysia | 12 216.1 | 12 |
| Pakistan | 9 402.3 | 9 |
| Brazil | 7 495.8 | 7 |
| Republic of Korea | 7 413.2 | 7 |
| Peru | 5 449.1 | 5 |
| Indonesia | 4 620.4 | 4 |
| Australia | 4 502.1 | 4 |

*Source:* ESCAP calculation based on fDi Intelligence data, 2015.
[a] In order to even out the volatile annual FDI flows, the total invested FDI flow during 2012-2014 is used.

## 2. India

FDI inflows to India have been steadily rising after a 32% decrease in 2012 compared with 2011. In 2014, India attracted FDI inflows amounting to $34 billion, a 22% increase. While this development is encouraging, the amounts received are about a quarter of total FDI received in China in 2014. FDI outflows from India picked up from very low level in 2013, bouncing back to $9.8 billion in 2014 (figure 3.17).

### Figure 3.17. FDI flows in India, 2009-2014

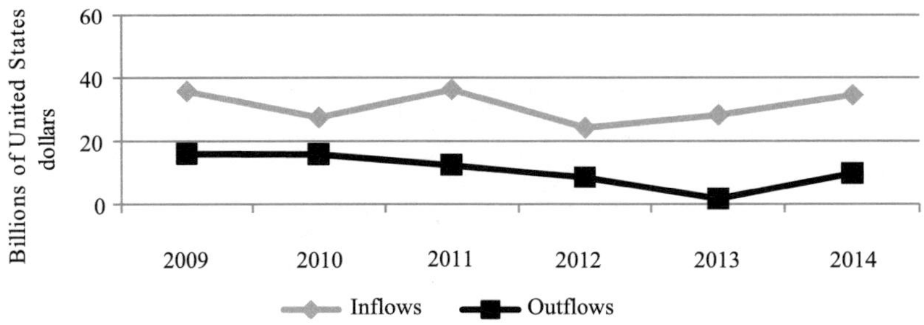


*Source:* ESCAP calculation based on UNCTAD, 2015.

With the improved performance of the economy, large-scale divestments from large Indian MNEs have stopped and some international expansions have resumed. This upward trend is expected to continue in the foreseeable future. The Government has liberalized FDI in sectors such as defence, railways, construction development, medical devices and insurance since Narendra Modi became Prime Minister in 2014 (Economist Intelligence Unit, 2014d). In addition, the Government is pursuing simplification of the business environment by reducing excessive regulation and increasing predictability in the country's trade and investment regimes (Indo Asian News Service, 2015). Also, the "Make in India" programme[13] could attract some new FDI in the manufacturing sector.

While India has achieved higher economic growth than China, it still has a long way to go to match China's role in the region's trade and investment flows. India's success will depend on its ability to accelerate the implementation of necessary structural reforms in order to improve its business and investment environment. Currently, India faces various structural bottlenecks, including delays in project approval, ill-targeted subsidies, a low manufacturing base and low agricultural productivity, difficulty in land acquisition, weak transportation and power networks, and strict labour regulations and skill mismatches (WTO, 2015).

## 3. Least developed countries

FDI inflows to the least developed countries in the Asia-Pacific region have been modest but have steadily risen during the past decade. Collectively, the Asian-Pacific least developed countries attracted $5.1 billion worth in FDI in 2014 (figure 3.18), which is 2.8 times larger than the amount received in 2005, although the share is still relatively small overall at less than 1% of total FDI to the Asia-Pacific region. Despite its small contribution, these countries are steadily increasing their share in global FDI inflows – recording 0.41% in 2014, compared with 0.18% in 2005 (figure 3.18).

Asian least developed countries have improved their economic performance over time. The average annual growth rate of output per capita during 1991-2012 was more than 3.5%. The rates for least developed countries globally, and African least developed countries in particular, were 2.6% and 1.9%, respectively. Labour productivity also increased by an average of 4% per annum during 2000-2012. However, these economies continue to struggle with a poor business climate, lack of soft and hard infrastructure, insufficient government resources, and other macroeconomic and political constraints, which prevent them from attracting higher levels of FDI (UNCTAD, 2014a).

Figure 3.18. FDI inflows to Asia-Pacific least developed countries and their share in global FDI inflows, 2005-2014[a]

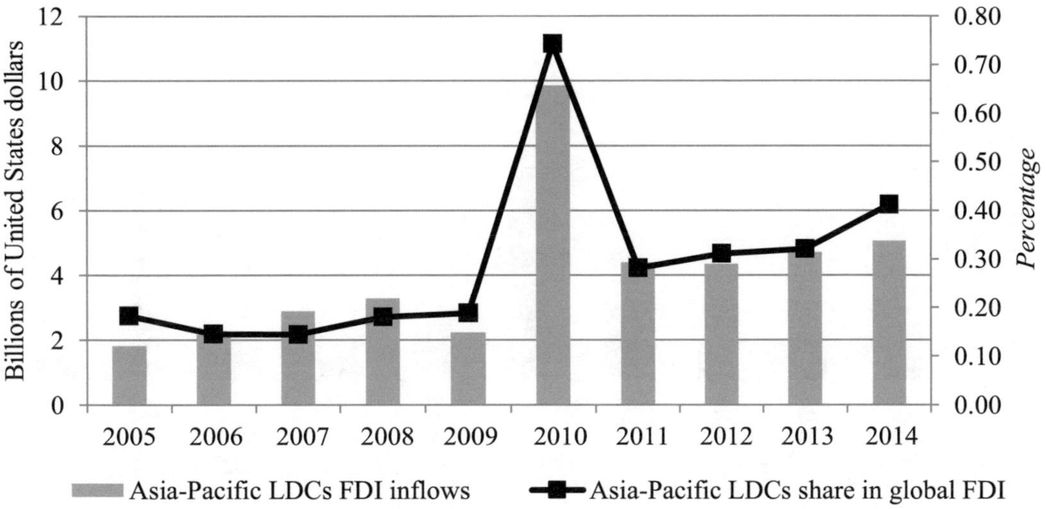


*Source:* ESCAP calculation based on UNCTADStat and UNCTAD, 2015.

[a] The peak in 2010 was mainly due to exceptionally large FDI inflows to a single country, Myanmar. FDI data for Myanmar in the World Investment Report 2015 showed dramatic changes from data of previous years, including the exceptionally large figure for 2010. It is explained by the fact that the national data source changed the system of data collection. This very recent development requires further research.

Different levels of government support and investment policies partly explain the varied performances across least developed countries in the Asia-Pacific region. For example, Bangladesh has promoted FDI for several decades with very liberal investment policies and incentive regimes. Coupled with low wages and preferential access to major export markets, this strategy has helped the country to attract a steady inflow of FDI, even if it has been concentrated mainly in the textiles and apparel sector. Nepal has become one of the most open and trade-dependent economies in the South Asian region (Sahoo, Nataraj and Dash, 2014), which has contributed to the sharp increase of FDI flows in the past decade – with $30 million FDI inflows in 2014, 15 times greater than that of 2005. However, the May 2015 earthquake destroyed much of Nepal's infrastructure and has since severely impeded economic activity in the country. Therefore, FDI inflows in infrastructural development are essential to enable the country to recover from this disaster. However, the lack of advanced infrastructure (apart from other issues that contribute to the high costs of doing business in Nepal) discourages FDI. Nepal therefore needs to implement policies that will help it to escape from this catch-22 situation, in particular through more effective regional economic integration.

The least developed countries in the Pacific subregion also fall under the category of small island developing States, i.e. Kiribati, Solomon Islands, Tuvalu and Vanuatu. The structural characteristics of these economies limit FDI options – a lack of adequate transport, communications and energy infrastructure, poor quality human capital, inefficient labour markets, low productivity capacities and the concentration on a narrow set of commodities/sectors – are limiting exports and inhibiting the establishment of global production networks (ESCAP 2015b; UNCTAD, 2014b; Feeny, Iamsiraroj and McGillivray, 2014). In addition, all Pacific least developed countries have very small economies and, therefore, small domestic markets, which further discourages FDI. Their FDI flows tend to be volatile and dependent on individual projects. For example, there is no record of any FDI inflow to Tuvalu during the past decade. Even relatively bigger countries, such as the Solomon Islands, have recorded fluctuating annual FDI flows ranging between $19 million and $238 million during the past decade.

Least developed countries in the region still rely heavily on natural resources for attracting FDI. However, the manufacturing and services sectors are making inroads, as they are attracting increasing amounts of FDI inflows (figure 3.19).

Figure 3.19. FDI inflows to Asia-Pacific least developed countries, by sector, 2005-2014

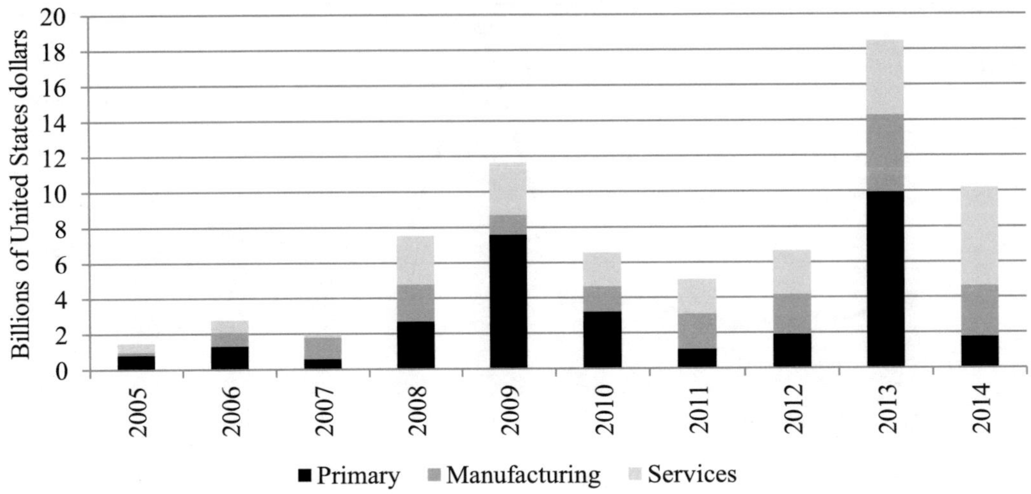


*Source:* ESCAP calculation based on fDi Intelligence data, 2015.

## D CONCLUSION

The Asia-Pacific region has continued to be a major player in the global FDI scene. The region has not only received significant amounts of FDI despite the decline of FDI globally, it has also continued to grow as a major source of outward investment in the global FDI market. Economies in the region have been the key drivers of the increasing role that developing economies are playing globally.

In addition to the increasing share of the Asia-Pacific region in global FDI flows, the region is also experiencing structural changes in the types of investment it attracts. Globally, the services sector has become the biggest sector for FDI. In Asia and the Pacific, manufacturing is still strategically important for several economies, especially those in South-East Asia where increasing amounts of FDI have been invested in manufacturing as a result of increased labour costs in China. However, a number of economies have strategically strived to attract investment in services- and technology-related areas.

The mode of investment shows signs of shifting. The Asia-Pacific region has experienced an exceptionally sharp increase in M&A but only a rather modest increase in greenfield FDI. A direct comparison between these two modalities is not possible, given the different data collection methods. However, the importance of greenfield FDI in Asia and the Pacific is still high, although M&A are increasingly being favoured by investors.

Of all the subregions in Asia and the Pacific, East and North-East Asia as well as South-East Asia have outperformed the others, in terms of both FDI inflows and outflows. While some economies in the region have experienced a noticeable fall in FDI, in general the region as a whole has performed well for various reasons.

First, the investment environment in most economies has improved further, with national and regional investment measures addressing liberalization, facilitation and promotion of FDI. Among the least developed countries, Bangladesh has managed to attract a steady inflow of FDI for several decades as a result of its liberal investment policy and incentive regimes. Historically, the Asia-Pacific region has benefited from mostly non-coercive Governments as well as strong markets and private sector-driven economies.

Second, deeper levels of economic integration in Asia and the Pacific have helped to increase intraregional FDI flows as well as overall FDI flows to and from the region. In particular, South-East Asian countries are moving towards deeper levels of integration with the forthcoming establishment of the ASEAN Economic Community, which will facilitate intraregional trade and investment flows. China is also continuing to pursue investment in nearby countries, especially in ASEAN, Pakistan and Sri Lanka. In addition, China has launched the "going global" strategy and the "One Belt One Road" initiative. Mega regional trade agreements such as RCEP and TPP will further promote intraregional and interregional investment flows. China has already invested heavily in infrastructure in the region, a strategy that has contributed to a better integrated market environment that attracts intraregional investors as well as investors from outside the region.

Despite the success of the region as a whole, uneven development between economies persists. The region has fast-developing star performers but is also home to countries where many live in extreme poverty. Least developed countries in the Asia-Pacific region have improved their capacities over time; however, they continue to rely on natural resources or labour-intensive industries and face a poor business climate, a lack of infrastructure and government resources, and other macroeconomic and political constraints that prevent them from attracting higher levels of value-added FDI flows. These small and vulnerable economies could benefit considerably from FDI, but they need enhanced regional cooperation to benefit from global and regional value chains.

Finally, the limitation on data availability prevent a more comprehensive intraregional analysis. In order to examine pressing issues, such as the impact of various modalities of FDI, improvements in the collection and availability of data in areas such as bilateral and sectoral FDI flows would further enhance the quality of analysis of international investment patterns and the determinates of their changes.

## ENDNOTES

[1] All FDI data are from UNCTADStat and the UNCTAD World Investment Report 2015 with the exception of data on the value of announced greenfield FDI projects, which were collected from FDi Intelligence database.

[2] The data on greenfield FDI are from fDi Intelligence, which tracks greenfield FDI project announcements on a global basis. The data are based on information available at the time of the project announcement and, therefore, differ from official FDI flows that are based on balance of payments and international investment position (IIP) statistics. Discrepancies may arise from the timing of the investment, as the database does not take any phasing of the investment into account. In addition, fDi Intelligence also uses its own estimates of capital investment if such data are not given in the project announcement. Additionally, some of the announced investment capital may be raised locally, meaning that only a part of the capital invested may manifest itself as actual FDI flows.

Due to different data collection methods, the direct comparison between announced greenfield FDI projects and value of cross-border M&As is not possible. However, this report attempts to provide some insights by observing the trends and changes over time.

[3] The values of greenfield FDI projects were collected from fDi Intelligence, except for the world total figure which is from the UNCTAD World Investment Report 2015 and which excludes the financial centres in the Caribbean.

[4] Due to the limited access to data on cross-border M&As at the country level, intraregional and country level analyses as well as a sectoral analysis mainly depend on greenfield FDI data.

[5] Data are retrieved from the Asia-Pacific Trade and Investment Agreements Database (APTIAD) at www.unescap.org/resources/asia-pacific-trade-and-investment-agreements-database-aptiad .

[6] Sectoral FDI trends are further examined in later sections under subregions and highlights of selected countries.

[7] FDI inflows to developing Pacific countries are too small for meaningful subregional interpretation. Instead, they are discussed in section C.3. on least developed countries.

[8] Individual ASEAN countries will have to make many adaptations in order to enable the implementation of the ASEAN Economic Community. In Thailand, for example, the National Reform Council has identified 106 Thai laws that need to be amended in order to fully implement the action plans outlined in the AEC Blueprint.

[9] The World Bank's Ease of doing business index ranks economies according to how conducive the regulatory environment is to business operations. The index averages the country's percentile rankings on 10 topics covered in the World Bank's Doing Business report. The ranking of each topic is the simple average of the percentile rankings of its component indicators. The index is available from http://data.worldbank.org/indicator/IC.BUS.EASE.XQ.

[10] The high increase in Hong Kong, China, could be explained by its role as a connector and a conduit for investment. It is argued that foreign investors use Hong Kong, China as a base from which to invest in the rest of China and the region, and that Chinese companies increasingly use Hong Kong, China as a platform to make global investment and acquisitions. It is likely that round-tripping between Hong Kong, China and mainland China are included in the figure, however, as it has been a continuous problem and would not be the only reason for the high increase in 2014.

[11] The "Going Global" strategy was adopted by the Government of China in 2001, under which Chinese firms are encouraged to look for opportunities overseas. This

strategy took another step forward in 2013 with adjustments in the regulatory framework for outward FDI in order to help Chinese firms to be competitive abroad.

[12] The "One Belt One Road" initiative is aimed at jointly building a "Silk Road Economic Belt" and "21st Century Maritime Silk Road", strongly advocated by China. Discussions on the implications and benefits are discussed among the associated countries and the Asia-Pacific region as a whole. Some experts claim it could potentially bring in opportunities for Chinese investments in infrastructure as well as lead to a potential increase in bilateral trade.

[13] "Make in India" is a long-term strategy aimed at increasing the share of manufacturing in GDP (from 16% to 25%) in a decade as well as the creation of 100 million jobs, according to Prime Minister Narendra Modi. It is hoped that this strategy will boost the country's automotive industry and provide the opportunities for new FDI in this sector. However, some hurdles exist that cannot be ignored, such as whether: (a) the focus on the manufacturing sector is really appropriate for India; (b) the demand constraints and excess capacity domestically and globally has been examined properly; and (c) the import substitution strategy will be helpful for import-dependent India.

[14] Small island developing States are recognized by the United Nations Conference on Environment and Development (UNCED) as a distinct group of developing countries facing specific social, economic and environmental vulnerabilities. For more information, refer to the UN-OHRLLS website at http://unohrlls.org/about-sids/.

## REFERENCES


ASEAN Secretariat (2014). *ASEAN Investment Report 2013-2014 – FDI Development and Value Chains.* Jakarta. Available from www.asean.org/resources/item/asean-unctad-launches-asean-investment-report-2013-2014-2

Calderon, Cesar, Norman Loayza and Luis Serven (2004). Greenfield foreign direct investment and mergers and acquisitions: feedback and macroeconomic effects. World Bank Policy Research Working Paper, No. 3192. Washington, D.C.

China Today (2014). China's changing pattern of FDI, 7 November. Available from www.chinatoday.com.cn/english/economy/2014-11/07/content_650645.htm.

Coonan, Clifford (2015). Slowing Chinese growth sees shift to manufacturing – 'For Sale in China' replacing 'Made in China'. *Irish Times,* 10 March. Available from www.irishtimes.com/business/economy/slowing-chinese-growth-sees-shift-to-services-from-manufacturing-1.2131997.

Economist Intelligence Unit (2014a). China economy: quick view – FDI records a slump in July. ViewsWire. Available from: viewswire.eiu.com.

_____ (2014b). China Going Global Investment Index 2014. Available from www.eiu.com/Handlers/WhitepaperHandler.ashx?fi=China-going-global-2014-English.pdf&mode=wp&campaignid=ChinaODI2014

_____ (2014c). Slow progress on ASEAN financial-market integration. *Economist,* 4 October. Available from www.eiu.com/industry/article/1862351370/asean/2014-10-04.

_____ (2014d). India: Investment regulations. *Economist,* 1 November. Available from viewswire.eiu.com/index.asp?layout=VWArticleVW3&article_id=472553631

Feeny, Simon, Sasi Iamsiraroj and Mark McGillivray (2014). Growth and foreign direct investment in the Pacific island countries. *Economic Modelling,* vol. 37, pp. 332-339.

Indo Asian News Service (2015). Structural bottlenecks barrier to higher growth in India: WTO. 4 June. Available from news.chennaionline.com/international/Structural-bottlenecks-barrier-to-higher-growth-in-India--WTO/2e9a0b2d-7ffc-4616-803b-b8596b33d733.col

*Nation* (2014). Cross-border M&A still low despite approach of AEC, 10 Octob. Bangkok.

Nocke, Volker, and Stephen Yeaple (2007). Cross-border mergers and acquisitions vs. greenfield foreign direct investment: the role of firm heterogeneity. *Journal of International Economics,* vol. 72, pp. 336-365.

Sahoo, Pravakar, Geethanjali Nataraj and Ranjan K. Dash (2014). *Foreign Direct Investment in South Asia: Policy, Impact, Determinants and Challenges.* New Delhi: Springer.

United Nations Conference on Trade and Development (2014a). *The Least Developed Countries Report 2014.* Sales No. E.14.II.D.7. Available from http://unctad.org/en/PublicationsLibrary/ldc2014_en.pdf

_____ (2014b). FDI in small island developing States: its limitations and potential. Global Investment Trends Monitor, No. 17, 1 September. Available from http://unctad.org/en/Pages/DIAE/Research%20on%20FDI%20and%20TNCs/Global-Investment-Trends-Monitor.aspx

_____ (2015). *World Investment Report 2015.* Sales No. E.15.II.D.5. Available from http://unctad.org/en/pages/PublicationWebflyer.aspx?publicationid=1245

United Nations, Economic and Social Commission for Asia and the Pacific (2011). *Asia-Pacific Trade and Investment Report 2011: Post-crisis Trade and Investment Opportunities.* Sales No. E.11.II.F.8. Available from www.unescap.org/resources/asia-pacific-trade-and-investment-report-2011-post-crisis-trade-and-investment.

_____ (2014). *Asia-Pacific Trade and Investment Report 2014: Trends and Developments.* Sales No. E.15.II.F.2. Available from www.unescap.org/resources/asia-pacific-trade-and-investment-report-2014-recent-trends-and-developments.

_____ (2015a). *Financing for Transformation: From Agenda to Action on Sustainable Development in Asia and the Pacific.* Sales No. E.15.II.F.6. Available from www.unescap.org/sites/default/files/Financing-for-Transformation-Final.pdf.

_____ (2015b). *Asia-Pacific Countries with Special Needs Development Report 2015: Building Productive Capacities to Overcome Structural Challenges.* Sales No. E.15.II.F.9. Available from www.unescap.org/sites/default/files/Asia-Pacific%20CSN%20Development%20Report%20 2015.pdf.

World Bank (2015). The dawn of a new economic era? Russia Economic Report, No. 33. Washington D.C. Available from www.worldbank.org/en/country/russia/publication/russia-economic-report-33

World Trade Organization (2015). Trade policy review: report by the secretariat – India. 28 April. WT/TPR/S/313. Available from: www.wto.org/english/tratop_e/tpr_e/s313_e.pdf.

## ONLINE DATABASES

ASEAN Secretariat (2015). Foreign Direct Investment Statistics. Available from: www.asean.org/news/item/foreign-direct-investment-statistics

Financial Times Ltd. fDi Intelligence, fDi Markets: Crossborder investment monitor. Available from www.fdimarkets.com (accessed May and June 2015).

United Nations Conference on Trade and Development. UNCTADStat. Available from unctadstat.unctad.org/ReportFolders/reportFolders.aspx?sCS_referer=&sCS_ChosenLang=en (accessed June 2015).

# 4 TRENDS AND DEVELOPMENTS IN TRADE FACILITATION

Recent global events, such as the successful conclusions of the WTO Trade Facilitation Agreement (TFA) negotiations (December 2013),[1] the fifth Global Review of Aid for Trade on the theme of reducing trade costs, and the adoption of the Addis Ababa Action Agenda (both in July 2015), have brought trade facilitation into sharp focus. It is clear that the WTO TFA implementation will become the new baseline for trade facilitation as a means of reducing trade costs as well as maintaining trade and investment competitiveness. In this regard, data collected by ESCAP as part of the Global Survey of Trade Facilitation and Paperless Trade Implementation (hereinafter referred to as the Global Survey) show that although the situation varies widely from country to country, many Asia-Pacific developing countries have already made considerable progress vis-à-vis WTO TFA implementation. As such, new opportunities for progress exist within the region through the adoption of innovative "next generation" trade facilitation measures that complement the WTO TFA. The ongoing negotiations among ESCAP Members of an intergovernmental agreement for cross-border paperless trade facilitation present such an opportunity to cooperate in order to promote the seamless exchange of information and documents along international supply chains.

Section A of this chapter presents updated data on trade costs for the Asia-Pacific region as well as an overview of regional and global trade facilitation implementation efforts. Section B looks at the ways in which regional cooperation is being fostered in the areas of trade facilitation and cross-border paperless trade in the Asia-Pacific region. While continuing to maximize efficiency in "soft infrastructure", i.e. the procedures and processes involved in meeting the documentation and other regulatory requirements involved in international trade, it is also important for countries in the Asia-Pacific region to tackle infrastructure and services bottlenecks in order to enhance their overall connectivity. Taking measures on both of these fronts is necessary to ensure that countries in the region can move towards seamless supply chains. As such, section C of this chapter also presents data on how the international supply chain connectivity of countries in the Asia-Pacific region has evolved.

## A TAKING STOCK OF TRADE COST REDUCTION AND TRADE FACILITATION IMPLEMENTATION

Trade costs can be defined as "all costs incurred in getting a good to a final user, other than the cost of producing the good itself – transportation costs (both freight costs and time costs), policy barriers (tariffs and non-tariff barriers), information costs, contract enforcement costs, costs associated with the use of different currencies, legal and regulatory costs and local distribution costs (wholesale and retail)" (Anderson and van Wincoop, 2004). Trade costs play a significant role in shaping regional and global trade patterns, determining the locations and types of actors which can reap the greatest benefits from the trade. Trade costs also shape consumer welfare as a factor determining the price and the diversity of goods available.

*"Reducing trade costs is critical to furthering regional economic integration and connectivity for sustainable development."*

The trade and development community recommitted to addressing trade costs, in particular to ensure that the benefits could be reaped by the least developed countries (WTO, 2015b). The Addis Ababa Action Agenda (United Nations, 2015) also highlighted the role that reducing trade barriers and trade facilitation measures could play in promoting regional economic integration and connectivity for inclusive growth and sustainable development.[2] In order to effectively reduce trade costs, policy interventions must address the "soft infrastructure" related to the simplification of procedures and documents associated with trading of goods as well as the "hard infrastructure" related to the physical infrastructure for supporting the trade of goods.

## 1. Trade costs in the Asia-Pacific region: an update

In relation to the intraregional and extraregional trade costs presented in the *Asia-Pacific Trade and Investment Report (APTIR) 2013*, it would appear that trade costs have remained at similar levels – over time – across the Asia-Pacific region.[3] Figure 4.1 shows the trade costs of Asia-Pacific subregions in trading with key developed country markets, and their evolution from 1996 to 2012. Trade costs vary widely across subregions. East Asia-3 has the lowest trade costs of the region, on a par with those of the European Union (EU)-3. While trade costs of North and Central Asian economies remain nearly three times higher than those of East Asia-3, the former appears to have made significant progress in reducing trade costs since 1996. Trade costs of South Asian economies (SAARC-4) also appear to have decreased, as have those of East Asia and EU-3. In contrast, trade costs of ASEAN-4 with key developed country markets, while already relatively low, have not fallen during the reporting period. Trade costs remain the highest in the Pacific island developing economies and no clear trend towards lower trade costs is apparent in that subregion.

The latest data from the ESCAP-World Bank Trade Costs Database[4] also suggests that regional integration remains uneven, as some regional groupings face lower intraregional trade costs, while for other groupings the trade costs remain prohibitively high.

### Figure 4.1. Trade costs of Asia-Pacific subregions with developed economies, 1996-2012

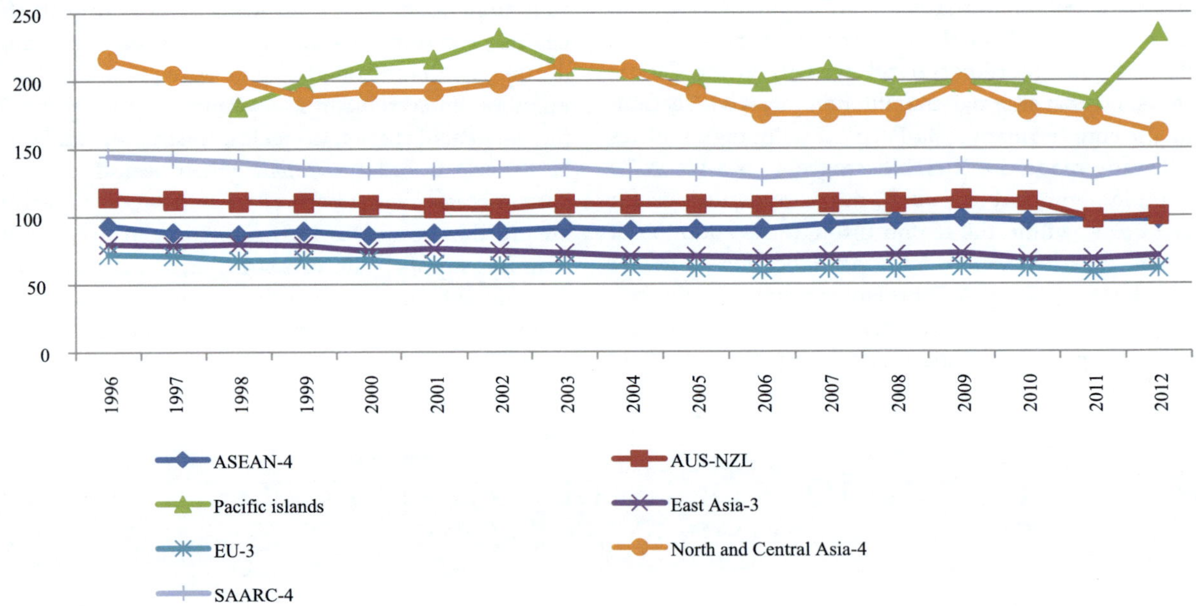


*Source:* ESCAP-World Bank Trade Costs Database (accessed September 2015).
*Notes:* ASEAN-4 – Indonesia, Malaysia, the Philippines and Thailand; AUS-NLZ – Australia and New Zealand; East Asia-3 – China, Japan and the Republic of Korea; EU-3 – Germany, France and the United Kingdom; Pacific islands – Fiji and Papua New Guinea; North and Central Asia-4 – Georgia, Kazakhstan, Kyrgyzstan and the Russian Federation; and SAARC-4 – Bangladesh, India, Pakistan and Sri Lanka. Trade costs shown are tariff equivalents calculated as trade-weighted average trade costs of countries in each subregion with the three largest developed economies (Germany, Japan and the United States of America).

## Table 4.1. Intra- and extraregional comprehensive trade costs in the Asia-Pacific region (excluding tariff costs)

*(Percentage)*

| Region | ASEAN-4 | East Asia-3 | North and Central Asia-4 | Pacific islands | SAARC-4 | AUS-NZL | EU-3 |
|---|---|---|---|---|---|---|---|
| ASEAN-4 | 76 | | | | | | |
| East Asia-3 | 75 | 51 | | | | | |
| North and Central Asia-4 | 351 | 177 | 121 | | | | |
| Pacific islands | 175 | 174 | 368 | 133 | | | |
| SAARC-4 | 128 | 125 | 282 | 317 | 114 | | |
| AUS-NZL | 101 | 89 | 338 | 73 | 142 | 54 | |
| EU-3 | 108 | 85 | 152 | 211 | 114 | 109 | 43 |
| United States | 85 | 63 | 180 | 163 | 109 | 100 | 67 |

*Source:* ESCAP-World Bank Trade Costs Database (accessed June 2015).
*Note:* Trade costs shown are average trade costs during 2008-2013 and may be interpreted as tariff equivalents. See figure 4.1 for the list of economies considered under each region.

Of the regional groupings in the Asia-Pacific region (table 4.1), East Asia-3 exhibits the lowest intraregional trade costs (51%) for 2008-2013 followed by AUZ-NZL (54%). In addition, intraregional trade costs of East Asia-3 show a 5% decrease during 2008-2013 when compared with 2002-2007 while that subregion's extraregional trade costs with all the regional groups also fell between 2008-2013 and 2002-2007. The Pacific islands have the highest intraregional trade costs (133%), which is more than double the intraregional trade costs of the regional benchmark, East Asia-3. The highest extraregional trade costs are between North and Central Asia-4 and the Pacific islands. This result is in line with expectations, given the high intraregional trade costs of both of those subregions and the geographical obstacles of being landlocked and sealocked, respectively. Furthermore, the volume of trade between the two subregions is low as there may be greater incentives to trade with countries that have higher connectivity and closer proximity.

*"Regional integration remains uneven in the Asia-Pacific region as some subregions continue to exhibit high intraregional trade costs."*

The intraregional trade costs for ASEAN-4 during the period under review are 76%, which is comparable with, and indeed marginally higher than the extraregional trade costs between ASEAN-4 and East Asia-3 (75%). The intraregional trade costs within SAARC-4 are 114%. While the sources and causes of the trade costs are likely to be different, 114% was also the recorded bilateral trade costs between SAARC-4 and EU-3. This may signify the need for enhanced trade facilitation efforts and improved connectivity within the SAARC-4 subregion. The findings from the ESCAP-World Bank Trade Costs Database indicate that it is often cheaper for developing countries in the Asia-Pacific region to trade with partners outside the region rather than within the region.

## 2. Trade facilitation implementation status in the Asia-Pacific region and beyond

Research by ESCAP has shown a strong correlation between the level of implementation of trade facilitation measures and the international trade costs of the Asia-Pacific countries (figure 4.2). This highlights the benefits of pursuing trade facilitation measures with a view to reducing trade costs.

### Figure 4.2. Trade facilitation implementation and trade costs of Asia-Pacific economies[a]

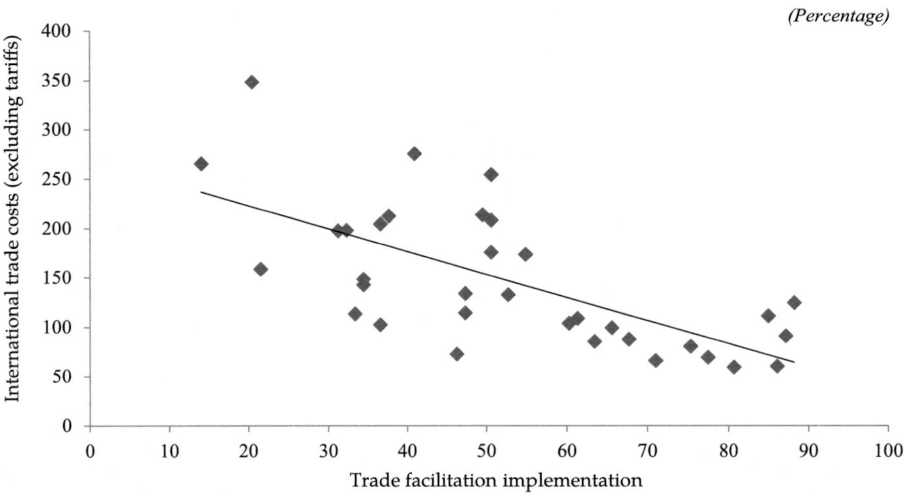


*Source:* ESCAP, 2015a.

[a] Country trade costs are based on average comprehensive bilateral trade costs with Germany, China and the United States (2008-2013) and expressed as ad valorem equivalents (percentage).

### Figure 4.3. Trade facilitation implementation around the world (excluding cross-border paperless trade measures), 2015[a]

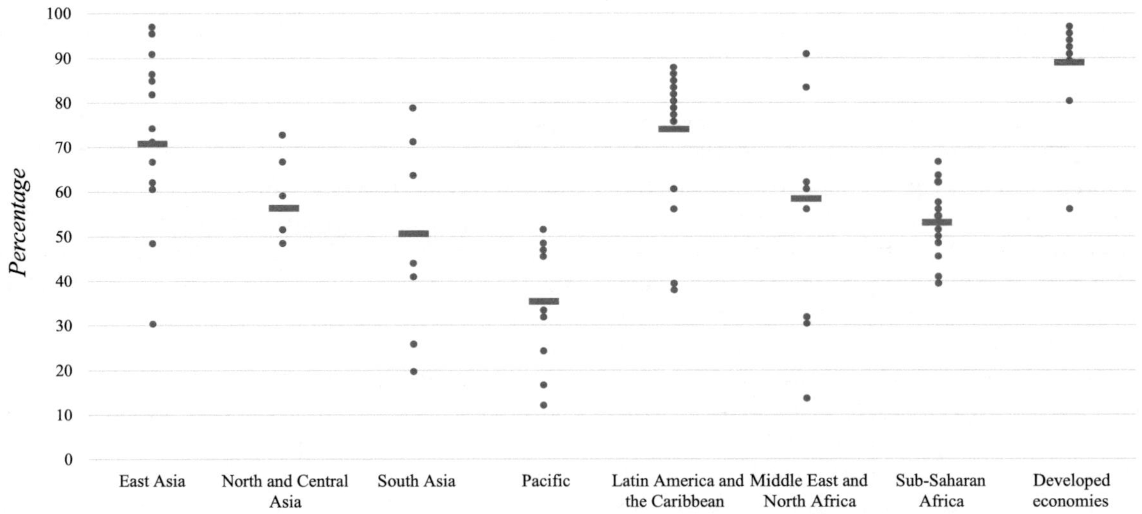


*Source:* UNRC Survey on Trade Facilitation and Paperless Trade Implementation (June, 2015).

*Notes:* This figure presents average trade facilitation implementation levels (in percentage) of each region (red bars) as well as implementation by individual economies within each regions (green dots).

[a] Based on a preliminary analysis of the Global Survey data presented at the fifth Global Aid for Trade Review. See http://unnext.unescap.org/survey/GlobalSurveyPPT.pdf

The United Nations Regional Commissions (UNRCs) initiated the Global Survey in October 2014 (ESCAP, 2015a) in order to (a) better understand and monitor progress on implementation of trade facilitation and paperless trade measures in the Asia-Pacific region, (b) support evidence-based policy-making, and (c) highlight capacity-building and technical assistance needs.[5] Led by ESCAP, the Global Survey collected data on 38 trade facilitation measures.[6] The Global Survey goes beyond the scope of the WTO TFA by including measures related to paperless trade[7] and cross-border paperless trade; thus, it reflects the prospective regional arrangement on cross-border paperless trade facilitation currently under negotiation by ESCAP member States (ESCAP, 2015b).

As shown in figure 4.3,[8] the results reveal wide disparities between regions in trade facilitation implementation levels. The highest average levels of trade facilitation implementation in the regions were recorded in developing countries in Latin America and the Caribbean, and in East Asia.[9] The Pacific region is lagging significantly behind most other regions in this area. The results also show that the three least globally implemented WTO TFA-related measures are: (a) the establishment and publication of average release times; (b) trade facilitation measures for authorized operators; and (c) the electronic Single Window system.

> *"Trade facilitation implementation rates vary greatly across economies of the Asia-Pacific region, and Pacific islands are lagging behind."*

In the Asia-Pacific region, data were compiled for 44 economies (figure 4.4). Overall, the average level of trade facilitation implementation by the 44 Asia-Pacific economies, based on an ambitious set of 31 trade facilitation and paperless trade measures, is 46.5%. Within the Asia-Pacific region there is great variation in trade facilitation implementation rates. Australia, the Republic of Korea and Singapore have obtained scores in excess of 85%, while other countries have yet to achieve 15% implementation levels. While the larger and developed economies tend to achieve higher levels of trade facilitation implementation, there are some notable exceptions to this trend. For example, Cambodia and the Lao People's Democratic Republic (both least developed countries) have achieved trade facilitation implementation scores well in excess of the regional average.

## Figure 4.4. Overall implementation of trade facilitation measures in 44 Asia-Pacific economies, 2015

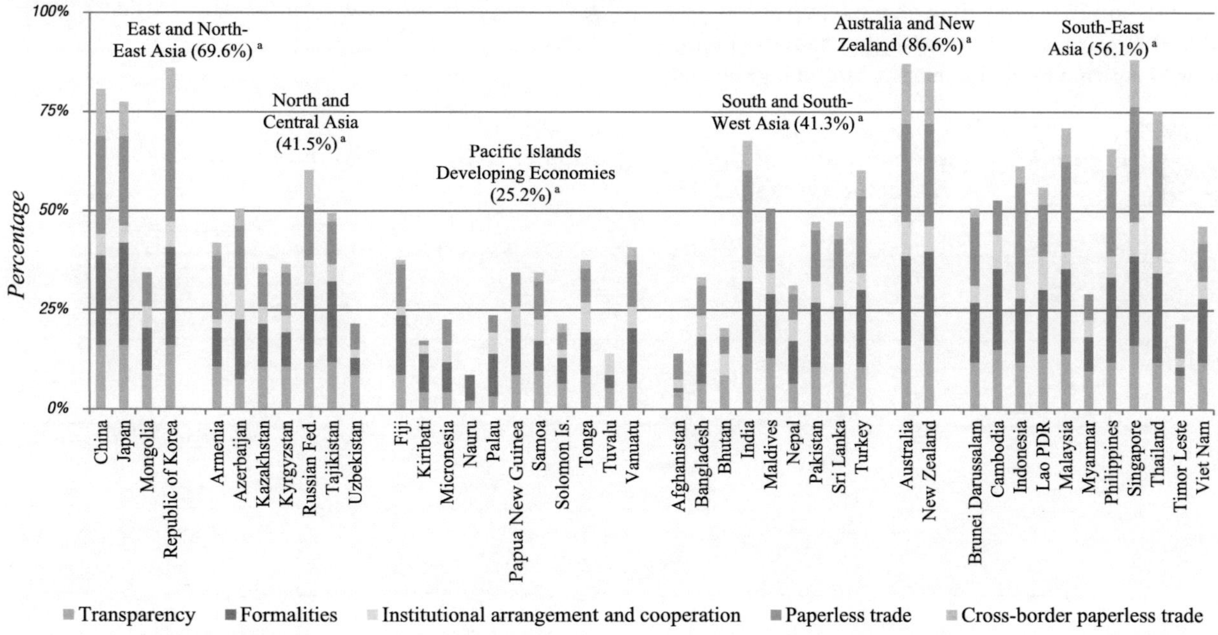


*Source:* Duval and others (2015).
[a] Subregional average implementation rate.

Figure 4.5 provides a more detailed look at trade facilitation implementation within the Asia-Pacific region and disaggregates the findings by the categories of (a) least developed countries (b) landlocked developing countries, and (c) small island developing States.

### Figure 4.5. Trade facilitation implementation by individual economies in Asia-Pacific subregions and in countries with special needs, 2015

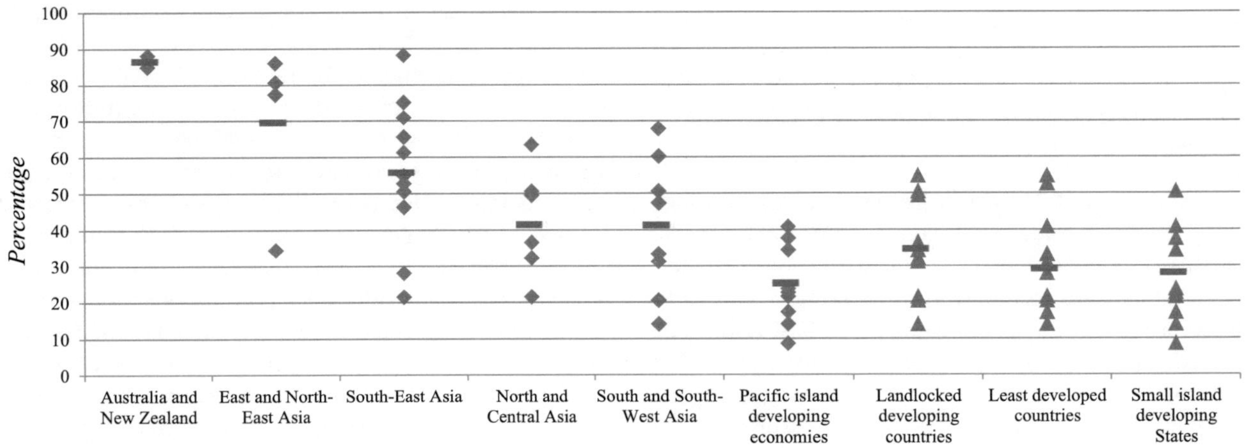


*Source:* ESCAP (2015a).

*Notes:* Trade facilitation implementation levels (in percentage) of individual economies within each subregion (blue diamonds) as well as within groups of economies with special needs (green triangles).

— Average trade facilitation implementation of the group (%).

Countries with special needs face particular challenges in trade facilitation implementation. This is reflected in the average implementation levels of such countries, which vary between 25% and 35% depending on the group of countries considered (figure 4.5). Interestingly, least developed countries as a group appear to have achieved higher trade

> *"Nearly all economies in the Asia-Pacific region have taken steps towards the implementation of paperless trade."*

### Figure 4.6. Implementation of different groups of trade facilitation measures: Asia-Pacific average, 2015

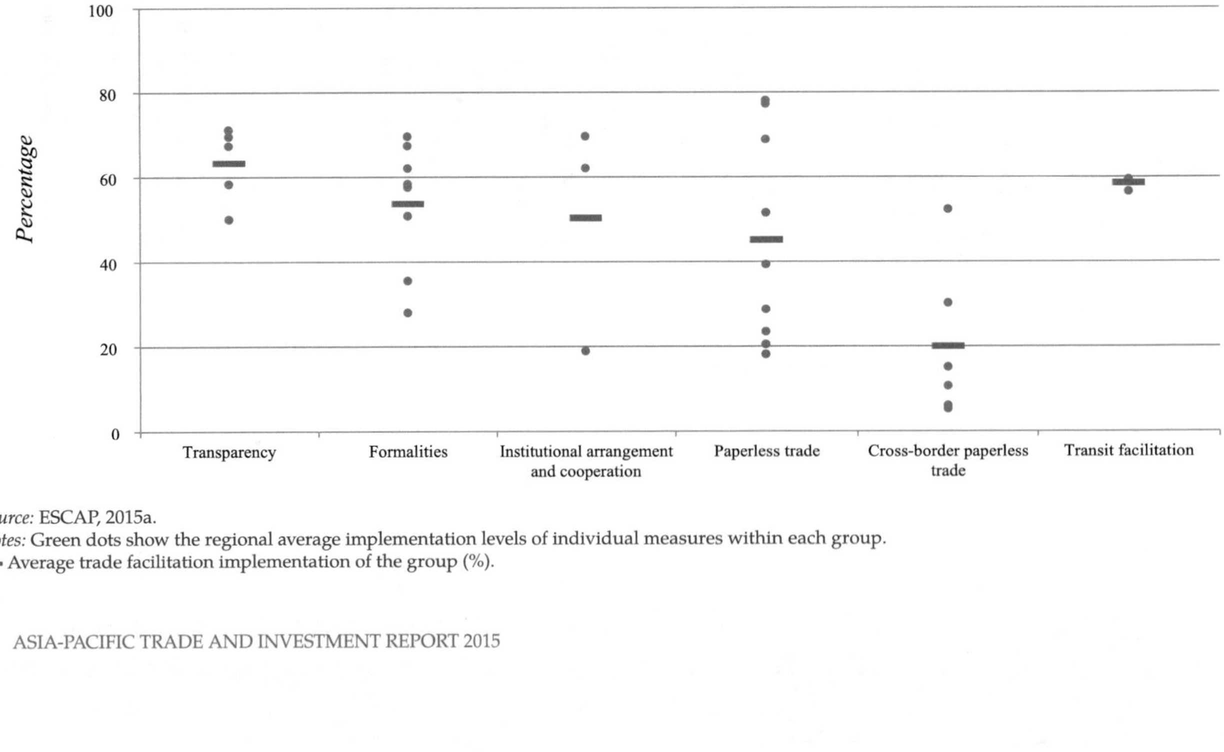


*Source:* ESCAP, 2015a.

*Notes:* Green dots show the regional average implementation levels of individual measures within each group.

— Average trade facilitation implementation of the group (%).

facilitation implementation levels, on average, than landlocked developing countries or small island developing States.

The progress of countries in relation to specific trade facilitation measures is also mixed. The trade facilitation measures related to enhancing transparency and reducing formalities recorded the highest levels of implementation as all countries in the Asia-Pacific region are engaged in the implementation of such measures (figure 4.6). Implementation disparities are greatest among paperless trade measures. Overall, the least implemented measures in the region are those in the cross-border paperless trade category. While essentially all economies in the Asia-Pacific region have taken steps towards the implementation of paperless trade, nearly one quarter of the economies in the region have not implemented – even the pilot stage – any measure related to cross-border paperless trade, i.e. the exchange and legal recognition of electronic trade data and documents across borders with trade partners. Yet, for countries that have already implemented the majority of the WTO TFA-related measures, the implementation of cross-border paperless trade remains an important opportunity to cut down trade costs.

> *"Full implementation of the WTO TFA could reduce trade costs by up to 17% in the Asia-Pacific developing economies."*

## 3. WTO TFA – the new baseline for trade facilitation implementation

The WTO TFA will enter into force once two-thirds of the WTO members have formally ratified the Agreement.[10] Once this occurs, developing WTO members will endeavour to implement the trade facilitation measures contained within the Agreement. Based on the Global Survey data, it has been estimated that full implementation of the WTO TFA

**Figure 4.7. Implementation of WTO TFA-related measures in the Asia-Pacific region, 2015**

*(Percentage of countries)*

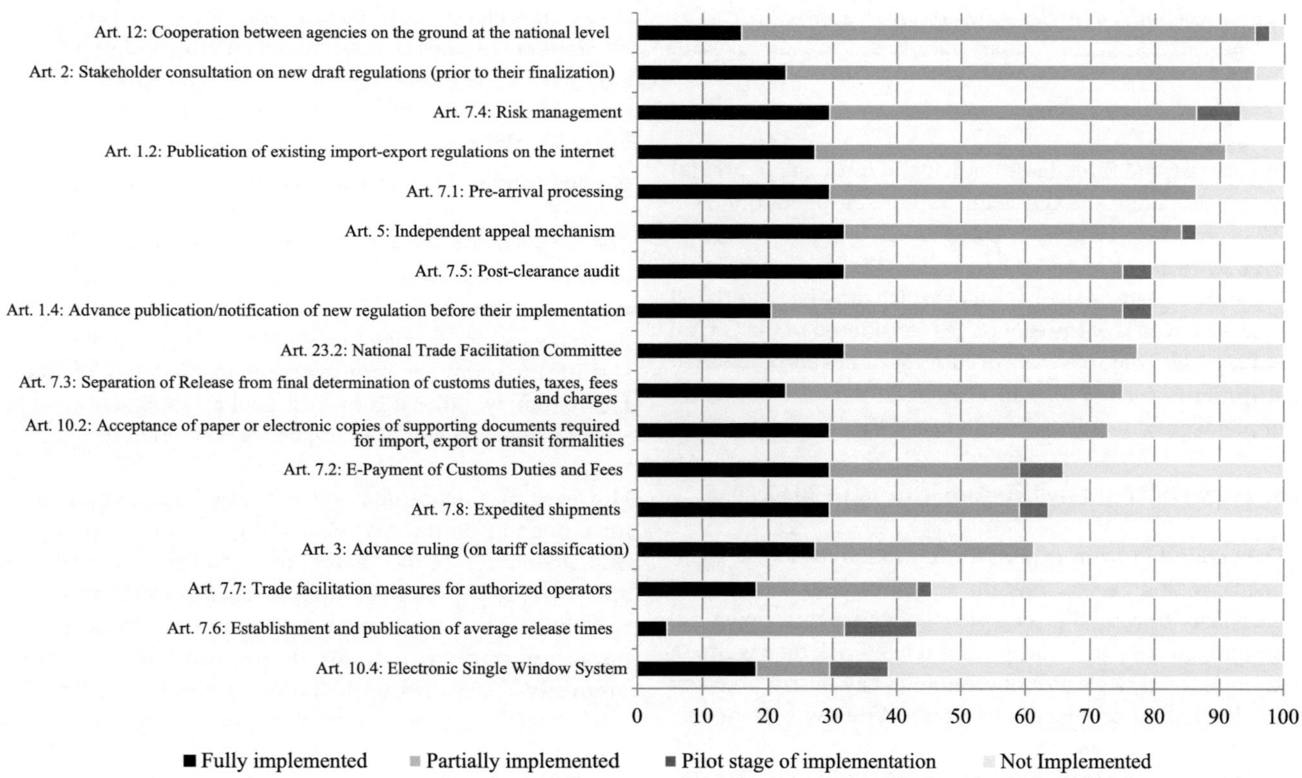


*Source:* Duval and others, 2015.

CHAPTER 4

measures could bring down trade costs by up to 17% on average in the Asia-Pacific developing economies (Duval and others, 2015).

Figure 4.7 shows the extent to which the 17 WTO TFA-related measures included in the Global Survey have been implemented. Of these 17 measures, 14 (more than 80%) have been at least partially implemented in more than half of all 44 Asia-Pacific countries surveyed, indicating that the WTO TFA implementation in the region is already significantly underway.[11] The four most implemented (fully, partially or on a pilot basis) WTO TFA-related measures in Asia-Pacific countries are: (a) cooperation between agencies (Art.12 of the WTO TFA); (b) stakeholder consultation on new draft regulations (Art. 2); (c) risk management (Art.7.4); and (d) publication of existing import-export regulations (Art.1.2), with the implementation ongoing in 90% of the Asia-Pacific countries. However, cooperation between agencies is among the least "fully implemented" measures considered in the Global Survey.

*"Cooperation among agencies is one of the least fully implemented WTO TFA-related measures in the Asia-Pacific region."*

In contrast, the three least implemented measures are: (a) trade facilitation measures for authorized operators (Art. 7.7 of the WTO TFA); (b) establishment and publication of average release times (Art.7.6); and (c) the electronic Single Window system (Art.10.4), all of which have been initiated in less than 50% of the economies considered in the Global Survey. Electronic payment of customs duties and expedited shipments (Art. 7.2) has also been partially or fully implemented in only 60% of the Asia-Pacific economies.

## 4. Focus of trade facilitation efforts in 2014-2015

Data collected from experts in 30 economies in the Asia-Pacific region[12] reveal that the region has put the greatest emphasis during the past year on improving (existing) automated customs systems and related risk management systems. Many Asia-Pacific economies have also worked on implementing an electronic Single Window system and other paperless trade measures as well as on adopting new legislation and regulations for trade facilitation. Finally, implementation of post-clearance audits (a measure that is particularly complementary to risk management) and the establishment of National Trade Facilitation Committees (a measure required under the WTO TFA) also received particular attention during the past year across the Asia-Pacific region.

Looking ahead, the surveyed experts identified the lack of coordination between Government agencies and limited human resource capacity as the two most serious challenges facing the implementation of trade facilitation measures in 21 out of 30 economies. The lack of political will, no clearly designated lead agency and financial constraints were also mentioned in at least 16 economies.

## 5. Moving towards cross-border paperless trade

Figure 4.8 shows implementation of trade facilitation as a step-by step process, based on the groups of measures included in the Global Survey. Trade facilitation begins with the setting up of the institutional arrangement needed to prioritize and coordinate implementation of trade facilitation measures. The next step involves making the trade processes more transparent by sharing information on existing laws, regulations and procedures as widely as possible, and by consulting with stakeholders when developing new ones. Designing and implementing simpler and more efficient trade formalities is the third step. The re-engineered and streamlined processes may first be implemented based on paper documents, but can then be further improved through information and communications technology and the development of paperless trade systems. The ultimate step is to enable electronic trade data and documents exchange by traders, Governments and service providers within national (Single Window and other) systems to be used and re-used in order to provide stakeholders in partner countries with the information they need to speed up the movement of goods and reduce the overall costs of the supply chain.

The regional and subregional cumulative trade facilitation implementation levels shown in figure 4.8 demonstrate that, while East and South-East Asia are performing well above the Asia-Pacific average, together the subregions still have significant room for improvement in all areas of trade facilitation, whether it is institutional arrangements or the further enhancement of inter-agency cooperation.

However, the Global Survey results also highlight the need for economies in the Asia-Pacific region to go beyond the implementation of the general trade facilitation measures and towards paperless trade. Asia-Pacific economies may, in particular, endeavour to move towards cross-border paperless trade, which entails the implementation of innovative measures with the potential to significantly

*"Cross-border paperless trade implementation provides opportunities for Asia-Pacific economies to cut their trade costs further and maintain their competitive advantage."*

## Figure 4.8 Moving up the trade facilitation ladder towards seamless international supply chains, 2015[a]

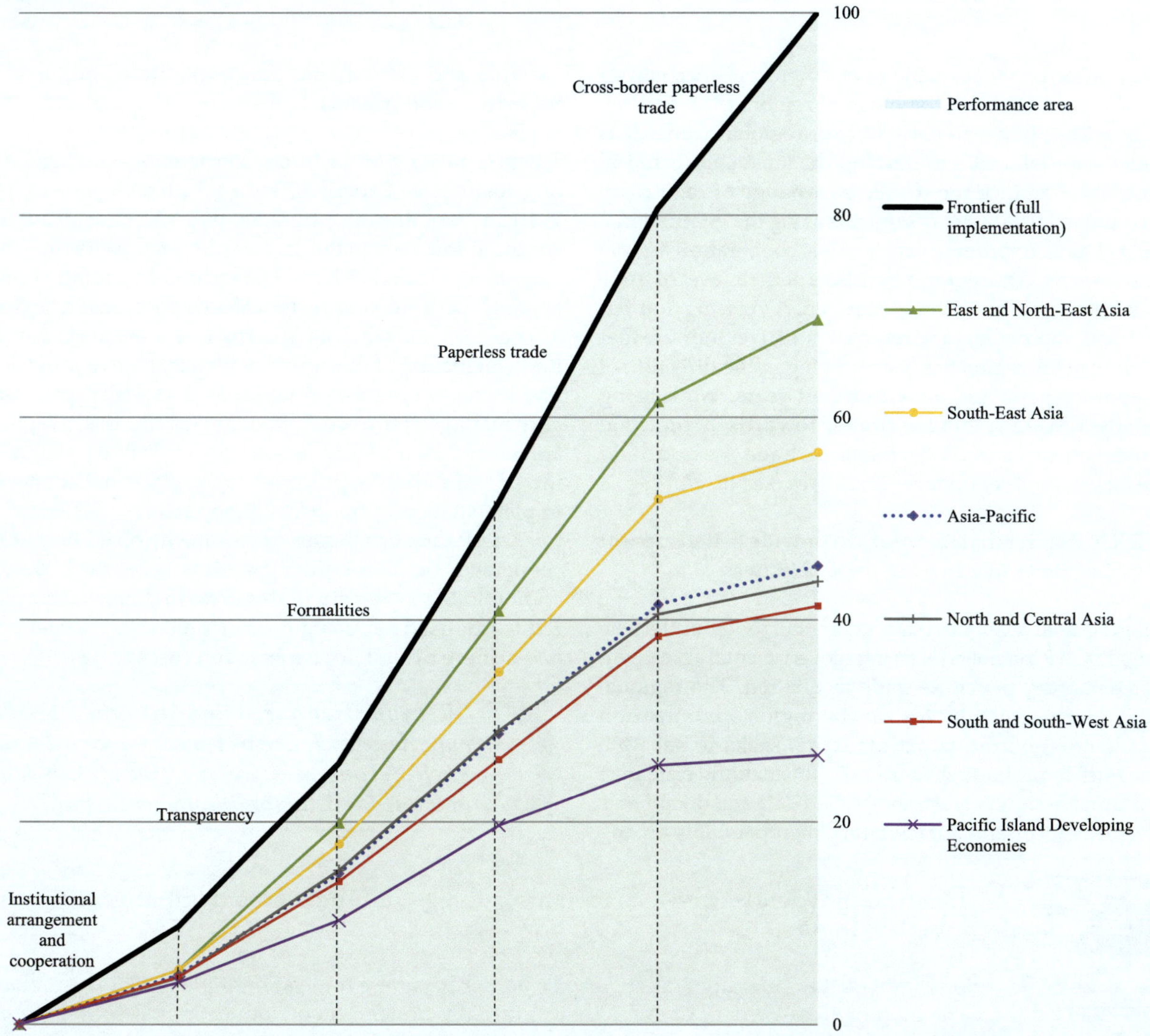


*Source:* ESCAP, 2015a.

*Notes:* The figure shows the cumulative trade facilitation implementation scores of the Asia-Pacific subregions for five groups of trade facilitation measures included in the Global Survey. The scores are based on equally weighted implementation of 31 trade facilitation measures. The number of measures in each group varies. Full implementation of all measures equals 100.

[a] This step-by-step process is inspired by and generally consistent with the UN/CEFACT step-by-step approach to trade facilitation towards a Single Window environment.

reduce trade costs and promote greater regional integration in Asia and the Pacific.[13] Research by ESCAP indicates that full region-wide implementation of cross-border paperless trade can bring about export gains in the order of $257 billion annually (ESCAP, 2014). The time required to export would fall by as much as 24% (i.e. to 44%), and the direct costs would decline by up to 17% (i.e. to 31%), depending on the implementation scenario considered. As a result, the total direct cost savings across all trade in the Asia-Pacific region would be approximately $1 billion annually in the case of partial reform, and $7 billion annually in the case of full implementation. Taken together with the Global Survey results, this suggests that the Asia-Pacific region has yet to reap the significant benefits provided by cross-border paperless trade.

## B FOSTERING REGIONAL COOPERATION ON CROSS-BORDER PAPERLESS TRADE

Cross-border paperless trade is an important mechanism for reducing trade costs, enhancing regional integration, and boosting intraregional and extraregional trade. It is necessary for countries to develop the legal and technical protocols needed for the seamless exchange of regulatory and commercial data and documents along the international supply chains. In order to achieve this, cooperation among countries across the region, regardless of their level of trade facilitation implementation, is required. A growing number of bilateral, subregional and regional initiatives indicate that the Asia-Pacific region has been moving in the direction of cross-border paperless trade in recent years. Work being done by ESCAP member States towards a regional arrangement on cross-border paperless trade seeks to build synergies with other ongoing initiatives (see Box 4.1).

The ESCAP secretariat also seeks to provide better support to member States in achieving these objectives.

At the regional level, negotiations are currently underway among ESCAP members on an intergovernmental agreement for cross-border paperless trade facilitation. The regional arrangement, which builds on the region's momentum towards cross-border paperless trade, seeks to set up a framework to promote such trade by (a) enabling exchange and mutual recognition of trade-related data and documents in electronic form, and (b) facilitating interoperability among national and subregional Single Window and/or other paperless trade systems.

The first meeting of the Intergovernmental Steering Group on Cross-border Paperless Trade, which took place in April 2015 in Bangkok, established two working groups to continue improving the text of the prospective regional agreement (ESCAP, 2015c). The technical working group is charged with making technical revisions of the regional agreement as well as drafting a roadmap for the implementation of the agreement's substantive provisions. The legal working group will review the legal provisions and manage the overall revision of the draft regional agreement. While trade facilitation levels in the region are mixed and step-wise processes are in place for the effective implementation of trade facilitation reform, it is beneficial for Asia-Pacific economies to become involved in regional cooperation on cross-border paperless trade at an early stage and build their capacity in this area. In doing so, they will reduce the need for re-engineering processes at a later point and achieve overall implementation cost savings.

> *"Regional cooperation on cross-border paperless trade can be beneficial for all Asia-Pacific economies, irrespective of their level of trade facilitation implementation."*

### Box 4.1 Identifying synergies between regional, subregional and bilateral initiatives for cross-border paperless trade

The Asia-Pacific region is moving towards cooperation in cross-border paperless trade at multiple levels. The regional agreement on the facilitation of cross-border paperless trade, currently under negotiation at ESCAP, seeks to build synergies with such initiatives and provide a framework that can strengthen and reinforce ongoing work. A number of countries in the region are currently working together bilaterally in the area of cross-border paperless trade. For example, Tajikistan and Afghanistan initiated a bilateral project for cross-border data exchange among trade regulatory agencies. This project, which is aimed at improving the monitoring of trade and borders as well as ensuring trade facilitation and supply chain security, will be expanded to other economies in the region, such as Pakistan and the Islamic Republic of Iran, and assist in the future formation of transit corridors (ESCAP, 2015d). The prospective regional arrangement on cross-border paperless trade will serve to reduce the work and negotiations necessary for establishing such bilateral arrangements for cross-border paperless trade.

On the subregional level, the ASEAN Single Window (ASW) was established in order to enhance economic integration among ASEAN members. The objective of ASW is to expedite cargo clearance by providing infrastructure for electronic data exchange and communication among ASEAN members. As part of this initiative, ASEAN members have each committed to implement a National Single Window (NSW) that will serve as a single point of communication with the NSWs of other ASEAN members, thereby enabling direct data exchange in a closed secure network via the ASW Gateway (United Nations Network of Experts for Paperless Trade, 2015b). The regional arrangement on cross-border paperless trade under negotiation at ESCAP can provide a useful framework for ASEAN members to (a) learn from the experience of non-ASEAN members in exchanging data and information across borders for trade facilitation as well as (b) ensure that the electronic data exchange protocols eventually developed through this broader regional arrangement will be built upon the work done by the ASEAN members in the context of ASW (United Nations Network of Experts for Paperless Trade, 2015b).

## C TOWARDS SEAMLESS SUPPLY CHAINS: INTERNATIONAL CONNECTIVITY

Moving towards seamless supply chains not only involves the seamless exchange of data and documents; it also requires efficient movement of physical goods themselves along the supply chain and across borders. Maritime connectivity has long been identified as a critical component of efficient and seamless supply chains. In terms of volume, approximately 80% of traded goods are transported through seaports (UNCTAD, 2014). In addition, research by ESCAP has found that maritime connectivity and services can account for 16%-18% of policy-related, non-tariff trade costs (ESCAP, 2012). Addressing logistics performance is also cited as an important policy measure for reducing trade costs (OECD, 2015). This section reviews the progress made by economies in the Asia-Pacific region in efficiently moving goods along international supply chains using the ESCAP International Supply Chain Connectivity Index (ISCCI). The index, constructed using trade across border (TAB) indicators[14] of the World Bank Doing Business Report and the UNCTAD Liner Shipping Connectivity Index (LSCI),[15] measures countries' performance along international supply chains. Equal weighting is given to import procedures, export procedures (from TAB indicators) and liner shipping performance (from LSCI) in ISCCI. Taken together, these indicators provide information about how well countries are connected to international supply chains and, hence, shed light on potential barriers and obstacles to trade.

Data from ISCCI shows that the top global performers in terms of international supply chain connectivity remain continue to be in the Asia-Pacific region, i.e.: Singapore; Hong Kong, China; the Republic of Korea, Malaysia and China (table 4.2). The ISCCI 2015 top five performers remain largely unchanged compared with the ISCCI 2012 rankings (ESCAP, 2013). Singapore ranks first globally for international supply chain connectivity and for trading across borders (i.e. efficiency of import and export procedures). While China remains the global leader in liner shipping connectivity (first place ranking in LSCI), it has fallen from sixty-eighth in 2012 to ninety-eighth place in 2015 in the TAB indicators, placing it behind Malaysia in terms of overall supply chain connectivity. A comparison of China and Singapore suggests that port efficiency and connectivity is an essential component of overall international supply chain connectivity. However, it is also evident that improving the efficiency of import and export procedures can greatly benefit economies that may be lagging in liner shipping connectivity because of their size, inconvenient geographic location or lack of funds to upgrade port infrastructure.

**Table 4.2. Performance rankings according to ISCCI, TAB and LSCI, 2015**

| Economy | ISCC rank 2015 | TAB rank 2015 | LSCI rank 2015 | Economy | ISCC rank 2015 | TAB rank 2015 | LSCI rank 2015 |
|---|---|---|---|---|---|---|---|
| Singapore | 1 | 1 | 3 | Pakistan | 73 | 108 | 69 |
| Hong Kong, China | 2 | 2 | 4 | Philippines | 74 | 65 | 98 |
| Republic of Korea | 3 | 3 | 5 | Myanmar | 94 | 103 | 144 |
| Malaysia | 4 | 11 | 6 | Azerbaijan | 98 | 166 | 32 |
| China | 5 | 98 | 1 | Lao People's Democratic Republic | 100 | 156 | 45 |
| United States | 7 | 16 | 10 | Russian Federation | 104 | 155 | 46 |
| Germany | 10 | 18 | 7 | Bhutan | 114 | 165 | 40 |
| Japan | 20 | 20 | 20 | Nepal | 119 | 171 | 41 |
| Thailand | 31 | 36 | 44 | Cambodia | 130 | 124 | 141 |
| Sri Lanka | 34 | 69 | 28 | Kyrgyzstan | 138 | 183 | 47[a] |
| Viet Nam | 39 | 75 | 38 | Kazakhstan | 142 | 185 | 48[a] |
| New Zealand | | 27 | 94 | Bangladesh | 147 | 140 | 124 |
| Australia | | 49 | 72 | Uzbekistan | 148 | 189 | 49[a] |
| Mongolia | | 173 | 2[a] | Islamic Republic of Iran | | 148 | 108 |
| India | | 126 | 39 | Tajikistan | | 188 | 71[a] |

*Notes:* TAB rankings are based on the World Bank Doing Business Report 2015 and UNCTAD LSCI 2015.
[a] The LSCI ranking of landlocked countries is based on the ranking of the main transit country. ISCCI rankings are based on ESCAP calculations.

> *"Enhancing port efficiency is essential to enhancing overall international supply chain connectivity."*

Figure 4.9 shows the relative contribution of import procedures, export procedures and liner shipping connectivity performance to international supply chain connectivity performance. The generally observed trend in the Asia-Pacific region is consistent with the findings of the Global Survey and the ESCAP-World Bank Trade Costs Database – performance across the Asia-Pacific is heterogeneous, with the region being home to both some of the world's best and worst performers. Countries of East and North-East Asia are among the global leaders in international supply chain connectivity, whereas the performance of land locked deveioping countries and small island developing States lags behind. It can be inferred that, for the top performing economies, the contributions of import and export facilitation procedures and shipping liner connectivity are relatively equal. The notable exception is China, whose liner shipping connectivity performance is the largest contribution to its overall international supply chain connectivity. In part, due to sheer scale of effects, maritime connectivity in China is maximal,[16] suggesting that increased attention is required for improving the efficiency of the import and export procedures as well as logistics performance (Bang, Greve and Westergaaard-Kabelmann, 2014).

For small island developing States especially those in the Pacific, liner shipping connectivity remains a particularly marginal contribution to overall international supply chain connectivity. However, it is possible for small island countries to make progress in this area. For example, the Maldives has improved its position in relation to liner shipping connectivity in recent years, although from a relatively low base.

In the case of landlocked countries, especially as they do not have control over port operations in their transit countries, improvement of their international supply chain connectivity performance could be achieved through the simplification of trade procedures, documentation requirements and automation of procedures, where possible. Furthermore, since landlocked countries are dependent on the seaport of the transit countries, it is particularly important for them to connect to the most efficient and connected port. A case in point would be Mongolia, whose liner shipping connectivity performance and, hence, overall ISCCI score was boosted by utilizing the port connectivity of its main transit country, China. However, for other landlocked countries that must rely on the ports of transit countries with lower levels of liner shipping connectivity, improving trade procedures should be the focus of policymaking attention.

**Figure 4.9. Contribution of export, import and liner shipping connectivity performance to international supply chain connectivity, 2015**

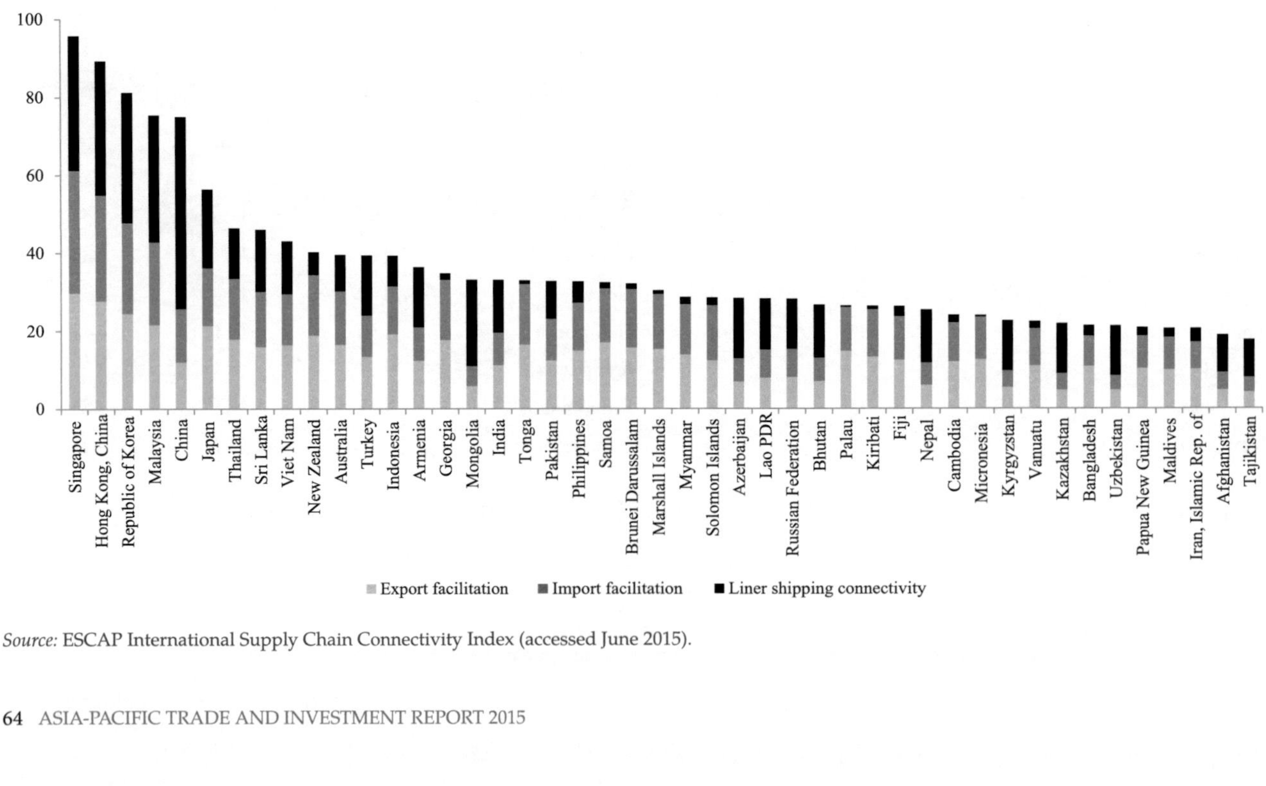


*Source:* ESCAP International Supply Chain Connectivity Index (accessed June 2015).

Overall, economies in the Asia-Pacific region have been making progress in international supply chain connectivity in recent years (figure 4.10).[17] Most countries of East, North-East and South-East Asia continue to make steady progress, and remain the regional and global frontrunners. However, these subregional groupings also have the widest gap between the top and bottom performers. For example, in contrast to the rest of the East and North-East Asia subregional grouping, Mongolia is the lowest performing country and exhibits a downwards trend in terms of international supply chain connectivity while Hong Kong, China – the top performer in East and North-East Asia – shows an upwards trajectory and is one of best performers, globally. For the South and South-West Asia subregion, the Islamic Republic of Iran, Bangladesh and Pakistan have demonstrated stagnant or downwards trends in international supply chain connectivity performance between 2009 and 2015. Sri Lanka stands out as top performer in the South and South-West Asia subregion, with the subregion's highest international supply chain connectivity scores as well as showing steady and significant progress in recent years.

> *"Improving the efficiency of import and export procedures is particularly important for economies lagging in maritime connectivity."*

The subregion that has shown the greatest progress in international supply chain connectivity between 2009 and 2015 is the North and Central Asia. In particular, Uzbekistan, the Russian Federation, Kazakhstan and Azerbaijan have each improved their connectivity level by more than 30%. The greatest momentum of this progress was between 2009 and 2012. While the progress has tapered off slightly between 2012 and 2015, the trend remains positive. This may be due, in part, to the improvements in liner shipping connectivity made by the Russian Federation, the main transit port for many of the Central Asian economies, in recent years; this demonstrates the fact that progress in transit countries can have knock-on benefits and result in improved international supply chain connectivity throughout a subregion.

## Figure 4.10. Evolution of performance by economies in the International Supply Chain Connectivity Index, 2009-2015

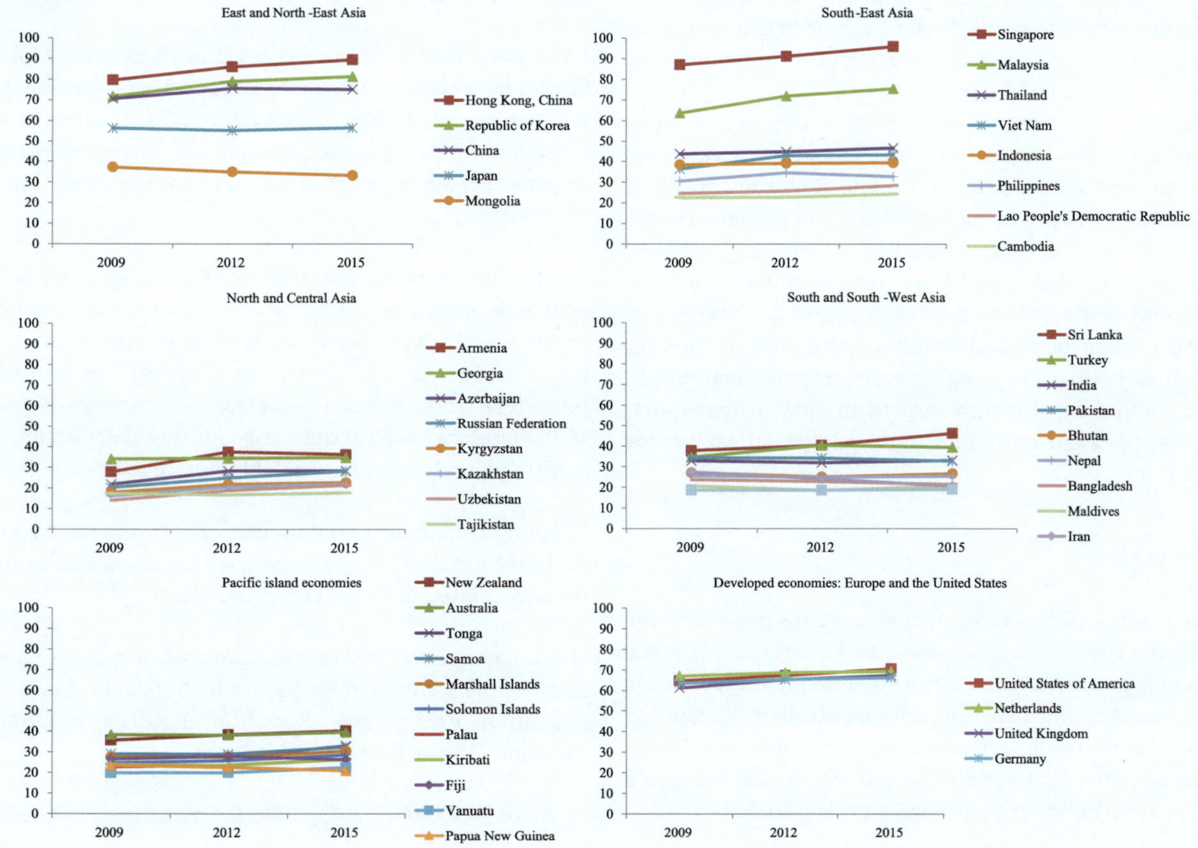


*Sources* : ESCAP, ISCCI data for 2015.

# D CONCLUSION

While the performance of individual countries has been mixed in Asia and the Pacific, the region as a whole has been making steady progress towards improving its trade facilitation and connectivity levels. Ongoing regional and global developments provide further opportunities for the countries of the Asia-Pacific region to access technical assistance and capacity-building in order to advance their trade facilitation efforts. In particular, developing countries stand to benefit from the capacity-building support available in relation to WTO TFA implementation. As the data from the Global Survey prove, the economies in the Asia-Pacific region have already implemented, or are in the process of implementing significant portions of the WTO TFA. In order to strengthen the overall region's competitive advantage, Asia-Pacific economies should look towards implementing more advanced measures, including paperless trade and cross-border paperless trade measures. The Asia-Pacific region has yet to take full advantage of the potential gains associated with electronic exchange of data and documents between stakeholders along the international supply chain. The work being done by ESCAP members to facilitate such seamless and secure international flows of information holds promise for the whole region.

At the same time, in order to achieve trade cost reductions as quickly and as efficiently as possible, it will be important for countries to continue implementing comprehensive and pragmatic national trade facilitation reform programmes. Such programmes should not be limited to customs facilitation or simplification, or exchange of documents but should instead be aimed at identifying and addressing procedural bottlenecks along the entire international supply chain, including through improvements in transport, logistics, payment and other trade-related infrastructure and services.[18]

## ENDNOTES

[1] "The Trade Facilitation Agreement contains provisions for expediting the movement, release and clearance of goods, including goods in transit. It also sets out measures for effective cooperation between customs and other appropriate authorities on trade facilitation and customs compliance issues. It further contains provisions for technical assistance and capacity-building in this area" (WTO, 2015a).

[2] This was covered by Area D of the Addis Ababa Action Agenda Action (United Nations, 2015).

[3] APTIR 2013 considered trade cost data for 2006-2011.

[4] The ESCAP-World Bank Trade Cost Database is the first database of its kind to systematically measure bilateral trade costs. The international trade costs captured by the database are the broad aggregate form, including direct trade costs, indirect trade costs associated with regulatory import and export requirements as well as costs resulting from currencies, language, culture, geography and distance. The recently updated database, which now covers almost 180 developed and developing economies, provides trade costs data for the manufacturing and agricultural sectors. Domestic and international shipping and logistics costs associated with imports and exports are also included.

[5] This first Global Survey builds on an annual regional survey undertaken by ESCAP since 2012, and has been conducted in close collaboration with UNCTAD, OECD, International Trade Centre (ITC), Oceania Customs Organization (OCO) and Latin American and Caribbean Economic System (SELA). For details, visit http://unnext.unescap.org/UNTFSurvey2015.asp.

[6] The trade facilitation measures considered in the Global Survey have been grouped into 4 categories: (a) general trade facilitation measures (Institutional Arrangement and Cooperation, Transparency, Formalities); (b) paperless trade; (c) cross-border paperless trade; and (d) transit facilitation (ESCAP, 2015a).

[7] In the Survey, paperless trade measures refer to those that enable the electronic exchange of trade data and documents between traders, Government agencies and other stakeholders domestically. In contrast, cross-border paperless trade refers to electronic exchanges between stakeholders located in different countries. For details, visit http://unnext.unescap.org/UNTFSurvey2015.asp.

[8] This figure is based on data from 102 countries, covering 22 trade facilitation measures, which are all essentially directly related to WTO TFA provisions.

[9] East Asia: Brunei Darussalam, Cambodia, China, Indonesia, Lao People's Democratic Republic, Malaysia, Mongolia, Myanmar, Philippines, Republic of Korea, Singapore, Thailand, Timor-Leste and Viet Nam.

[10] As of 20 October 2015, 50 WTO members have ratified the Agreement.

[11] This is reinforced by ESCAP's previous analysis of WTO TFA Category A notifications in the region, which indicates that on average, 15 Asia-Pacific economies that have already

submitted their Category A notifications to WTO have fully notified nearly 70% of all substantive provisions in the WTO TFA. This indicates that they have either fully implemented – or have full intention to implement within a short time frame – these measures.

[12] Anecdotal data from trade facilitation experts in 30 countries: ESCAP (2015a).

[13] The methodology used for this analysis assesses the potential impacts of cross-border paperless trade using the current reality of cross-border paperless trade implementation compared with the outcomes under a series of possible reform scenarios. The two reform scenarios considered in the analysis are: (a) all countries in the region achieve at least partial implementation of cross-border paperless trade; and (b) all countries in the region achieve full implementation of cross-border paperless trade.

[14] The World Bank Doing Business Trading Across Borders Indicators measure "the time and cost (excluding tariffs) associated with exporting and importing a standardized cargo of goods by sea transport [as well as] the time and cost necessary to complete four predefined stages (document preparation; customs clearance and inspections; inland transport and handling; and port and terminal handling) for exporting and importing goods are recorded; however, the time and cost for sea transport are not included. All documents needed by the trader to export or import the goods across the border are also recorded."

[15] LSCI comprises five components: fleet deployment – number of ships; container carrying-capacity; number of companies that deploy their container ships from a country's ports; number of liner services; and maximum vessel size.

[16] China controls a fifth of the world's container fleet, and many of the world's largest container ports are in China *(Economist, 2015).*

[17] On average, between 2009 and 2015 the region saw a 10% increase in the international supply chain connectivity scores.

[18] This may be done by applying the Business Process Analysis methodology developed by the United Nations Network of Experts for Paperless Trade and Transport in Asia and the Pacific. Available from unnext.unescap.org.

## REFERENCES

Anderson, James E., and Eric van Wincoop (2004). Trade costs. *Journal of Economic Literature*, vol. 42, No. 3, pp. 691-751.

Bang, John Kornerup, Majbritt Greve and Thomas Westergaard-Kabelmann (2014). *A Leading Trade Nation: the Role of Container Shipping and Logistics in Enhancing Trade and Economic Growth in China.* Maersk Technical Report, February 2014. Available from www.maersk.com/en/the-maersk-group/sustainability/~/media/90CB21A1C49E4335BD01 D79732E397E3.ashx%20 .

Duval, Yann, and others (2015). Trade facilitation implementation in Asia-Pacific 2015: moving towards paperless trade. Trade Insights, No. 12. Bangkok: ESCAP. Available from www.unescap.org/publications/trade-insights-series

*Economist* (2013). China's foreign ports – the new masters and commanders, 8 June. Economist Website. Available from www.economist.com/news/international/21579039-chinas-growing-empire-ports-abroad-mainly-about-trade-not-aggression-new-masters .

Organisation for Economic Co-operation and Development/World Trade Organization (2015). Aid for Trade at a *Glance 2015: Reducing Trade Costs for Inclusive, Sustainable Growth.* Paris: OECD Publishing. Available from www.oecd-ilibrary.org/development/aid-for-trade-at-a-glance-2015_aid_glance-2015-en

United Nations (2015). The Third International Conference on Financing for Development. United Nations Website. Available from: www.un.org/esa/ffd/ffd3/

United Nations Conference on Trade and Development (2014). Maritime connectivity and trade. Policy Issues in International Trade and Commodities Research Study Series, No. 70. Available from http://unctad.org/en/PublicationsLibrary/itcdtab72_en.pdf

United Nations, Economic and Social Commission for Asia and the Pacific (2012). *Growing Together: Economic Integration for an Inclusive and Sustainable Asia-Pacific Century.* Theme study 2012. ST/ESCAP/2629. Bangkok. Available from www.unescap.org/sites/default/files/themestudy2012-full.pdf.

_____ (2013). *Asia-Pacific Trade and Investment Report 2013: Turning the Tide – Towards Inclusive Trade and Investment.* Sales No. E.14.II.F.2. Available from www.unescap.org/resources/asia-pacifictrade-and-investment-report-2013-turning-tidetowards-inclusive-trade-and

_____ (2014). *Estimating the Benefits of Cross-border Paperless Trade: a Report in Support of Implementation of ESCAP Resolution 68/3.* Bangkok. Available from www.unescap.org/resources/estimating-benefits-cross-border-paperless-trade.

_____ (2015a). *UNRCs Trade Facilitation and Paperless Trade Implementation Survey 2015: Asia and the Pacific Report.* Bangkok. Available from www.unescap.org/resources/unrcs-trade-facilitation-and-paperless-trade-implementation-survey-2015-asia-and-pacific .

_____ (2015b). Draft text of the regional arrangement for the facilitation of cross-border paperless trade. First Meeting of the Interim Intergovernmental Steering Group on Cross-border Paperless Trade Facilitation, Bangkok, 1-3 April. Working Paper E/ESCAP/PTA/IISG(1)/WP.1, 19 January. Available from www.unescap.org/sites/default/files/PTA_IISG1_WP1_E.pdf .

_____ (2015c). First Meeting of the Intergovernmental Steering Group on Cross-border Paperless Trade Facilitation, Bangkok, 1-3 April. Available from www.unescap.org/events/first-meeting-intergovernmental-steering-group-cross-border-paperless-trade-facilitation .

_____ (2015d). ESCAP-UNCITRAL Capacity Building Workshop on Cross-border Paperless Trade Facilitation: Challenges and Issues for Enabling Environment, Bangkok, 31 March. Available from www.unescap.org/events/escap-uncitral-capacity-building-workshop-cross-border-paperless-trade-facilitation .

United Nations Network of Experts for Paperless Trade and Transport in Asia and the Pacific (2015a). Global Survey on Trade Facilitation and Paperless Trade Implementation: 2014-2015. Available from http://unnext.unescap.org/tfforum14-survey.asp

_____ (2015b). Towards an enabling environment for paperless trade – ASEAN Single Window: a regional Single Window for ASEAN connectivity. UNNExT Brief No. 13, May 2015. Bangkok: ESCAP. Available from http://unnext.unescap.org/pub/brief13.pdf .

World Trade Organization (2015a). Fifth Global Review of Aid for Trade: Reducing Trade Costs for Inclusive, Sustainable Growth, Geneva, 30 June-2 July. Available from https://www.wto.org/english/tratop_e/devel_e/a4t_e/global_review15prog_e/global_review15prog_e.htm .

_____ (2015b). Trade facilitation. Available from www.wto.org/english/tratop_e/tradfa_e/tradfa_e.htm.

## ONLINE DATABASES:

ESCAP-World Bank Trade Cost Database. Available from http://artnet.unescap.org/databases.html#first

# 5 OPENING DOORS OR BUILDING FENCES? REGIONAL TRENDS IN TRADE POLICY

The trade policy landscape in the Asia-Pacific region is continuing to evolve rapidly. Progress in the two "mega-regional" trade agreements – the Trans-Pacific Partnership (TPP) and the Regional Comprehensive Economic Partnership (RCEP), with each involving several Asia-Pacific economies – holds out considerable promise for further trade and investment liberalization (see chapter 6 for more details). Several bilateral trade agreements between economies in the region have also been concluded recently or are under negotiation. However, policy changes made unilaterally by national Governments have mixed greater liberalization with new protectionist measures. Governments around the world, including the Asia-Pacific region, continue to introduce new trade-restrictive measures with potentially detrimental consequences for growth, employment and welfare. In the context of slowing regional trade growth and the continued global economic uncertainties documented in chapters 1 and 2, the sustained rise in the stock of trade-restrictive measures remains cause for concern.

## A RECENT TRADE POLICY DEVELOPMENTS

New trade-restrictive measures notified to the WTO include increases in tariffs imposed on imported goods and other policies, such as quotas or bans, which are clearly restrictive of imports or exports.[1] From mid-November 2013 to mid-May 2015 (henceforth, the reporting period)[2] the global stock of trade-restrictive measures continued to increase at a rate of more than 14 new measures per month, although a rise was also recorded in the number of trade-liberalizing measures (WTO, 2014a and 2015a). In the Asia-Pacific region six new restrictive measures were introduced each month on average, compared with just over four liberalizing measures. The WTO has estimated that since October 2008 less than one quarter of the 2,416 trade-restrictive measures introduced have subsequently been withdrawn (WTO, 2015a).

*"The global stock of trade-restrictive measures increases by 14 new measures per month."*

In the most recent reporting period, 272 trade-restrictive measures were introduced globally (table 5.1). If trade remedy measures are also included, new measures in this period covered global merchandise imports with a value of $483.5 billion. In Asia and the Pacific, 108 new trade-restrictive measures were recorded in the same period, compared with 80 liberalizing measures (table 5.1). Asia-Pacific economies accounted for 40% of the trade-restrictive measures introduced globally, up from 38% in the previous period, but only 27% of liberalizing measures. Indonesia and India were responsible for the largest number of new trade-restrictive measures (28 and 22 measures, respectively). The majority of new trade-restrictive measures were tariff increases, although as in the previous period, the Asia-Pacific region accounted for a disproportionately high share of export restrictions (around two thirds of the global total). For example, in early 2014 Indonesia introduced restrictions on the export of raw minerals in the hope that the requirement for domestic processing would support industrialization and local employment (*Financial Times*, 2014).

*"In the most recent reporting period, 108 trade-restrictive measures were introduced by countries in Asia and the Pacific, compared with 80 liberalizing measures."*

Trade measures vary greatly in their impact; some can have significant commercial consequences for trading partners while others make relatively little difference. Gauging the impacts of individual trade measures requires observations of price and income elasticities as well as estimates of the price impacts of the restrictive (or liberalizing) measure(s). In many instances, however, these data are not available, making it difficult to quantify the commercial impacts of an individual measure. Simple tracking of the trade-restrictive and/or trade-liberalizing measures enacted is not by itself sufficient to allow a comprehensive evaluation of the global trade environment. It does, however, provide a good sense of the trending usage of restrictive measures around the world. Moreover, counting the instances of new measures in addition to previously instituted measures that are still in place allows for a better understanding of total trade costs, as the impacts of trade-restrictive measures are cumulative. However, despite the challenges, some studies have attempted to quantify the overall impacts of trade-restrictive measures introduced since the recent global financial crisis. One study that used a gravity-based model found that in the case of the least developed countries alone, the value of foregone exports caused by trade distortions implemented between 2009 and 2013, totalled $265 billion (Evenett and Fritz, 2015).

**Table 5.1. New trade and trade-related restrictive measures, mid-November 2013 to mid-May 2015**

| Type of measure | World | Asia-Pacific region |
|---|---|---|
| Import | 196 | 62 |
| *of which tariffs* | *(86)* | *(35)* |
| Export | 54 | 35 |
| Other | 22 | 11 |
| Total | 272 | 108 |

*Source:* ESCAP calculation based on data from WTO, 2014a and 2015a.

In contrast to the previous reporting period, globally trade-liberalizing measures slightly exceeded trade-restrictive measures; however, this was not the case in the Asia-Pacific region. India (23) recorded the most liberalizing measures (13) followed by the Eurasian Customs Union (17) (comprising Belarus, the Russian Federation and Kazakhstan at the time of recording) and China (15). Unilateral tariff reductions were by far the most common form of trade liberalizing measures, accounting for 86% of liberalizing measures globally and 70% in the Asia-Pacific region (table 5.2).

**Table 5.2. New trade liberalizing measures, mid-November 2013 to mid-May 2015**

| Type of measure | World | Asia-Pacific region |
|---|---|---|
| Import | 265 | 67 |
| *of which tariffs* | *(228)* | *(47)* |
| Export | 21 | 13 |
| Other | 5 | 0 |
| Total | 291 | 80 |

*Source:* ESCAP calculation based on data from WTO, 2014a and 2015a.

Trade remedy measures allow Governments some flexibility in the application of their WTO commitments in order to enable them to respond to particular situations, typically by imposing temporarily higher tariffs on imports from particular sources. Typical trade remedy measures are anti-dumping duties, countervailing duties and safeguards. Anti-dumping measures can be introduced to curtail imports from companies selling at unfairly low prices; countervailing duties are permitted to counteract subsidies by national authorities that enable their companies to export at lower prices; and safeguards allow Governments to suspend import surges temporarily – not in response to any unfair practices but in order to grant local industries time to adjust to increased foreign competition on national markets. Governments can also come under pressure to deploy these measures as a protectionist tool on behalf of domestic companies; thus monitoring their usage helps gauge the overall restrictiveness of the trading environment. Indeed, trade remedies are now deployed as much, or more than, more traditional measures of protection.

During the reporting period, 263 new trade remedies were initiated, with 97 by Governments in the Asia-Pacific region (table 5.3), a modest decrease from the previous period. Both globally and in the Asia-Pacific region, initiations slightly outstripped terminations, leading to a small increase in the overall number of barriers to trade. By far the most common form of trade remedies remained anti-dumping initiations. India was the top initiator of new trade remedies, introducing 34 during the period. It was, however, also the top terminator of actions, with 24 trade remedies discontinued. Interestingly, the number of overall terminations – that is, the removal of previously imposed measures – increased from the previous period, and in the Asia-Pacific the number of terminations almost doubled. This may be because post-crisis measures introduced in 2008 and 2009 have reached their five-year "sunset clauses"[3] and Governments have decided not to renew them.

**Table 5.3. Trade remedy measures, mid-November 2013 to mid-May 2015**

| Trade remedies | | World | Asia-Pacific region |
|---|---|---|---|
| **Initiation** | **Total** | **263** | **97** |
| | Anti-dumping | 208 | 78 |
| | Safeguards | 29 | 15 |
| | Countervailing | 26 | 4 |
| **Termination** | **Total** | **243** | **87** |
| | Anti-dumping | 195 | 66 |
| | Safeguards | 27 | 17 |
| | Countervailing | 21 | 4 |

*Source:* ESCAP's calculation based on data from WTO, 2014a and 2015a.

### Box 5.1. Has the balance swung away from protectionism in the G-20?

The G-20 includes the world's largest trading economies. As such, trade-restrictive actions taken by G-20 members result in especially significant repercussions for many countries' commercial interests. Since the global financial crisis, G-20 leaders have frequently pledged to resist or rollback any additional protectionist measures; however, critics have complained that the reality has frequently fallen short of the rhetoric (Evenett, 2013). The WTO, in conjunction with OECD and UNCTAD, provides monitoring of this commitment and reports frequently on the trade measures implemented by these systemically important economies.

The most recent WTO-OECD-UNCTAD overall assessment report on G-20 measures covered mid-October 2014 to mid-May 2015. It found that during that period G-20 members had implemented fewer trade-restrictive measures per month than at any time since 2013. In total, 119 new measures were introduced during that period, 25 of which were in Asia-Pacific G-20 members. In contrast, the introduction of trade-liberalizing measures remained stable. While this can be taken as evidence of members exercising some restraint in introducing new trade restrictions, the WTO warned that it was not yet clear that this positive deceleration in the introduction of new trade-restrictive measures would continue. The longer-term trends provide further cause for concern. Of the 1,360 restrictions recorded since 2008, less than 25% have been eliminated, leaving the total number of remaining restrictive measures at 1,031. G-20 members, including those in Asia and the Pacific, need to show renewed leadership in maintaining and strengthening the open global trading regime.

*Source:* WTO-OECD-UNCTAD, 2015.

Not all potentially trade-restrictive measures are captured in WTO reporting because members are not required to notify measures falling outside WTO rules coverage. For example, subsidized financing which many Governments used during the global financial crisis in the form of "bailouts" for crisis-hit industries were not captured by WTO reporting. This has raised concerns that by using less-transparent forms of protectionism, governments are continuing to implement (directly or indirectly) trade-restrictive policies on a scale not captured by the WTO. The Global Trade Alert (GTA) initiative attempts to correct this problem of under-reporting by gathering data from a wider variety of sources. GTA data indicates that the resort to post-crisis protectionism has been broader than originally thought and that there was a renewed increase in trade-restrictive measures from 2012 in response to the slowing global economic recovery. In general, increases in types of restrictions bound by multilateral rules were smaller than for more less transparent or "murky" measures not covered by binding disciplines such as some domestic subsidies, investment restrictions or discriminatory procurement arrangements. Including consideration of less-transparent measures shows that over the same reporting period as used by the WTO, the Asia-Pacific region was responsible for introducing 556 out of a total of 999 trade-restrictive measures introduced globally. Manufacturing and agricultural sectors were most commonly affected by these measures (figure 5.1).

**Figure 5.1. Sectoral composition of new restrictions, including less-transparent measures (share of total), mid-November 2013 to mid-May 2015**

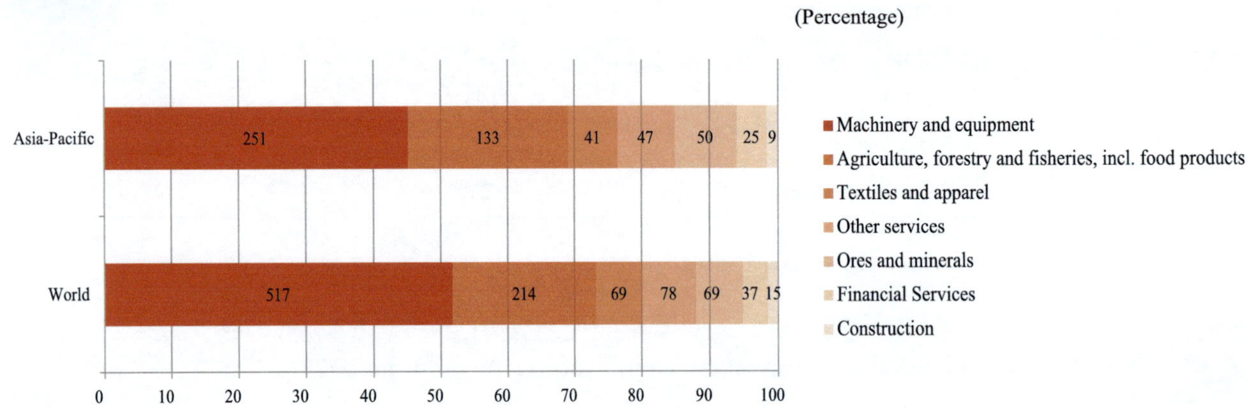


*Source:* ESCAP calculations based on data from Global Trade Alert, 2015.

According to GTA monitoring, India and the Russian Federation have been the most active among those countries imposing new trade-restrictive measures, introducing 184 and 144 measures, respectively. In terms of countries most affected, data show that Chinese products have been targeted more than those from any other country. Estimates are that, since the global economic crisis, 1,804 measures have harmed Chinese commercial interests (Evenett, 2013). This is higher than for the European Union (1,637), the United States (1,319) or Japan (911). During 2012-2015, red measures also frequently targeted products from the Republic of Korea (361), which was the second most affected economy in the Asia-Pacific region after China, followed by products from Japan (300), India (280) and Thailand (268).

*"WTO monitoring does not capture many less-transparent forms of protectionism."*

**Table 5.4. Ranking of Asia-Pacific countries according to the overall number of red measures implemented, 2012-2015**

| Implementing jurisdiction | Number of red measures |
|---|---|
| India | 184 |
| Russian Federation | 144 |
| Indonesia | 57 |
| Japan | 52 |
| China | 43 |
| Australia | 42 |
| Turkey | 41 |
| Kazakhstan | 39 |
| Viet Nam | 22 |
| Republic of Korea | 18 |

*Source:* ESCAP calculations based on data accessed from Global Trade Alert, 2015.

**Table 5.5. Top 10 targeted jurisdictions in the Asia-Pacific region, 2012-2015**

| Targeted jurisdiction | Number of red measures |
|---|---|
| China | 707 |
| Republic of Korea | 361 |
| Japan | 300 |
| India | 280 |
| Thailand | 268 |
| Indonesia | 227 |
| Malaysia | 217 |
| Russian Federation | 212 |
| Turkey | 210 |
| Singapore | 190 |

*Source:* ESCAP calculations based on data accessed from Global Trade Alert, 2015.

# B SHIFTING SANDS: CHANGES IN THE RELATIVE IMPORTANCE OF TARIFF AND NON-TARIFF MEASURES

The trends in the use of trade measures by regional economies, as detailed above, provide a useful guide to the direction in which the trade environment is being steered. It is, however, also useful to place these changes within the broader context of longer-term trends in trade policies. Two are worth documenting in greater detail: (a) the fall in average applied tariffs during recent decades; and (b) the rising importance of non-tariff measures as an impediment to regional trade.

In line with global trends, the average applied tariff rates in most Asia-Pacific economies are considerably lower now in comparison with earlier eras. Reductions have occurred as a product of: (a) unilateral liberalization as countries have adopted more trade-oriented development strategies; (b) the spread of preferential trade agreements providing greater market access to agreement partners; and (c) progress in multilateral liberalization through WTO. In 2012, average applied tariff rates in developed countries were below 2%, having been around 6% in 1995, while for developing economies the equivalent figures were 8% and 17%, respectively (World Bank, 2012). These aggregate figures, however, conceal substantial variation across sectors. Tariffs on agricultural products, for example, remain much higher than for manufactured products.

Even while reducing average tariff rates, developing countries have retained substantial "policy space" because bound rates remain substantially higher than applied rates (figure 5.2). This means that policymakers in developing countries can respond to import surges by raising applied rates without contravening commitments under WTO disciplines; safeguards can also be used for these purposes in some contexts. In addition, substantial shares of tariff lines remain "unbound" in many developing and least developed economies, especially on so-called "sensitive products,"[4] where there is no agreed-upon tariff rate ceiling. In consequence, binding tariff rate coverage varies substantially between developing countries. For example, Bangladesh had a binding coverage of only 15.5% of tariff lines in 2013 compared with 75.4% in India and 100% in the Lao People's Democratic Republic.

**Figure 5.2. Bound and applied MFN tariff rates in selected Asia-Pacific economies (all products, simple averages)**

(Percentage)

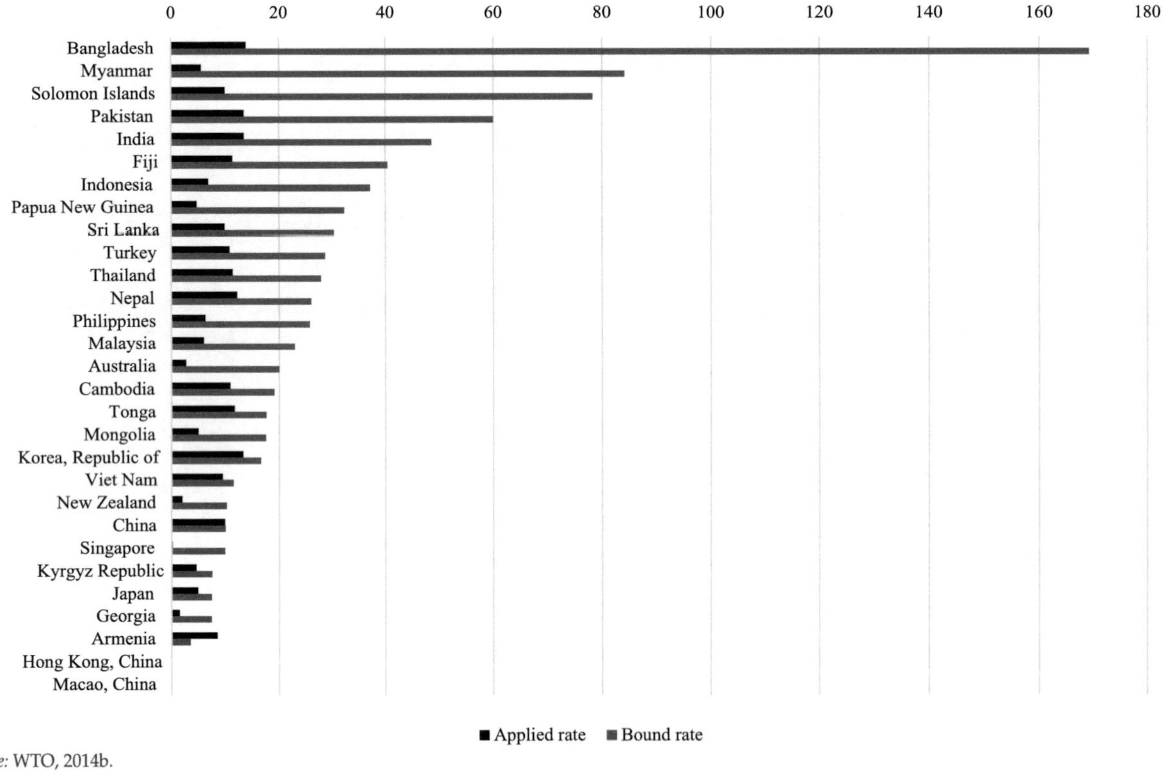


*Source:* WTO, 2014b.

Market access depends not only on tariff levels but also on other policies and regulations. Export subsidies can also have an impact on the ability of other countries to take advantage of opportunities for trade (see box 5.2). Non-tariff measures encompass numerous and diverse regulations that can have substantial impacts on trade, often unintended.

*"Technical non-tariff measures can be used as a disguised form of protectionism."*

Among the various types of non-tariff measures (NTMs), "Technical NTMs" have emerged as being particularly important to exporters. Common types of these technical NTMs include technical barriers to trade (TBT), such as product labelling standards, and sanitary and phytosanitary (SPS) measures, which cover regulations on plant and animal health (for more details see Heal and Palmioli, 2015, chapters 3 and 4). While they serve important public policy objectives, these measures can sometimes be used as a disguised form of protectionism and can be a significant impediment to trade. This is especially true in the case of low-income developing or least developed countries that often lack the laboratory facilities or certification processes to ensure compliance with the measures, thus further exacerbating disparities in the region. Because technical NTMs are more complex than tariffs, and because their impacts on trade are more difficult to assess, they can be a convenient tool for Governments wishing to discriminate against imported products without raising dispute.

Since 2002 the number of newly-initiated technical NTMs notified to WTO increased from around 1,200 in 2002 to surpass 2,500 for the first time in 2013 (improved recording of measures through the WTO I-TIP platform may also partially explain the rising numbers). Around one fifth of new measures originated in the Asia-Pacific region. The rise in technical NTMs has been ascribed in part to the growing importance of health and environmentally conscious middle-class consumers in rapidly expanding emerging economies (Cadot and Malouche, 2012). This has created greater pressure on policymakers to take regulatory steps to ensure, for example, that foodstuffs are free from dangerous pesticide residues. In this context, it is of little surprise that economies with a fast-growing middle class, most importantly China, are now responsible for a large and still expanding share of NTMs.

## Figure 5.3. Growing initiations of TBT and SPS measures in the Asia-Pacific region

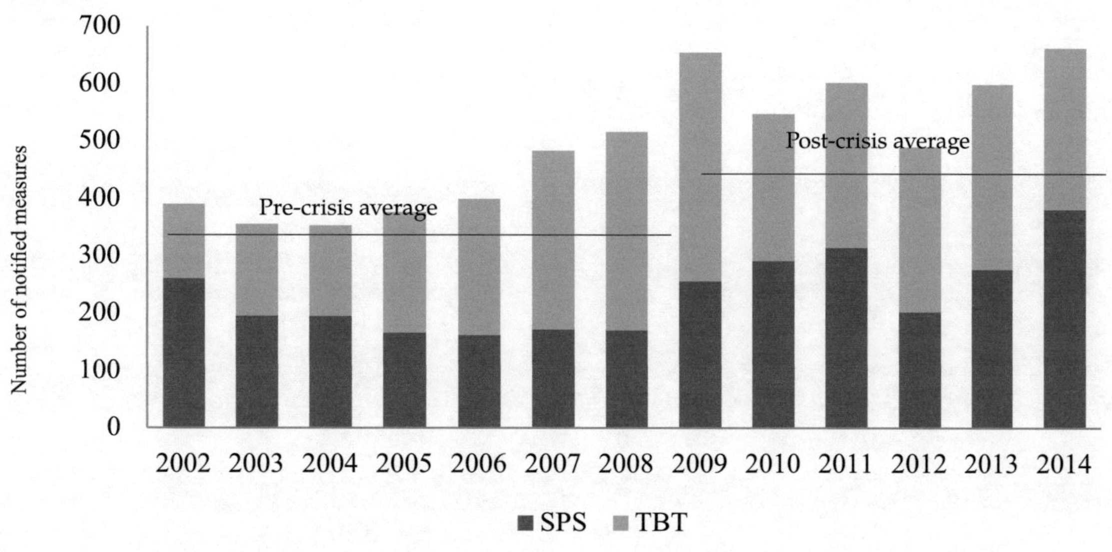


*Source:* ESCAP calculation using data accessed from WTO I-TIP Database, accessed August 2015.

Figure 5.3 shows the rising number of TBT and SPS measures adopted in the Asia-Pacific region, particularly alongside the global financial crisis-induced economic slowdown. The countries responsible for the largest shares of new NTMs in Asia and the Pacific were generally considerably more active in bringing forward new measures during 2008-2013 than in previous years. China and the Republic of Korea, which are important markets for other developing Asia-Pacific producers, were responsible for big surges in the use of NTMs (Heal and Palmioli, 2015).

Calculating the precise trade impacts of NTMs is even more difficult than in the case of tariffs. However, given that average tariffs have fallen during the period in which the number of NTMs has risen, it is believed that NTMs now represent a larger barrier to trade and cause higher trade costs than tariffs in many sectors (UNCTAD, 2012). Agricultural and food products are particularly prone to high levels of NTMs, which is disadvantageous to developing countries whose comparative advantage in these produces could be diminished or eliminated by the use of NTMs in the importing markets. One recent study provides ad valorem (tariff) equivalents (AVE) of NTMs as global averages for different merchandise sectors (Cadot and Gourdon, 2015). These averages are based on recent, more detailed NTM data arising out of the multi-agency Transparency in Trade initiative, which offers a more comprehensive identification of NTMs than had previously been available (table 5.6). The average AVE across sectors is 8.8%; however it is as high as 26% in the live animals sector where both SPS (such as sanitary certificates) and TBT measures (such as labelling requirements) are significant.

**Table 5.6. Non-tariff measures ad-valorem equivalents, by HS Section and NTM Chapter**

Percentage

| | SPS (A)[a] | TBT (B)[a] | Other (C, D and E)[b] | Total |
|---|---|---|---|---|
| Live animals | 12.9 | 10.1 | 3.2 | 26.2 |
| Vegetables | 10.3 | 8.1 | 1.3 | 19.6 |
| Fats and oils | 6.9 | 7.8 | 0.5 | 15.2 |
| Beverages and tobacco | 8.0 | 7.5 | 1.8 | 17.3 |
| Minerals | 1.6 | 6.6 | 0.8 | 9.0 |
| Chemicals | 1.1 | 5.6 | 0.7 | 7.3 |
| Plastics | 1.3 | 4.7 | 0.4 | 6.4 |
| Leather | 2.8 | 2.2 | 2.6 | 7.6 |
| Wood products | 4.7 | 1.4 | 0.4 | 6.5 |
| Paper | 0.8 | 1.7 | 0.7 | 3.2 |
| Textiles and clothing | 0.8 | 4.2 | 1.4 | 6.4 |
| Footwear | 0.7 | 3.2 | 0.9 | 4.8 |
| Stone and glassware | 1.8 | 4.9 | 0.6 | 7.3 |
| Pearls | 1.0 | 4.3 | 0.7 | 6.0 |
| Metals | 1.4 | 3.4 | 0.8 | 5.6 |
| Machinery | 1.6 | 4.6 | 1.0 | 7.1 |
| Vehicles | 0.4 | 9.3 | 1.2 | 10.9 |
| Optical and medical instruments | 0.7 | 7.5 | 1.6 | 9.9 |
| Arms | 0.0 | 0.5 | 0.3 | 0.8 |
| Miscellaneous | 0.7 | 4.4 | 0.3 | 5.3 |
| Works of art | 0.0 | 2.6 | 0.0 | 2.6 |
| **Average** | **2.8** | **5.0** | **1.0** | **8.8** |

*Source:* Cadot and Gourdon, 2015.

[a] The letters A, B, C, D and E refer to the "Chapters" used for classifying different kinds of NTMs used in the new UNCTAD classification (UNCTAD, 2013). Technical measures (Chapters A and B) refer to product-specific properties such as characteristics, technical specifications, and production process of a product. Non-technical measures (Chapters C to O) refer to trade requirements, such as shipping requirements, custom formalities, trade rules, taxation policies etc.

[b] Chapter C refers to "Pre-shipment inspection and other formalities;" Chapter D refers to "Contingent trade protective measures;" and Chapter E refers to "Non-automatic licensing, quotas, prohibitions and quantity-control measures other than for SPS or TBT reasons."

Several studies have highlighted how the emergence and spread of global value chains has reinforced the importance of maintaining an open and predictable trade policy regime (see review in OECD, 2013). With production increasingly dispersed across countries, intermediates cross borders many times before final assembly. Countries participating in international trade are doing so less and less by producing a product in its entirety. Instead, they are specializing in performing specific tasks at different points in the supply chain, which means that success in international markets requires the ability to cheaply and efficiently source imports of goods and services.[5] Even small additional costs arising from barriers to imports, such as NTMs, generally hurt the competitiveness and ability of countries to compete in export markets. This could deter investment from multinational companies seeking production locations. Similarly, even small reductions in non-tariff barriers can support cost reductions and efficiency gains for businesses in complex global supply networks (Yi, 2003). Therefore it is especially important to tackle the issue of NTM-based protectionism, although this requires continued efforts to improve available data on the prevalence and impact of NTMs.

### Box 5.2. Export subsidies: China-United States dispute highlights use of trade distorting measures

On 22 April 2015, the United States formally requested that a dispute settlement panel be formed at the WTO to consider a case against alleged Chinese export subsidies. This move followed two unsuccessful rounds of negotiations between the two countries after the United States had submitted a request for consultations on 11 February 2015. The European Union, Japan and Brazil, among others, have already joined the proceedings as third parties. The case involves targeted support provided by the Government of China to firms operating in several different industrial clusters, known as "demonstration bases." Firms operating in these bases – covering sectors including textiles, agriculture, medical products, light industry, special chemical engineering, new materials and hardware/building materials – were provided with grants and reduced-price or free services through "Common Service Platforms." The United States estimates that $1 billion was provided during a three-year period to Common Service Platform providers of services (Ringle and others, 2015).

The issue critical to the dispute is the claim that the subsidies provided through the demonstration bases were contingent upon export performance. As such, they would be prohibited under Article 3 of the WTO Agreement on Subsidies and Countervailing Measures. Under the Agreement, subsidies are divided into three categories: prohibited; actionable; and non-actionable. Export-contingent subsidies or those contingent on the use of domestic instead of imported goods are prohibited and thereby subject to the WTO dispute settlement procedures. They can be challenged by the injured party, whether it happens to be the importing country or an adversely affected third country. The subsidy must be immediately withdrawn if it is ruled prohibited; if this does not take place the complainant is authorized to take countermeasures.

The case also raises the issue of prohibited export subsidies in the Asia-Pacific region more broadly. Evidence from the Global Trade Alert indicates that Asia-Pacific economies introduced 50 "red" and 22 "amber" export subsidy measures during 2008-2014. India was responsible by far for the largest number of measures, accounting for almost half of the total, followed by China and Pakistan.

**Table A. Recorded export subsidy measures in Asia-Pacific economies, 2008-2014**

| Country | Red | | Amber | |
|---|---|---|---|---|
| | Total | Implemented | Total | Implemented |
| Armenia | 1 | 1 | 0 | 0 |
| Australia | 1 | 1 | 0 | 0 |
| Bangladesh | 0 | 0 | 2 | 0 |
| China | 11 | 11 | 0 | 0 |
| India | 24 | 15 | 9 | 9 |
| Indonesia | 1 | 1 | 0 | 0 |
| Japan | 1 | 1 | 1 | 1 |
| Kazakhstan | 1 | 1 | 1 | 1 |
| Malaysia | 0 | 0 | 2 | 2 |
| Nepal | 0 | 0 | 1 | 1 |
| Pakistan | 4 | 4 | 3 | 3 |
| Russian Federation | 3 | 3 | 2 | 2 |
| Sri Lanka | 0 | 0 | 1 | 0 |
| Thailand | 2 | 1 | 0 | 0 |
| Uzbekistan | 1 | 1 | 0 | 0 |
| Total | 50 | 40 | 22 | 19 |

*Source:* Global Trade Alert, 2015.
*Note:* "Red" refers to measures that have been implemented and almost certainly discriminate against foreign commercial interests. "Amber" refers to measures that have been implemented and may be discriminatory against foreign interests, or measures that have been announced and which would almost certainly be discriminatory if implemented.

Another source of evidence regarding the extent to which export subsidies are deemed to impose costs on trade partners can be gleaned from the use of countervailing duties (CVD). Such duties can be charged after the importing country has shown, through an investigation, that a product is being subsidized by the exporter and that this is causing injuries to domestic industries. The subsidized exporter can agree to raise its export prices as an alternative to its exports being charged countervailing duty. Examining the imposition of CVD by importers thus gives some indication of the scale of export subsidies perceived to be harmful. WTO data shows that between 1995 and June 2014 there were, globally, 193 implemented CVDs. Most of the CVD measures (53 out of 193) were raised against Chinese exports, while products from India attracted 34 CVD (table B).

It is important to note that export subsidies can harm not only firms in the importing country but also firms in third countries who lose out on potential export opportunities. There is evidence that firms from least developed countries have been substantial losers from export incentives imposed in both developed and developing countries in the wake of the global financial crisis. Evenett and Fritz (2015) found that G-20 export incentives were responsible for 86.5% of the harm done to exports by least developed countries during the crisis era (2009-2013). In addition, they estimated that exports by least developed countries would have been 31.5% higher in the absence of trade distortions, including export incentives, imposed around the world during the crisis.

**Table B. Countervailing duty measures: exporters vs reporting countries, 1995-2014**

| Exporter | Australia | China | European Union | Japan | New Zealand | Turkey | United States | Other countries | Total |
|---|---|---|---|---|---|---|---|---|---|
| Australia | | | 1 | | | | | | 1 |
| China | 6 | | 4 | | | | 27 | 16 | 53 |
| European Union | | 2 | | | 1 | | | 9 | 12 |
| India | | | 13 | | | 1 | 8 | 12 | 34 |
| Indonesia | | | 2 | | | | 4 | 2 | 8 |
| Iran (Islamic Republic of) | | | 1 | | | | | | 1 |
| Republic of Korea | | | 2 | 1 | | | 6 | | 9 |
| Malaysia | | | 2 | | | | | 1 | 3 |
| Pakistan | | | 1 | | | | | 1 | 2 |
| Philippines | | | 1 | | | | | 1 | 2 |
| Sri Lanka | | | | | | | | 1 | 1 |
| Thailand | | | 1 | | | | 1 | 1 | 3 |
| Turkey | | | | | | | 1 | | 1 |
| United States | 1 | 4 | 1 | | | | | 2 | 8 |
| Viet Nam | | | | | | | 2 | | 2 |
| Other countries | 2 | | 5 | | 3 | | 30 | 13 | 53 |
| **Total** | **9** | **6** | **34** | **1** | **4** | **1** | **79** | **59** | **193** |

*Source:* ESCAP calculations based on WTO CVD statistics, 2014.

## C TOWARDS TRADE POLICIES THAT BENEFIT ASIA-PACIFIC LEAST DEVELOPED COUNTRIES

Twelve countries in the Asia-Pacific are classified as least developed countries in recognition of the severe structural impediments to growth and sustainable development that they face.[6] These countries display huge diversity in population size and geography; Tuvalu, the smallest, has a population of just 10,000 while the population of Bangladesh now numbers more than 150 million. Excluding Bangladesh, the average population in the Asian and Pacific least developed countries hovers at around just 12.5 million. In addition, countries such as Afghanistan, Bhutan, the Lao People's democratic Republic and Nepal are landlocked, while Kiribati, the Solomon Islands, Timor-Leste, Tuvalu and Vanuatu are islands, giving them all different sets of unique challenges as they attempt to develop. The common challenges they face, however, are similar in terms of economic marginalization and the need for structural transformation.

Trade is a vital part of many of the least developed countries' development strategies. The recently agreed Sustainable Development Goals recognize the importance of trade as a means of implementation and set a target of doubling the least developed countries' share of global exports by 2020 (United Nations, 2015). In recent years, they have experienced some success in terms of increasing exports volumes; consequently, the share of the Asia-Pacific region's least developed countries in global exports increased from 0.17% in 2003 to 0.29% in 2013. However, without supportive policies in major markets, the ability of those countries to expand their exports will be constrained. In particular, if least developed countries are to grow and diversify their exports, it requires both a steady increase in world trade and a meaningful market access for their goods and services.

In the case of trade in merchandise goods, non-reciprocal preferences have helped least developed countries gain access to markets both in developed and in some developing economies (table 5.7). These schemes include the Generalized System of Preferences (GSP) and, more recently, Duty-Free Quota-Free (DFQF) programmes. The DFQF programmes were first introduced at the 2005 WTO Ministerial Conference in Hong Kong, China, and then as part of the WTO "Bali package" in 2013, developed countries agreed to offer DFQF access to at least 97% of products originating from least developed countries on a tariff line basis. At present, all developed economies meet this requirement, with the exception of the United States and the Russian Federation (WTO, 2015b).[7] The schemes are of greatest value to least developed countries when they: (a) cover export products where least developed countries have a comparative advantage at present or a clear potential of developing one in future; (b) offer "true" preferential market access – over and above what is offered to other developing countries through GSP; (c) have simple rules of origin (RoO)[8] that (i) reflect the current reality of international commerce where much of the trade is in parts and components, rather than finished goods, (ii) are easy to comply with, (iii) are sensitive to sectors of importance now and in the future, and (iv) allow cumulation over least developed countries.

> *"The Sustainable Development Goals set a target of doubling the least developed countries' share of global exports by 2020."*

**Table 5.7. Duty-Free Quota-Free schemes for least developed countries in selected major markets, 2014**

| Provider | Duty-free coverage (major exclusions) | Number of dutiable tariff lines |
|---|---|---|
| Australia | 100% | 0 |
| Canada | 98.6% (dairy, eggs and poultry) | 105 |
| China (2013)[a] | 61.5% (chemicals, machinery, paper and wood products, cotton, textiles, steel products) | 3 170 |
| European Union | 99% (arms and ammunition) | 91 |
| India[b] | 94.1% (Meat and dairy products, vegetables, coffee, tobacco, iron and steel products, copper products) | 674 |
| Japan | 97.9% (rice, sugar, fishery products, articles of leather) | 197 |
| New Zealand | 100% | 0 |
| Republic of Korea | 90.4% (meat, fish, vegetables, food products) | 1 180 |
| Russian Federation (2012) | 38.1% (exclusions cover a wide range of tariff lines including petroleum products, copper, iron ore, articles of leather, articles of apparel) | 6 885 |
| Turkey (2011) | 79.7% (meat, fish, food, steel products) | 2 384 |
| United States | 82.6% (dairy products, sugar, cocoa, articles of leather, cotton, articles of apparel, other textiles and textile articles, footwear, watches) | 1 864 |

*Source:* WTO, 2015b and 2015c.

[a] China has extended DFQF coverage for least developed countries to 95% of its tariff lines in 2013. It has reported in WTO meetings that an updated notification in this regard would be submitted soon.

[b] India extended DFQF coverage to 98% in 2014, although the WTO notification in this regard has not been submitted.

Least developed countries have indicated that reforming RoO in preferential arrangements is a priority. The 2013 WTO Ministerial Conference in Bali, Indonesia adopted the first set of multilateral guidelines on preferential RoO as one measure in a package of reforms designed to help least developed countries. This decision formally requests members to consider certain guidelines when developing their RoO frameworks for least developed countries; it was, however, not legally binding. In October 2014, the least developed countries' group at WTO presented a report to the WTO Committee on Rules of Origin, calling for a more effective design of preferential RoO. They urged that RoO be reformed to reflect current global value chains, not least by adopting lower percentage requirements for the calculation of domestic content. The least developed countries' group's proposal was to allow foreign inputs to a maximum of 75% of value in order for a good to qualify for benefits under least developed countries preferential trade arrangements (International Centre for Trade and Sustainable Development, 2015a). The least developed countries pointed to the reforms of RoO by the European Union and Canada as promising models for other trading partners and suggested that the reforms in those countries had already boosted trade and investment.

Beyond the RoO applicable in preferential trade arrangements, other non-tariff measures continue to be a major obstacle for least developed countries. Reliable market access for exporters now depends at least as much on ability to comply with regulatory measures, such as food safety standards, in the destination markets as on the absence of prohibitive tariffs.

> *"Least developed countries request urgent reform in preferential rules of origin."*

The growth in the number of NTMs, especially in the Asia-Pacific, raises particular concerns for least developed countries. First, where these measures impose quality and safety standards that are above multilaterally accepted norms, the cost of compliance can be higher in low-income countries because their capability for meeting the requirements is more limited. Infrastructure gaps, weak export services, and less advanced production and testing facilities all play a role. In addition, least developed countries are often required to outsource services such as laboratory testing and certification of food products, which can be expensive. These higher costs can erode the advantages that developing countries have from lower labour costs.

Naturally, NTMs vary substantially by sector. Typically the food and agriculture sectors have the heaviest concentration of SPS measures, whereas TBT measures apply to a broader range of sectors including manufactured goods and electronics. By considering the export baskets of Asia-Pacific least developed countries and comparing it with the average NTM ad-valorem tariff equivalent in different product sectors (table 5.6), it is possible to estimate which least developed countries have export baskets most likely to be exposed to high NTM barriers. Figure 5.4 shows those least developed countries with the highest concentration of exports in sectors with higher estimated NTM ad valorem equivalents, i.e. where the ad valorem equivalent for NTMs is estimated to be high globally, and where a specific Asia-Pacific least developed country has a high share of exports in that sector. This method indicates that the Pacific Island economies are the most potentially exposed to impacts from NTMs as a result of their exports being concentrated in fish exports, a sector in which both SPS and TBT measures are significant (table 5.8). Continued technical assistance and capacity-building for developing country exporters and Governments – focusing on improving compliance with the standards required to access potential markets–will continue to be a worthwhile investment with large potential returns in terms of increasing exports to higher value-added sectors. Aid for Trade and other international funds should also continue to prioritize these programmes.

## Figure 5.4. Estimated exposure of least developed countries' exports to non-tariff measures

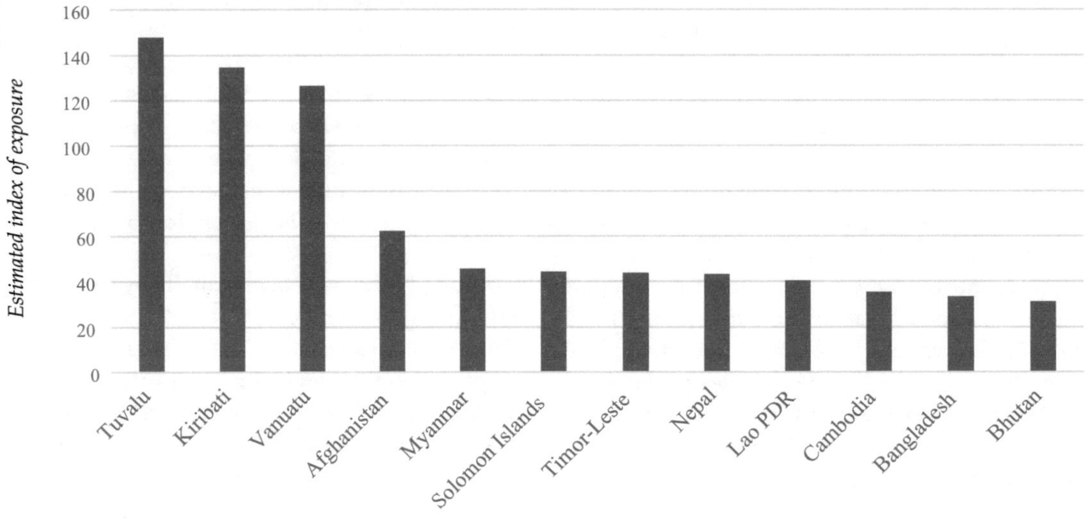


*Source:* ESCAP calculation based on export data from the World Bank WITS database, accessed July 2015, and NTM AVE estimates from Cadot, 2015.
*Note:* NTM exposure estimates were obtained by multiplying the share of exports from a particular sector with the estimated NTM AVE for that sector and then averaging across the export basket.

In addition to securing meaningful market access in merchandise trade, least developed countries are also seeking improved opportunities for their exporters of services. In 2012, services exports comprised 18% of total exports from Asia-Pacific least developed countries, and represent a much higher share in some economies, such as the Pacific island economies, where tourism is a major economic driver. In contrast to merchandise trade, where least developed countries could benefit from GSP and DFQF access in many markets, least developed countries services exports did not obtain any preferential market access. To improve on this situation, the WTO Ministerial Conference in 2011 adopted the WTO services waiver (lasting 15 years) with the objective of providing the legal framework for allowing countries to give better-than MFN treatment for services and service suppliers from least developed countries.

Implementation of the services waiver after 2011 has not been quick. Reliable data on least developed countries' services exports have been hard to obtain; conceptually the offer of preference in services sectors governed by complex regulations is more complex than in the case of tariffs when a simple numerical reduction in rates is possible. The WTO Bali Ministerial decision in December 2013, however, gave new impetus to the process and agreed on a work programme for implementation of the least developed countries services waiver provisions.

A meeting of the WTO Services Council in February 2015 made some progress; 25 WTO members attending the meeting provided indications of the preferential access they were prepared to offer least developed countries in their services sectors, and across modes of supply. Subsequently, of those 25 members, 11 submitted their official notifications to the WTO by August 2015, i.e.: Australia; Canada; China; Hong Kong, China; Japan; New Zealand; Norway; the Republic of Korea; Singapore; Switzerland; and Taiwan Province of China.

Preferential treatments run across 12 major sectors and are granted based on the countries' ability and willingness to give preferential access. A majority of the sectors collectively requested by the least developed countries' group are covered to some extent. Specifically, sectors included in the offers, primarily across modes 1 (cross-border trade) and mode 3 (commercial presence), are: (a) professional and other business services; (b) construction; (c) distribution; (d) financial services; (e) travel and tourism; and (f) maritime and air transport. However, the limited progress on Mode 4 access, covering the movement of natural persons – for example, through visa requirement waivers – shows that preferential access will fall short of meeting least developed countries' full request. However, timely progress towards implementation remains important as the life span of the waiver extends only until 2026.

## Table 5.8. Top five export sectors in Asian and Pacific least developed countries

*Percentage share of total merchandise exports*

| Tuvalu | Kiribati | Vanuatu | Afghanistan | Myanmar | Solomon Islands | Timor-Leste | Nepal | Lao People's Democratic Republic | Cambodia | Bangladesh | Bhutan |
|---|---|---|---|---|---|---|---|---|---|---|---|
| Live Animals (94.7) | Live animals (96) | Live animals (91.7) | Vegetables (47.8) | Minerals (42.1) | Wood (67.8) | Minerals (96.7) | Textiles and clothing (35.1) | Minerals (29.5) | Textiles and clothing (69.2) | Textiles and clothing (90) | Metals (74) |
| Machinery (2.2) | Vehicles (2) | Vegetables (2.5) | Textiles and clothing (21.9) | Vegetables (10.5) | Live animals (5.8) | Vegetables (1.9) | Vegetables (11.3) | Wood (25.9) | Vegetables (6.1) | Live animals (2.1) | Chemicals (14.7) |
| Metals (1) | Vegetables (6) | Beverages and tobacco (2.4) | Minerals (10.9) | Wood (15.4) | Beverages and tobacco (7.2) | Machinery (0.6) | Beverages and tobacco (11.5) | Vegetables (6.4) | Footwear (9.7) | Vegetables (0.6) | Beverages and tobacco (1.5) |
| Miscellaneous (0.6) | Machinery (0.5) | Vehicles (1.2) | Metals (7.3) | Textiles and clothing (10.9) | Fats and oils (5.5) | Vehicles (0.2) | Metals (13.1) | Metals (19.1) | Vehicles (4.2) | Leather etc. (1.6) | Plastics (3.1) |
| Vehicles (0.3) | Beverages and tobacco (0.2) | Fats and oils (0.7) | Leather etc. (3.8) | Pearls (11.4) | Pearls (13) | Metals (0.3) | Plastics (7.1) | Textiles and clothing (7.3) | Beverages and tobacco (1.2) | Footwear (2.3) | Minerals (2.2) |

*Source:* World Bank WITS database (accessed July 2015).

### Box 5.3. India's duty-free scheme for least developed countries: Are benefits limited by non-tariff measures?

India was among the first developing countries to extend its Duty-Free Tariff Preference (DFTP) scheme to all least developed countries. Coverage, as measured by tariff lines, was originally 94% but was expanded to reach 98% as of 1 April 2014. India is an important market for Asia-Pacific least developed countries (especially in South Asia), which recorded exports worth $2.8 billion to India in 2013. However, exports to India only rose by around 28% between 2008 and 2013 compared with growth of more than 230% in least developed countries' exports to China during the same period. Up-to-date data on the share of Asia-Pacific least developed countries' exports entering India duty-free are currently unavailable. There is some evidence, however, that non-tariff measures are limiting the scheme's potential beneficial impact because of the inability of least developed countries to meet India's most recent and complex regulations.

A business survey by the International Trade Centre, Geneva, reported by the International Centre for Trade and Sustainable Development (2015b), has identified products facing barriers in the Indian market because of new regulations. Findings showed that affected products include cashews, coffee, cotton and textiles, beans, chemicals, precious and semi-precious stones, raw hides, fruits and vegetables, wood articles and metals. Most of these products are covered under India's DFTP scheme but least developed country exporters may not be benefitting fully from the improved market access provided by Indian reduced import tariffs.

Recent legislation has introduced new regulations, in particular concerning sanitary and phytosanitary measures, for instance the Indian Plant Quarantine Order, 2003 (revised, 2011) and the Food Safety and Standards Act (FSSA), 2006. Under the FSSA, all imports must meet quality and packaging requirements before receiving customs clearance. In addition, at the time of importation, the products must have a valid shelf life of no less than 60% of their original shelf life. Further, pre-shipment inspection for imports of certain goods has been made mandatory. Covered products include unshredded metallic waste and scrap, and shredded metallic waste and scrap. The International Trade Centre found that many least developed countries, suffering from a lack of domestic capacity for testing and certification, were therefore facing additional barriers in accessing the Indian market.

India has made efforts to simplify the preferential RoO requirements in DFTP. Under the DFTP scheme, the local value-added content in the beneficiary country must be at least 30%. However, some least developed country exporters are still expressing concern over the subjectivity in application of the rules by Indian authorities. In this regard, further outreach by India to least developed country exporters and the provision of technical assistance, as provided for under the DFTP scheme, will be welcomed. Asia-Pacific beneficiary countries can use assistance to improve understanding among their exporters and potential exporters on India's food safety and sanitary and phytosanitary regulations.

*Source:* International Centre for Trade and Sustainable Development, 2015b.

## D CONCLUSION

While the balance between liberalizing and restrictive measures has tipped slightly away from the latter, this should not be a cause for complacency among regional policymakers. The stock of total trade-restrictive measures remains much higher than in the period before the global financial crisis. New trade-restrictive measures as well as trade remedies harm the commercial interests of many regional economies, including developing economies and least developed countries. While often invisible or difficult to trace, the damage imposed by these new measures has real impacts on growth, jobs and welfare.

The Sustainable Development Goals recognize the importance of trade as an engine of growth and development, and prioritize the expansion of least developed countries' engagement in international trade. If the ambitious goal of doubling the share of global exports from least developed countries is to be met, it will require further action to ensure meaningful market access for least developed countries' goods and services. This will include simplifying barriers, such as restrictive RoO, that prevent least developed countries taking full advantage of DFQF access as well as taking further steps to implement and improve preferential access for service exports, in line with the least developed countries' collective request in this area.

## ENDNOTES

[1] WTO Trade Policy Reviews provide monitoring of several types of trade restrictive measures. On the import side these include tariffs, customs procedures, taxes, quantitative restrictions and other measures. On the export side they include duties, quantitative restrictions and other measures.

[2] WTO data presented in this chapter are derived from two reports to the WTO Trade Policy Review Body – WT/TPR/OV/17 covering mid-November 2013 to mid-October 2014 and WT/TPR/OV/W/9 covering mid-October 2014 to mid-May 2015.

[3] The "sunset clause" sets a five-year term limit on all anti-dumping duties from the time of their imposition. The duty may remain in force if authorities determine in a review initiated before that date that the expiry of the duty would likely lead to continuation or recurrence of dumping (Anti-dumping Agreement, Chapter 11.3).

[4] Sensitive products are designated by each country and are not subject to tariff bindings.

[5] Services are gaining an increasing share in a value of both tradeable and non-tradeable goods. See Anukoowattaka and others (2015) for more details.

[6] The Asia-Pacific least developed countries are Afghanistan, Bangladesh, Bhutan, Cambodia, Kiribati, Lao People's Democratic Republic, Myanmar, Nepal, Solomon Islands, Timor-Leste, Tuvalu and Vanuatu.

[7] As of 2014 (or latest available year), the United States Duty-Free Quota-Free coverage was 82.6% of all tariff lines, while the Russian Federation Duty-Free Quota-Free coverage was 38.1% of all tariff lines.

[8] According to WTO (Introduction, p. 2), RoO are "the criteria needed to determine the national source of a product. Their importance is derived from the fact that duties and restrictions in several cases depend upon the source of imports. There is wide variation in the practice of Governments with regard to the Rules of Origin. While the requirement of substantial transformation is universally recognized, some Governments apply the criterion of change of tariff classification, others the ad valorem percentage criterion and yet others the criterion of manufacturing or processing operation."

## REFERENCES

Anukoonwattaka, Witada, Marco Scagliusi and Mia Mikic (2015). Servicification and industrial exports from Asia and the Pacific. Trade Insights, No. 10. Bangkok: ESCAP. Available from www.unescap.org/resources/servicification-and-industrial-exports-asia-and-pacific-trade-insights-issue-no-10 .

Cadot, Olivier, and Julien Gourdon (2015). NTMs, preferential trade agreements and prices: new evidence. CEPII Working Paper. Paris. Available from www.cepii.fr/PDF_PUB/wp/2015/wp2015-01.pdf.

Cadot, Olivier, and Mariam Malouche, eds. (2012). Chapter 1: Overview. In *Non-Tariff Measures–A Fresh Look at Trade Policy's New Frontier.* Washington, D.C.: World Bank.

Evenett, Simon (2013). *What Restraint? Five Years of G20 Pledges on Trade.* London: Centre for Economic Policy Research. Available from www.globaltradealert.org/14th_GTA_report .

Evenett, Simon, and Johannes Fritz (2015). *Throwing Sand in the Wheels: How Trade Distortions Slowed LDC Export-Led Growth.* London: Centre for Economic Policy Research. Available from http://www.voxeu.org/content/throwing-sand-wheels-how-foreign-trade-distortions-slowed-ldc-export-led-growth .

Financial Times (2014). Indonesia slaps ban on mineral exports, 12 January Available from www.ft.com/cms/s/0/d643e66e-7b71-11e3-a2da-00144feabdc0.html#axzz3ZnRrALeH.

Heal, Adam, and Giovanni Palmioli (2015). Trade and non-tariff measures: impacts in the asia-pacific region. *Emerging Issues in Trade and Investment*, vol. 1. Bangkok: ESCAP. ST/ESCAP/2719. Available from www.unescap.org/sites/default/files/NTM%20Flagship%20-%2025%20May.pdf .

International Centre for Trade and Sustainable Development (2015a). LDCs prompt WTO discussions on rules of origin. Bridges Africa, 6 May. Available from www.ictsd.org/bridges-news/bridges-africa/news/ldcs-prompt-wto-discussions-on-rules-of-origin.

_____ (2015b). How do NTMs constrain the effectiveness of

India's preferential scheme for LDCs? Bridges Africa, 4 March. Available from www.ictsd.org/bridges-news/bridges-africa/news/how-do-ntms-constrain-the-effectiveness-of-india%E2%80%99s-preferential.

Organisation for Economic Co-operation and Development (2013). Trade policy implications of global value chains. Paris. Available from www.oecd.org/sti/ind/Trade_Policy_Implicatipns_May_2013.pdf.

Ringle, Brooke, and others (2015). U.S. requests WTO dispute settlement panel in China export subsidies case. Available from www.lexology.com/library/detail.aspx?g=74172043-55ac-4869-83f2-4f101e821584.

United Nations Conference on Trade and Development (2012). *Non-tariff Measures to Trade: Economic and Policy Issues for Developing Countries.* UNCTAD/DITC/TAB/2012/1. Geneva. Available from http://unctad.org/en/pages/PublicationWebflyer. aspx?publicationid=625 .

_____ (2013). *Classification of Non-Tariff Measure – February 2012 version.* Geneva. UNCTAD/DITC/TAB/2012/2. Available from http://unctad.org/en/PublicationsLibrary/ditctab20122_en.pdf.

United Nations, Department of Economic and Social Affairs (2015). Transforming our world: the 2030 agenda for sustainable development. Available from https://sustainabledevelopment.un.org/post2015/transformingourworld .

World Bank (2012). *A Fresh Look at Non-Tariff Measures.* Washington, D.C. Available from www.siteresources.worldbank.org/INTRANETTRADE/Resources/Pubs/NTMs_A_Fresh_Look_Complete.pdf.

World Trade Organization (2014a). Overview of developments in the international trading environment: annual report by the Director-General. Trade Policy Review Body. 24 November. WT/TPR/OV/17.

_____ (2014b). *World Tariff Profiles 2014.* Geneva. Available from www.wto.org/english/res_e/publications_e/world_tariff_profiles14_e.htm.

_____ (2015a). Report to the TPRB from the Director-General on Trade-related developments (Mid-October 2014 to Mid-May 2015). Trade Policy Review Body. 3 July. WT/TPR/OV/W/9.

_____ (2015b). Duty-free and quota-free (DFQF) market access for least-developed countries: report by the secretariat. Committee on Trade and Development. 26 November. WT/COMTD/W/206.

_____ (2015c). Notification of preferential tariff treatment for LDCs (as per paragraph 2 of WT/L/304 and WT/L/759) and transparency mechanism for preferential trade arrangements (as per WT/L/806 and WT/COMTD/73). Council for Trade in Goods, Committee on Trade and Development. 23 July. G/C/W/714 and WT/COMTD/N/46

WTO-OECD-UNCTAD (2015). Reports on G-20 trade and investment measures (mid-October 2014 to mid-May 2015). Available from https://www.wto.org/english/news_e/news15_e/g20_joint_summary_june15_e.pdf.

Yi, Kei Mu (2003). Can vertical specialization explain the growth of world trade? *Journal of Political Economy,* vol. 111, No. 1, pp. 52-102.

**ONLINE DATABASES**

Global Trade Alert Database. Available from www.globaltradealert.org . Accessed July and August 2015.

World Bank Development Indicators. Available from www.data.worldbank.org/sites/default/files/wdi-2014-book.pdf. Accessed July and August 2015.

World Trade Organization. Countervailing Duties Statistics. Available from www.wto.org/english/tratop_e/scm_e/scm_e.htm. Accessed July and August 2015.

# 6 PREFERENTIAL TRADE POLICIES AND AGREEMENTS

Once considered an example of the benefits of autonomous trade liberalization, Asia-Pacific economies have turned into major contributors to a global build-up of preferential trade agreements (PTAs).[1] Stalled multilateral trade negotiations under the Doha Round plus a considerable slowdown in economic activities globally have provided a strong incentive to use preferential trade agreements for both offensive and defensive liberalization. This has led to the negotiation of trade deals being treated almost as a substitute for trade policymaking.

Currently, Asia-Pacific region economies are participating in a wide variety of preferential agreements, at both the bilateral and plurilateral (regional) levels. They are parties to 155 (59%) of the global total of 262 "physical"[2] PTAs that are currently in force. While fewer new agreements are being completed on an annual basis, almost all of them that were enacted in 2014 and January-June 2015 involve at least one economy from Asia and the Pacific.

Although it is unlikely that economies in the Asia-Pacific region will lessen their reliance on preferential liberalization in the foreseeable future, there are signs that they may be reviewing their approach to, and engagement in preferential liberalization initiatives with a view to turning largely dormant plurilateral blocs in Asia and the Pacific into more effective drivers of regional economic integration. Several concurrent initiatives are nudging Governments and other stakeholders towards reviewing their countries' position in the regional economic architecture and to rethink the ways in which trade can contribute to their development. These initiatives are: (a) the establishment of the ASEAN Economic Community at the end of 2015; (b) success in reaching agreement under the Trans-Pacific Partnership; (c) ongoing promising efforts in negotiations on the Regional Comprehensive Economic Partnership; and (d) the region-wide economic cooperation and integration process that members of ESCAP have entrusted the secretariat to develop. The fact that global trade growth at 3% per annum continues to linger behind the growth of global GDP for the fourth consecutive year (WTO, 2015), together with and a high level of skepticism about the likely outcome of the tenth Ministerial Conference of WTO in December 2015, are adding to the realization that business as usual with regard to multilateral trade agreements may not be an option for much longer.

The ESCAP secretariat monitors trends and developments in the area of economic integration in Asia and the Pacific[3] by assessing (a) trends in the creation of new PTAs as well as changes in the patterns and nature of the PTA landscape involving members and associate members of ESCAP, and (b) the relevance of PTAs for, and interaction with regional and global trade.[4] Monitoring is based on several elements traditionally used to assess PTAs and their outcomes: the number of PTAs; PTA partners and coverage of trade among them; the type[5] and scope of agreements;[6] and their status.[7] Furthermore, as 2016 will mark the tenth anniversary of the General Council's Decision on the transparency mechanism of regional trade agreements (RTAs), this chapter reviews the notification process to WTO under this transparency mechanism and argues in support of the need to convert it into a mandatory and permanent system to assist further assessment of the impacts of PTAs.

# A TRENDS IN PREFERENTIAL TRADE AGREEMENTS: SELECTED FEATURES AND STYLIZED FACTS

### 1. It takes longer to enact preferential trade deals due to both longer negotiations and longer ratification processes

The expectations built in the aftermath of the ninth WTO Ministerial Conference in 2013 and the agreed Bali Package regarding the revival of multilateralism implied that there could be less need to pry markets open through preferential trade deals. However, this was not followed by a significant drop in the immediate efforts to continue along the preferential path. Still, in reviewing the medium term since the peak of the financial crisis in 2009, a small but continuous drop can be found in the number of PTAs enacted annually by Asian economies. While it would be rewarding to link this situation with renewed confidence in the multilateral outcomes, fewer agreements could also be a sign that they are getting more complex in nature and/or involve more difficult partners, so it may take longer to negotiate and ratify them. In many cases, the ratification process is prolonged by more challenging public scrutiny arising from many economies having rightly adopted transparent procedures related to preferential trade agreements and providing the public with the opportunity to request information on each agreement prior to a formal ratification.

All these factors tend to extend the time associated with putting a PTA in place. For example, some of the bilateral PTAs signed or enacted in 2015 date from mid-2000s (e.g. Canada-Republic of Korea, 2005; Australia-Japan, 2007; and China-Australia, 2005). Similarly, when the two mega-regionals – negotiated either exclusively among or with a significant number of partners from Asia and the Pacific– were initiated, government representatives were optimistic in terms of the end-date for the completion of those negotiations. However, it took five years to finally reach an agreement under the Trans-Pacific Partnership (TPP) in early October 2015 (with expectations of a long ratification process to still come). Similarly, in spite of recent progress in the tenth round of negotiations under the Regional Comprehensive Economic Partnership (RCEP) Agreement, it is highly unlikely that it will be signed, as planned, by the end of 2015.

*"Asia-Pacific economies are enacting fewer trade agreements, but still contribute more than half of the global number of agreements."*

### 2. Most PTAs are among developing economies in the region, but Asia-Pacific economies are increasingly pursuing deals with extraregional partners

It is easy to see why export-driven economies of Asia and the Pacific have embraced preferential trade liberalization as one of the important ways of keeping markets open for their products, services and investment. With the continued economic slowdown in traditional export markets, PTAs have become a chosen strategy for finding new ones. Given the lack of progress under the Doha Round, even the strongest believers in multilateralism in the region had to embrace PTAs as the only option to defend themselves from trade diversion. The majority of the 155 agreements put in place by economies in the Asia-Pacific region has partners among other developing countries and provide a dynamic force behind South-South trade and cooperation. However, as shown in figure 6.1, the number of preferential deals among developing countries is growing at a diminishing rate. Between 2010 and 2014 the Asia-Pacific economies put into force an average of 6.5 trade agreements per year (5.4 bilateral ones) compared with an average of 9 (7.4 bilaterals) during 2005-2009. Of the total number of PTAs in force, 80 link economies within Asia and the Pacific. However, in the observed period since January 2014, most of the bilateral agreements signed or put into force were between partners in different geographical regions including, for example, China-Switzerland, China-Iceland, Hong Kong, China-Chile, Republic of Korea-Canada and Thailand-Peru.

**Figure 6.1. Cumulative number of PTAs (notified and non-notified to WTO) enacted by Asia-Pacific economies, 1971-June 2015**

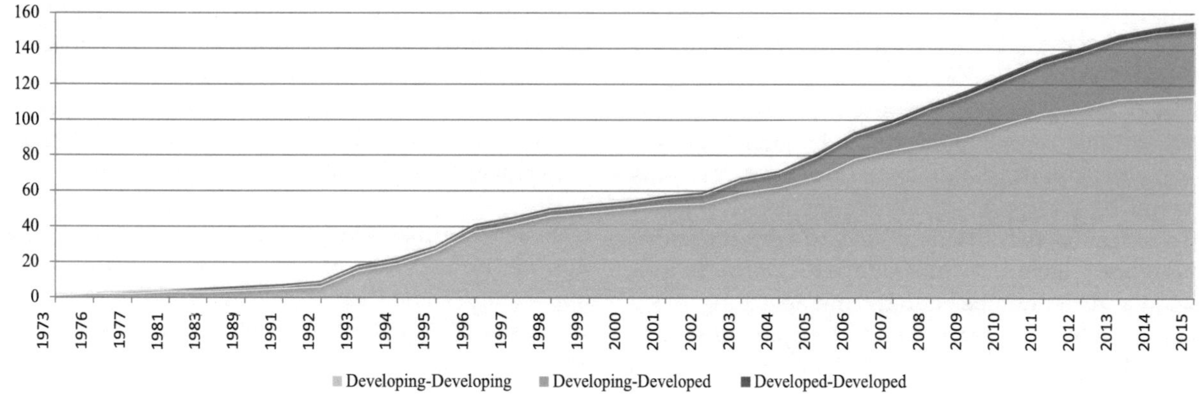


*Source:* ESCAP calculation based on data from the Asia-Pacific Trade and Investment Agreement Database (APTIAD). [8]

### 3. Number of PTAs and trade intensity among partners not strongly linked

The ESCAP members and associate members are grouped into five subregions: East and North-East Asia (ENEA), North and Central Asia (NCA), South-East Asia (SEA), South and South-West Asia (SSWA) and the Pacific. Apart from ENEA, all have put in place at least one trade agreement as a vehicle for regional integration. Members of these blocs are also linked by many bilateral agreements. However, the levels of intra-bloc trade for these subregions are, in principle, low and not growing noticeably in terms of relative size (i.e. as a share in total trade of the countries involved).

Slightly more than half of the 80 PTAs with exclusive Asia-Pacific membership have been signed among neighbouring economies in the same subregion. NCA leads other subregions in terms of high average propensity towards negotiating within a subset of arguably more "similar" economies. Most NCA economies have agreements either within their own subregion or with partners outside Asia and the Pacific (figure 6.2, column a). However, when it comes to intra-bloc trade, only about 11% of their total imports are purchased from the other economies in NCA; a further 35% comes from other Asia-Pacific economies while more than half of their imports are sourced from economies outside Asia and the Pacific (figure 6.2, column b).

**Figure 6.2. Number of PTAs among economies of subregions and their import intensity**

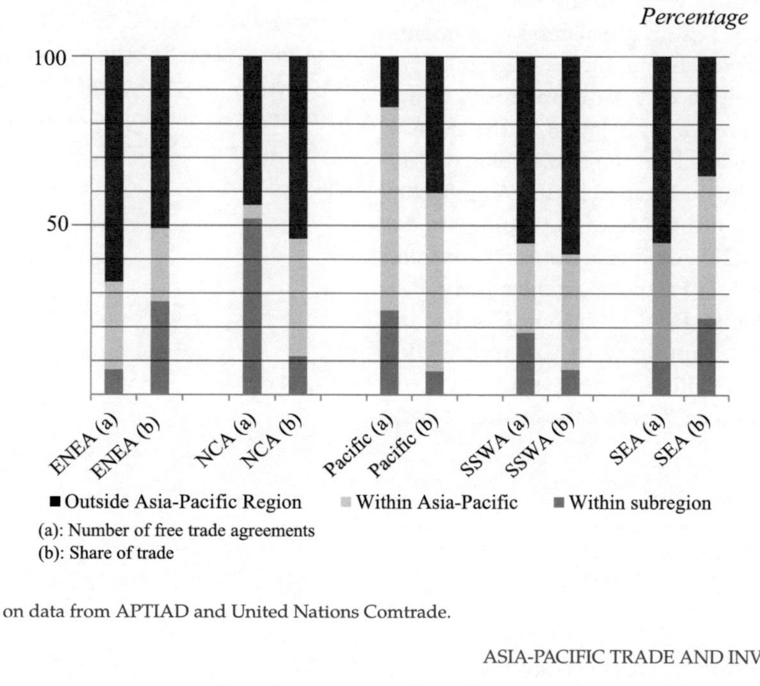


*Source:* ESCAP calculation based on data from APTIAD and United Nations Comtrade.

In contrast, there is no subregion-wide PTA in East and North-East Asia, while individual economies have only a few bilateral PTAs within the subregion (not all of which are in force).[9] However, the level of imports from other economies in the subregion, as a share of their total imports, is much higher (27.6%) compared with the share of formal agreements (7.4%) with those partners. The other subregion exhibiting a somewhat similar characteristic is South-East Asia, where the share of imports from subregional partners outweighs their participation in the formal agreements (22.8% and 10%, respectively). While the above is just a casual observation, the obvious absence of a direct positive link between a level of intra-trade with partners in a subregion and the number of agreements among those partners has already been noted and examined earlier (ESCAP, 2011a).

These findings feed the view that trade agreements are often not signed for the purpose of simply expanding merchandise trade, but for many other reasons, including non-economic related ones. This argument notwithstanding, given the overall impression of a low utilization of existing trade agreements by businesses, the opinion is now perhaps moving towards the view that if agreements are not meant to lead to more trade, investment and business, then they should not be pursued. This also suggests that further research into the selection of trading partners for PTAs is needed, as the issues of low utilization rates within the existing PTAs may indicate that the true potential of preferential market access is not being reached.

### 4. Three's a crowd: the preference is for bilateral agreements

The preference among the Asia-Pacific economies has been to sign bilateral deals, resulting in 124 out of the existing155 agreements being bilateral, of which 57 are with members from outside the region.[10] Within plurilateral agreements existing in the region, parties still continue to sign bilateral agreements (e.g. India, with a number of members in the South Asian Free Trade Area, and Japan with ASEAN members). In the "noodle bowl" of the agreements (figure 6.3) that are currently being negotiated by the Asia-Pacific economies, the majority are bilateral (32) followed by country-bloc negotiations (25). Another feature of the current negotiations among the Asia-Pacific economies is the fact that they are now negotiating PTAs with countries that are outside the region (for example with Canada, Chile, European Free Trade Association, European Union, Gulf Cooperation Council, Mexico, Peru and the United States).

### 5. Too many agreements may cause lower utilization and/or higher trade costs

The proliferation of bilateral PTAs has contributed to multiple overlapping agreements – the so-called "noodle bowl" (figure 6.3). The jury is still out on the impact of the "noodle bowl" on effectiveness of PTAs as there are a number of factors that may be at play in affecting trade costs and efficiency of trade under PTAs. There are two main issues with regard to the "noodle bowl" phenomenon:

(a) Businesses unable to fully use the negotiated preferences due to the lack of appropriate information on new opportunities and/or due to trade rules density, lack of transparency and possible conflict among the trade rules; and

(b) The adverse effects on costs of trade (including additional procedural costs, cost of compliance, and search costs).

> ***"In the Asia-Pacific "noodle bowl" there are currently 124 bilateral deals, 57 of which are with partners outside the region."***

Because there are no readily available statistics on the preferential trade flows of developing countries, the only way to gauge the effectiveness of PTAs – at least from the perspective of trade flow expansion – is to survey firms involved in exports and imports as well as appropriate regulators. Recent findings based on perception and other surveys (Economist Intelligence Unit, 2014; Ing and Urata, 2015) have indicated that the ultimate beneficiaries of the PTAs do not find them easy to use and that, in many cases, businesses forego using preferential trade terms as they prove to be too complicated, costly or even impossible to comply with. As ESCAP (2011a) argued, complicated rules of origin and certification procedures might add up to extra trade costs, reaching from 3% of the value of exports for companies in developed countries to 8% or higher in some lower income countries.

## Figure 6.3. Asia-Pacific "noodle bowl"

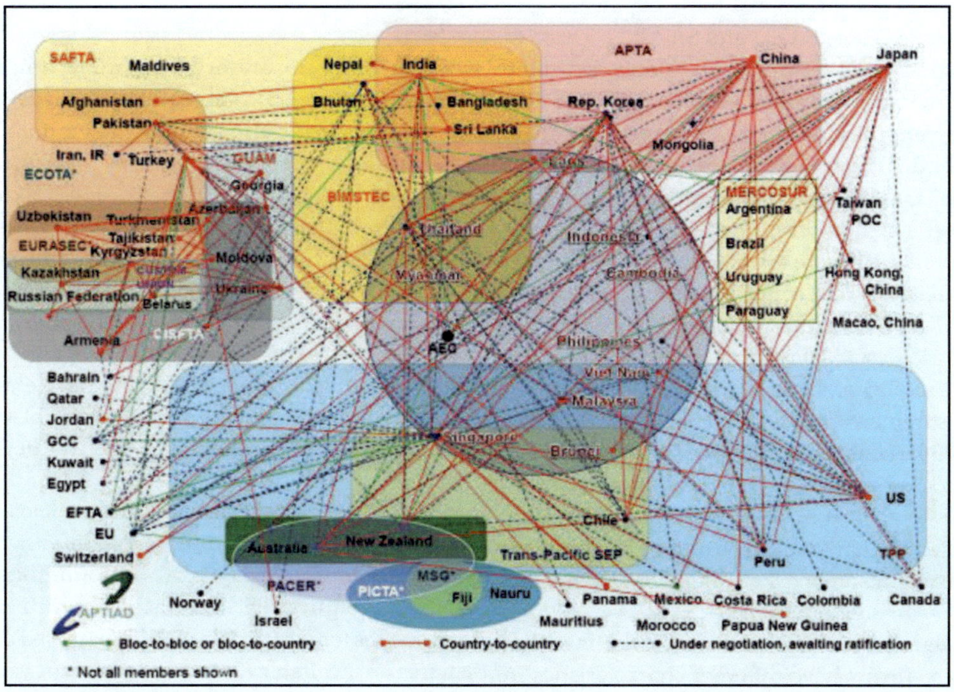


*Sources:* ESCAP and APTIAD database 2015.

### 6. Asia-Pacific economies tend to avoid forging deeper integration

More than half of all trade agreements put into force by Asia-Pacific economies relate to free trade agreements or areas for trade in (merchandise) goods, while close to a further 39% of agreements allow free trade of both goods and services (figure 6.4). Therefore, more than 88% of PTAs are presented as free trade deals on goods or goods and services. In contrast, only 10% (15 agreements) are declared as having partial scope (i.e. "Others" in figure 6.4), and only 2% (three PTAs) are customs unions. Of the three customs unions, two involve North and Central Asian countries. The rarity of the "custom unions" category is, on the whole, consistent with the behaviour observed in other parts of the world as well as the acceptance of the obstacles to successfully completing negotiations and then later implementing the agreement.

## Figure 6.4. Breakdown of trade agreements, by type and number of partners

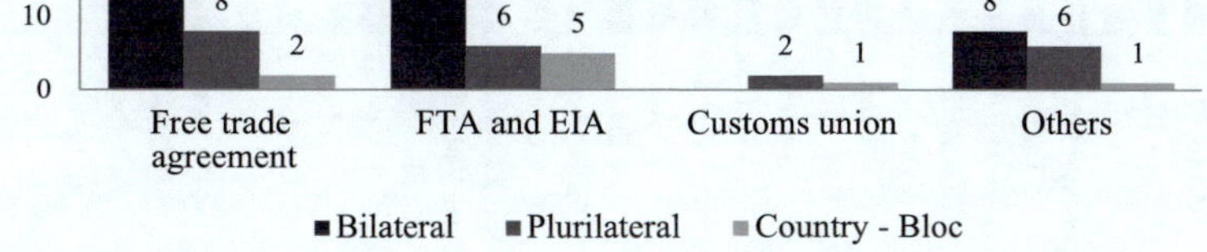


*Source:* ESCAP calculation based on APTIAD data.

CHAPTER 6

There are 22 plurilateral trade agreements[11] with an average of 9.7 members per agreement. These plurilateral deals coincide in most cases with the subregional blocs, which tend to have broader goals than just trade expansion (for example, ASEAN, PACER+, EAEU and SAARC). Three of the plurilateral agreements are groupings established at the global level, and members from Asia-Pacific in those PTAs work towards strengthening South-South cooperation (GSTP, D8-PTA and PTN). All three are so-called "partial scope agreements" that use a gradual and selective approach to reducing tariff barriers while not addressing other obstacles to cooperation. There are also at least five in this group of 22 plurilaterals that comprise basically the same economies but reflect the various versions or stages of their attempts towards the establishment of regional blocs (the case at hand is a group of Central Asian economies that feature in various frameworks, but which in most cases are defunct or inactive variants of one or two regional initiatives). This situation occurs because of the lack of effort by Asia-Pacific economies to abolish or annul bilateral agreements between economies that have moved on and signed regional or plurilateral agreements among the same set of economies.[12]

Co-existence of agreements is explained by the fact that these parallel agreements have different characteristics in terms of liberalization content, even though they cannot be clearly aligned from low to high openness, for example. They are not formulated in such a way that would allow each subsequent agreement to include all of the content of the previous ones as well as add something new, so that it would be possible to simply annul all but the latest agreement. This is in contrast to the way in which the European Union integrated itself through increasingly deeper forms of market integration, starting with the formation of a customs union and ending with an economic union extended to a monetary union for a subset of members. The approach of Asia-Pacific economies to PTAs is to use them as a vehicle to expand trade, investment and business, but not to drive integration of markets for goods, services, labour and capital, as has been the case with the European Union.

A reluctance to undertake a more ambitious form of integration is a good indicator of the level of political will to support even more shallow integration. While in many cases the success of a free trade agreement can only be achieved by the efforts of the business sector, other forms of integrated markets require a top-down approach and a firm political commitment to integration, including a willingness to give up some (or much) policymaking autonomy in areas of common interest to all members.

7. **Many existing bilateral PTAs have elements of "next generation" agreements, but many also just deal with unfinished business from the twentieth century**

Many countries have already undertaken significant tariff liberalization in the trading of goods, either through WTO commitments or unilateral (autonomous) trade policy reforms. Figure 6.5 illustrates the situation among 40 economies for which data on MFN-applied duty-free import shares are available (2014 or most recent year). While some dozen economies have opted to not levy MFN duties on more than half of, and up to 100% of their merchandise imports, there are still almost 30 economies that demonstrate much less affinity for free trade. For those economies that still have a high level of import tariffs, it is likely that other less transparent barriers will also prevail; it is those economies which first need to remove these nineteenth or twentieth century issues before continuing with the new areas of liberalization. Bilateral or regional PTAs for such economies may be just what are needed to give them the confidence to build up their multilateral liberalization efforts.[13]

**Figure 6.5. Share of tariff lines with zero duty on total non-agriculture merchandise imports, by Asia-Pacific economy, 2014**

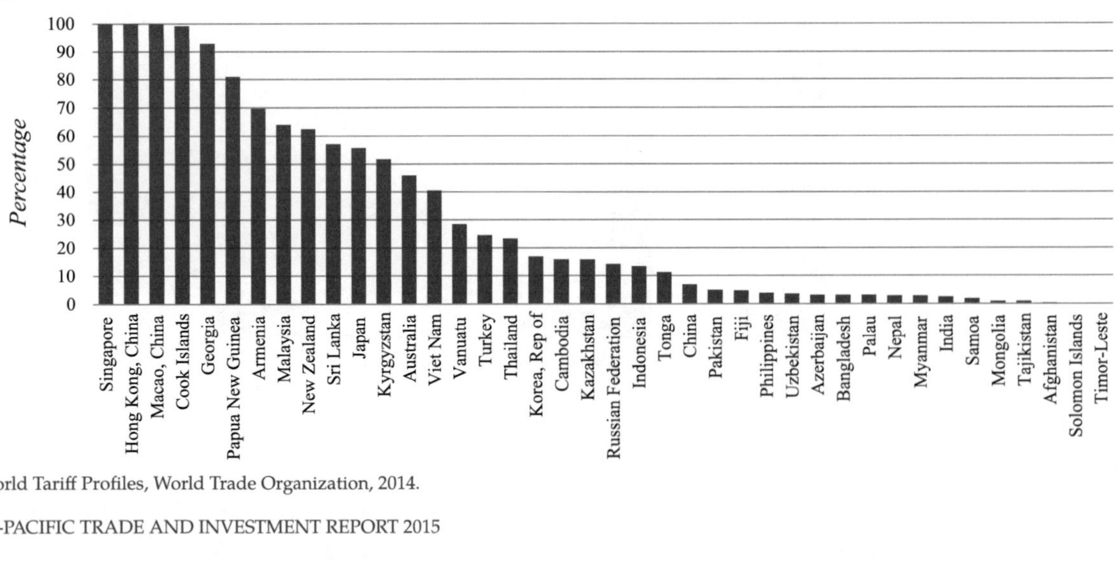


*Source:* World Tariff Profiles, World Trade Organization, 2014.

However, while more than half of the economies appear conservative in terms of maintaining a tariff wall (even if it is much lower), a number of economies have undertaken to allow liberalization in areas that are not currently covered by WTO disciplines, such as competition, investment and government procurement. The number of agreements containing these areas of liberalization featuring "next generation" trade agreements is still low (figure 6.6).

The most prominent types of regional trade agreements that include not only standard WTO-plus but also many "WTO-beyond" areas, such as competition, government procurement and investment, are RCEP and TPP agreements (see box 6.1). The third, relatively new regional bloc evolving in Asia is the Eurasian Economic Union (EAEU) that, at present, has five members. As declared, its features appear to be much closer to those of the European Union, with members having undertaken commitments to forming a customs union or harmonizing macroeconomic policies and having the Eurasian Economic Commission as a permanent regulatory body of the EAEU.

**Figure 6.6. Areas of liberalization pursued by Asia-Pacific PTAs**

*(Percentage)*

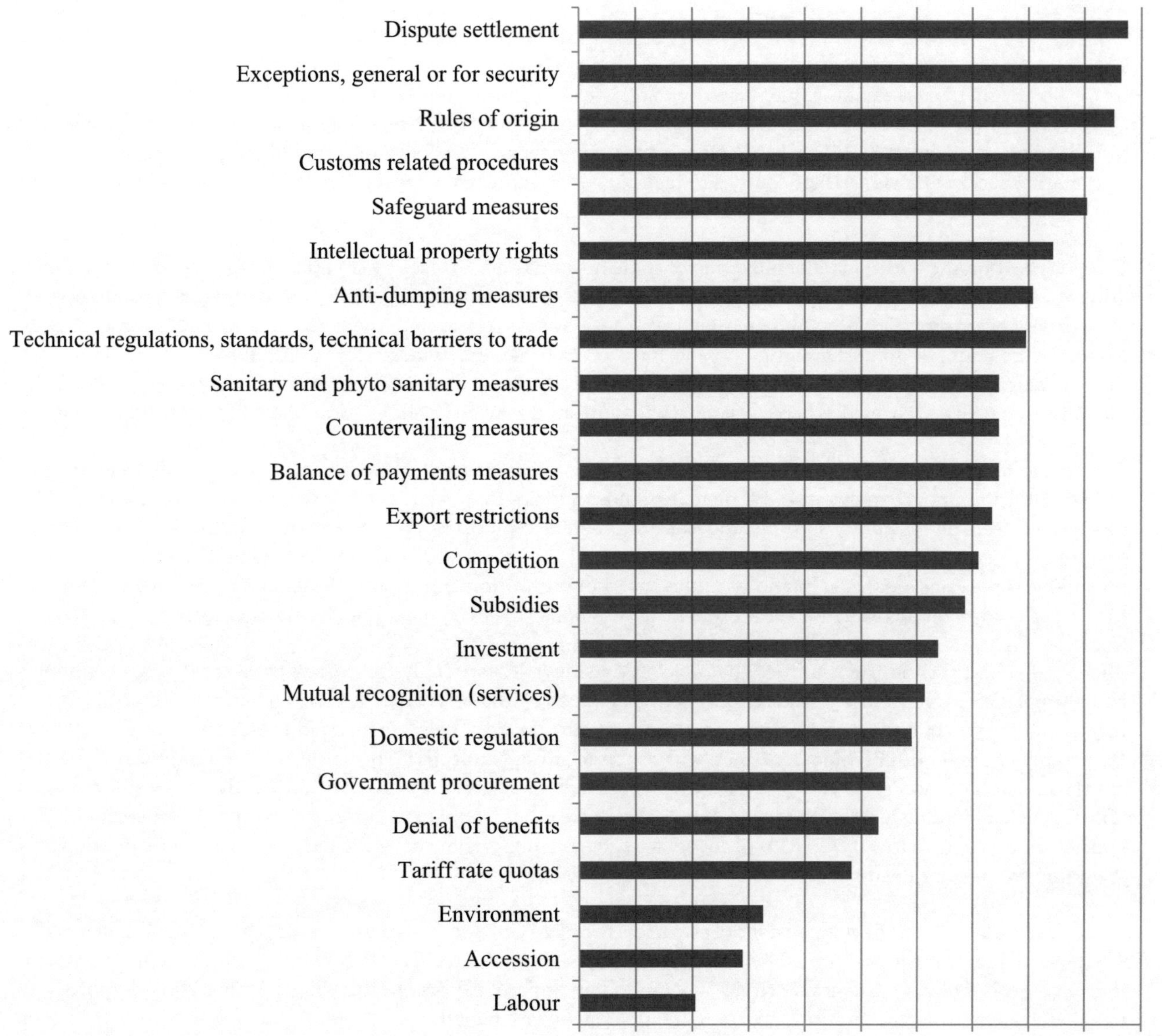


*Source:* World Trade Organization, RTA-IS accessed September 2015.

Even prior to the mega-blocs an increasing number of bilateral agreements had "next generation" features, including investment, competition or government procurement. An uptake of these WTO-beyond features by the regional (plurilateral) deals, some of which comprise important global and regional traders, is significant in two contrasting ways. On the positive side, switching from bilateral to plurilateral agreements of high quality may help in sorting out "noodle bowl" problems (for more details see below). On the negative side, if the plurilateral deals that provide up to 30%-40% of world trade or GDP are faster in putting in place new disciplines going above and beyond those of WTO, there is a potential for them to undermine the existing WTO system of rules. One area that is frequently mentioned in this regard is dispute settlement; however, competition, investment and other regulatory-heavy areas that are actually not part of a current multilateral system are good contenders too.

*"Recent agreements are more comprehensive in scope."*

### Box 6.1. Trans-Pacific Partnership finally arrives

The Trans-Pacific Partnership Agreement (known simply as "TPP") evolved from a small agreement among four countries (Brunei Darussalam, Chile, New Zealand and Singapore) into a comprehensive trade and integration agreement between 12 major trading nations. The additional eight countries – Australia, Canada, Japan, Malaysia, Mexico, Peru, the United States and Viet Nam – brought extensive diversity into the initial grouping. The overall TPP market accounts for a GDP of nearly $28 trillion, which represents approximately 40% of global GDP, 30% of world imports and more than 11% of the global population.

TPP goes beyond the traditional liberalization of trade in goods and services by covering areas such as investor-state arbitration, intellectual property protection, environmental and labour standards, the privileges of state-owned enterprises and government procurement practices. These issues – considered "next generation" issues – traditionally belong to the realm of domestic regulation and have yet to be seriously tackled in a multilateral setting. However, they are slowly being added to the menu of preferential trade deals. Once their inclusion in negotiated preferential liberalization deals, such as TPP, becomes more widespread, it may be easier to adopt them at the multilateral level.

The precise terms of liberalization in TPP have yet to be publicly released. However, even if all details were known, doing an a priori impact analysis of TPP members and countries that have been left outside the agreement may not be very helpful. The constantly shifting landscape of bilateral and plurilateral agreements, not to mention the larger economic environment, means that understanding the real impacts of such comprehensive liberalization can be only obtained in an ex post analysis. In addition, the speed of ratification among the 12 signatories is a key element, as the longer it takes for all of them to enact the deal, the smaller the overall benefits for the members.

The negative impacts on the countries that are left outside TPP, especially the rest of the Asia-Pacific economies, namely other ASEAN members, China, India and the Republic of Korea, will depend on the change in their competitive conditions, i.e. size of trade diversion and preference erosion. Luckily, because many of these countries already have PTAs with a number of TPP members, they will not be so strongly affected. The countries that might fare the worst are those that have no PTAs with TPP countries, and trade goods and services with them that have still not been liberalized at the multilateral level. Some estimates that take into account existing levels of commitments under WTO – for example, high shares (up to 50% or more) of duty-free imports at the MFN basis or up to 100% bindings for low tariff rates – raise the hope of likely low trade diversion impacts.

Some developing or least developed countries currently utilize GSP schemes that most of the TPP members provide. The potential for them to be harmed by preference erosion exists if other TPP members are direct competitors with the same exportables. One example could be Cambodian apparel exports to the United States. These exports will now have to face competition from other TPP members who will benefit from lower barriers than before. However, looking at such possible producers, one discovers that they already enjoy significant preferences, either through GSP or through PTAs. Thus, big impacts should not be expected to come from trade liberalization provisions in TPP. It is more likely that any adverse effects will come as a result of investment provisions included in TPP. Meanwhile, the benefits of removing other so-called behind-the-border barriers are difficult to restrict to TPP members only (e.g. trade facilitation, or other regulatory measures) and thus the agreement's comprehensive regulatory reforms – if they indeed happen – are expected to produce sizable positive "externalities" effects for non-members.

On a broader scale, a positive outcome of TPP is it potential use as a pathway (or stepping stone) to wider liberalization and integration, specifically in the Asia-Pacific Economic Cooperation where countries are waiting to embark on the Free Trade Area of the Asia-Pacific (FTAAP). As TPP is a larger and deeper liberalization effort than achieved under the so-called P4 agreement, it is possible to imagine that FTAAP could likewise use TPP as a stepping stone for consolidating existing PTAs and reducing the effect of the "noodle bowl".

In thinking about the policy response to TPP, non-TPP countries should wait for the full provisions of TPP to become available before evaluating the costs and benefits to their own trade and investment patterns. They should also evaluate their national regulations and TPP obligations in the "next generation issues" to make an assessment about the changes that they will need implement on the domestic front and the associated challenges if they want to join TPP.

# B TRADE WITH PREFERENTIAL TRADE AGREEMENT PARTNERS

The extent to which economies in the Asia-Pacific region trade with their PTA partners varies considerably (figure 6.7). Only 35% of exports and 45% of imports are transacted with the PTA partners (as a simple average for 2011-2013). Most of the least developed countries show a very high share of exports to their PTA partners, typically neighbouring nations – e.g. Afghanistan (72%), Bhutan (88%), the Lao People's Democratic Republic (86%) and Myanmar (92%). Some South-East Asian countries also have a much higher dependence on trade with PTA partners. At the other end of the spectrum, the Pacific island countries export less than 10% of their total exports, on average, to PTA partners. While averages can hide important specifics (i.e. the liberalizing quality of PTAs), it is worth noting that the figure for North and Central Asian economies is only 16%. Import patterns are similarly diverse. Some economies show a much higher propensity to import from the PTA partners compared with their export pattern – e.g. Bangladesh (60%), Cambodia (90%), Sri Lanka (51%) and Macao, China (60%) – while some others tend to import much less from PTA partners than what they export to them (e.g. in the case of Afghanistan, Bhutan and some Pacific island nations).

No fixed pattern is observed from this analysis as there are variations in the trade patterns of the individual economies, although small economies' share of trade with neighbouring PTA partners is still significant. On the export side, Brunei Darussalam directs almost 100% of its exports to its PTA partners.

An ideal situation would be to have the preferential trade data to do this analysis. Unfortunately, these data are not available for most of the economies in the Asia-Pacific region; thus the total trade with PTA partners is used as the best proxy when analysing benefits from PTAs.

*"An average Asia-Pacific economy buys less than 40% of its imports from its PTA partners."*

## Figure 6.7. Share of trade with PTA partners,

*(Percentage, average for 2011-2013)*

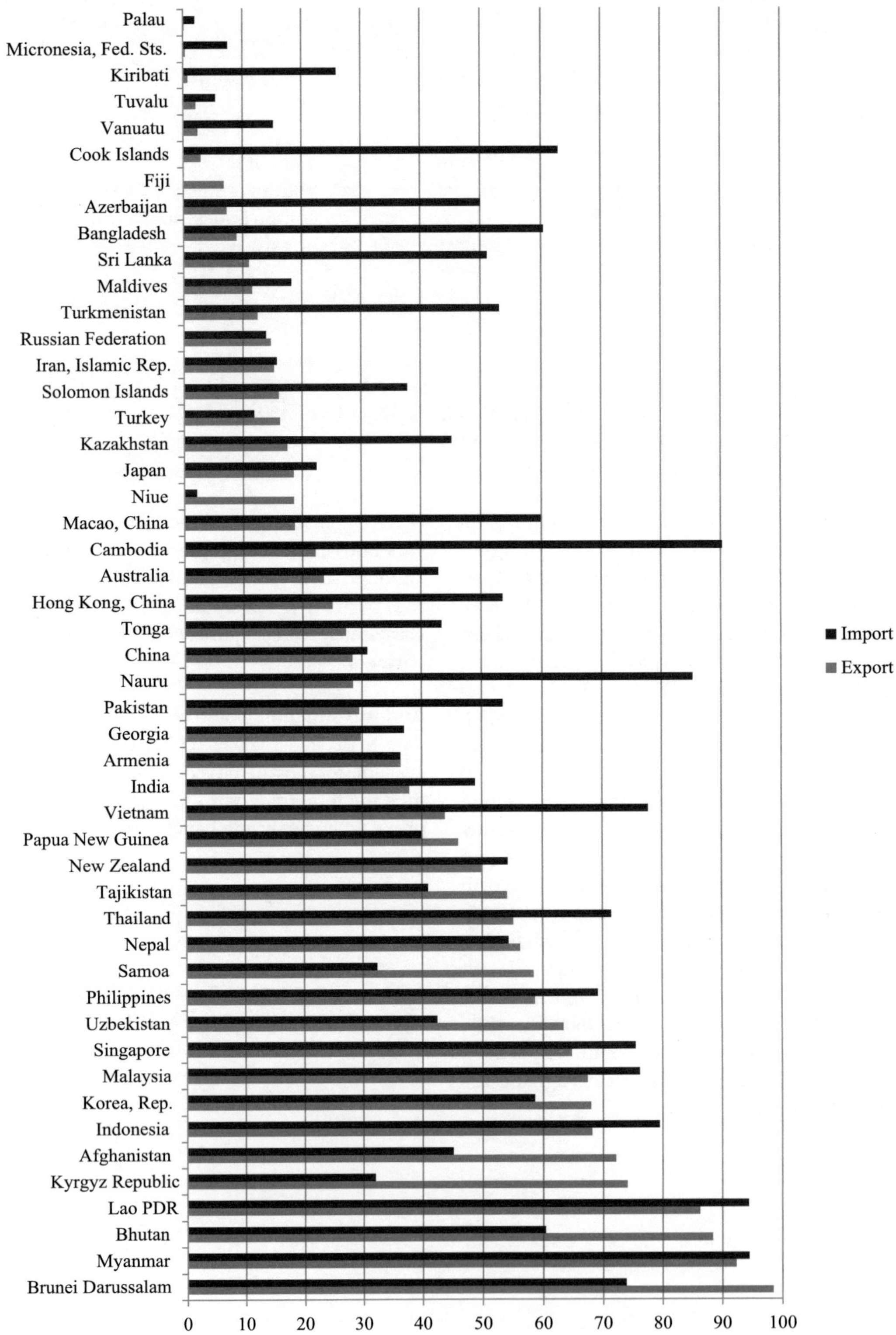


*Source:* ESCAP calculation based on United Nations Comtrade data downloaded from WITS and APTIAD databases (accessed July 2015).

Three developed economies are also dissimilar, with Japan relying on much of its trade with non-partners, New Zealand's exports and imports are more or less balanced (50% and 54%, respectively) while Australian imports from PTA partners hold a higher share (43%) compared with exports (24%).

## C TRANSPARENCY AND PREFERENTIAL TRADE AGREEMENTS: THE RECORD OF ASIA-PACIFIC ECONOMIES[14]

The existence of PTAs was "legalized" under the multilateral trading system rules early on by the GATT Article XXIV, which allowed formation of a customs union or free trade area. Article XXIV. 7(a) and &(c) provides for a transparency mechanism[15] under which the WTO members are required to notify details of PTAs to the WTO Secretariat. Despite this requirement, in practice most of the members did not comply as prescribed under the rules and therefore this concern was incorporated into the Doha Round agenda. Moreover, on 14 December 2006, the General Council established, on a provisional basis, a new transparency mechanism for all RTAs. It envisages that Members would review and, if necessary, modify the decision, and replace it with a permanent mechanism adopted as part of the overall results of the Doha Round.[16]

At present, the WTO Members are required to notify the WTO Secretariat of the details of their preferential trade deals[17] under the following conditions:

(a) Early Announcement. Members participating in new negotiations aimed at the conclusion of an RTA should inform the WTO Secretariat of such negotiations;

(b) Notification of ratification. The PTA should be notified as early as possible and, in general, no later than the parties' ratification of the PTA, or on the application of an agreement and before the application of preferential treatment between the parties;

(c) Subsequent notification and reporting. Any changes affecting the implementation of a PTA, or an already implemented PTA, should also be notified to WTO; and

(d) RTA implementation period. The parties must submit to WTO a short written report on the realization of liberalization commitments in the RTA as originally notified.

Of all agreements involving at least one Asian or Pacific economy, 155 are enforced, 12 are pending ratification and 64 are being negotiated. With regard to RTA transparency, notification is required for all of these categories. However, only 151 of these PTAs have been notified to WTO by the Asia-Pacific economies (133 of which are in force, 2 are pending ratification and 16 are still under negotiation). In addition, the largest number of PTAs that have not been notified to WTO are in the "under negotiation" category (figure 6.8). The exact reason for no notification is not known; however, one possibility could be a lack of awareness of the notification procedure.

**Figure 6.8. Preferential trade agreements with WTO notification, June 2015**

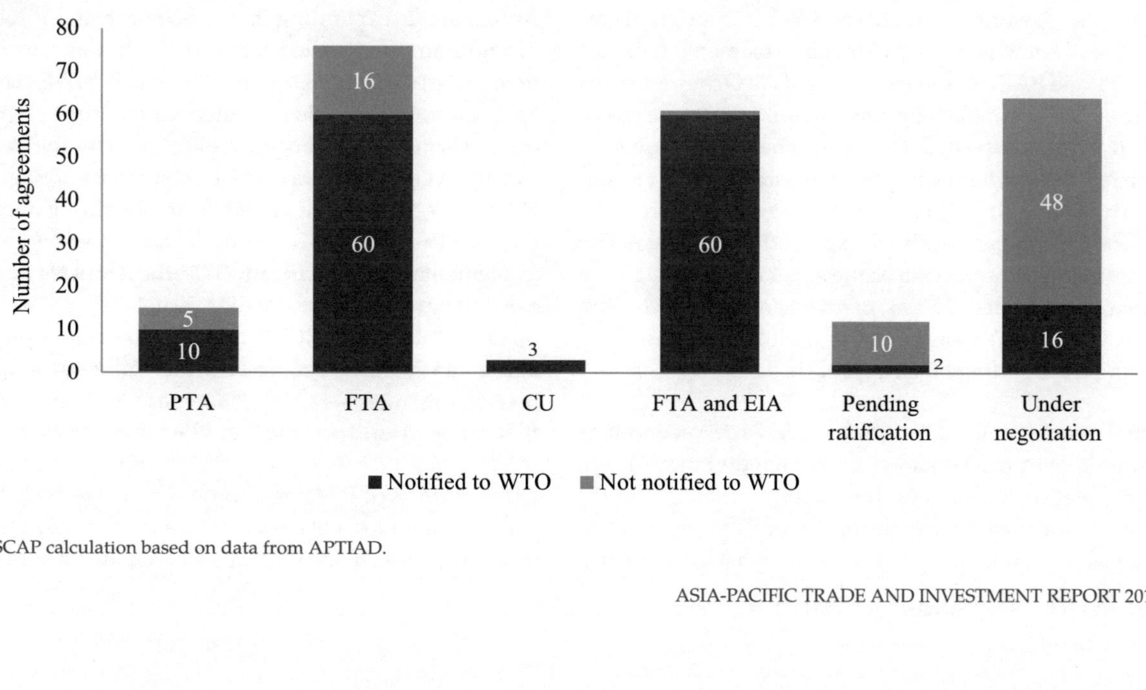


*Source:* ESCAP calculation based on data from APTIAD.

CHAPTER 6

Another important issue related to the transparency mechanism is submission of data by the PTA parties.[18] As shown earlier in this chapter, it can be difficult to get data, even for total MFN trade, for calculating trade with PTA partners. In several Asia-Pacific economies there is a big time lag in data availability (e.g. on some cases, even data for 2013 were not available in July 2015).

The transparency mechanism requires WTO Members to notify import statistics, especially those for each party's imports from the rest of the world, broken down into the country of origin in terms of value. It also recognizes the constraints facing developing countries in collecting the data. It would be useful to have the total MFN trade data as well as preferential trade data in order to carry out a complete analysis of benefits and losses of PTA. It is important for the developing and least developed countries to make an effort to capture the preferential trade data for inclusion in their trade statistics. Unfortunately, most of those economies do not have the preferential trade data, neither within the government domain nor in the public domain. This creates greater challenges for policymakers as they cannot draw on their past assessments for negotiating new agreements, not can they evaluate actual trade under each PTA and whether or not the agreement really benefits their economy.

The WTO transparency provision is an important step in getting countries to make the effort to capture and then disseminate preferential trade data. Such a step will be useful for various assessments of the ex post facto analysis of the PTAs. At the same time, most of the preferential trade remedies cannot be taken due to the lack of this data. In most of the stakeholders' consultations in preparation for PTA negotiations, the industry is often given to understand that the preferential trade remedial measures will be available. However, due to the lack of preferential trade data the industry fails to establish the fact that the surge in preferential imports is causing damage to the domestic industry and thus no remedial actions can be taken. This leads to a situation where the Governments initiate global remedial measures, thus penalizing those exporters who have not been the cause of such preferential surge and resulting in the creation of more barriers than necessary to legitimately protect the domestic industry.

RTA transparency could therefore be an important tool for economies when building their capacity and seeking technical assistance in developing a mechanism for capturing preferential trade data. This would also be useful for policymakers when assessing which PTA is more useful for exports and imports, as it would enable them to make an informed decision on consolidating PTAs.

# D CONCLUSION

Asia-Pacific economies, initially considered to be latecomers to reciprocal preferential negotiations, have advanced rapidly to claim a leading position and contribute the largest share of PTAs, both in terms of the overall number and in adding new agreements to the list. However, Asia-Pacific economies are now looking towards "next generation" agreements – covering areas beyond WTO through mega-blocs. These "new generation" mega-agreements (such as RCEP, TPP and EAEU) cover areas beyond WTO commitments and are aimed at establishing new disciplines in these areas. Thus, it can be expected that a number of agreements negotiated some time ago might be revisited with a view to not only deepening their current, relatively shallow liberalization content but also to expand their coverage. The ultimate objective appears to be the generation, through the web of a critical mass of PTAs, of a consensus for including these beyond WTO areas in future multilateral agenda by following the building block approach.

One of the remaining challenges for Asia-Pacific economies is the multiplicity of PTA known as the "noodle bowl". There is no correlation between (a) the number of PTAs and (b) the share of trade and its expansion under PTAs. Economies with a lesser number of agreements often have are greater share of intra-PTA trade than those that sign a large number of PTAs. It is therefore important that economies start reducing the complexity of negotiated terms and attempt to consolidate their multiple PTAs, which will ease the terms of trade transactions. A few such efforts in the Asia-Pacific region appear to be underway. The Asia-Pacific Trade Agreement is expanding its membership and is looking to provide an open-ended agreement that any developing member of ESCAP can join. It remains to be seen if the agreement can be also opened to the three developed countries in the Asia-Pacific region and if, at the same time, it can convert itself into a high-standard free trade agreement. Other agreements that are emerging as strong alternatives are RCEP, and TPP. It is not certain whether, after the implementation of RCEP and TPP, the ASEAN+1 and other existing agreements (more than 50 in total) will be nullified or not. Only when RCEP and TPP become open-ended agreements and overtake all other bilateral agreements between its members, can true consolidation be achieved that can truly address the "noodle bowl" problem.

Transparency of PTAs is another challenge that the Asia-Pacific economies will have to address. Some 23 agreements, especially those in the Central Asia region (14 agreements), out of 156 agreements in force have not been notified to WTO despite the transparency mechanism under which WTO members are required to provide details of PTAs to the WTO secretariat. Another issue regarding the transparency mechanism is the submission of data as discussed in this chapter. The lack of data may create disadvantages for policymakers as well as domestic industries as various data-based analysis and assessments of the PTAs cannot be produced. The availability of preferential trade data will be useful not only to researchers, but also to policymakers, since they would be able to evaluate in actual terms the benefits and gains from the PTAs. This will be useful to future negotiations as well as policymaking.

## ENDNOTES

[1] In line with much of the existing literature, this report also uses the term "preferential trade agreement (PTAs)" as a generic term for any form of negotiated reciprocal preferential trade agreement between two or more economies. The WTO convention is to use "regional trade agreements" as the generic term encompassing both bilateral and multi-country (plurilateral) agreements. However, because of the specific characteristics of the economic integration process in Asia and the Pacific, which comprises five subregions that are all pursuing some form of "regional" liberalization, it was thought that using preferential trade agreement as a generic form would lessen terminological use of "noodle bowl". The key features of any generic term here is that it must describe a process that is both reciprocal and discriminatory in the context of not providing trade preferences for all WTO members; however, preferences that are provided are on a reciprocal basis. A summary of the applied taxonomy is provided in the Annex.

[2] This number refers only to the so-called "physical" agreements reported by the WTO as of 6 May 2015 (see website at http://rtais.wto.org/UI-publicsummarytable.aspx). Normally, the WTO reports the number of trade agreements based on notification requirements, which means that if a trade agreement includes both goods and services, it will be counted as two notifications – one for goods and the other for services – even though it is physically one trade agreement. To prevent unnecessary inflation of the number of agreements, only the physical number of trade agreements is reported here, counting goods and services between the same partners as one.

[3] In addition to the agreements notified to WTO, the Asia-Pacific Trade and Investment Agreements Database (APTIAD) records agreements that have not been notified to WTO, which has resulted in the increased number.

[4] For example, previous issues of the Asia-Pacific Trade and Investment Report (ESCAP, 2009, 2010, 2011a, 2011b, 2012a, 2012b , 2013 and 2014) as well as other publications by the ESCAP Trade and Investment Division, including APTIAD Briefing Notes.

[5] Classified as Partial Scope Agreements (partial tariff reduction commitments), free trade agreements (FTAs), custom unions (CU), and economic integration agreements (EIAs), which in the WTO taxonomy are reserved for services only.

[6] Classified as bilateral, plurilateral or country-bloc agreements.

[7] Classified as "in force", "pending country ratification" or "under negotiation".

[8] The numbers presented in figure 6.1 are based on the established WTO practice of self-classification by economies with regard to their development level. Following that practice, only three Asia-Pacific economies are "developed" and the remainder are "developing", including the special category of least developed countries, despite the fact that a number of them have a high rate of GDP per capita and a not-insignificant share in world trade.

[9] This number ignores the deal signed between China and Taiwan Province of China, which is still not in force (according to the WTO RTA-IS database at http://rtais.wto.org/UI/PublicShowMemberRTAIDCard.aspx?rtaid=713). In addition, the Mongolia-Japan FTA was signed but has not yet been ratified.

[10] There are 92 bilateral PTAs between developing economies, 28 between developing and developed economies and 4 between developed economies.

[11] From the number of parties to the nature of the agreement, 22 plurilateral agreements are very diverse. The agreement with the largest membership is GSTP (44 members). Some agreements have the same core membership but are able to present themselves as different PTAs. Some of these emanate from the political split among the original membership (e.g. Commonwealth of Independent States Free Trade Area (CISFTA) and Commonwealth of Independent States (CIS)).

[12] In fact, while Asia-Pacific economies do not notify inactive agreements (apart from Turkey), there is no economic rationale for not cancelling inactive agreements or those that have been surpassed by more advanced versions. Australia and New Zealand did so when they reached a new agreement in 1982 and placed their previous agreement, signed in 1965, into the "inactive" category. There are several candidates for cancellation among agreements categorized as "in force" at present (e.g. the Lao People's Democratic Republic-Thailand partial scope trade agreement notified in 1991).

[13] Despite the official titles given to the agreed texts, WTO members are able to choose only among four different "types" when notifying their agreements. These four types are: free trade agreements and customs unions (for goods); economic integration agreements (for services); and partial scope agreements (only for agreements between developing countries).

[14] Please refer to endnote 1 with regard to interchangeability of use of terms PTAs and RTAs.

[15] A similar provision exists under Article 5 of the General Agreement on Trade in Services (GATS).

[16] The new transparency mechanism provides for early announcement and notification to WTO of any RTA. Members will consider the notified RTAs on the basis of a factual presentation by the WTO Secretariat. The Committee on Regional Trade Agreements will consider RTAs falling under Article XXIV of the General Agreement on Tariffs and Trade (GATT) and Article V of GATS. The Committee on Trade and Development will consider RTAs falling under the Enabling Clause (trade arrangements between developing countries).

[17] The details include information related to the official name of a PTA, its scope, date of signature, any foreseen timetable for its entry into force or provisional application, relevant contact points and/or website addresses, and any other relevant unrestricted information.

[18] Annex of WTO Document WT/L/671.

## REFERENCES


Economist Intelligence Unit (2014). *FTAs: fantastic, fine or futile? Business views on trade agreements in Asia–A survey by the Economist Intelligence Unit.* Available from https://globalconnections.hsbc.com/downloads/ftas_fantastic_fine_or_futile.pdf

Ing, Lili Yan, and Shujiro Urata, eds. (2015). The use of FTAs in ASEAN: survey-based analysis. ERIA Research Project Report 2013, No. 5. Jakarta: Economic Research Institute for ASEAN and East Asia. Available from www.eria.org/publications/research_project_reports/FY2013/No.5.html

United Nations, Economic and Social Commission for Asia and the Pacific (2009). *Asia-Pacific Trade and Investment Report 2009: Trade-led Recovery and Beyond.* Sales No. E.09.II.F.19. Available from www.unescap.org/resources/asia-pacific-trade-and-investment-report-2009-trade-led-recovery-and-beyond

____ (2010). *Asia-Pacific Trade and Investment Report 2010: Recent Trends and Developments.* ST/ESCAP/2590. Bangkok. Available from www.unescap.org/resources/asia-pacific-trade-and-investment-report-2010-recent-trends-and-developments .

______(2011a). *Asia-Pacific Trade and Investment Report 2011: Post-crisis Trade and Investment Opportunities.* Sales No. E.11.II.F.8, Available from www.unescap.org/resources/asia-pacific-trade-and-investment-report-2011-post-crisis-trade-and-investment

______(2011b). *Statistical Yearbook for Asia and the Pacific 2011.* Sales No. E.11.II.F.1, Available from www.unescap.org/stat/data/syb2011/escap-syb2011.pdf .

______(2012a). *Asia-Pacific Trade and Pacific Report 2011: Update March 2012.* Bangkok. Available from www.unescap.org/tid/ti_report2011/download/Asia-Pacific-Trade-and-Investment-Report-2011-Update-March-2012.pdf.

______(2012b). *Asia-Pacific Trade and Investment Report 2012: Recent Trends and Developments.* ST/ESCAP/2650. Bangkok. Available from www.unescap.org/resources/asia-pacific-trade-and-investment-report-2012-recent-trends-and-developments .

______(2013). *Asia-Pacific Trade and Investment Report 2013: Turning the Tide – Towards Inclusive Trade and Investment.* Sales No. E.14.II.F.2 Available from http://www.unescap.org/resources/asia-pacific-trade-and-investment-report-2013-turning-tide-towards-inclusive-trade-and

______(2014). *Asia-Pacific Trade and Investment Report 2014: Recent Trends and Development.* Available from www.unescap.org/resources/asia-pacific-trade-and-investment-report-2014-recent-trends-and-developments

World Bank (2005). *Global Economic Prospects 2005.* Available from www.worldbank.org/content/dam/Worldbank/GEP/GEParchives/GEP2005/GEP2005Chap2.pdf.

World Trade Organization (2015). Falling import demand, lower commodity prices push down trade growth prospects. Press Release PRESS/752, 30 September. Available from www.wto.org/english/news_e/pres15_e/pr752_e.htm.

________(2014) World Tariff Profiles 2014. Available from www.wto.org/english/res_e/booksp_e/tariff_profiles14_e.pdf


## ONLINE DATABASES


United Nations, Economic and Social Commission for Asia and the Pacific. Asia-Pacific Trade and Investment Trade Agreements Database. Available from http://artnet.unescap.org/databases.html#second

United Nations, Statistics Division, Department of Economic and Social Affairs. UN Comtrade database. Available from www.comtrade.un.org.

World Trade Organization, Regional Trade Agreements Information System. Available from rtais.wto.org/UI/PublicMaintainRTAHome.aspx

# Annex

## Taxonomy of trade agreements

| Scope of beneficiaries | Method of implementation: Reciprocal | Method of implementation: Non-reciprocal (unilateral) |
|---|---|---|
| Preferential to selected countries (bilateral or plurilateral) | ATIGA, SAFTA, EAEU and other PTAs* | Generalized System of Preferences, Everything but Arms, other unilateral preferential arrangements** |
| Non-discriminatory and given at MFN basis to all members of WTO | WTO multilateral agreements | Autonomous (unilateral) liberalization |

*Source:* Adapted from World Bank, 2005.
*Notes:* The database is available at http://ptadb.wto.org/?lang=1.
* Examples are provided from the pool of PTAs involving Asia-Pacific economies.
**All developed countries and a number of developing economies have put in place some non-reciprocal trade preferential arrangements.

# PART 2

## SUPPORTING PARTICIPATION IN VALUE CHAINS

# 7 GLOBAL VALUE CHAINS AND INTERCONNECTEDNESS OF ASIA-PACIFIC ECONOMIES

The term "global value chains" (GVCs) has been used to describe the sequence of all functional activities required in the process of value creation involving more than one country (UNCTAD, 2013).[1] According to UNCTAD (2013), "about 60 per cent of global trade, which today amounts to more than $20 trillion, consists of trade in intermediate goods and services that are incorporated at various stages in the production process of goods and services for final consumption."[2]

Global Value Chains will become increasingly influential in determining future trade and FDI patterns as well as growth opportunities. Experience from the Asia-Pacific region shows that the benefits from participation in GVCs are multilayered, ranging from the company level where GVCs can bolster productivity of participating enterprises and provide opportunities for creation of high(er)-skilled and better paid jobs, to the macro level with enhanced economic growth and higher per capita income.[3] An effective development strategy will now require policy approaches to effectively facilitate dynamic insertion of local companies into GVCs.

Informed policies require good data and analysis. It is therefore essential to understand how GVCs work in Asia and the Pacific, and especially how policies can help countries strengthen their GVC participation. Drawing on alternative indicators of GVC involvement, the objective of this chapter is to improve understanding of current and emerging issues related to GVC development in Asia and the Pacific. It sets out the main evidence as well as the implications of trade and trade-related policies for strengthening GVC participation by Asia-Pacific economies. Systematic investigation shows how policies related to trade and trade facilitation could strengthen the role of Asia-Pacific exporters in GVC-trade networks. In addition, the different capacities of Asia-Pacific economies to engage in that process should not be taken for granted. Asia-Pacific economies at different development levels have different styles of engagement with these networks. At one extreme are low-income economies whose firms specialize in tasks that rely on low-wage/unskilled labour and may have limited opportunities to benefit from technology dissemination and skills upgrading. At the other extreme are the high-income economies that tend to control the knowledge-intensive tasks of the network. Finally, the chapter informs policymakers of the different policy needs for facilitating the adjustment process of GVC participation by economies of different development levels.

# A CONCEPTS AND DEVELOPMENT BENEFITS OF GVCS

## 1. What are GVCs?

The concept of "value chain" implies a full range of functions (or activities) undertaken to collect various inputs and assemble them into final products (figure 7.1). At each individual function in this process, a certain value is added; these values are then accumulated in a final product.[4]

> *"A Global Value Chain is a sequence of all functional activities required in the process of value creation involving more than one country."*

A decline in trade costs due to trade liberalization and the technological advancement of communications, logistics, shipping and transport allows for most if not all individual functions in a value chain – which earlier had to be performed within a smaller geographical area (typically one country) – to be located where they could be produced most efficiently anywhere in the world (taking into consideration a combination of price, quality, timeliness and other factors). This separability of functions or tasks allowed for value chains to evolve in the international context where there is "trade in tasks" between countries participating in the same value chain.

Although the nature of GVCs may be sector-specific, they typically involve the movement of intermediate goods through successive countries within the global network system of multinational companies (MNCs). The global production strategies of MNCs result in shifting the focus of global trade from trade in final consumer items (goods and services) to trade in intermediate inputs.

**Figure 7.1. A simplified value chain**

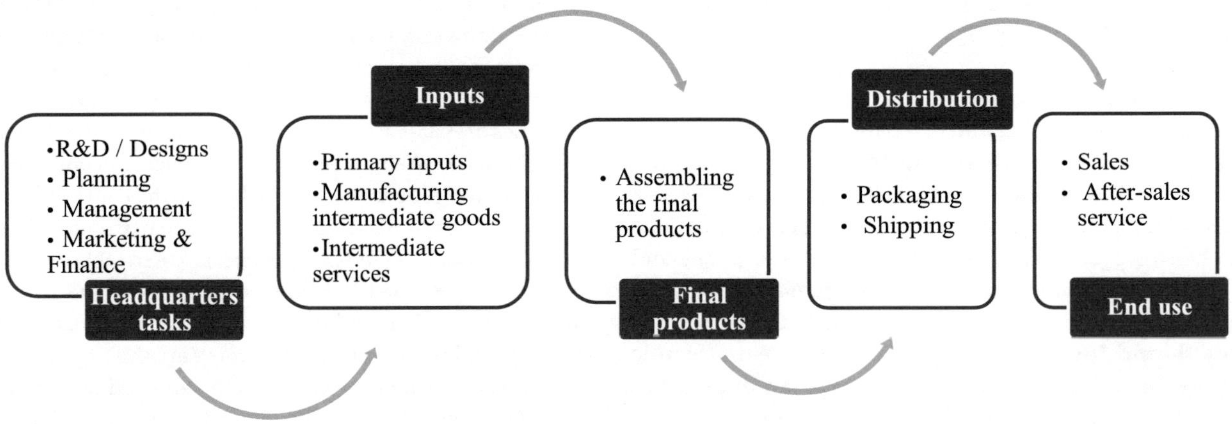


*Source:* ESCAP.

The development of GVCs has taken place in various sectors, such as apparel and footwear, automobiles, electronics and the agro-food industry.[5] Although GVCs have sector-specific characteristics, they typically involve the movement of intermediate goods through a series of countries where, in each one, a new value is designed, coordinated and implemented through the global network system. This has enabled some local enterprises in developing countries to also participate as providers of inputs (goods and services) based on their expertise.

While the term GVCs is widely used, in general, researchers have not differentiated between GVCs and "global production networks". There are also other terms related to the GVC phenomenon that are used interchangeably in the economics literature, such as "disintegration of process", "international production sharing" and "international unbundling of production".[6] The term "international product fragmentation" is also often used in the economics literature when describing the split of the production process in the GVC phenomenon across countries.

The unbundling of the production process in the GVC phenomenon can be both geographical (across countries) and organizational (across firms). According to Cattaneo and others (2013), when the fragmented process of production takes place within a firm but at its foreign locations, it is called "offshoring" or "offshore production". The offshoring activities are conducted via vertical foreign direct investment (FDI), and trade within a respective GVC is considered to be an intra-firm trade.[7] In contrast, if the activities are subcontracted to independent contractors and suppliers, the term "outsourcing" is often used to highlight the fact that trade within a respective GVC is at an arm's length in nature. In this context, Antràs and Helpman (2004) simplify the possible organizational and geographical structure of GVCs into a matrix of four sourcing strategies (figure 7.2). Operations can take place inside the lead firm and in its home country, which is referred to as domestic in-house production (the upper left quadrant of the matrix). Second, production stages can take place inside the firm but with some operated in a foreign country through offshore production via vertical FDI (the lower left quadrant of the matrix). Alternatively, firms can outsource activities to independent suppliers. This is called "arm's length relationship". If the arm's length suppliers are based in the same country as the lead firm, the strategy is called domestic outsourcing (the upper right quadrant of the matrix). An alternative strategy is to offshore outsourcing, which implies that the arm's length suppliers operate in a foreign location. It is important to note that the possible sourcing strategies described and defined above can apply to any stage of the production and business process, from the design stage to the final assembly stage.

These global sourcing strategies result in greater FDI, especially of the vertical type, and increased intra-firm trade as well as vertical arm's length trade between a lead firm and its suppliers. According to UNCTAD (2013), the ratio between global FDI stock and trade has almost doubled from around 50% in the mid-1990s to more than 100% in 2010. UNCTAD estimates that around 80% of global trade (in terms of gross exports) is linked to the international production networks of MNCs (either as intra-firm trade, contract manufacturing, licensing or franchising), or through arm's length transactions involving at least one MNC. In general, the rise of GVCs is linked in particular to greater efficiency-seeking FDI, through which MNCs seek to locate discrete parts of their production process in low-cost locations (box 7.1). Efficiency-seeking FDI increases the amount of trade taking place within the international production networks of MNCs.

**Figure 7.2. Simplified illustration of sourcing strategies in GVCs**

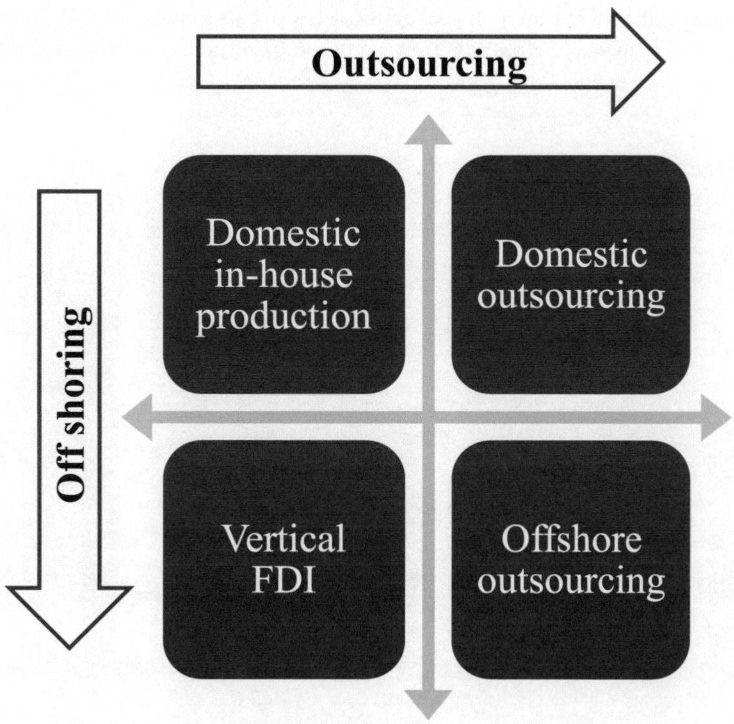


*Source:* ESCAP (adapted from Antràs and Helpman, 2004).

## Box 7.1 Outward FDI, trade cost and India's participation in GVCs[a]

Integration into international production networks or GVCs is viewed as a key to developing the manufacturing sector in India, which generates about 20% of GDP. However, India's level of participation in GVCs has remained lower than that of the other developing economies in Asia (Athukorala, 2011). As India is slowly starting to integrate into GVCs, it is important to examine the factors that may promote or create a hindrance to this process. A brief examination is made here of the impact of India's manufacturing outward FDI, on the one hand, and bilateral trade costs on the other hand, on production-network related exports from India to the FDI host countries.

The production network-related (or GVC) exports refer to exports of parts and components by manufacturing industries. Production network-related trade is dominant in certain manufacturing industries (e.g. machinery and electronics). However, there is no single measure of production network-related trade as it varies depending on the use of trade classification, coverage of industries and countries, level of disaggregation used, nature and intensity of such trade etc. (see, for example, Ando and Kimura, 2005; Athukorala, 2010; and Amighini, 2012). Nevertheless, in this note, the classification developed by Athukorala (2010) is used as it can capture production network-related trade in a wide range of manufacturing industries and is thus not limited to machinery parts and components only.

India's exports of parts and components have been growing at a slower pace than the country's overall manufacturing exports. As a result, the share of parts and components in total manufacturing exports has remained low (figure A). Similarly, manufacturing outward FDI has been growing slower than total outward FDI. Nevertheless, manufacturing outward FDI constitutes a significant fraction of total outward FDI (figure B), although its level does not change much.

The findings of the empirical analysis (see annex 7A) suggest that manufacturing outward FDI has a significant positive impact on exports of parts and components to the FDI host countries, even when inward FDI to India from the partner country does not change. On the other hand, bilateral trade costs have a significant negative impact on production network-related exports.

The results have a pertinent implication for policy. In particular, encouraging outward FDI in the manufacturing sector could significantly improve India's participation in international production networks. On the other hand, in line with existing wisdom, trade costs reduce exports of parts and components to the FDI host countries of India.

### Figure A. India's exports of parts and components

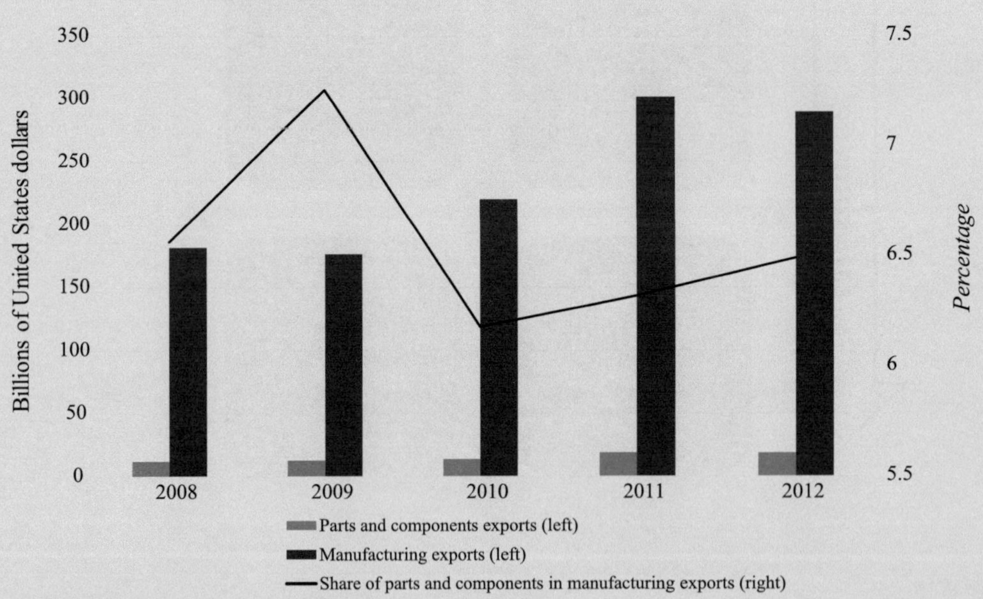


*Source:* Author's compilation from United Nations Comtrade (using SITC Rev. 3 data)

**Figure B. Outward FDI by Indian firms**

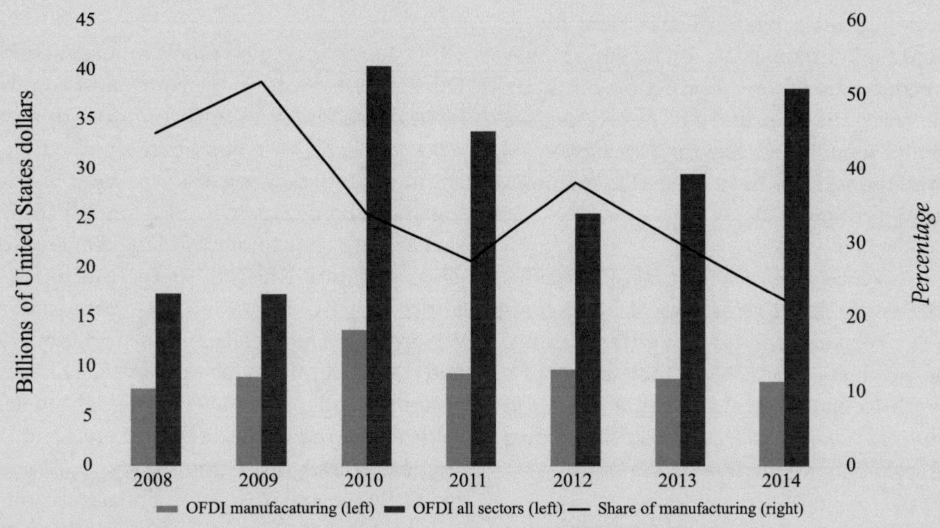


*Source:* Author's compilation from Reserve Bank of India (using firm-level outward FDI data).

[a] Box 7.1 and annex 7A were prepared by Khanindra Ch. Das, Assistant Professor, Rajiv Gandhi Indian Institute of Management, India.

## 2. What are the main drivers of GVCs?

The current GVC phenomenon has some distinctive features that have attracted research attention worldwide. One is the pace and scale of GVC expansion, which is now faster and wider than ever before. In addition, international sharing of production is no longer restricted to developed countries, but increasingly involves developing countries, including emerging ones.[8] Factors influencing the decision by firms to internationally fragment their production are discussed by a large body of literature.[9] Based on that literature, figure 7.3 identifies three groups of factors that are linked to: (a) cost efficiency; (b) market access; and (c) low international trade costs. The main categories or examples of each of these are also listed in figure 7.3.

> *"For GVCs to emerge, trade costs must be low enough to enable firms utilizing country-specific advantages related to cost efficiency and/or market access."*

**Figure 7.3 Main factors behind GVCs**

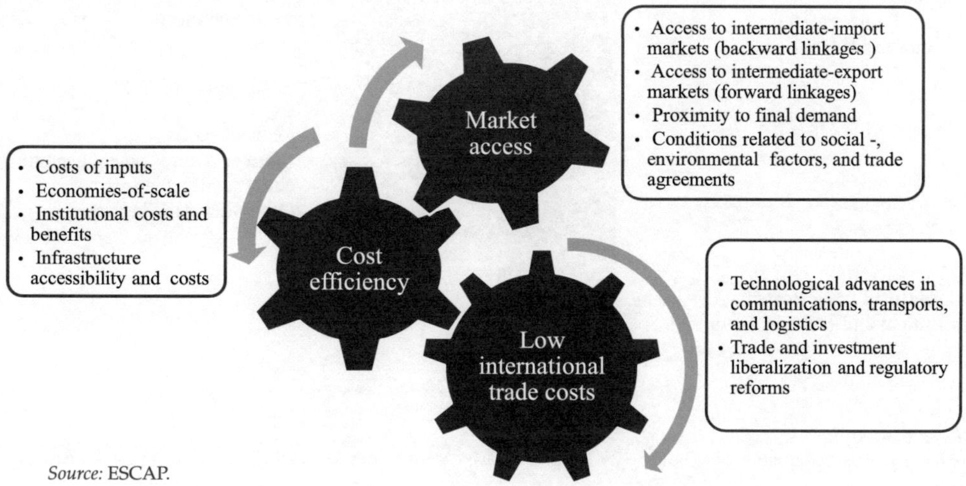


*Source:* ESCAP.

International production sharing in GVCs takes place on different geographic scales (regional and global). As described by Jones and Kierzkowski (2001), the level of fragmentation depends on a trade-off between lower production costs and higher trade costs. By locating stages of production in economies where production costs are lower, firms can decrease the marginal cost of production; however, they may then incur higher fixed and variable costs that correspond to all the services links needed to maintain production in several locations.

The pace and scale of GVC expansion in the past two decades are associated with a significant reduction of trade costs (OECD, 2013b). A precondition for the international unbundling of the production process is that trade costs must be low enough to enable firms to utilize location advantages of countries arising from factor-price differences and economies-of-scale (Anukoonwattaka, 2011).[10]

Trade costs include the whole range of costs incurred by a firm when bringing goods or services from the place of production to where users or consumers are located.[11] GVC operations require intermediate inputs to be manufactured in one or more countries and then shipped to another destination for final assembly, and a portion of trade costs are incurred each time a good-in-process crosses a border. An important cost element related to GVCs is coordination costs, as geographically dispersed activities have to be managed in a consistent way. Even a minor reduction in one or more trade cost elements can result in the cost of a vertically-integrated good being reduced considerably due to a cumulative effect of a change in tariffs.

Other factors can also result in a reduction of trade costs. During past decades, transport and communication costs have decreased first and foremost due to technological advances such as in container shipment or Internet-based communication. Progress has been made all along the logistics chain, ensuring the smooth flow of goods and services in a coordinated and inexpensive way. Lower trade costs are not limited to technological change. The improvements in trade cost-related infrastructure and services such as logistics, transportation, and information and communications technology (ICT), streamlined customs clearance, and more efficient financial and insurance services have helped reduce trade costs. Duval and Utoktham (2010) suggested that tariff trade costs in Asia and the Pacific generally account up to 10% of bilateral comprehensive trade costs, while other policy-related trade costs (i.e. of a non-tariff nature) account for 60% to 90% of bilateral trade costs (figure 7.4).

A trade cost reduction may make it profitable for firms, which had previously kept all of their production stages in one country, to move some stages of the production process to locations overseas. Firms that have already internationally fragmented their production are also likely to increase their flows of the component trade when trade costs decline.

**Figure 7.4. Contribution of various policy-related factors to changes in trade costs**

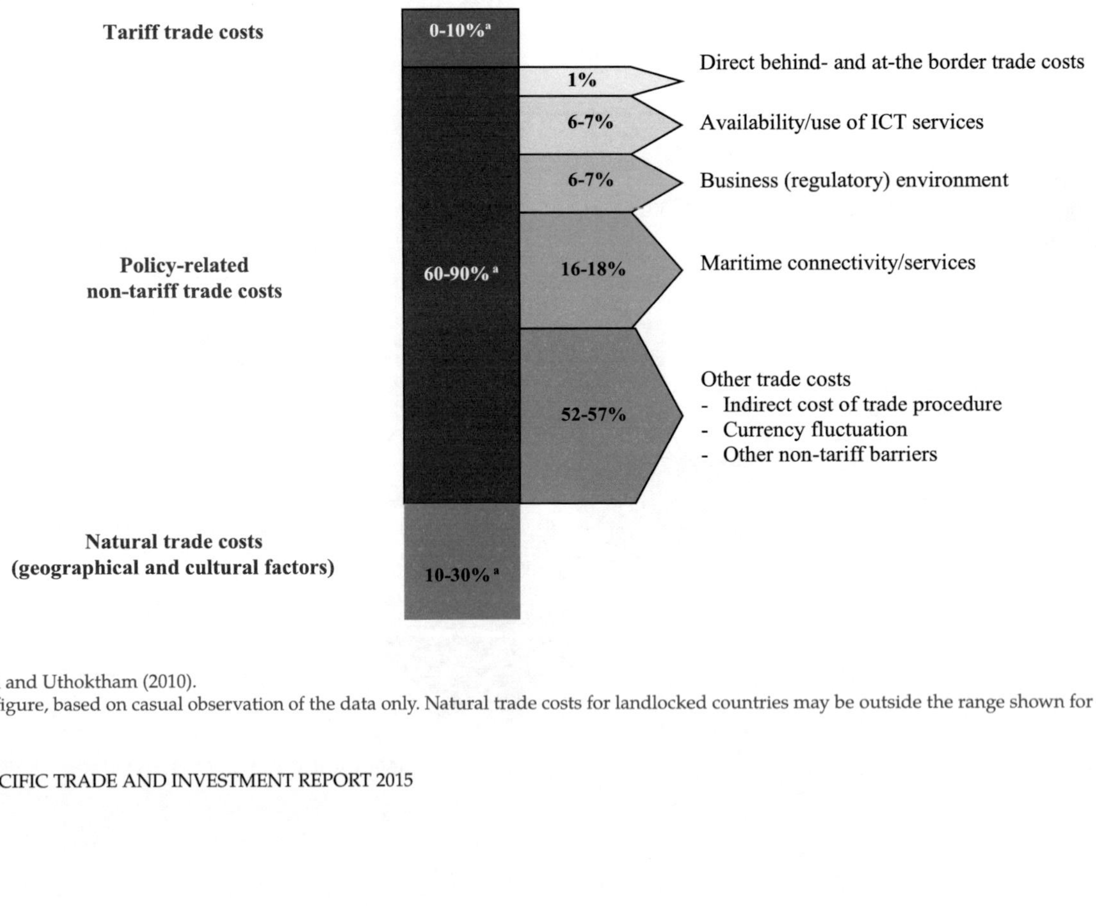


*Source:* Duval and Uthoktham (2010).

[a] Illustrative figure, based on casual observation of the data only. Natural trade costs for landlocked countries may be outside the range shown for natural trade costs.

Another motivation for firms to internationally fragment their production is the opportunity to increase efficiency, as growing competition in domestic and international markets forces firms to become more efficient and focused on lowering costs. Spreading production stages over different countries may allow an MNC to achieve necessary production cost savings because some required inputs such as labour, natural resources, and intermediate goods and services, may be available in some countries at cheaper rates than in the home country of the MNC.[12]

However, resource endowment is not the only source of location advantages. For certain tasks of the value chains that involve high fixed costs, the potential for achieving scale economies becomes a dominant factor explaining why a country has been able to participate in some parts of GVCs.[13] Institutional and infrastructure factors also have impacts on cost competitiveness. In addition, the availability of infrastructure and related costs, tax incentives, preferential trade arrangements and existing regulatory frameworks are among the factors that determine the participation by a country in GVCs (Bhattacharya and Moazzem, 2013).

Another important form of motivation is entry into new markets and access to strategic inputs. In a GVC context, backward linkages mean that a country imports intermediate goods to be used in its exports, while forward linkages exist when a country exports inputs to be used in exports by other countries. The efficiency of backward linkages requires that GVC-participating firms are able to access the most efficient inputs either from domestic markets or imports. At the same time, the efficiency of forward linkages requires access to downstream producers who will further process the exports (if those exports are intermediate goods) or consumers (if those exports are final products). It is important to note that the spread of fragmented production is not necessarily across countries; instead, it may be concentrated in a certain region. The issue is emphasized in the literature on "New Economic Geography", which shows there are "agglomeration effects" that draw firms to cluster in a certain area in order to benefit from positive externality in the form of knowledge spillovers and backward- and forward-linkages. Conditions for certain locations to provide benefits from the agglomeration effects are related to social, environmental, geographical and trade agreements.[14] This report gives particular attention to exploring how trade agreements and regional integration have an impact on the location of GVCs.

## 3. How are regional integration and GVCs related?

The expansion of GVCs has opened opportunities for firms to strengthen their regional components in order to support deeper integration within Asia and the Pacific by allowing economies to pursue the division of labour and specialization in tasks as opposed to product-based comparative advantages. For example, technology-intensive parts and components of electronics products are produced in relatively advanced industrial countries of the region, such as Japan, and the Republic of Korea, while the assembling of different intermediates into finished products is taking place elsewhere in the region, i.e. in emerging economies such as China and Viet Nam. The regional nature of GVCs has been confirmed by empirical literature using inter-country input-output tables. For example, Baldwin (2013) pointed out that much of the value-added distribution in GVCs tends to be within regional blocs that are broadly defined as "Factory Europe", "Factory North America" and "Factory Asia". Backer and Yamano (2012) indicated that around three-quarters of the intermediates embodied in exports from the European Union are sourced within Europe. Similarly, Canada and Mexico are heavily oriented towards the other North-American Free Trade Agreement (NAFTA) members; more than 50% of the imported intermediates embodied in their exports originate somewhere in the NAFTA zone.

> *"Regional integration initiatives are driving GVCs, but are also themselves driven by GVCs."*

The regional nature of GVCs may be related to the role played by trade costs. Other things being equal, countries appear to source intermediates from nearby countries in order to minimize transportation costs that are an important part of trade costs. Regional integration agreements may partly reduce trade costs between countries within a respective region, especially if such agreements provide for deep integration beyond market access. In other words, integration agreements that include liberalization of services trade, investment provisions, intellectual property rights protection, and the harmonization of standards and regulations will make cross-border production more efficient.

The empirical literature is rich with evidence pointing to a positive association between the existence of regional trade agreements and existence of regional value chains (regional production fragmentation) (see, for example, Johnston and Noguera, 2012; Hayakawa and Yamashita 2011; Blyde, Graziano and Martincus, 2014; and Orefice and Rocha, 2014). It appears that these two phenomena are mutually supporting; the deeper and more comprehensive trade integration agreements will go hand-in-hand with more expansive production sharing across borders in the region.

However, there is also the possibility of reverse causality. Orefice and Rocha (2014) found that the higher levels of trade in GVCs raised the likelihood of signing deeper agreements, especially between countries of different development levels. In addition, they found that the evidence appeared to be relatively strong for Asian countries. For example, following the implementation of NAFTA and the signature of the Mexico-European Union Free Trade Agreement, Japanese automobile manufacturers found themselves in a disadvantaged position and pushed the Government to sign an FTA with Mexico. In addition, Japanese FTAs often include beyond-the-border issues that help to improve the efficiency of international production networks such as trade facilitation, investment protection and facilitation, technical cooperation and international financial policy cooperation (Jerzewska, 2011).

## 4. How do GVCs contribute to development?

The ultimate development objectives of a country are socio-economic upgrading with more and better-remunerated jobs, a more sustainable use of resources, and better governance and political stability at large. Socio-economic upgrading often occurs as a process of "industrial upgrading", which now often occurs through the process of industrial transformation and trade within GVCs (WTO, 2014). Prior to the mid-1980s, achieving industrialization was largely synonymous with building the whole supply chain within one economy. This was done successfully through decade-long learning-by-doing by early entrants such as Japan, the Republic of Korea and Taiwan Province of China. Nowadays, a greater division of labour and segmentation of production on a global scale in GVCs allows more economies to benefit from trade. It is not necessary to develop vertically integrated industries in order to participate in global trade; it is enough to develop capacities in specific segments (stages of production, tasks or business functions) of the value chain. The learning process involved is then less complex and, as a result, industrialization is easier to achieve (Baldwin, 2011).[15] In other words, even small developing economies with limited capacities to develop a whole value chain now have a chance to operate tasks previously executed in developed economies, creating local jobs and value-added etc.

> *"GVCs bolster economic efficiency through productivity improvement and efficient allocation of resources."*

In terms of productivity and competitiveness upgrading, the GVC phenomenon offers an alternative outward-looking development model driven by trade and competitiveness. Firms participating in GVCs are pressured to become more competitive and engaged in innovative activities. The pressure arises from engaging in exporting, by operating in a market exposed to imports or by being exposed to foreign affiliates of MNCs. Also, the outsourcing and offshoring of less efficient activities to more efficient producers can increase the productivity of firms. Interactions between foreign affiliates and domestic firms in host countries increase the potential of knowledge and technological spillovers. Direct investment by MNCs may also positively affect productivity in host countries to the extent that they are more likely to offer training and on-the-job learning.

Evidence clearly shows that GVC-driven trade has brought investments in new productive capacity and infrastructure improvements in developing economies (OECD, 2013a). Key producing countries such as China, have developed enormous factory complexes whose output is sent to world markets through vast new port facilities (Stone and Shepherd, 2013). Participation in GVC activities has boosted employment, enabled increased specialisation and larger scale production, driven more efficient geographical allocation of industrial activities, and increased the availability of a variety of intermediate goods in the developing world (Gereffi, 2006).

## 5. Why are GVCs particularly important for small emerging economies?

> *"Participating in GVCs appears to provide a pathway for small economies to engage in global-scale production as well as entry to higher value-added activities."*

GVC participation enhances the possibilities for access to new types of production and to upgrade towards higher value-added activities. If and when they are able to participate in the international production networks of MNCs, the benefit for developing economies will be critical as it will unlock their development disadvantages arising from being a small domestic market as well as from insufficient capital and the lack the experience to meet international standards. In fact, the competitiveness improvements can be felt beyond the GVC-participating firms and export sectors. Local firms, in general, can achieve greater success in their own markets by combining domestic and imported intermediate inputs.

With regard to long-term development, preserving participation in GVCs requires greater attention to "upgrading" the segment in which firms and economies are involved. Business strategies in GVCs are dynamic. Participating firms have to be able to adjust quickly to changes in demand factors such as consumers' tastes and purchasing power, and supply factors affecting competition between producers at each stage of production. For emerging economies that, in general, started their participation in GVCs in the low-skilled, labour-intensive segments, economic growth and expansion of relatively labour-intensive segments will be followed by increasing real wages. Preserving a country's participation in GVCs for long-term development then requires upgrading, or moving up the value chain, which is also desirable from the perspective of higher benefits that will be received by an economy when it can participate in a higher value-added GVC segment.

As described by Humphrey and Schmitz (2002), there are four types of upgrading for enterprises within a value chain:

(a) Process upgrading – transforming inputs into outputs more efficiently by recognising the production system or introducing superior technology;

(b) Product upgrading – moving into more sophisticated product lines in terms of increased unit values;

(c) Functional upgrading – acquiring new, superior functions in the chain, such as design or marketing; and

(d) Intersectoral upgrading – applying the competences acquired in a particular function to move into a new sector.

Economies with limited capacity to upgrade into at least one of these four dimensions will eventually no longer be able to preserve their participation in GVCs.

# B GVCs AND ASIA-PACIFIC COUNTRIES: STYLIZED FACTS

The use of descriptive statistics allows for the identification of several stylized facts and trends as detailed below. [16]

## 1. Participation of Asia-Pacific economies in GVCs

*"The region is a major exporter of GVC final products, but not yet a major source of final demand."*

While it is clear that Asia-Pacific economies have been an important exporter of GVC products, final demand still comes mainly from developed economies outside the region. In 2013, about 45% of global GVC-related exports of final products came from the Asia-Pacific region, with exports by China representing half of the region's final exports (figure 7.5). In contrast, the region's imports of GVC final products accounted for just 26% of global imports. Imports of GVC final products are dominated by the United States and countries in the European Union.

**Figure 7.5. Major exporters and importers of GVC-final products, 2013**

*(Percentage share of total exports and imports)*

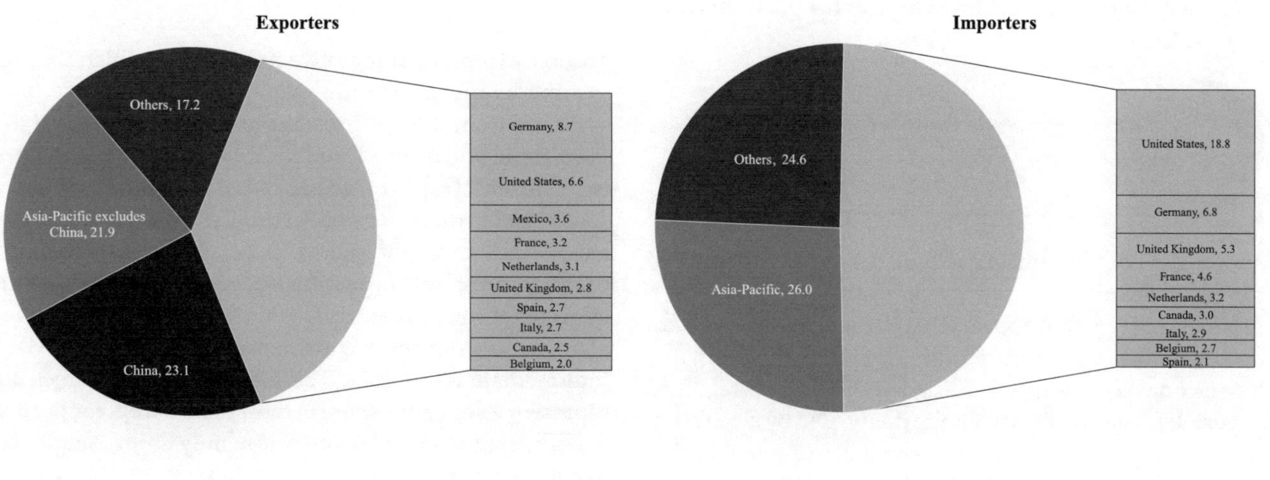


*Source:* ESCAP calculation based on data from the United Nations Comtrade database.
*Note:* See online appendix A for product list.

CHAPTER 7

## 2. In which countries are GVC trade opportunities mainly concentrated?

*"GVC participation of Asia and the Pacific appears to be largely concentrated in just 10 countries"*

While China dominates final products exports, other countries in the region have captured a significant share in the global trade of GVC-intermediate products. In 2013, 43% of global GVC-intermediate exports came from the Asia-Pacific region. At the same time, 38% of global GVC-intermediate imports went to the region. However, 90% of these trade flows are concentrated in just 10 countries, i.e. Australia, China, Japan, India, Indonesia, Malaysia, the Republic of Korea, Singapore, Thailand and Turkey (figure 7.6).

**Figure 7.6. Major exporters and importers of GVC-intermediate products, 2013**

*(Percentage share of total exports and imports)*

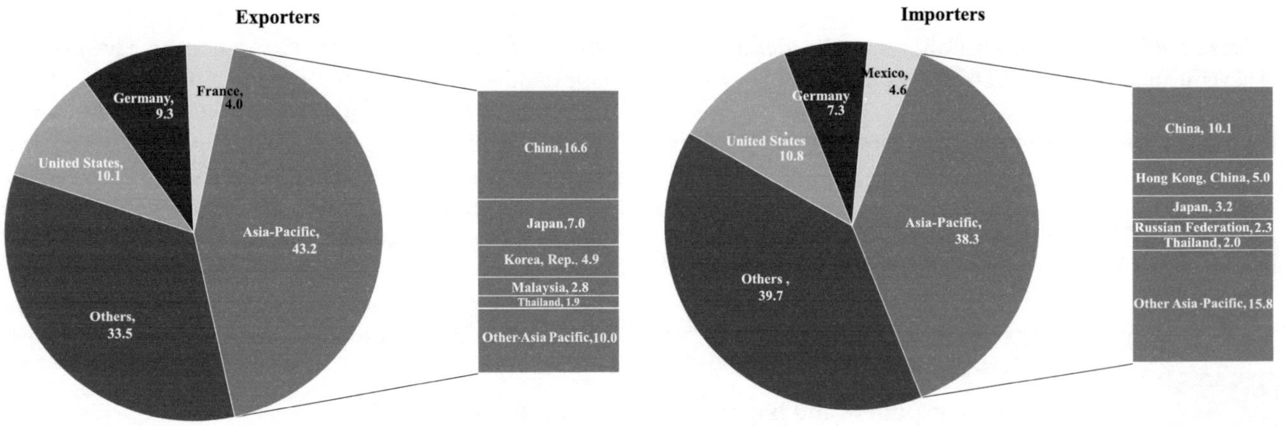


*Source:* ESCAP calculation based on data from the United Nations Comtrade database.
*Note:* See online appendix A for product list.

## 3. Does national income level matter for participation in GVCs?

*"The low-income economies are largely bypassed by GVCs."*

Although GVCs in principle should promote economies of different development levels to jointly take part in a production process, it appears that participants in GVCs are mostly in the high- and middle-income categories while low-income economies are being left out. In general, GVC exports by Asia and the Pacific are dominated by electronics from the upper-middle income economies (figure 7.7). The region is also prevalent in the exports of other product groups, except for automotive products, of which the high income countries are the major exporters. There is no evidence from the GVC-related trade data to the fear that everything will be produced in China; countries specialize in different product groups. For example, China is specialized in the exports of electronics. Turkey and Thailand have significant export shares, especially in the final exports of automotive and agriculture products. Malaysia is the largest exporter of processed agriculture intermediates while also accounting for a considerable share in exports of intermediate electronics. The low-income economies still represent a negligible share in most cases except for the final export of apparel and footwear, mainly from Bangladesh and Cambodia.-

Figure 7.7. Shares of Asia-Pacific economies by income groups in GVC export sectors, 2013

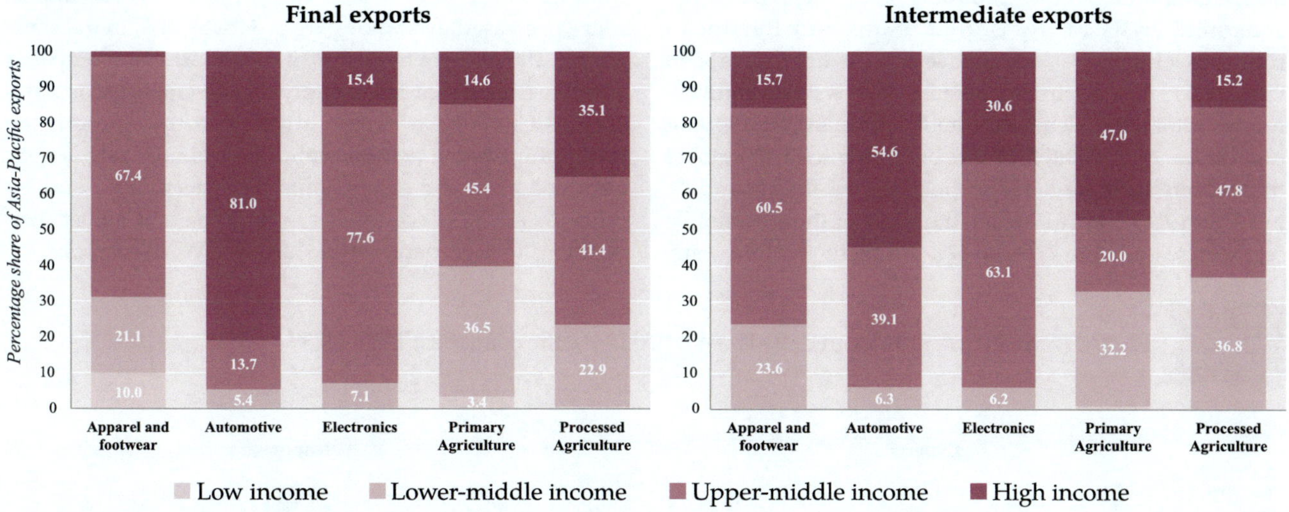


*Source:* ESCAP calculation based on data from the United Nations Comtrade database.
*Note:* See online appendix B for country list.

## 4. How did the recent global economic crisis affect GVCs?

> *"Core of demand for final goods has started to shift towards Asia and the Pacific."*

The 2008/2009 economic crisis in developed countries has accelerated global demand shift from the United States and the European Union towards developing economies. The Asia-Pacific region has significantly increased its stake in final imports by 7 percentage points, from 19% in 2007 to 26% in 2013 (figure 7.8). Exporters in developed countries are also aware of the drop in demand at home and are shifting their focus to emerging markets. An example is the case of Spanish group Inditex (Zara), which has opened retail outlets in China, India, Kazakhstan, the Republic of Korea and the Russian Federation with the hope of improving its financial performance after the crisis.

Figure 7.8. Shares of Asia and the Pacific in global trade of GVC final products, before and after the 2008-2009 global economic crisis

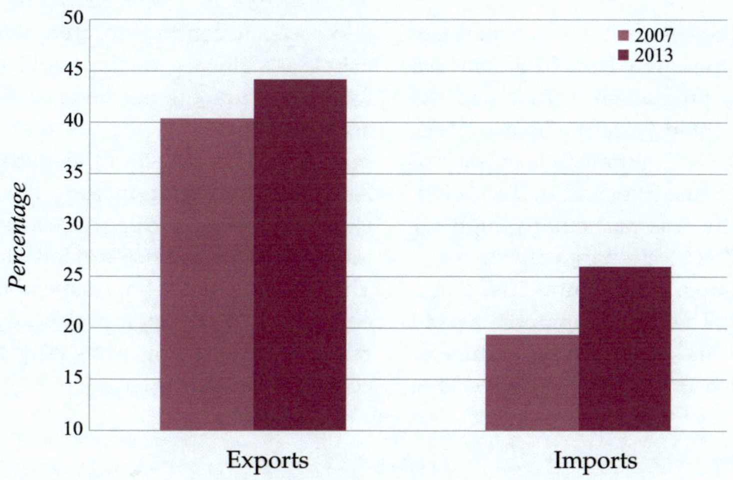


*Source:* ESCAP calculation based on data from the United Nations Comtrade database.

CHAPTER 7

The shifts in global demand appear to be triggering a restructuring of GVC intermediate trade. For example, there has been a significant drop in demand for final and intermediate electronics products since the start of the economic crisis in the United States and European countries.[17] In contrast, automotive intermediates have been less affected than electronics because there is still a relatively robust automotive demand from fast-growing developing economies. As a result, the share of electronics in the global trade of intermediate goods dropped significantly from 53% in 2006 to 25.5% in 2013 while the share of the automotive sector increased from 29.5% to 42% during those same years.

These global shifts have been reflected in the export structures of Asia and the Pacific. The share of intermediate electronics in the region's total intermediate exports dropped from 73% in 2006 to 43% in 2013 (figure 7.9). The import share decreased even more, from 74% to 38%, in the same period. The stronger reduction of the import share compared with the export share may imply that assembling countries such as China have already diversified their production towards upstream activities and, hence, now rely less on imported parts and components. This has put pressure on other Asia-Pacific economies to upgrade and adjust their positions in accordance with shifting GVC dynamics.

**Figure 7.9 Structure of intermediate trade by Asia-Pacific countries, 1995-2013**

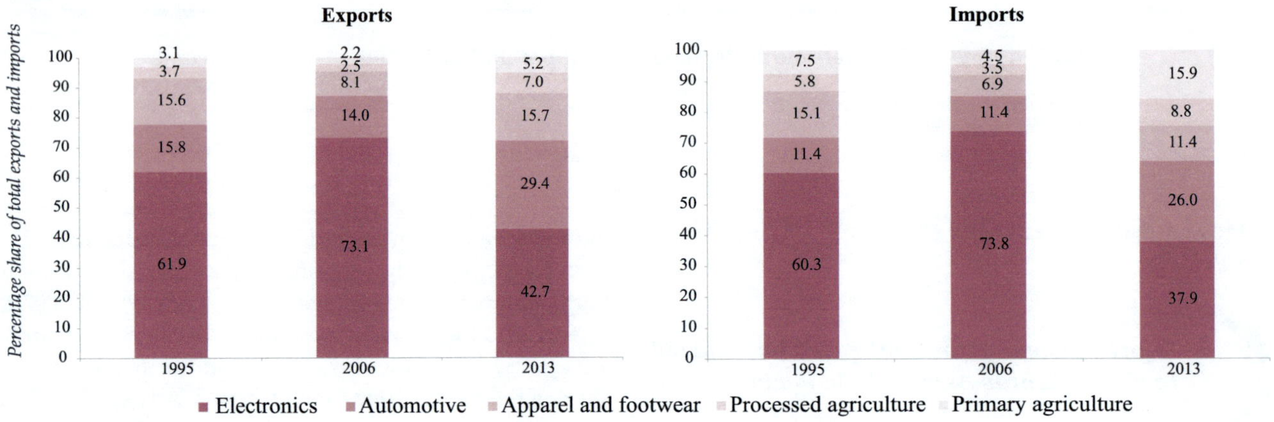


*Source:* ESCAP calculation based on data from the United Nations Comtrade database.

## 5. How is intraregional trade affected by GVCs?

> *"Intraregional trade, especially South-South trade, playing an increasing role."*

The share of intraregional exports in total intermediate exports by Asia-Pacific countries grew from 52.6% in 1995 to 58% in 2013. GVC-related production in Asia and the Pacific relies heavily on intraregional intermediate imports. In 2013, more than 65% of the GVC intermediate imports of Asian and Pacific economies came from within the region. The regional import intensity was particularly high for apparel and footwear as well as electronics, with shares of intraregional intermediate imports as high as 91.5% and 82%, respectively (figure 7.10). The regional import intensity was moderate for automotive and processed agriculture, of which the regional intermediate imports were 60% and 55%, respectively, in 2013. In contrast, the regional intensity for primary-agriculture imports was relatively low at 22%.

For final products, the regional export intensity of GVC final exports from Asia and the Pacific increased rapidly from 30.7% in 2007 to 37% in 2013. The regional trade intensity is expected to continue to strengthen if the region reaffirms its role as a global growth pole. However, the opportunities for rising intraregional trade in final products will differ across sectors. The sectors that have a relatively high potential to benefit from the global demand shift towards Asia and the Pacific include the apparel/footwear and electronics sectors, which have a high share of intraregional import at 86.5% and 76.6% of total final imports, respectively. These shifts in global final demand towards large developing economies in the region also add to the importance of regional integration, especially for smaller developing economies in the region.

## Figure 7.10. Shares of intraregional trade, 1995-2013

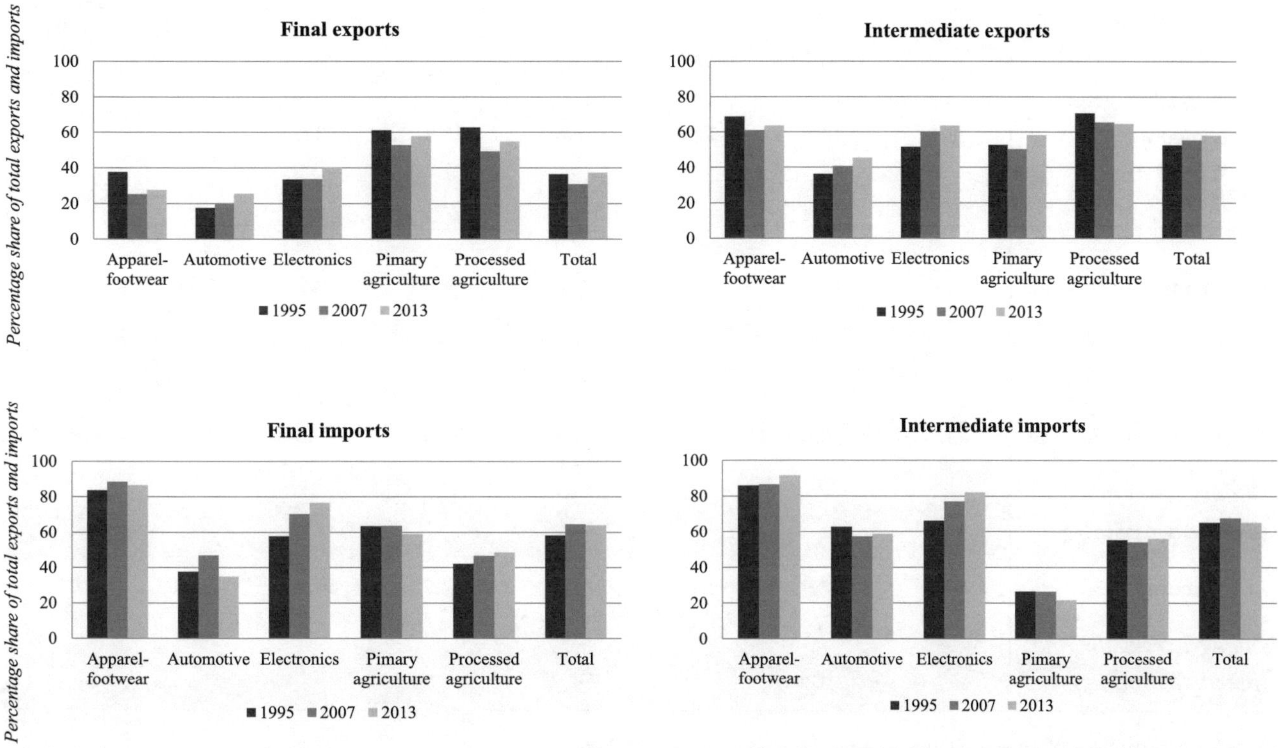


With the rising intraregional trade intensity of GVCs in Asia and the Pacific, there is also growing intraregional (South-South) trade among developing economies excluding those in the high-income category (hereafter referred to as "non-high income economies"). Trade statistics shows an increasing dependence of low-income economies' exports on middle-income markets, especially the upper-middle income countries, between 1995 and 2013 (table 7.1). Exports from low-income countries to the upper-middle-income countries in the Asia-Pacific region accounted for more than 66% of their intraregional intermediate exports and 33% of their intraregional final exports in 2013, which is a significant increase by 58 and 23 percentage points, respectively, from the export shares in 1995. Similarly, upper-middle-income Asia-Pacific countries as a group have become a major destination for intraregional exports from other income groups with shares of about 40.6% to 53% of the high-income countries' intraregional final and intermediate exports, 36.6% to 46% of those of the lower-middle income group, and 11.7% to 18.9% of the exports from the same group. In contrast, intraregional exports to the region's high-income countries have grown at a much slower rate. As a result, although intraregional exports to high-income countries are still significant, their shares of total intraregional exports have dropped considerably. For instance, the final exports to high-income economies accounted as much as 43.7% of the final exports by lower-middle income countries in 2013. However, that is a decrease by 39.1 percentage points compared to their share in 1995.

**Table 7.1. Intraregional exports of GVC products, by income group, 2013 and changes from 1995**

*(Percentage share of intraregional exports)*

| | Final goods | | | | Intermediate goods | | | |
|---|---|---|---|---|---|---|---|---|
| Importer / Exporter | High | Upper-middle | Lower middle | Low | High | Upper-middle | Lower-middle | Low |
| **High income** | **45.1** | **40.6** | **12.6** | **1.6** | **26.9** | **53.0** | **19.0** | **1.0** |
| *Changes from 1995 (percentage points)* | -30.0 | 23.3 | 6.2 | 0.6 | -25.6 | 15.6 | 10.1 | -0.1 |
| **Upper-middle income** | **74.4** | **11.7** | **11.8** | **2.1** | **58.0** | **18.9** | **18.0** | **5.1** |
| *Changes from 1995 (percentage points)* | -20.3 | 9.1 | 9.8 | 1.5 | -22.4 | 7.2 | 11.8 | 3.4 |
| **Lower-middle income** | **43.7** | **36.6** | **16.1** | **3.6** | **30.0** | **46.0** | **14.4** | **9.7** |
| *Changes from 1995 (percentage points)* | -39.1 | 27.2 | 10.4 | 1.6 | -38.1 | 24.5 | 8.5 | 5.1 |
| **Low income** | **50.6** | **32.9** | **16.4** | **0.0** | **12.7** | **66.2** | **20.4** | **0.7** |
| *Changes from 1995 (percentage points)* | -10.6 | 23.3 | -10.3 | -2.4 | -42.7 | 58.1 | -9.4 | -6.1 |

*Source:* ESCAP calculation based on data from the United Nations Comtrade database.

## 6. What is the role of services in the development of GVCs in Asia and the Pacific?

*"Services create a significant value in the process of manufacturing, distribution and marketing of goods in GVCs."*

The recognition of the value created, directly or indirectly, by services used in the process of manufacturing, distribution and marketing of goods has become known as "servicification" (ESCAP, 2013). GVCs rely intensively on services to link and coordinate the activities located in different countries (Gereffi and others, 2001). In addition, increasing liberalization of trade in services as well as the advancement of communications and transportation technologies have increased tradeability of services, and consequently generate a higher share of foreign services in industrial exports.

Using the data on trade in value-added from the OECD-WTO TiVA database,[18] research by ESCAP has estimated that services accounted for 29.4% of the total value-added in industrial exports by Asia and the Pacific in 2009(Anukoonwattaka and others, 2015).[19] The share of services is predominant in high-technology sectors, i.e. electrical and optical equipment (32.5%), machinery (30.8%), transport equipment (30.6%), and chemicals and non-metallic mineral products (30%), while it lags behind in agriculture, hunting, forestry and fishing (18.5%), mining and quarrying (21.8%), and food products (25.2%). These results are in line with the global trend, where transport equipment and high-tech sectors are the most service-intensive industries (World Bank, 2013).[20] Much of the intermediate services areimported, particularly business services that are an essential input to the export production of manufacturing goods, especially electrical, machinery, transport equipment and chemical products. The share of imported services in industrial exports increased from 7% in 1995 to 11% in 2009. The increase of services imports has been particularly rapid in the case of business services. Furthermore, the share of intraregional imports of services increased, especially in GVC-related industrial exports.

# C DETERMINANTS OF GVC-RELATED EXPORTS: EVIDENCE AND IMPLICATIONS FOR TRADE-RELATED POLICIES

GVCs have been an important feature of the trade, investment and production of Asia-Pacific countries. As mentioned above, the process of industrialization in many countries appears to accelerate after entering GVCs and expanding GVC-related exports (WTO, 2014; and Baldwin, 2011). However, the opportunities to engage in GVC-related activities have been opened only to a limited number of countries in the region. Therefore, a question for Asia-Pacific policymakers is how to create an enabling environment to enhance the opportunity to further integrate into GVCs in order to reap the long-term benefits from participation.

With a presumption that the combination of natural and policy-related factors determine a country's participation in GVCs, this section explores which policy variables are the most relevant and it provides policy advice for improving the ability of developing Asia and the Pacific to integrate into GVCs. The analysis also draws on suggestive stylized evidence from the previous section which indicates that policy advice should take into account differences across development levels, sectors and stages of production. For example, a policy designed for a country exporting final goods might differ from that designed for a country exporting intermediate products; these may differ even further, depending on a country development level. It is also argued that, in a world with GVCs where exports include a significant amount of imported inputs, import barriers (at- and behind-the-border) imposed by an exporting country could be as harmful as trade barriers imposed in the export market.

To investigate these issues, an augmented gravity model of trade is estimated. The model is estimated to assess the impacts of changes in trade and trade-facilitation policies on exports of Asia-Pacific economies through GVCs after controlling for fixed effects of time, exporting and importing countries, and sectors (box 7.2). The empirical framework, based on Baldwin and Taglioni (2011), is suitable for capturing GVC-related trade where trade in intermediate goods is important.[21] In order to control for differences in the patterns of trade in final and intermediate products, the gravity equations are estimated for final and intermediate exports separately. Furthermore, the models for intraregional exports of those products are also estimated to investigate if the patterns differ between trade in global and regional value chains.

In addition to the gravity model of the whole Asia-Pacific region, separated gravity models of exports by each income group are estimated in order to provide specific policy advice to countries with different development levels. This study includes all Asia-Pacific economies, both developed and developing. Country classification by income group is based on the World Bank's income classification in 2014. Countries are categorized into four income groups: high upper-middle lower-middle and low-income economies.[22] It should be noted that high-income countries include developed and some developing economies (see country lists in online appendix B).

### Box 7.2. Augmented gravity model of GVC-related exports by Asia-Pacific economies

The augmented gravity model of bilateral exports is estimated to measure the effects of policy factors on GVC-related exports of final and intermediate goods by Asia-Pacific economies from 1995 to 2013. The focus is on trade-related polices that include trade-policy measures, trade facilitation and behind-the-border obstacles to trade and FDI. In order to avoid multi-collinearity between policy variables and fixed effects, the gravity model of GVC-related exports is divided into two parts: (A) a gravity model with only trade-policy variables; and (B) a gravity model with not only trade policy variables but also trade facilitation and behind-the-border factors. The baseline specifications are:

(A) Gravity model with only trade-policy variables:

$$X^l_{ijkt} = \beta_0 + \beta_1 mass_{ijt} + \boldsymbol{\beta_2 T}^l_{ijkt} + \boldsymbol{\beta_3 T}^l_{jikt} + \beta_4 RTA_{ijt} + \boldsymbol{\beta_5 G}_{ij} + \delta_{it} + \delta_{jt} + \delta_{kt} + \varepsilon^l_{ijkt}\ .$$

(B) Gravity model with trade facilitation and behind-the-border factors:

$$X^l_{ijkt} = \beta_0 + \beta_1 mass_{ijt} + \boldsymbol{\beta_2 T}^l_{ijkt} + \boldsymbol{\beta_3 T}^l_{jikt} + \beta_4 RTA_{ijt} + \boldsymbol{\beta_5 G}_{ij} + \boldsymbol{\beta_6 F}_{it} + \boldsymbol{\beta_7 F}_{jt} + \delta_i + \delta_j +$$

CHAPTER 7

$\delta_k + \varepsilon^l_{ijkt}$, where

$X^l_{ijkt}$ is the bilateral exports of product l in sector k from country i to country j in year t, and $mass_{ijt}$ is the economic mass measured under the method suggested by Baldwin and Taglioni (2011).[23]

The role of policies imposed by both the exporting country i and the import country j are investigated through the estimated coefficients of policy variables included in the model: $\boldsymbol{T}^l_{ijkt}$, $\boldsymbol{T}^l_{jikt}$, $RTA_{ijt}$ $\boldsymbol{F}_{it}$ and $\boldsymbol{F}_{jt}$. $\boldsymbol{T}^l_{ijkt}$ is a vector of product-variant trade-policy variables imposed by country i faced by country j related to trade in product l of sector k at time t. The set of policy variables include applied MFN tariffs and non-tariff measures. Similarly, $\boldsymbol{T}^l_{ijkt}$ is a vector of the same set of policies faced by country i when exporting product l to country j at period t. $RTA_{ijt}$ is a dummy variable capturing the regional trade agreement (RTA) relationship between country i and country j at time t. $\boldsymbol{F}_{it}$ and $\boldsymbol{F}_{jt}$ are the vectors of behind-the-border indicators at time t of country i and country j, respectively. The vectors include indices measuring behind-the-border conditions of a country such as availability of ICT (proxied by Internet users per 100 people), port and logistics conditions (based on international supply chain connectivity or ISCC index) and behind-the-border conditions, which reflect business environment (Doing business – distance to frontier), are country-time specific variables. In addition, $\boldsymbol{G}_{ij}$ is a vector that includes time-invariant controlled variables as per standard gravity model, i.e., distance, contingency and common official language. $\delta_i$, $\delta_j$, and $\delta_k$, are included in the model to capture unobserved time-invariant fixed effects by country and sector levels. Adding *t* to the subscript, the variables become time-variant fixed effects.

The dataset covers all Asia-Pacific countries whose data were available during the study period. The dataset combines trade and policy data from several databases. Trade data are from United Nations Comtrade, downloaded from World Integrated Trade Solution (WITS). The geographical distances between most populated cities (in kilometres), contiguity and bilateral common language dummy variables were obtained from CEPII (www.cepii.fr). GDP, value-added data of the manufacturing sector in current US dollars, GDP deflator and income group data were obtained from World Bank's World Development Indicators (WB-WDI). For policy variables, tariff data were from the UNCTAD TRAINS database, downloaded through WITS. Non-tariff measures were obtained from WTO's Integrated Trade Intelligence Portal (WTO-ITIP). RTA data were from de Sousa (2012). Trade facilitation data, cross-border proxy, and ISCC index were obtained from the ESCAP database (http://artnet.unescap.org/databases.html#fourth). Since ISCC data include some components in trading across borders in the ease of doing business indicator, the study calculates modified ease of doing business index (distance to frontier), excluding the trading across border component. The data were downloaded from Doing Business (www.doingbusiness.org). Internet users per 100 people, which is the proxy of efficiency in paperless trade facilitation, were obtained from WB-WDI (see annex 7B).

The analysis covers GVC-related final and intermediate exports of five sectors: apparel and footwear; automobiles; electronics; agricultural primary; and processed agricultural products.[24] The product lists proposed by Sturgeon and Memedovic (2010) were utilized to identify GVC final and intermediate products of the apparel and footwear, automobile and electronics sectors.[25] In addition, the final and intermediate exports of primary and processed agricultural products are identified, based on the Broad Economic Categories (BEC) categorization of household consumption for final goods, and industrial uses for intermediate goods users (see online appendix A). Exports by a country are measured based on data reported by its trading partners (importers). Using mirrored export data helps to partially eliminate the missing data, especially in the case of countries with limited export statistics.

## 1. General requirements for enhancing GVC participation

(a) A comprehensive trade liberalization

Tariffs and the numbers of non-tariff measures (NTMs) are used as suggestive indicators of trade protection while an RTA dummy represents the existence of a formal trade agreement between two trading partners. As presented in figure 7.11 and table 1 of online appendix C, there is evidence that tariff liberalization is a critical step in competitively engaging in the value chains, both globally and regionally. The impacts of tariffs imposed and faced by Asia-Pacific exporting countries at the product level (HS-6 digits) are investigated through the gravity model with trade policy variables. The estimated tariff coefficients suggest that a tariff reduction could enhance GVC-related exports of final and intermediate products, both to global and to intraregional markets. For the tariff faced by an exporting country, a tariff reduction by 1% is associated with an increase between 1% to 1.7% of GVC-related exports (see table 1 of online appendix C for details).

Furthermore, import barriers of a country could impede its capacity to export through GVCs. Based on the estimated coefficients, a 1% increase in its own tariff protection is associated with a decrease by 2%-5% of GVC-related exports. This finding appears to confirm that a country's own protection is harmful to its export capacity in GVCs. It is important to note that tariffs are measured at the product level (HS 6-digits). Thus, the results suggest that an adverse impact of tariff protection could happen even at the disaggregated level of intra-industry trade.

> ***"1% increase in own tariff is linked with a 2%-5% decrease of GVC-related export through GVCs."***

The sizes of tariff coefficients indicate that a country's exports might suffer from its own protection measures more than from the protection measures of its import partners. A possible explanation could be related to the back-and-forth intra-industry trade at different stages of production in GVCs. Export competitiveness in GVCs then requires efficiency in import procurement even at a highly disaggregated product level. This means that policymakers must give much more consideration to facilitate imports, as they traditionally focus on promoting exports, if they want to support exports through participation in GVCs.

The results imply that the way in which trade policy is conceived requires some reordering. Although, in general, tariffs have declined substantially during the past few decades as a result of trade liberalization, both by unilateral and multilateral actions, tariffs remain an important impediment to trade in GVCs (see chapter 5 in this report for the current review). One reason is that there is a great diversity in levels of applied (and bound) tariffs in developing countries. More importantly, the impact of existing tariffs – however low those tariffs may be – is magnified due to the fact that when intermediate goods are traded across borders several times, before being assembled into a final exportable product, the applied tariffs get added on top of each other. The GVC-participating firms are therefore affected by a tariff at both ends of the chain, both as additional costs of their intermediate goods and as a barrier (affecting their competitiveness) in the market for which the exportable final good is destined.

Therefore, protection against imported inputs will increase the costs of GVC exports and reduce producers' ability, especially those in the small and medium-sized enterprise (SME) sector, to compete in export markets. In addition, as accumulated tariffs could reach quite a high level by the time the finished good reaches customers, their effect on either reduction of profit margins or demand, if being shifted to the consumers, might dampen production and investment at all stages of the value chain. For example, the effective burden for China's exports, when measured by tariffs on the domestic value-added, was higher than 37% for agricultural exports and 20% for manufacturing products in 2009. This is much higher than when measured by tariffs on gross exports, which show tariffs facing a Chinese exporter were 22% for agricultural exports and less than 5% for manufacturing exports (OECD, 2013b).[25]

> ***"Trade liberalization for the development of GVCs implies more than just tariff elimination."***

The estimated coefficient of NTMs confirms that removing trade barriers for the promotion of participation in GVCs should go beyond tariff elimination. The NTM coefficients are negative. It means that the more NTMs are imposed, or are faced by an exporting country, the lower will be their exports. However, as is frequently the case in the estimation of trade impacts, when quantifying the impact resulting from changing the number of imposed NTMs on the volume of exports, the result does not give large numbers. Based the statistical evidence, an additional NTM imposed by an exporting country is associated with a reduction of that country's own exports by 0.3% for final exports and 0.5% for intermediate exports. On the other hand, an additional NTM faced by an exporting country is associated with a reduction of 0.1% of final exports.

The estimated NTM coefficients are quite small compared to tariff coefficients. However, it does not imply that NTMs should be interpreted as negligible impediments to exports in GVCs. It shows that without knowing the tariff-equivalence of NTMs it is impossible to properly quantify a change in trade barriers attributed by NTMs (Heal and Palmioli, 2015). Since such tariff equivalents are not available across countries studied here, the number of NTMs reported by WTO members is used as a proxy. This is far from a perfect proxy because of the likely discrepancy between reported NTMs (as used in the model) and implemented NTMs if countries did not notify or update their real NTM status to WTO. It is also not true that countries necessarily underreport, as there are also possible cases where some measures, such as technical regulations, have been withdrawn without proper notification to WTO. In addition, the availability of data becomes an issue when the estimates focuses on intraregional trade.

## Box 7.3. How to interpret figures 7.11 and 7.12

Figures 7.11 and 7.12 are constructed to help explain the results of the econometric analysis (the tables of complete regression outputs can be found in online appendix C). The econometric analysis assesses the impacts of policy variables on GVC-related exports by Asia-Pacific countries. Figure 7.11 highlights the roles of trade-policy variables, while figure 7.12 illustrates the impacts of trade facilitation and behind-the-border conditions on exports of final and intermediate goods of Asia-Pacific countries through the global and regional value chains. The gravity models are estimated separately for global and intraregional exports of final and intermediate goods as categorized in the four models in figures 7.11 and 7.12. The horizontal axis shows the dependent variables of each model. Estimated coefficients from each gravity model are presented by dots along a vertical line. Only the coefficients of focused variables with. statistically significant relationships at the 1% to 5% level are presented in the figures. A dot above a horizontal axis is a coefficient with a positive value, while a dot below a horizontal axis is a negative coefficient. Interpreting the coefficients follows standard econometric practice, i.e. a positive coefficient indicates a positive association between an independent variable (dot label) and a dependent variable (a category on a horizontal axis). Along a vertical line, the distance of a dot from a horizontal axis indicates the size of a respective coefficient. It then implies the elasticity of exports to a change in the respective policy measures.

## Figure 7.11. Impacts of trade policy factors on exports in GVCs (estimated coefficients)

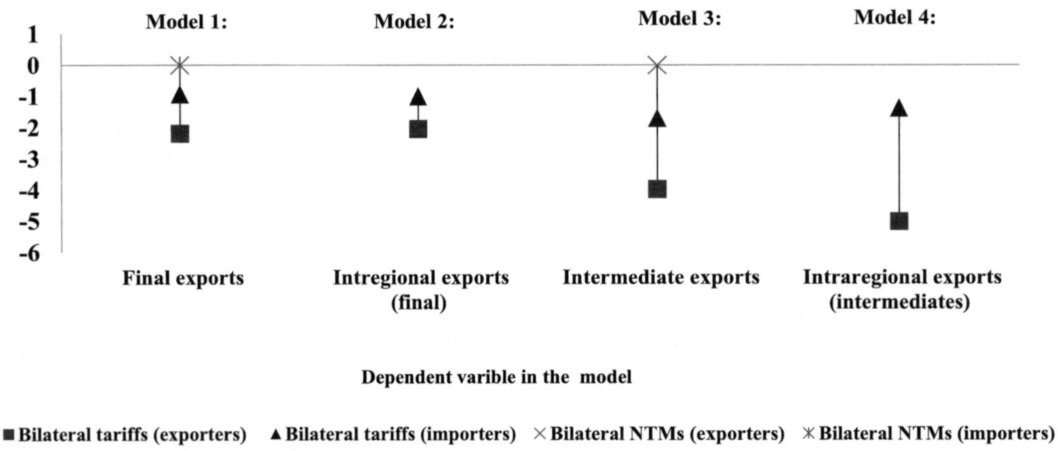


*Source:* ESCAP estimates.
*Note:* Estimated coefficients that are statistically significant at the 1% to 5% level are illustrated in the figure. See table 1 of online appendix C for details of the regression output.

It is also important to note that the phenomenon of servicification, as already mentioned, indicates the need for comprehensive coverage of liberalization policy across economic sectors (see also chapter 8). Removing barriers to cross-border movements of goods will not suffice for strengthening the competitiveness of national producers from the perspective of participation in GVCs. Appropriate liberalization of services sector, including trade in services, and movements of capital and labour are also necessary for the development of GVCs.

> *"Liberalization of trade in services and investment could help facilitate participation in GVCs."*

Servicification is very important in GVCs of industrial goods. It requires a comprehensive approach when formulating policies to strengthen GVC participation. While liberalizing trade in goods is a starting point for opening new trade opportunities, the value chains in the production of industrial goods also requires efficient services. Improvements in the performance of the service sectors, including through liberalization of services trade, would thereby enhance the competitiveness of manufacturing firms and facilitate their participation in global production networks. In addition, trade in services under modes 3 and 4 also relate to the liberalization of investment and movement of professionals.

In addition, facilitating business in GVCs requires minimizing behind-the-border obstacles (see next section for more details). This relates to the quality of regulatory institutions, which includes a broader set of domestic policy reform, deregulation and improvement of the transparency and efficiency of law enforcement. For example, a strong legal system to protect intellectual property rights and contract enforcement is crucial for participating in GVC tasks related to R&D, design, innovation and branding. Countries that have political stability, open to foreign investment and adhere to international standards are likely to succeed in attracting foreign investment and becoming a part of GVCs.

(b) Improving behind-the-border and border trade facilitation

Fast and efficient procedures at the border are essential to the operation of GVCs because goods cross borders many times as both inputs and final products. The efficient customs and simplified administrative procedures at the border are thus a critical factor for participation in GVCs as they will have an impact on the overall trade costs.

In order for a firm to be able to better connect to GVCs, improvement of hard infrastructure, such as port connectivity, transport, logistics and the information communication network, is required. The accessibility and high quality of these physical infrastructure features are critical to helping firms minimize trade costs and thereby increase their opportunities for connecting with global production networks.

To investigate the roles of infrastructure and trade facilitation, the estimation takes into account these elements by three indices on the export and import sides. The International Supply Chain Connectivity (ISCC) index reflects the efficiency of moving goods from the factory to export markets. It takes into account the availability and quality of ports, shipping, inland transportation, customs and procedures at the border. Availability and ease of access to the Internet is used as a proxy for efficiency in information flows and communication technologies. Sub-indicators related to the behind-the-border business environment from World Bank's Doing Business database are aggregated to quantify the relative position of countries in terms of regulations and institutions including contract enforcement, the legal system, credit accessibility, etc.

*"ICT is important for expanding production and trade networks from the regional to the global level."*

As presented in figure 7.11 and table 2 of online appendix C , the coefficients of internet users in exporting and importing countries are positive and statistically significant for GVC-related exports of final and intermediate products at the global level. This is consistent with the hypothesis that the efficiency of communication technologies is important for coordinating business activities along a GVC. The improvement of ICT, either in importing or exporting economies, could lead to increases in exports to the global market.[27] However, the coefficients show that Internet connectivity does not significantly affect intraregional trade. This may be due to the fact that other factors help facilitate information flows between Asia-Pacific nations. For example, communication between business entities in the value chains may be easier when the countries are in close proximity, sharing similar cultures or having historical and social linkages.

*"Asia-Pacific exporters may lose their competitive edge in the GVC-related exports if they start lagging in logistics and customs procedures."*

The empirical results confirm the expectation that an improvement in logistics and custom clearance in exporting economies would help their export performance. The ISCC coefficients show that better logistics (measured as an improvement in the ISCC score) in an exporting economy helps exports of final products through GVCs afte controlling for the logistics in an import destination. A 1% improvement in the ISCC score of an exporting economy is associated with an increase of its final exports between 0.9% to 1%. There is no evidence that better logistics plays a significant role in intermediate exports.

In contrast, better logistics and ICT connectivity of an import partner that reduce the cost of GVC-related trade transaction with distant destinations also may reduce export opportunities for the Asia-Pacific region. In the other words, better logistics in an importing economy may increase its imports from any exporter in the world at the expense of Asia-Pacific exporters that used to leverage their location advantages. The contrasting impacts of logistics and ICT connectivity in exporter and importer economies lead to the conclusion that Asia-Pacific exporters need to match their import partners in improving logistics to avoid losing their competitive position in GVCs.

*"Exports in GVCs are highly sensitive to rules and obstacles of doing business in importing countries."*

The estimated coefficients of the Doing Business indicator reflect a strong link between behind-the-border factors in importing economies and exports in GVCs. The indicator is used in the regression as a proxy of quality of regulatory institutions, including rules, regulations and the legal system. The positive coefficients indicate that GVC-related exports are directed more to destinations with relatively good regulatory conditions. Estimated coefficients on doing business for importing economies are positive and significant at 1% to 5%. The coefficient magnitude is particularly large for intraregional trade compared with the coefficient estimated from total trade.

Based on this dataset, the estimation is still not conclusive enough to confirm that local regulations and rules in exporting countries matter. However, it is important to keep in mind that in the Asia-Pacific region foreign investments and exports related to GVCs often take place in export processing zones, which are meant to shelter foreign investors and the exporters from the red tape and other regulatory burden generated by local rules.

These results appear to confirm that GVCs require the reassessment of trade facilitation measures. As countries become strongly connected through GVC participation, the need for international coordination on regulatory reform and harmonization are stronger than ever before. Regional coordination is particularly important in the context of Asia and the Pacific because economies in the region are strongly connected in the value chains.

**Figure 7.12. Impacts of trade facilitation factors on exports in GVCs (estimated coefficients)**

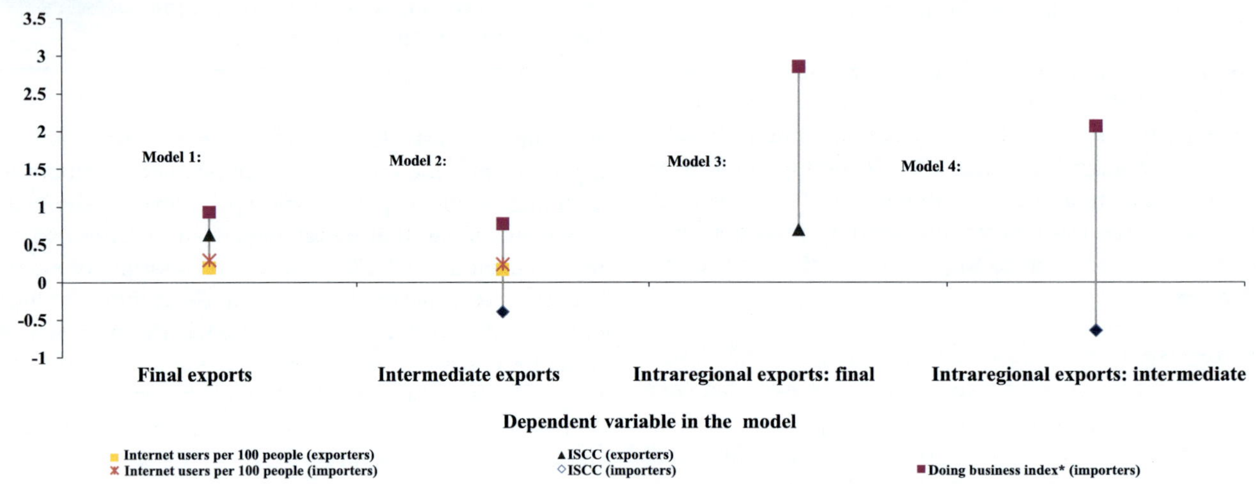


*Source:* ESCAP estimates.

*Note:* Estimated coefficients that are statistically significant at less than or equal to the 5% level are illustrated in the figure. See table 2 of annex 7B for details of the regression output.

(c) Supporting GVC development through regional integration frameworks

> *"RTAs appear to be helping expansion of exports related to GVCs."*

Casual observations suggest that regional integration could enhance GVC participation by economies in the Asia-Pacific region. The results based on systematic investigation confirm the positive impacts of regional integration on GVC-related exports of Asia-Pacific region economies. The estimated RTA coefficients, which are positive and statistically significant, suggest that having a formal trade agreement appears to enhance bilateral export through GVCs (table 7.2). Based on the coefficients of RTA-dummy variables, GVC-related exports by Asia-Pacific economies in general could be at least 58.6% higher with an RTA than without an RTA (see details of regression output in table 1 of online appendix C). There are two possible interpretations of the panel data analysis. On the one hand, it may reflect that GVC-related exports from Asia-Pacific economies to a particular import partner appear to increase after a formal trade agreement is signed. On the other hand, it could also mean that GVC-related exports by Asia-Pacific economies appear to be destined more to countries with which those economies have a trade agreement compared to other countries with which they do not have a trade agreement, given that they are similar in other characteristics.

However, RTAs alone will have limited benefits without the improvement of connectivity with global trade partners through unilateral or multilateral trade and investment liberalization and facilitation. The RTA coefficients appear to be somewhat higher for global exports than for intraregional exports when the same type of export is considered. Having an RTA may increase final global exports by 73.9% and intraregional exports by 58.6%. For intermediate exports, the coefficients show that the impacts are 78.9% for global exports and 73.1% for intraregional exports. This may imply that an RTA is particularly supportive of GVC-related exports to destinations outside the region. A possible explanation could be that a formal trade agreement may not be important at the intraregional level because Asia-Pacific countries are already connected in the regional production networks even without an RTA, due to geographical advantages, historical factors etc.

In addition, the effectiveness of RTAs in helping GVC-related export appears to depend on the development levels of exporters and importers. For example, while significantly helping low-income economies to export to high-income countries, having a formal trade agreement does not play a significant role in exports to non-high income economies. When looking at exports from high-income countries, the results show that RTAs do not help their exports to countries in the same peer group. In contrast, having an RTA plays a significant role in helping lower-middle income economies increase their exports to intraregional markets regardless of the level of income.

Although the results are quite mixed, the general conclusion is that having an RTA with high-income import partners may be a useful strategy for Asia-Pacific exporters, both in the low and the middle-income groups. Given the fact that high-income countries are likely be a large market for intermediate and final products in GVCs, this finding implies that an RTA strategy that may effectively help GVC-related exports by low- and middle-income Asia-Pacific economies would be market-driven RTAs.

**Table 7.2. Estimated RTA coefficients from the gravity models, by group of exporters and importers**

| | Exports by type of products and income level at destinations | | | | | | | |
|---|---|---|---|---|---|---|---|---|
| | Final | | Intermediate | | Final (intraregional) | | Intermediate (intraregional) | |
| **Asia-Pacific exporters** | **High** | **Non-high** | **High** | **Non-high** | **High** | **Non-high** | **High** | **Non-high** |
| Low-income[a] | 1.732 | | 1.531 | | | | 1.586 | |
| Lower-middle income [b] | | 1.908 | 0.515 | | 0.790 | 1.798 | 1.482 | 1.396 |
| Upper-middle income[c] | 0.735 | | 0.386 | | 0.663 | | | 0.806 |
| High-income[d] | | 1.062 | | 1.266 | | 0.722 | | 1.211 |
| All Asia-Pacific[e] | 0.739 | | 0.789 | | 0.586 | | 0.731 | |

*Note:* Each column of the table presents estimated RTA coefficients obtained from differentgravity models of GVC-related exports. The models are controlled for conditions related to trade protections, trade facilitation, and fixed effects of countries and years. Only the RTA coefficients with statistical significance at the 1% to 5 % level are presented in the table.
[a] Based on regression output shown in tables 3 and 4 of online appendix C.
[b] Based on regression output shown in tables 5 and 6 of online appendix C.
[c] Based on regression output shown in tables 7 and 8 of online appendix C.
[d] Based on regression output shown in tables 9 and 10 of online appendix C.
[e] Based on regression output shown in table 1 of online appendix C.

## 2. National priorities for different income groups

Asia-Pacific economies are significantly diverse, both in terms of development levels and patterns of their exports in GVCs. Policy formulation to enhance GVC participation by Asia-Pacific economies should highlight market-specific and country-specific factors. Therefore, regressions are estimated separately by income group of exporters and importers as well as by types of exports. The results are presented in tables 7.3 to 7.5. They indicate that in addition to general policy conditions, the focus and priority of policymaking could vary between income groups. This, in turn reflects specificities of how a development stage of an economy affects its participation in GVCs, and indicates custom-made policies to support its GVC participation.

> *"Infrastructure investment to improve connectivity is the key to entering GVCs."*

(a) Policy priorities for low-income economies

Low-income economies are mainly at the entry stage of GVC participation. Many of them have advantages in terms of availability of primary inputs such as natural resources and/or low-cost labour. However, their potential to participate in GVCs is often obscured by obstacles of geographical isolation and small domestic markets.

For low-income Asia-Pacific economies, statistical evidence shows that a tariff reduction by, and having an RTA with their import partners appears to help the GVC-related exports of the latter, especially to high-income markets. In addition, improvements in their connectivity and efficiency of logistic systems (as measured by ISCC) and in their ICT could enhance their opportunities to export through GVCs, especially to high-income markets (table 7.3). Some specifications show an unexpected result, which may be related to the incompleteness of the data on the low-income economies.

**Table 7.3. Estimated coefficients of policy variables from the gravity models of GVC-related exports, by low-income Asia-Pacific exporter**

| | Exports by types of products and income level at destinations | | | | | | | |
|---|---|---|---|---|---|---|---|---|
| | Final | | Intermediate | | Final (intraregional) | | Intermediate (intraregional) | |
| **Policy variables** | **High** | **Non-high** | **High** | **Non-high** | **High** | **Non-high** | **High** | **Non-high** |
| Tariffs (exporters) | x | | | | | | | |
| Tariffs (importers) | -3.46 | | -2.262 | | -2.117 | | -1.999 | -3.475 |
| RTA | 1.732 | | 1.531 | | 1.586 | | 1.732 | |
| Internet users (exporters) | 0.274 | x | | | | | 0.274 | |
| ISCC (exporters) | 2.675 | 9.422 | | | | x | 2.675 | x |
| Doing business (exporters) | x | | | | | 3.035 | | |
| Internet (importers) | | | 1.211 | | | | | |
| ISCC (importers) | | | | | | | | |
| Doing business (importers) | | | | | | | | |

*Note:* The table presents the estimated coefficients shown in tables 3 and 4 of online appendix C. Only the policy coefficients that are statistically significant at the 1% to 5 % level are presented in the table. The coefficients with unexpected results are denoted by "x". The models are controlled for conditions at the border and behind-the-border that may affect GVC-related export capacity. Fixed effects are also controlled at the country, year and sector levels. The NTM coefficient cannot be estimated due to the fact that NTM data are missing for most of the low-income economies.

(b) Lower-middle income economies

> ***"Reforms of trade and investment policies, especially trade facilitation, are the sine qua non for these countries to become a major player in GVCs."***

Lower-middle income economies in the Asia-Pacific region are already involved in GVCs to a significant level. A major policy question, then, is how to enhance their performance in GVCs in order to maximize benefits for their further development. The estimated coefficients of policy variables shown in table 7.4 suggest that exports by lower-middle income economies to non-high income economies appear to be particularly sensitive to tariff reductions by their import partners and RTA memberships. This may reflect the fact that there is a room for tariff reductions to increase the margin of preference in trade between them. The evidence for the negative impact of NTMs is statistically significant, although the coefficient magnitude is quite small. In addition, there are cases where evidence shows that improved logistics and simplification of rules and regulations in lower-middle income economies could increase their GVC export opportunities. Similar to the findings in the model of GVC-related exports by the Asia-Pacific region overall, there is a negative association between infrastructure improvement in an importing country and the export opportunity of an Asia-Pacific lower-middle income exporter. This finding appears to confirm the earlier statement that better connectivity of an import partner may reduce the advantage of Asia-Pacific exporters in regional value chains. The better connectivity reduces the cost incurred by distance when importing, especially from a distant exporting source. Therefore, Asia-Pacific countries that enjoy location advantages may lose their export competitiveness.

**Table 7.4. Estimated coefficients of policy variables from the gravity models of GVC-related exports, by lower-middle income Asia-Pacific exporters**

| | Exports by types of products and income level at destinations | | | | | | | |
|---|---|---|---|---|---|---|---|---|
| | Final | | Intermediate | | Final (intraregional) | | Intermediate (intraregional) | |
| **Policy variables** | **High** | **Non-high** | **High** | **Non-high** | **High** | **Non-high** | **High** | **Non-high** |
| Tariffs (exporters) | x | | | | | | | |
| Tariffs (importers) | -1.413 | -1.805 | | -3.357 | -1.369 | -3.658 | | -5.255 |
| RTA | | 1.908 | 0.515 | 1.482 | 0.79 | 1.798 | | 1.396 |
| NTMs (exporters) | -0.009 | -0.016 | -0.005 | -0.009 | | -0.021 | | -0.021 |
| NTMs (importers) | -0.002 | | | | | | | |
| Internet users (exporters) | | | | | -0.38 | | | |
| ISCC (exporters) | 1.171 | 1.224 | | | | 1.616 | | |
| Doing business (exporters) | | | | | | -3.628 | x | |
| Internet (importers) | 0.355 | | | | | -0.37 | | |
| ISCC (importers) | | | -0.738 | | -1.288 | | | |
| Doing business (importers) | | 1.663 | 1.416 | | 9.06 | | | |

*Note:* The table presents the estimated coefficients shown in tables 5 and 6 of online appendix C. Only the policy coefficients that are statistically significant at the 1% to 5 % level are presented in the table. The coefficients with unexpected results are denoted by "x". The models are controlled for conditions at the border and behind-the-border that may affect GVC-related export capacity. Fixed effects are also controlled at the country, year and sector levels.

(c) Upper-middle income economies

*"Investing in technologies and enhancing market integration to facilitate upgrading process within a value chain."*

Upper-middle income economies appear to be already well-connected in the GVC web. Their positions in GVCs appear to be in transition. A priority for them is how to diversify their GVC participation into the higher value-added activities. The high value-added manufacturing sectors, by nature, are technologically intensive. This implies that upgrading vertically along the value chains to higher value-addition segments may, in turn, have some adverse effects on employment. To mitigate issues with potential rise in unemployment, some initiatives could simultaneously be undertaken to expand and diversify production horizontally into new products.

The empirical finding appears to suggest that upper-middle income economies need a different set of policies to support their GVC participation. Policy actions that would apparently help the export capacity of low- and lower-middle income economies in fact turn out to have the opposite impact on the export capacity of upper-middle income economies (table 7.5). Supporting GVC participation by upper-middle income Asia-Pacific exporters may require a set of policies that has not been included in the model. For example, the policy priorities may need to focus on facilitating production transformation towards a higher stage of value addition in value chains. A priority might be policies related to skills upgrading, technology transfer and innovation (see chapter 9), and outward FDI to maintain or enhance their export capacity (box 7.1). However, the evidence remains strong for the importance of ICT connectivity. This may reflect the fact that once developing countries reach the upper-middle-income stage, their GVC participation also moves towards higher value-added activities. Their GVC participation becomes more communication-intensive in order to respond quickly to changes in demand (just-in-time delivery) or to the need to adapt quickly to new designs or new production technology. Moreover, an RTA coefficient suggests that having a formal trade agreement could increase their chance to export to high-income countries.

**Table 7.5. Estimated coefficients of policy variables from the gravity models of GVC-related exports, by upper-middle income Asia-Pacific exporter**

| | Exports by types of products and income level at destinations | | | | | | | |
|---|---|---|---|---|---|---|---|---|
| | Final | | Intermediate | | Final (intraregional) | | Intermediate (intraregional) | |
| **Policy variables** | **High** | **Non-high** | **High** | **Non-high** | **High** | **Non-high** | **High** | **Non-high** |
| Tariffs (exporters) | | x | -1.358 | | x | x | | |
| Tariffs (importers) | | -2.728 | -2.509 | -3.913 | x | -3.82 | | -7.328 |
| RTA | 0.735 | | 0.386 | | 0.663 | | | 0.806 |
| NTMs (exporters) | | x | x | -0.005 | | | x | |
| NTMs (importers) | -0.003 | | -0.004 | | | | | |
| Internet users (exporters) | 0.236 | x | 0.291 | 0.699 | 0.517 | | | |
| ISCC (exporters) | | | | | | x | 1.045 | |
| Doing business (exporters) | x | x | | | x | x | | |
| Internet (importers) | | 0.187 | | | | | | |
| ISCC (importers) | | | | | -1.363 | | -1.223 | |
| Doing business (importers) | | | | | 5.217 | | | |

*Note:* The table presents the estimated coefficients shown in tables 7 and 8 of online appendix C. Only the policy coefficients that are statistically significant at the 1% to 5 % level are presented in the table. The coefficients with unexpected results are denoted by "x". The models are controlled for conditions at the border and behind-the-border that may affect GVC-related export capacity. Fixed effects are also controlled at country, year and sector levels.

# D CONCLUSION

The rapid expansion of GVCs has been driven by technological progress and trade policy reforms that allowed multinational corporations to geographically disperse their stages of production across national borders. This phenomenon has created a finer division of labour between countries – at the level of specialization in tasks, rather than in products – both within the same region and across regions.

The experience of many Asia-Pacific countries appears to show that the emergence of GVCs offers a richer menu of options for diversification, industrialization, growth and development. However, the development of GVCs in Asia and the Pacific is centred on countries in North-East Asia and South-East Asia. In addition, integration into GVCs could open the door to industrialization and economic development, but it does not ensure long-term and sustainable economic development. Although it appears that participation in GVCs tends to be relatively successful in industrialization and in achieving high economic growth, for an economy to reap the long-term benefits from GVC participation, it is important to move towards higher value-added production activities and sectors supported by an enabling policy environment.

Policy formulation in response to the dynamics of interconnections in the global economy requires a comprehensive framework and long-term vision. The dynamic nature of GVCs implies that the specialization and comparative strengths of economies will continue to evolve, which will require further adjustment at the regional and national levels. For example, in recent years, the increasing global shift in demand for final products to developing Asia and the Pacific may lead to the deeper integration of the region in GVCs. In addition, the possibility for economies in the region to benefit from technological spillovers from high-value-added activities may increase because it is possible that research and designs as well as management may move to the region that is the major driver of final demand.

More fundamentally, policymakers will continue to be challenged by the global nature and operation of value chains. Informed policies related to GVCs will require the availability of good data and analyses. This chapter looks into the determinant of GVC-related exports for economies at different levels of GVC development. It informs policymakers about what is required on the national and the regional policy front in order to improve participation by firms and countries in GVCs, including:

(a) Trade cost reduction, which is essential for more effective participation in GVCs and for overcoming geographical disadvantages. Given the same level of production cost, trade costs are the key determinant of an economy's GVC performance. Trade cost reduction policies include liberalization of trade in goods, services and investment;

(b) Trade facilitation, the development of ICT infrastructure, improved logistics performance, regulatory transparency and other policies that reduce broader behind-the-border obstacles to trade;

(c) Regional economic integration agreements, which could be a catalyst for enhancing GVC participation by developing Asia-Pacific economies, provided the agreements are deep in commitments as well as broad in scope and coverage. However, bilateral and regional integration agreements will have little effect without the implementation of necessary domestic trade reforms and, in particular, trade facilitation;

(d) Enabling GVC development, which will increasingly require more international cooperation and coordination among Governments. The need to harmonize domestic rules and regulations with international standards is particularly strong in Asia and the Pacific, as burdens from domestic rules and regulations could be amplified and damage theregion-wide competitiveness in GVCs;

(e) The need to increase the involvement of low-income economies in GVCs. The dynamic nature of GVCs may offer new opportunities for economies that have thus far not been integrated into GVCs. The key to unlocking the potential of low-income economies is infrastructure development, especially where related to trade facilitation;

(f) Attention by Governments to removing behind-the-border obstacles after countries have become significantly integrated into GVCs. Domestic policy and regulatory reforms to facilitate trade and business operation would attract FDI and enable those countries to remain competitive in the face of intense competition in GVCs; and

(g) Investment in technologies in order to improve productivity and migration to other GVC segments with higher value addition. Due to cost increases, economies that have gone through the industrialization process will be under pressure to upgrade GVC participation to higher-value-added activities. A smooth transition from labour-intensive to skills-intensive segments of GVCs needs an enabling policy to facilitate the adjustment process through a well-designed labour market and social policies as well as through investment in education and skills. In addition, economic integration policies could also help to strengthen the flexibility of economies and the labour force in the changing environment.

## ENDNOTES

[1] Although the term GVC has been widely used since the 2000s, the concept is not actually new. The term "Commodity Chain" was used in a quite similar context since the late 1970s (OECD, 2012). For example, Gereffi (1994) used the term "Global Commodity Chain" to describe the apparel commodity chain starting from raw materials such as cotton, wool, and fibres to the final product which is garments. In the 2000s, there was a terminology shift from the global commodity chain to the global value chain. The latter term was influenced by Porter's study (1985) on the governance of value-added chains. Recently, the term "network" is often used instead of "chain". A reason is to highlight the complexity of the interactions among global producers which is more complicated than a simple circuit or a linear flow (Coe, Dicken and Hess, 2007).

[2] A much broader concept of GVCs that focuses on the "governance" nature of the supplier-buyer nexus is also mentioned in UNCTAD (2013). The definition subsumes intra-firm trade and intermediate trade as well as final goods bought for eventual sale by large retail establishments. In this view, GVCs might cover 70%-80% of world trade.

[3] There are costs, too. Integration into GVCs on its own does not ensure long-term and sustainable development. The high economic growth could come with increasing income inequality and environmental degradation unless governments, enterprises, and other stakeholders reconcile their short-term and long-term development strategies and remain mindful of their respective roles and responsibilities with respect to social justice and sustainable development.

[4] Since the late 1970s, the circular economy has attracted attention as a vibrant economic model to replace traditional linear production systems, such as the "take, make and dispose model". It emphasizes the efficient use of resources and energy, the recycling of used goods and materials or waste and the sustainability of integrated product value chains, even across borders. A circular economy can potentially cover a wide range of global value chains and integrate all of them into a non-linear, or circular, production system in order to optimize the efficiency of resources and production used in the system rather than seeking efficiency of individual components or functions separately within the value chain (Braungart and McDonough, 2002).

[5] The level of product fragmentation differs between products. Services, for example, are less prone to vertical specialisation because frequently the face-to-face contact between the provider and the consumer is required.

[6] The debate on which terms are most appropriate is beyond the scope of this study.

[7] OECD (2013a, p. 9) stated that "most trade today takes place within a production network (trade in intermediate goods and services represents 75% of global trade) or intra-firm."

[8] It is necessary to explain that ESCAP classifies countries by their development as described in UN DESA classification, meaning that only three countries in Asia and the Pacific belong to developed economies (Australia, Japan and New Zealand).

[9] Examples are Amiti, (2005), Athukorala (2008), Kimura (2006), Krugman and Venables (1995), Rugman and Verbeke (2004), Venables (1996), Venables and Baldwin (2011), and WTO (2008).

[10] In the case of goods, trade costs include land transport and port costs, freight and insurance costs, tariffs and duties, costs associated with non-tariff measures, and can be extended to also include mark-ups from importers, wholesalers and retailers (OECD, 2013a). In the case of services, transport costs are largely replaced with communication costs (although services can also be provided by natural persons that have to travel to the country where the consumer is located) and trade barriers are non-tariff measures.

[11] One way of thinking about these factors is as the "friction" associated with trade, or the set of economic forces that tends to reduce trade. Trade costs are the price equivalent of the reduction of international trade compared with the potential implied by domestic production and consumption in the origin and destination markets (Arvis and others, 2013).

[12] Comparative-advantage theory suggests that interactions between factor-intensity of fragmenting tasks and factor-price differences between potential trade-partner countries will determine the division of labour between the countries participating in GVCs. Empirically, Kimura (2006) reveals a fact about GVCs in East Asia that wage differential plays a crucial role for multinational firms when taking location decisions. Meanwhile, Athukorala (2008) indicates that significant differences in wages among the countries within the East and South-East Asian regions have provided the basis for rapid expansion of intraregional product-sharing systems, giving rise to increased cross-border trade in parts and components.

[13] The emergence of international production networks of automotive sector in ASEAN countries after the consolidation of Japanese operations in the ASEAN automotive sector in the early 2000s was an illustrative example of the combination

between lowering trade costs arising from regional trade liberalization programmes and the MNCs' attempts to seek for cost-efficiency through scale economies (Anukoonwattaka, 2007).

[14] Based on experiences of ASEAN and China, Athukorala (2008) indicated that site selection decisions by MNCs operating in assembly activities were strongly influenced by the presence of other key market players in a given country or in neighbouring countries. Moreover, the industrial relocation does not empty out the first location/nation but rather slows the growth of new manufacturing activity. As the second location's wages are driven up, a third location/nation emerges for offshoring. This is, in essence, the geographical dimension of the "flying geese" pattern whereby one East Asian nation after the other benefits from a cluster of industrial activity (Baldwin, 2013).

[15] Baldwin (2011) argues that because the learning process involved is less complex, industrialization is easier to achieve but it might also be less durable because capabilities are now narrower and therefore easier for competitors to replicate. Nonetheless, resisting GVC participation may be ineffective, because it hinders domestic firms in accessing inexpensive or more sophisticated inputs, thereby potentially causing their products to be uncompetitive in world markets. Consequently, Baldwin (2011) advised economies to learn from experiences of those that have industrialized through GVCs, such as Thailand from the late 1980s, rather than from the early model of industrialization that involve building whole supply chain within one economy.

[16] This study combines the classification of Sturgeon and Memodevic (2010) and the Broad Economic Categories (BEC) Classification of the United Nations to examine GVC-related trade in final- and intermediate- products of the agro-food, apparel and footwear, automotive, and electronics sectors using trade data available in the United Nations Comtrade database. Sturgeon and Memodevic (2010) approach allows a distinction between GVC-related products and general products on the basis of product differentiation. They adopt a concept of product differentiation which does not only focus on the differentiation of final products but also include customized intermediate inputs which tend to be utilized in the production of differentiated final products.

[17] The findings seem to be consistent with that of Milberg and Winkler (2010). They observe that the share of trade among developing countries jumped to 50% of world intermediate goods trade in 2009 compared to about 25% in 2000.

[18] It is based on data from the May 2013 version of OECD-WTO TiVA database. It covers 18 industries classified under 1 digit-ISIC Rev.3, which comprises 11 industrial sectors (agriculture, mining, food products, textiles and apparel, wood and paper, chemicals and minerals, basic metals, machinery, electrical equipment, transport equipment, other manufactures and utilities) and 7 service sectors (construction, wholesale and retail, transport and telecoms, finance and insurance, business services and other services).

[19] See Anukoonwattaka, Scagliusi and Mikic (2015).

[20] Distribution, business-coordination, and logistics are among the most important service inputs for the production of Asia-Pacific industrial exports. These services account for 9% and 7.5%, respectively, of industrial exports by Asia-Pacific region in 2009 (Anukoonwattaka and others, 2015). It is found that the shares of business services are particularly high in the exports of electrical equipment, machinery, and transport equipment. These industries are mentioned as the sectors involve intensively with the global operation of MNCs.

[21] An important feature of Baldwin and Taglioni (2011) framework is allowing trade flows to be driven not only by final demand but also intermediate demand. Following from this feature, the drivers of intermediate trade flows would be, in addition to factors affecting consumer income, factors affecting the production cost of the whole value chains.

[22] The World Bank's income groups are based on Gross National Income per capita which certainly has some limitations in representing the development level of a country. However, grouping countries by income levels provide better information about country's development status compared to other types of country grouping.

[23] Based on the framework of Baldwin and Taglioni (2011), the feature of GVC-related trade is controlled through the adjusted "mass" variable in the gravity model. This adjusted "mass" variable is defined as:

$$mass_{ij} = \frac{C_{it}E_{jt}}{\omega_{it}P_{jt}}$$

where

$C_{it} = VA_{it}^{mfg} + \sum_{j \neq o} m_{ijt}^{itm}$

$E_{jt} = GDP_{jt} + \sum_{i \neq o} m_{jit}^{itm}$

$\omega_{it} = \sum GDP_{jt} \times (dist_{ij})^{1-\sigma \; \frac{1}{1-\sigma}}$ where $\sigma = 4$

$P_{jt}$ = GDP deflator of destination j at time t

[24] The study does not include mining and petroleum sectors which have peculiar characteristics.

[25] The product lists set out by Sturgeon and Memedovic (2010) is based on information from industrial survey related to differentiation and customization of products to identify GVC-related products under the Broader Economic Category (BEC) and Standard Industry and Trade

Classification (SITC) Revision 3.

[26] Consistent with this analysis is Debaere and Mostashari (2010) that find tariff reductions in the exporting countries give the way to new goods being exported to the United States between 1989 and 1999. In addition, OECD (2013b) indicate the larger the share of imported inputs and the longer supply chains, the higher tariff costs embedded in the gross exports. This is because goods cross borders many times in GVCs, as inputs and then as final products, and tariffs are levied on the gross value, not just the value-added, of these goods every time they cross a border. Therefore, the longer the value chains, the more times the goods would cross borders and the magnifier of tariff embedded in the final value.

[27] Estimated coefficients on Internet users in exporting and importing countries are positive and significant at 1% to 5%.

### REFERENCES


Amighini, Alessia (2012). China and India in the international fragmentation of automobile production network. *China Economic Review*, vol. 23, No. 2, pp. 325-341.

Amiti, Mary (2005). Location of vertically linked industries: agglomeration versus comparative advantage. *European Economic Review*, vol. 49, No. 4, pp. 809–32.

Ando, Mitsuyo, and Fukunari Kimura (2005). The formation of international production and distribution networks in East Asia. In T. Ito and A. Rose, eds., *International trade in East Asia, NBER-East Asia seminar on Economics*, vol. 14, pp. 177-213 (Chicago: University of Chicago Press).

Antràs, Pol, and Elhanan Helpman (2004). Global sourcing. *Journal of Political Economy*, vol. 112, No. 3, pp.552-580.

Anukoonwattaka, Witada (2007). Trade liberalization and vertical integration of a multinational: a theoretical model and empirical evidence from outsourcing of Toyota, Southeast Asia, Bangkok: Thammasat University.

____ (2011). Driving forces of Asian international production networks: a brief history and theoretical perspectives. In *India: A New Player in Asian Production Networks?*, Studies in Trade and Investment No. 75. ST/ESCAP/2624. Bangkok: ESCAP. Chapter 1, pp. 7-22.

Anukoonwattaka, Witada, Marco Scagliusi and Mia Mikic (2015). Servicification and industrial exports from Asia and the Pacific. Trade Insights, No. 10, May 2015, Bangkok: ESCAP.

Arvis, Jean-François, and others (2013). Trade costs in the developing world: 1995 – 2010. Policy Research Working Paper No. 6309. Washington D.C.: World Bank.

Athukorala, Prema-chandra (2008). Singapore and ASEAN in the new regional division of labor. *Singapore Economic Review*, vol. 53, No. 3, pp. 479-508.

____ (2010). Production networks and trade patterns in East Asia: regionalization or globalization?, ADB Working Paper Series on Regional Economic Integration No. 56. Manila: Asian Development Bank.

____ (2011). Asian trade flows: trends, patterns, and projections. ADB Economics Working Paper Series, No. 241. Manila: Asian Development Bank.

Backer, Koen, and Norihiko Yamano (2012). International comparative evidence on global value chains. OECD Science, Technology and Industry Working Paper 2012/3. Paris.

Baldwin, Richard (2011). Trade and industrialisation after globalisation's second unbundling: how building and joining a supply chain are different and why it matters. In R.C. Feenstra and A.M. Taylor, eds., *Globalization in an Age of Crisis: Multilateral Economic Cooperation in the Twenty-First Century*. Cambridge, M.A.: National Bureau of Economic Research.

____ (2013). Global supply chains: why they emerged, why they matter, and where they are going. In D. Elms and P. Low, eds., *Global Value Chains in a Changing World*, pp. 13-60. Geneva: World Trade Organization.

Baldwin, Richard, and Daria Taglioni (2011). Gravity chains: estimating bilateral trade flows when parts and components trade is important. NBER Working Paper No. 16672. Cambridge, M.A.: National Bureau of Economic Research.

Bhattacharya, Debapriya, and Khondaker G. Moazzem (2013). Least developed Countries (LDCs) in the global value chain (GVC): trends, determinants and challenges. CPD Working Paper No. 104. Dhaka: Centre for Policy Dialogue.

Blyde, Juan, Alejandro Graziano and Christian V. Martincus (2014). Economic integration agreements and production fragmentation: evidence on the extensive margin. *Applied Economics Letters*, vol. 22, No. 10.

Braungart, Michael, and William McDonough (2002). *Cradle to Cradle: Remaking the Way We Make Things*. New York: North Point Press.

Cattaneo, Olivier, and others (2013). Joining, upgrading and being competitive in global value chains: a strategic framework. Policy Research Working Paper No. 6406. Washington D.C.: World Bank.

Coe, Neil M., Peter Dicken and Martin Hess (2007). Global production networks: debates and challenges. Paper prepared for the GPERG workshop, University of Manchester.

Debaere, Peter, and Shalah Mostashari (2010). Do tariffs matter for the extensive margin of international trade? An empirical analysis. *Journal of International Economics*, vol. 81, No. 2, pp.163-169.

De Sousa, José (2012). The currency union effect on trade is decreasing over time. *Economics Letters*, vol. 117, No. 3, pp. 917–920.

Duval, Yann, and Chorthip Utoktham, (2010). Intraregional trade costs in Asia: a primer. Trade and Investment Division Staff Working Paper 01/10. Bangkok: ESCAP. Available from www.unescap.org/tid/publication/swp110.pdf

Gereffi, Gray (1994), The organization of buyer-driven global commodity chains: how US retailers shape overseas production networks. In G. Gereffi and M. Korzeniewicz, eds., *Commodity Chains and Global Capitalism*. Westport, C.T.: Praeger Publishers. pp. 95-122.

____ (2006), The new offshoring of jobs and global development. ILO Social Policy Lectures, Jamaica, December, 2005.

Gereffi, Gray, and others (2001). Globalisation, value chains and development. IDS Bullettin 32.3. Brighton, United Kingdom: Institute of Development Studies. Available from www.ids.ac.uk/files/dmfile/gereffietal323.pdf

Hayakawa, Kazunobu, and Nobuaki Yamashita (2011). The role of Preferential Trade Agreements (PTAs) in facilitating global production networks. IDE Discussion Paper. No. 280. Chiba, Japan: Institute of Developing Economies.

Heal, Adam, and Giovanni Palimioli (2015). Making market access meaningful: Implementation of Duty-Free Quota-Free Trade for Asia-Pacific least developed countries. Trade Insights No. 9. Bangkok: ESCAP. Available from www.unescap.org/resources/making-market-access-meaningful-implementation-duty-free-quota-free-trade-asia-pacific

Humphrey, John, and Hubert Schmitz (2002). How does insertion in global value chains affect upgrading in industrial clusters? *Regional Studies*, vol.36, No. 9, pp. 1017-1027. Available from www.uwi.edu/ccfc/wp-content/uploads/2013/11/How-Does-Insertion-in-GVCs-Affect-Upgrading-in-Industrial-Clusters.pdf

Jerzewska, Anna (2011). Japan's FTAs as tools for achieving companies' commercial interests: do Japanese corporations need a Region-Wide Trade Liberalization Treaty? *Asian Regional Integration Review*, vol. 3, pp. 1-17.

Johnson, Robert, and Guillermo Noguera (2012). Proximity and production fragmentation. *American Economic Review*, vol. 102, No. 3, pp. 407-411.

Jones, Ronald W., and Henryk Kierzkowski (2001). Horizontal aspects of vertical fragmentation. In Leonard K. Cheng and Henryk Kierzkowski, eds., *Global Production and Trade in East Asia*. New York: Springer Science+Business Media. pp. 33-51

Kimura, Fukunari (2006). International production and distribution networks in East Asia: eighteen facts, mechanics, and policy implications. *Asian Economic Policy Review*, vol. 1, No. 2, pp. 326-344.

Krugman, Paul, and Anthony J. Venables (1995). Globalization and the inequality of nations. *Quarterly Journal of Economics*, vol. 110, No. 4, pp. 857-880.

Milberg, William, and Deborah Winkler (2010). Trade crisis and recovery: restructuring of global value chains. Policy Research Working Paper Series No. 5294. Washington, D.C.: World Bank.

Olivero, Maria P., and Yoto V. Yotov (2012). Dynamic gravity: endogenous country size and asset accumulation. *Canadian Journal of Economics*, vol. 45, No. 1, pp. 64-92.

Orefice, Gianluca, and Nadia Rocha (2014). Deep integration and production networks: an empirical analysis. *World Economy*, vol. 37, No. 1, pp.106-136.

Organisation for Economic Co-operation and Development (2012). Mapping global value chains. Conference Papers for the OECD Policy dialogue on Aid for Trade. TAD/TC/WP/RD(2012)9. Paris. Available from www.oecd.org/dac/aft/MappingGlobalValueChains_web_usb.pdf

____ (2013a). Managing aid to achieve trade and development results: an analysis of trade-related targets. Conference Papers for the OECD Policy dialogue on Aid for Trade. Paris. Available from www.oecd.org/dac/aft/Managing_Aid_To_Achieve_Trade_Dev_Results.pdf

____ (2013b). Trade costs: what have we learnt? A synthesis report. OECD Trade Policy Paper No. 150. Available from www.oecd.org/officialdocuments/publicdisplaydocumentpdf/?cote=TAD/TC/WP(2013)3/FINAL&docLanguage=En

Porter, Michael E. (1985). *Competitive Advantage: Creating and Sustaining Superior Performance.* New York: The Free Press.

Rugman, Alan M., and Alain Verbeke (2004). A perspective on regional and global strategies of multinational enterprises. *Journal of International Business Studies*, vol. 35, pp. 3-18.

Stone, Susan, and Ben Shepherd (2013). Global production networks and employment: a developing countries perspective. OECD Trade Policy Paper No. 154. Paris: OECD.

Sturgeon, Timothy J., and Olga Memedevic (2010). Mapping global value chains: intermediate goods trade and structural change in the world economy. Working Paper 05/2010. Vienna.: United Nations Industrial

Development Organization. Available from www.unido.org/fileadmin/media/documents/pdf/Publications/110905/WP052010_Ebook.pdf

Trefler, Daniel (2004). The long and short of the Canada-U.S. free trade agreement. *American Economic Review*, vol. 94, No. 4, pp. 870-895.

United Nations Conference on Trade and Development (2013).*World Investment Report 2013: Global value chains – Investment and Trade for Development*. Sales No. E.13.II.D.5. Geneva. Available from unctad.org/en/PublicationsLibrary/wir2013_en.pdf

United Nations, Economic and Social Commission for Asia and the Pacific (2013). 2013). *Asia-Pacific Trade and Investment Report 2013: Turning the Tide – Towards Inclusive Trade and Investment*. Sales No. E.14.II.F.2. Available from www.unescap.org/resources/asia-pacifictrade-and-investment-report-2013-turning-tidetowards-inclusive-trade-and

Venables, Anthony J. (1996). Equilibrium locations of vertically linked industries. *International Economic Review*, vol. 37, No. 2, pp. 341-359.

Venables, Tony, and Richard Baldwin (2011). Relocating the value chain: off-shoring and agglomeration in the global economy. Discussion Paper No. 544. Oxford, United Kingdom: University of Oxford, Department of Economics.

World Bank (2013). Services linkages and the value added content of trade. Policy Research Working Paper No. 6432. Washington, D.C. Available from http://go.worldbank.org/NQ2JQADSD0

World Trade Organization (2014). *World Trade Report 2014: Trade and Development – Recent Trends and the Role of the WTO.* Geneva. Available from www.wto.org/english/res_e/booksp_e/world_trade_report14_e.pdf

## ONLINE DATABASES

Centre d'Etudes Prospectives et d'Informations Internationales (CEPII). Available from www.cepii.fr

OECD-WTO. Trade in Value Added (TiVA). Available from stats.oecd.org/Index.aspx?DataSetCode=TIVA_OECD_WTO

United Nations, Economic and Social Commission for Asia and the Pacific. International Supply Chain Connectivity Database. Available from artnet.unescap.org/databases.html#fourth

United Nations, Statistics Division, Department of Economic and Social Affairs. UN Comtrade database. Available from www.comtrade.un.org

World Bank. Doing Business. Available at www.doingbusiness.org

World Development Indicator (WB–WDI). Available from data.worldbank.org/data-catalog/world-development-indicators

World Integrated Trade Solution (WITS) database. Available from wits.worldbank.org/wits/

World Trade Organization. WTO Integrated Trade Intelligence Portal (WTO-ITIP). Available from www.wto.org/english/res_e/statis_e/itip_e.htm

# Annex A

## Outward FDI; trade cost and India's participation in GVCs: The gravity estimation

An empirical analysis was carried out using the "gold standard" gravity equation in the following form:

$$PC_{jt} = g(\pi_t + \chi_{jt} + \mu_j + \eta_1 TC_{jt} + \eta_2 OFDI_{jt} + \eta_3 X_{jt}) + \varepsilon_{jt}$$

Where $PC_{jt}$ stands for India's exports of parts and components to country *j* at time t. $TC_{jt}$ is bilateral trade cost; $OFDI_{jt}$ is India's outward FDI in the export-destination country *j*; and $X_{jt}$ stands for additional control variable. The subscript for exporter (i) is suppressed as the analysis pertains to exports from one country (India).

The estimation was done using (a) within-transformed (linear) fixed effects; and (b) fixed effects Poisson (Quasi-ML) regression to account for zero trade values. In addition; as the adjustment of trade flows to policy changes may not be instantaneous (Trefler; 2004; Olivero and Yotov; 2012); the regression uses 2009 and 2012 data (with a three-year interval).

### Data sources

Exports of parts and components were sourced from United Nations Comtrade. Following Athukorala (2010); the values of total exports of parts and components at the country level are obtained by aggregating the exports of the 5-digit SITC Rev. 3 commodities (list of parts and components available on request). The trade costs data are from the ESCAP-World Bank Trade Cost Database; outward FDI from Reserve Bank of India (i.e.; compiled by aggregating the firm-level data); and inward FDI from the Ministry of Commerce and Industry of India.

### Variable description

lpc = Natural log of parts and components exports of India to partner country *j*
pc = Parts and components exports of India to partner country *j*
tc = Trade cost in manufacturing sector
eq = Manufacturing outward FDI by India through equity mode in destination country *j*
eq_loan = Manufacturing outward FDI by India (equity plus loan mode) in destination country *j*
total = Manufacturing outward FDI by India (equity; loan and guarantee mode) in destination country *j*
ifdi = Inward FDI in India received from partner country *j*

**Baseline results**

| | Within-transformed fixed effects | | | Fixed effects Poisson (Quasi ML) | | |
|---|---|---|---|---|---|---|
| | lpc | lpc | lpc | pc | pc | pc |
| tc | -0.0045** | -0.0045** | -0.0046** | -0.0142* | -0.0145* | -0.0146* |
| | (0.0020) | (0.0020) | (0.0021) | (0.008) | (0.008) | (0.008) |
| eq | 0.0004* | | | 0.0004*** | | |
| | (0.0002) | | | (0.0001) | | |
| eq_loan | | 0.0005** | | | 0.0005*** | |
| | | (0.0002) | | | (0.0001) | |
| total | | | 0.0002 | | | 0.0003*** |
| | | | (0.0002) | | | (0.0001) |
| Constant | 19.0517*** | 19.047*** | 19.049*** | - | - | - |
| | (0.2915) | (0.292) | (0.304) | | | |
| Time dummy | Yes | Yes | Yes | Yes | Yes | Yes |
| | | | | | | |
| Observations | 94 | 94 | 94 | 60 | 60 | 60 |
| No; of countries | 64 | 64 | 64 | 30 | 30 | 30 |
| F test | 16.77*** | 16.50*** | 14.74*** | | | |
| Wald test | | | | 8.79e+08*** | 8.75e+08*** | 8.93e+08*** |
| R square | 0.31 | 0.31 | 0.33 | | | |
| Log likelihood | | | | -3.127e+08 | -3.147e+08 | -3.046e+08 |

*Note:* Robust standard error in the parentheses. Coefficients of time ($\pi_t$) and partner dummies ($\mu_j$) are not reported. However; the regression could not be run with partner-time ($\chi_{jt}$) dummies using this dataset. Log values of the dependent variable in the within-transformed model are generated after adding one to parts and components exports; i.e.; to overcome zero trade values. Results are similar with zero trade values. ***<0.01; **<0.05; *<0.10.

Economies covered: Australia; Austria; Belgium; Benin; Botswana; Brazil; Chile; China; Colombia; Cyprus; Czech Republic; Denmark; Dominican Republic; Egypt; Ethiopia; Finland; France; Gabon; Georgia; Germany; Hong Kong, China; Indonesia; Islamic Republic of Iran; Ireland; Israel; Italy; Japan; Jordan; Kazakhstan; Kenya; Republic of Korea; Kyrgyzstan; Luxembourg; Malaysia; Mauritius; Mexico; Morocco; Nepal; New Zealand; Nigeria; Oman; Panama; Peru; Philippines; Qatar; Romania; Russian Federation; Rwanda; Senegal; Singapore; South Africa; Spain; Sri Lanka; Switzerland; Syria; Tanzania; Thailand; Turkey; Ukraine; United Kingdom; United States; Uzbekistan; Viet Nam; and Yemen

**Robustness check: control for inward FDI**

| | Within-transformed fixed effects | | | Fixed effects Poisson (Quasi ML) | | |
|---|---|---|---|---|---|---|
| | lpc | lpc | lpc | pc | pc | pc |
| tc | -0.0366*** | 0.0367*** | -0.0399*** | 0.0347*** | -0.0354*** | 0.0356*** |
| | (0.0104) | (0.0104) | (0.0111) | (0.0108) | (0.0110) | (0.0110) |
| eq | 0.00035 | | | 0.0004*** | | |
| | (0.0002) | | | (0.0001) | | |
| eq_loan | | 0.00038 | | | 0.0004*** | |
| | | (0.0002) | | | (0.0001) | |
| total | | | 0.00019 | | | 0.0003*** |
| | | | (0.00015) | | | (0.0001) |
| ifdi | -0.00004 | -0.00003 | -0.00002 | -1.57e-06 | 3.57e-06 | 8.45e-06 |
| | (0.00004) | (0.00004) | (0.00004) | (0.00003) | (0.00003) | (0.00002) |
| Constant | 23.031*** | 23.030*** | 23.375*** | - | - | - |
| | (1.182) | (1.181) | (1.249) | | | |
| Time Dummy | Yes | Yes | Yes | Yes | Yes | Yes |
| | | | | | | |
| Observations | 72 | 72 | 72 | 48 | 48 | 48 |
| No of Countries | 48 | 48 | 48 | 24 | 24 | 24 |
| F test | 16.13*** | 16.14*** | 18.32*** | | | |
| Wald test | | | | 7.99e+08*** | 7.97e+08*** | 8.18e+08*** |
| R square | 0.69 | 0.69 | 0.69 | | | |
| Log likelihood | | | | -2.671e+08 | -2.678e+08 | -2.567e+08 |

*Note:* Robust standard error in the parentheses. Coefficients of time ($\pi_t$) and partner dummies ($\mu_j$) are not reported. However; the regression could not be run with partner-time ($\chi_{jt}$) dummies using this dataset. Log values of the dependent variable in the within-transformed model are generated after adding one to parts and components exports; i.e.; to overcome zero trade values. Results are similar with zero trade values. ***<0.01; **<0.05; *<0.10.

Economies covered: Australia; Austria; Belgium; Botswana; Brazil; Chile; China; Cyprus; Czech Republic; Denmark; Egypt; Finland; France; Germany; Hong Kong, China; Indonesia; Ireland; Israel; Italy; Japan; Kazakhstan; Kenya; Republic of Korea; Luxembourg; Malaysia; Mauritius; Mexico; Morocco; Nepal; New Zealand; Nigeria; Oman; Panama; Philippines; Qatar; Russian Federation; Singapore; South Africa; Spain; Sri Lanka; Switzerland; Tanzania; Thailand; Turkey; Ukraine; United Kingdom; United States; and Yemen.

# Annex 7B

## The gravity models for GVC-related exports by Asia-Pacific economies

Determinants of GVC-related exports by Asia-Pacific economies within and outside the region are systematically investigated in this study based on the framework suggested by Baldwin and Taglioni (2011). The focus of the study was finding effective policy strategies to strengthen the position of Asia-Pacific economies in GVC networks.

The study applies the Baldwin and Taglioni (2011) framework to developing augmented gravity models to understanding the policy impacts on GVC-related exports of final and intermediate products based on the experience of Asia-Pacific economies from 1995 to 2013.

A major distinction of the Baldwin and Taglioni (2011) gravity model from the standard benchmark is in the "mass" variable. Standard theoretical gravity is derived based on Anderson and Van Wincoop's (2003) consumer expenditure problem. As the GDP of home and destination economies are good proxies of mass variables for the gravity model of final traded goods, mass in Anderson and Van Wincoop (2003) is:

$$mass_{ijt} = \frac{GDP_{it}GDP_{jt}}{\omega_{it}P_{jt}}$$

However, in the presence of a global production network where intermediate goods are crucial factors in trade flows, GDP might not be a good proxy as it cannot be a good representation of true consumer and producer demand shifter. The study follows Baldwin and Taglioni (2011), who suggested the alternative mass that has been adjusted for consumer demand and demand for intermediate input as follows:

$$mass_{ij} = \frac{C_{it}E_{jt}}{\omega_{it}P_{jt}}$$

$$C_{it} = VA_{it}^{mfg} + \sum\nolimits_{j \neq o} m_{ijt}^{itm}$$

$$E_{jt} = GDP_{jt} + \sum\nolimits_{i \neq o} m_{jit}^{itm}$$

$$\omega_{it} = \left(\sum GDP_{jt} \times (dist_{ij})^{1-\sigma}\right)^{\frac{1}{1-\sigma}}$$

where $\sigma = 4$

$P_{jt}$ = GDP deflator of destination $j$ at time $t$

### Specification of the gravity models

In order to avoid multicollinearity in policy variables, and between policy variables and fixed effects, the gravity model of GVC-related exports is divided into two parts: (a) a gravity model with only trade-policy variables; and (b) a gravity model with, not only trade policy variables but also trade facilitation and behind-the-border factors.

For the model with only trade policy factors, most of trade policy choices are imposed by a particular economy at a specific time to specific partners. Therefore, exporter-time, importer-time and sector-time fixed effects are applied. The baseline specification is:

$$X_{ijkt}^{l} = \beta_0 + \beta_1 mass_{ijt} + \boldsymbol{\beta_2 T}_{ijkt}^{l} + \boldsymbol{\beta_3 T}_{jikt}^{l} + \beta_4 RTA_{ijt} + \boldsymbol{\beta_5 G}_{ij} + \delta_{it} + \delta_{jt} + \delta_{kt} + \varepsilon_{ijkt}^{l}\,.$$

For trade facilitation and behind-the-border conditions, data are country-time specific. The model then includes fixed effects separately by reporter, partner, time and sector:

$$X^l_{ijkt} = \beta_0 + \beta_1 mass_{ijt} + \boldsymbol{\beta_2 T}^l_{ijkt} + \boldsymbol{\beta_3 T}^l_{jikt} + \beta_4 RTA_{ijt} + \boldsymbol{\beta_5 G}_{ij} + \boldsymbol{\beta_6 F}_{it} + \boldsymbol{\beta_7 F}_{jt} + \delta_i + \delta_j + \delta_k + \varepsilon^l_{ijkt}$$

where

$X^l_{ijkt}$ is the bilateral exports of product l in sector k from country i to country j in year t.

$mass_{ijt}$ is the economic mass measured under the method suggested by Baldwin and Taglioni (2011).

$X^l_{ijkt}$ is a vector of product-variant trade-policy variables imposed by country i faced by country j related to trade in product l of sector k at time t. The set of policy variables include applied MFN tariffs and non-tariff measures.

$X^l_{ijkt}$ is a vector of the same set of policies faced by country i when exporting product l to country j at period t.

$RTA_{ijt}$ is a dummy variable capturing the RTA relationship between country i and country j at time t.

$\boldsymbol{F}_{it}$ and $\boldsymbol{F}_{jt}$ are the vectors of behind-the-border indicators at time t of country i and country j, respectively. The vectors include indices measuring behind-the-border conditions of a country such as availability of ICT (proxied by Internet users per 100 people), port and logistics conditions (based on ISCC) and behind-the-border conditions that reflect business environment (Doing Business – distance to frontier), are country-time specific variables.

$\boldsymbol{G}_{ij}$ is a vector includes time-invariant controlled variables as per standard gravity model, i.e., distance, contingency, and common official language.

$\delta_i, \delta_j,$ are $\delta_k$ included in the model to capture unobserved time-invariant fixed effects by country and sector levels. By adding t to the subscript, the variables become time-variant fixed effects.

**Data source, variable description and expected signs**

| Variable | Unit | Expected signs | Source | Description |
|---|---|---|---|---|
| ln_xij | US dollar | | WITS | Export of country *i* to destination *j*, through import flows[1] |
| mass | - | + | Author's calculation based on WB-WDI | See Baldwin and Taglioni, 2011 |
| dist | Kilometer | - | CEPII | Distance between source country *i* and host country *j* |
| contig | - | + | CEPII | Dummy variable indicating 1 if 2 countries share common border, 0 otherwise |
| comlang_off | - | + | CEPII | Dummy variable indicating 1 if 2 countries share common official language, 0 otherwise |
| tariff_ij | 1+percent | - | TRAINS through WITS download platform | Simple average tariff of country *i* charging on importation from country *j* |
| tariff_ji | 1+percent | - | TRAINS through WITS download platform | Simple average tariff of country *j* charging on importation from country *i* |
| NTM_num_ij | Number | - | Author's calculation based on WTO-ITIP | Number of NTM measures that country i imposes on country *j* |
| NTM_num_ji | Number | - | Author's calculation based on WTO-ITIP | Number of NTM measures that country *j* imposes on country *i* |
| RTA | - | + | de Sousa (2012) | Dummy variable indicating 1 if 2 countries have RTA, 0 otherwise |
| d2f_xtab_i | Score (0-100) | + | Doing Business | Ease of doing business index: distance to frontier (excluding electricity) of country *i* |
| d2f_xtab_j | Score (0-100) | + | Doing Business | Ease of doing business index: distance to frontier (excluding electricity) of country *j* |
| iscc_i | Index | + | UNCTAD | Liner shipping connectivity index of country *i* |
| iscc_i | Index | + | UNCTAD | Liner shipping connectivity index of country *i* /*j* |
| intusers_i | Users/100 people | + | WB-WDI | internet users per 100 people of country *j* |
| intusers_j | Users/100 people | + | WB-WDI | internet users per 100 people of country *j* |

[1] The study uses import flows of, for example, Thailand from the Republic of Korea to represent exports of the Republic of Korea to Thailand. This method solves the missing data problem, especially in small least developed economies.

**Empirical results are available from online Appendix C.**

# 8 SERVICES IN INDUSTRIAL VALUE CHAINS

Services value-added, across all world economies, accounted for 29% of global gross exports in 2009, according to research by ESCAP (2014). In addition, there has been an increase in the reliance on imported services at the expense of domestically-supplied ones. The increased importance of "servicification" implies that services have become a key to enhancing the competitiveness of economies, especially those exporting industrial products through global value chains (GVCs). In fact, GVC-related production and trade have spread more extensively through the Asia-Pacific region than in the rest of the world, indicating the high importance of servicification, inter alia, to the development of industrial exports of the region.

Taking into account the unique characteristics of the region, this chapter focuses closely on servicification in Asia and the Pacific. The analysis looks into the types of service inputs embedded in industrial exports of Asia and the Pacific, and explores sourcing patterns for these inputs. It also sheds light on appropriate policies for liberalization of trade and regional integration in services that are aimed at enhancing international competitiveness of Asia-Pacific economies.

## A CONTRIBUTION OF SERVICES IN ASIA-PACIFIC INDUSTRIAL EXPORTS[1]

The recognition of the value created, directly or indirectly, by services in the manufacturing, distribution and marketing process of goods has become known as "servicification" (ESCAP, 2013). The expansion of servicification is driven by many factors, most notably the reductions of barriers to trade in services as well as the spread of GVCs. According to Gereffi and others (2001), GVCs rely intensively on services to link and coordinate the activities located in different economies. In addition, the increasingly liberal trade in services as well as the advancement of communications and transportation technologies have increased the tradability of services, and consequently have generated a higher share of foreign services in industrial exports.

Based on data from the OECD-WTO TiVA database,[2] figure 8.1 depicts the share of services value-added embedded in gross industrial exports in 2009 in the Asia-Pacific region.[3] Service content in industrial exports from Asia-Pacific economies amounted to 29.4%.[4] The share of services is predominant in high-technology sectors, i.e., electrical and optical equipment (32.5%), machinery (30.8%), transport equipment (30.6%), and chemicals and non-metallic mineral products (30%); however, the share lags behind in agriculture, hunting, forestry and fishing (18.5%), mining and quarrying (21.8%), and food products (25.2%). These results are consistent with global trends, under which the transport equipment and high-tech sectors are the most service-intensive industries (World Bank, 2013). However, the share of services value-added could differ across economies of different development levels.[5] With reference to the correlation between the level of development and trade in services, the World Trade Report (WTO, 2014) estimated a gap in the share of services value-added in exports between developed and developing economies as big as 5 percentage points.

Domestic services account for 18.3% of total industrial exports from the Asia-Pacific, while the foreign services' contribution is 11.1%.[6] However, there is variation across industries. Notably, the share of imported services appears to be related to GVC-related exports. For example, the share of imported services is particularly high in the exports of electrical and optical equipment (16%) compared to the share in exports of other sectors, especially agriculture and mining.

Figure 8.1. Services content in gross exports of Asia-Pacific economies, by industrial sector, 2009

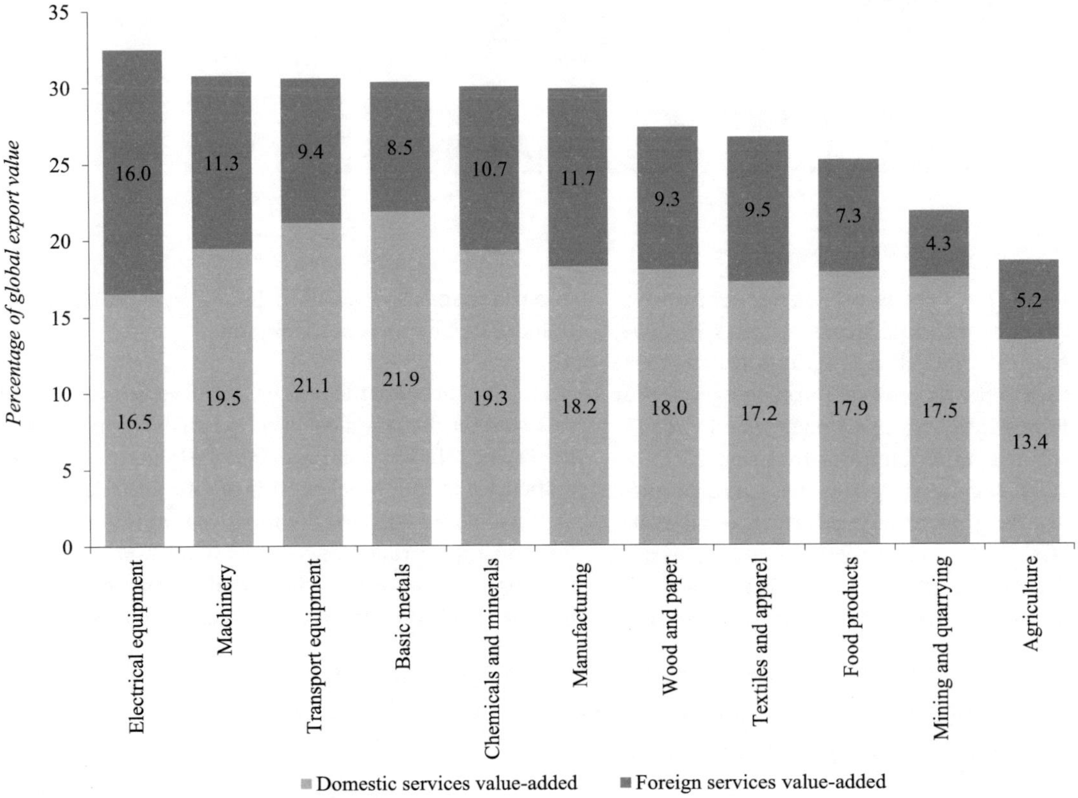


*Source:* ESCAP calculation based on the OECD-WTO TiVA database (accessed in March 2015).

During the past several decades, there has been substantial replacement of domestic services by imported ones, especially in the high-technology sectors (figure 8.2). Domestically-provided services fell dramatically in transport, machinery, electrical equipment and manufacturing. That decline has been more than replaced by the expansion of foreign services, which increased significantly by 5.7, 5.6 and 5.6 percentage points for the transport, machinery and the electrical sectors, respectively. Consistent with these findings, WTO (2015) indicated that developing economies experienced a dramatic decrease in domestic services and a sharp growth in foreign services value-added between 1995 and 2009. One of the reasons for the declining share of domestic services could be the increasing tendency of services offshoring, which has become a common element of the GVC phenomenon.[7]

Figure 8.2. Changes in the shares of services value-added in gross industrial exports by Asia-Pacific economies, 1995-2009

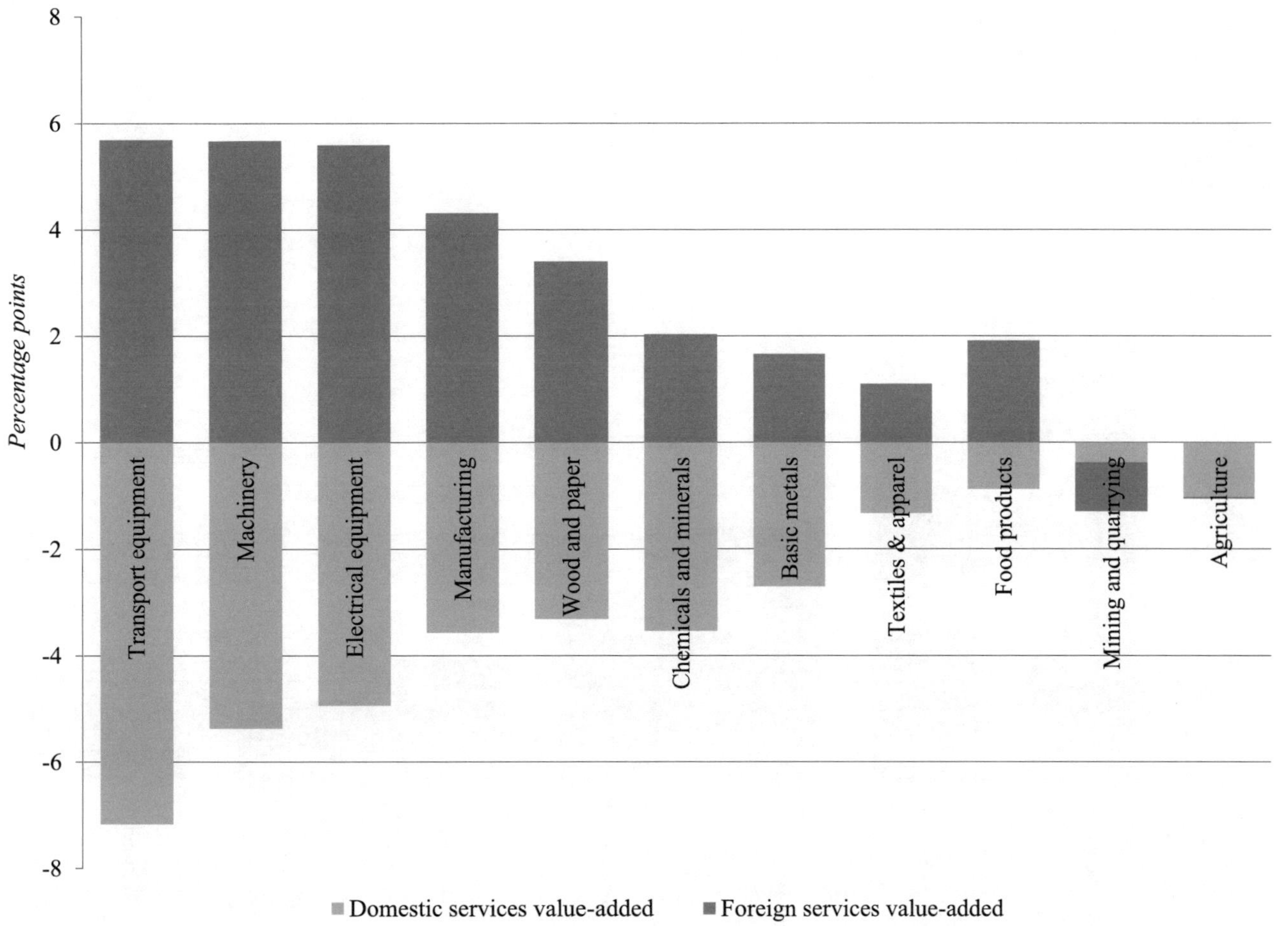


*Source:* ESCAP calculation based on the OECD-WTO TiVA database (accessed in March 2015).

In sum, the information above suggests that the spread of GVCs, especially in high-technology industries, appears to translate into a relatively high service intensity of production and exports. A large part of the rising service content has moved from domestic sources to imports, which implies that access to cost-efficient service imports may play an important part in enhancing an economy's competitiveness in the exports by high-technology industrial sectors.

## B KEY SERVICES FOR EXPORT COMPETITIVENESS OF ASIA-PACIFIC INDUSTRIES

Policies to promote the competitiveness of industrial exports should pay particular attention to the cost-efficiency of key service inputs. Services inputs related to distribution (wholesale, retail, hotel and restaurant services) are the most important, with a share of 9% in gross industrial exports (figure 8.3). In fact, the share of wholesale and retail trade, hotels and restaurants service in exports of Asia-Pacific economies is higher than the world average (8%). Business services and logistic-related services (transport and storage, post and telecommunications) are the other two major service inputs to the production of industrial exports, contributing 7.5% and 5.2% of gross industrial export value-added, respectively. The service sector with the lowest contribution is construction, amounting to approximately 0.6% just behind the residual category of other services with 1.6% share.

Due to their nature (services were historically perceived to be non-tradable), most services are likely to have relatively high domestic content, especially utility services (electricity, gas and water supplies) and construction services. Among the services embedded in industrial exports by Asia and the Pacific, electricity, gas and water supply as well as financial intermediation have the highest domestic-to-foreign value-added ratio: 3 and 2.2, respectively. Similarly, in the case of wholesale and retail trade, hotels and restaurants, domestic services account for about two thirds of the total value-added. In contrast, business services depend on the contribution from foreign suppliers for slightly more than half of the business services embedded in industrial exports by Asia and the Pacific.

Figure 8.3. Services inputs to gross industrial exports by Asia-Pacific economies, 2009

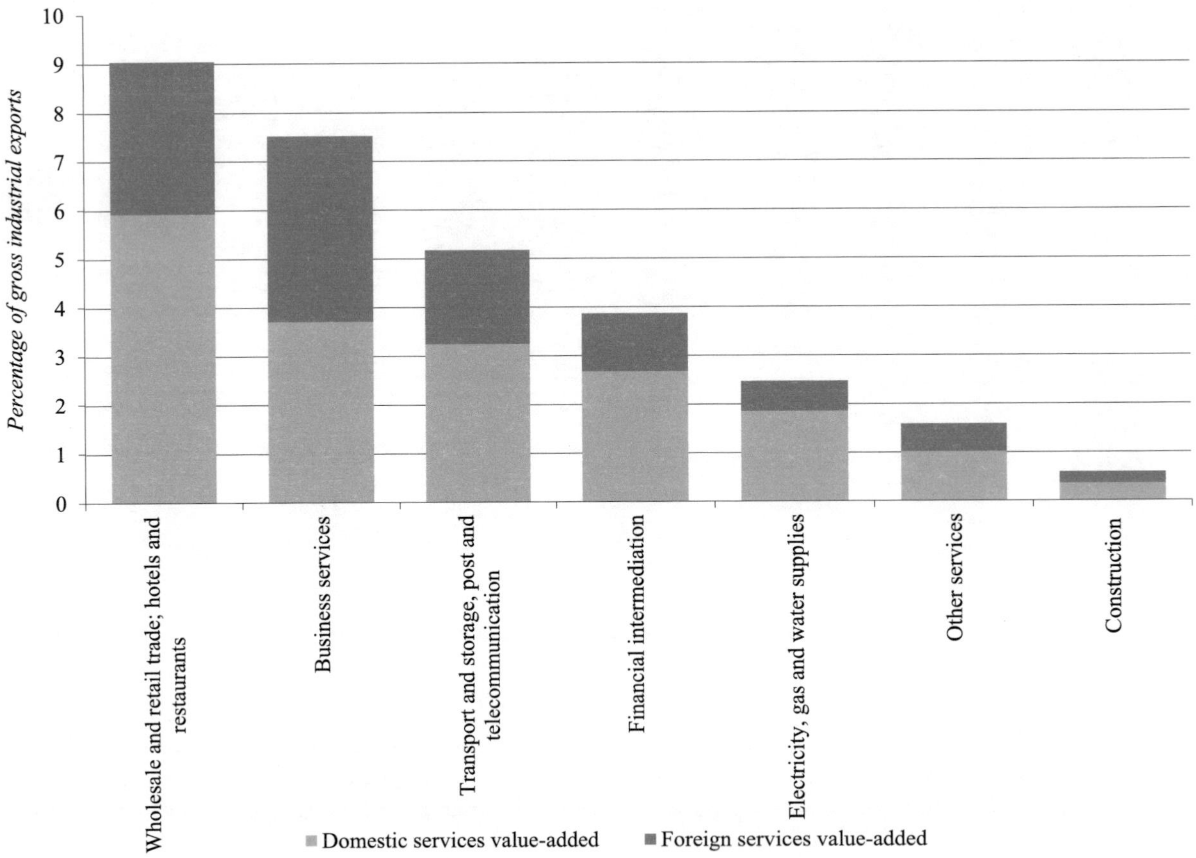


*Source:* ESCAP calculation based on the OECD-WTO TiVA database (accessed in March 2015).

Service offshoring appears to be taking place for all service inputs. There was a decline in the domestic content of all service inputs from 1995 to 2009 (figure 8.4). The move of service sourcing has been most striking in the cases of business services, where the domestic component decreased by 2.2 percentage points during those years.

## Figure 8.4. Changes in services value-added in gross industrial exports by Asia-Pacific economies, by source, 1995-2009

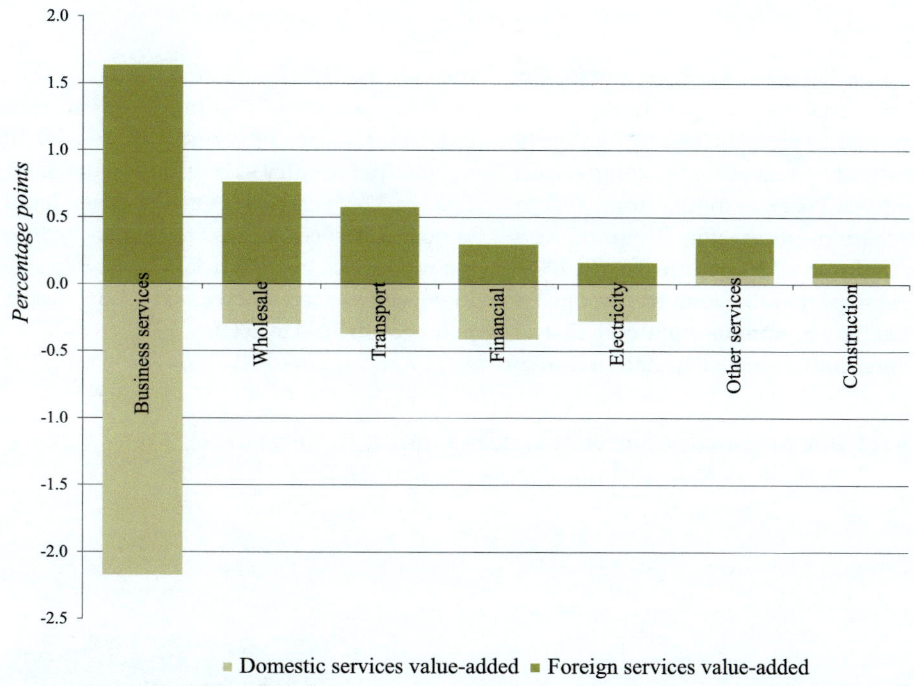


*Source:* ESCAP calculation based on OECD-WTO TiVA database (accessed in March 2015).

## Figure 8.5. Services inputs to gross industrial exports by Asia-Pacific economies, by the industrial sector, 2009

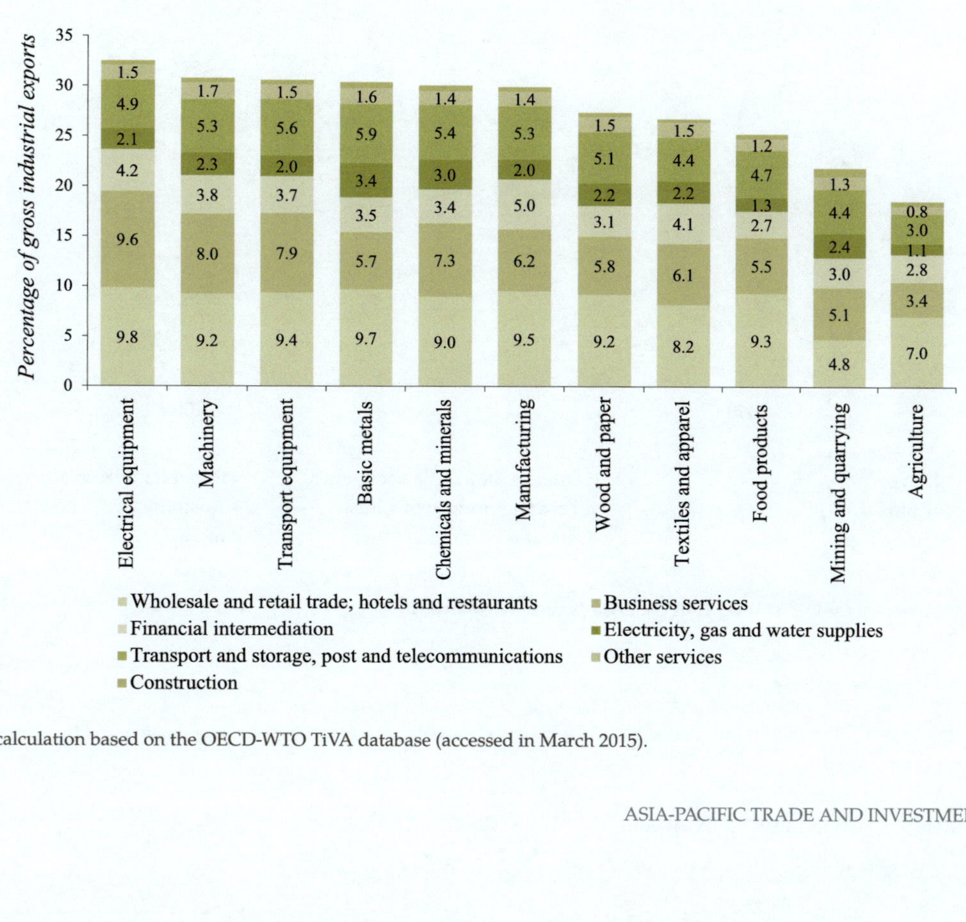


*Source:* ESCAP calculation based on the OECD-WTO TiVA database (accessed in March 2015).

# C INTRAREGIONALLY TRADED SERVICES IN INDUSTRIAL EXPORTS FROM ASIA-PACIFIC ECONOMIES

The increasing reliance on imported services mentioned above may boost intraregional trade opportunities if the rising demand for imported services can be met by supply (exports) from Asia-Pacific economies. A comparison between sources of imported service inputs from 2000 to 2009 reveals that the share of intraregional imports rose from 42.5% of service inputs to 47.3% (figure 8.6). In 2009, more than 80% of those imports were sourced from just 8 out of the 18 Asia-Pacific economies included in the database: Australia; China; India; Japan; Republic of Korea; Russian Federation; Hong Kong, China; and Taiwan Province of China.[8] Although Japan remains the most important source of services inputs for the Asia-Pacific region, that country's contribution declined from 16.4% in 2000 to 12.5% in 2009. On the other hand, the share of imported services sourced from other economies increased, mainly service exports from China, Republic of Korea and India, whose shares increased by 1.6, 1.4, and 1.3 percentage points from 2000 to 2009.

**Figure 8.6. Intraregional imports of services inputs in industrial exports of Asia and the Pacific, by source, 2000 and 2009**

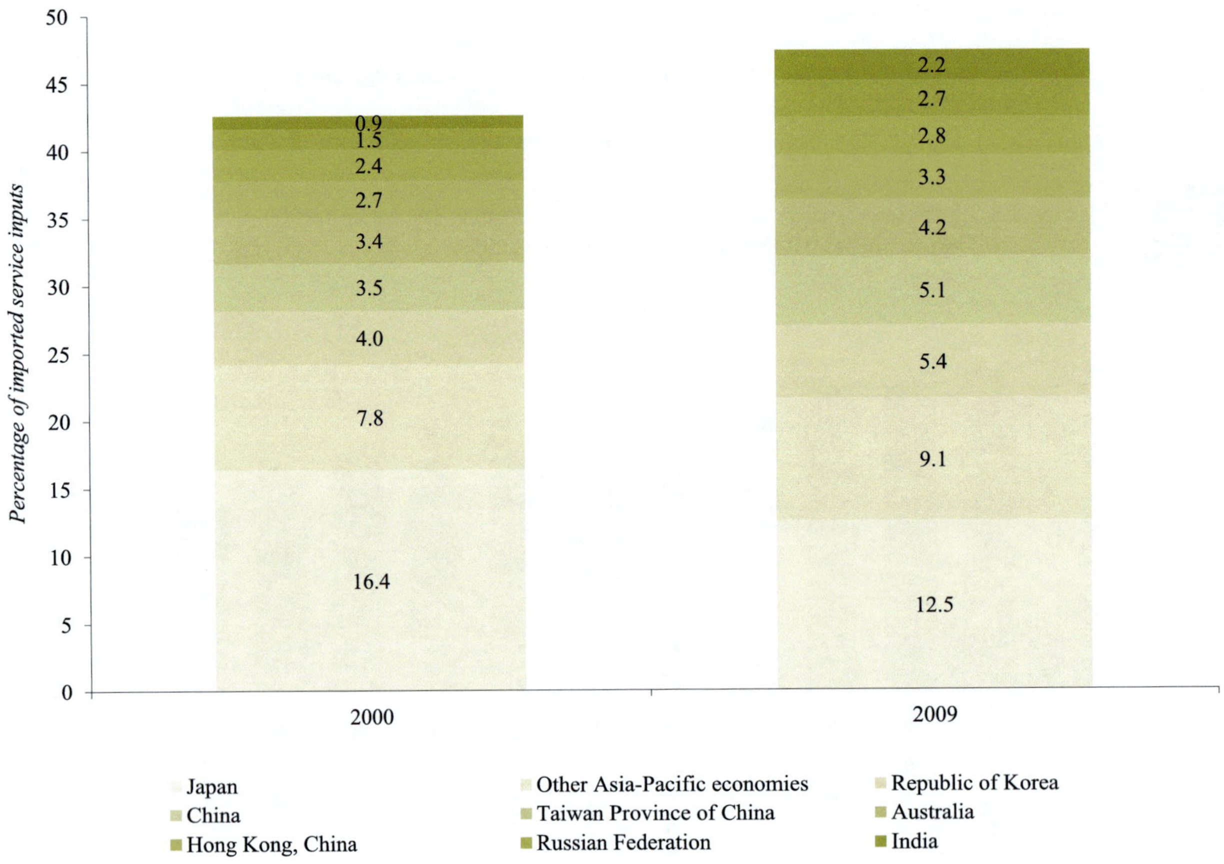


*Source:* ESCAP calculation based on the OECD-WTO TiVA database (accessed in March 2015).

# D CONCLUSION

Better statistical tracking of trade in value-added has uncovered the phenomenon of servicification, which had been a hidden part of trade values contained in the supply chains of goods. Using this new statistical source, this chapter confirms that services create a significant portion of the export value of industrial goods. In the Asia-Pacific economies covered by the OECD-WTO TiVA database, the value created by services as intermediate inputs represents about 29% of the total value-added in industrial exports. In electrical, machinery, transport equipment and chemical products as well as basic metals, directly and indirectly embodied services account for more than 30% of the value-added of exports.

GVCs heighten the need for coordination and efficient linking of production stages and locations, with services playing a particularly prominent role. They rely heavily on distribution, logistics, and information and communication technologies, and therefore on efficient network infrastructure and complementary services such as finance and insurance. In the OECD-WTO database, distribution, business coordination and logistics are among the most important service inputs for the cost-efficient production of Asia-Pacific industrial exports. At present, much of these key intermediate services are imported, in particular business services that are one of the essential inputs for production of exported manufacturing goods, especially electrical, machinery, transport equipment and chemical products.

The importance of servicification requires a comprehensive approach to policy formulation. While liberalizing trade in goods is a starting point for creating new trade opportunities, the value chains of industrial goods also require efficient services. Improvements in the performance of the service sector, including by liberalization of services trade, would therefore enhance the competitiveness of manufacturing firms and facilitate their participation in global production networks. In contrast, restricted service trade and rigid regulation, often found among some of the fastest-growing economies in the region, such as China, India, Indonesia, the Philippines, Malaysia and Thailand, could translate into negative effects on exports of goods (World Bank, 2012).

However, as imported services become an increasingly essential element of internationalized production, Governments will come under more pressure to find a balance between assisting domestic service providers and promoting the competitiveness of manufacturing exports in GVCs. There is also a risk that too much reliance on imported intermediate services and goods may lead to limited development spillovers from GVCs to the rest of the economy.

The general direction of service trade policy should then focus on creating competitive market conditions and developing a well-functioning domestic service sector that meets high regulatory standards. Measures will have to vary from sector to sector. For example, ensuring access to the grid or network for new entrants in the telecommunications or electricity sectors should help in creating equal opportunities and result in pro-competitive efficiency gains. The openness of financial services with a good regulatory framework could enhance competition and stability of the financial sector and contribute to macro-stability. In addition, it is important to have a comprehensive set of policies in place to encourage spillovers and technological diffusion from foreign to domestic providers. This may include, for example, public investment to upgrade and improve accessibility to backbone infrastructure such as railways, ports, health care and education. The provision of education and training (e.g., in information technology, languages and professional skills) as well as greater domestic and international labour mobility will enable domestic firms as well as individuals to take advantage of service-export opportunities.

## ENDNOTES

[1] More details are available in Anukoonwattaka, Scagliusi and Mikic (2015).

[2] The analysis is based on data on trade in value-added from the OECD-WTO TiVA database. The May 2013 version was the only available version at the time of preparing this report. The database covers 56 economies, of which 17 are ESCAP members (Australia; Brunei Darussalam; Cambodia; China; India; Indonesia; Japan; Republic of Korea; Malaysia; New Zealand; the Philippines; Russian Federation; Singapore; Thailand; Viet Nam; Turkey; and Hong Kong, China). As these 17 economies and Taiwan Province of China accounted for 97.4% of merchandise exports and 97.3% of merchandise imports by Asia-Pacific economies in 2013 they are taken as a representative sample of the region. The OECD-WTO TiVA database covers 18 sectors classified under 1 digit-ISIC Rev .3, which comprises 11 industrial sectors (agriculture, mining, food products, textiles and apparel, wood and paper, chemicals and minerals, basic metals, machinery, electrical equipment, transport equipment, other manufactures, and utilities) and 7 service sectors (construction, wholesale and retail, transport, telecommunications, finance and insurance, business services and other services). The May 2013 version

of the OECD-WTO TiVA database provides data for the years 1995, 2000, 2005, 2008 and 2009.

[3] Value-added in exports can be split into its three components: value-added from services; manufacturing; and primary products. Increasing the share of one of these components, ceteris paribus, leads to the decrease of the other two shares.

[4] Service content in world exports of industrial products was 29% in the same period (ESCAP, 2014).

[5] Following the United Nations classification, the economies analysed in this chapter comprise: one least developed economy (Cambodia); 13 developing economies (Brunei Darussalam; China; India; Indonesia; Malaysia; the Philippines; Republic of Korea; Singapore; Thailand; Turkey; Viet Nam; Hong Kong, China; and Taiwan Province of China); one economy in transition (Russian Federation); and three developed economies (Australia, Japan and New Zealand).

[6] Domestic services include direct, indirect and re-imported ones. Direct domestic services value-added is the value added by services exporting industry. Indirect domestic services value-added is the value added by other domestic services industries that provide intermediate inputs to exports of goods and other services. Re-imported domeatic services is the domestic contribution to goods and services that were exported and came back as intermediate imposts used by the industry in question.

[7] Another factor could be the relatively rapid increase in the value-added from the industrial sector.

[8] The graph shows the top eight performing economies in terms of services exported. The remaining 10 economies (Brunei Darussalam, Cambodia, Indonesia, Malaysia, the Philippines, New Zealand, Singapore, Thailand, Turkey and Viet Nam) are clustered in "Other AP economies".

## REFERENCES


Anukoonwattaka, Witada, Marco Scagliusi and Mia Mikic (2015). Servicification and industrial exports from Asia and the Pacific. Trade Insights, No. 10. Bangkok: ESCAP. Available from www.unescap.org/resources/servicification-and-industrial-exports-asia-and-pacific-trade-insights-issue-no-10

Gereffi, G., and others (2001). Globalisation, value chains and development. IDS Bulletin, No. 32.3. Brighton, United Kingdom: Institute of Development Studies. Available from www.ids.ac.uk/files/dmfile/gereffietal323.pdf

United Nations, Economic and Social Commission for Asia and the Pacific (2013). *Asia-Pacific Trade and Investment Report 2013: – Turning the Tide - Towards Inclusive Trade and Investment.* Sales No. E.14.II.F.2. Available from www.unescap.org/resources/asia-pacific-trade-and-investment-report-2013-turning-tide-towards-inclusive-trade-and

______ (2014). *Asia-Pacific Trade and Investment Report 2014: Recent Trends and Developments.* Sales No. E.15.II.F.2. Available from www.unescap.org/resources/asia-pacific-trade-and-investment-report-2014-recent-trends-and-developments

World Bank (2012). Policy barriers to international trade in services. Policy Research Working Paper, No. 6109. Washington, D.C. Available from http://elibrary.worldbank.org/doi/pdf/10.1596/1813-9450-6109

_____ (2013). Services linkages and the value added contents of trade. Policy Research Working Paper, No. 6432. Washington, D.C. Available from http://go.worldbank.org/NQ2JQADSD0

World Trade Organization (2014). *World Trade Report 2014.* Chapter II C. Washington, D.C. Available from https://www.wto.org/english/res_e/booksp_e/eport14_e.pdf

______ (2015). Services and global value chains – some evidence on servicification of manufacturing and services networks. Working Paper ERSD-2015-03. Geneva. Available from https://www.wto.org/english/res_e/reser_e/ersd201503_e.pdf


## ONLINE DATABASES


OECD-WTO. Trade in Value Added (TiVA). Available from http://stats.oecd.org/Index.aspx?DataSetCode=TIVA_OECD_WTO

# 9 GLOBAL VALUE CHAINS, TECHNOLOGY TRANSFERS AND INNOVATION

As discussed in the report so far, the rise of the global value chain (GVC) production model has modified the paradigm for trade and development policies.[1] An outward orientation remains a key to development prospects, but instead of needing to build up a complete domestic industry in order to engage in exporting, economies can now specialize in one task that forms part of that industry, such as the production of particular components. This expands the scope of industrial development and may significantly shorten the time it takes to become an industrial exporter.

From a development standpoint, as an economy evolves and accumulates human and physical capital, the prospect of moving upwards along the value chain emerges. The early stages of GVC participation typically involve labour-intensive low-value-added operations, such as product assembly. Upon reaching higher levels of development, however, there is the possibility to specialize in higher value-added tasks such as component manufacture, ultimately culminating in research and development (R&D). Higher value-added tasks are beneficial to an economy because they are often accompanied by positive spillovers in terms of technology, productivity and skills upgrading, and will ideally lead to endogenous technology creation. This modified trade and development paradigm therefore focuses on joining GVCs and – crucially – on "moving up" into higher value-added processes. Identifying the policies needed to support moving up is therefore a matter of critical importance to the region.[2]

Among economists there is a consensus that, under the right circumstances outward orientation including through participation in GVCs, is a viable development paradigm, even following the Global Financial Crisis (e.g. Haddad and Shepherd, 2011, or Evenett, Mikic and Ratnayake, eds., 2011). In fact, many policymakers from developing economies emphasize that outward orientation should be linked to participation in GVCs. However, they also express concern regarding the extent to which the GVC model actually allows for industrialization and development, i.e. there is the fear being that a country might join a GVC at a low value-added point and become stuck there. Instead of moving up the value chain, it would experience stagnating productivity and income growth. This chapter analyses evidence from firm-level surveys in order to establish whether or not such concerns are justified, and to identify examples of good practice to ensure that GVC participation is conducive to technological upgrading and technology transfer.

GVCs have a variety of economic effects in developing countries; however, not all of them can be discussed in detail here. From a development point of view, however, two processes lie at the core of making GVCs work positively – economic upgrading and "densification", i.e. the development of strong linkages among GVCs and an ever-widening range of domestic firms. Figure 9.1 shows the various economic mechanisms at work in the broad process of GVC participation, some of which are discussed in the present chapter as they touch on technology transfer. Taglioni and Winkler (2015) provide a complete review.

## Figure 9.1. GVC transmission channels

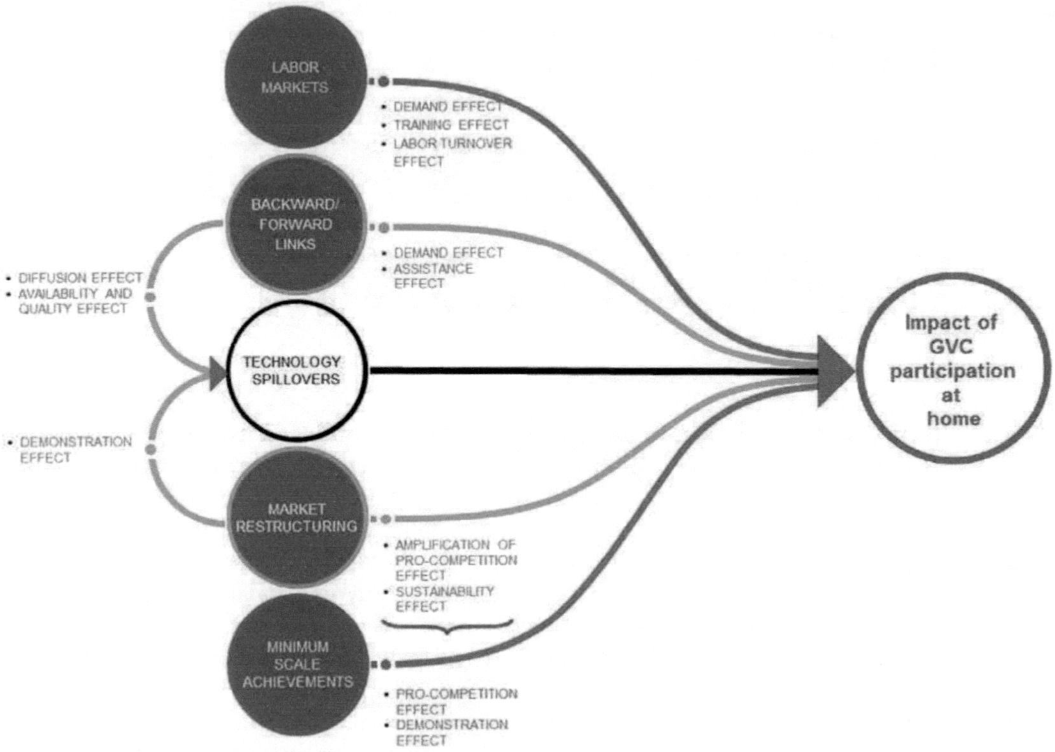


*Source:* Taglioni and Winkler, (2015).

To provide an empirical point of departure for considering the relationship between GVCs and technology, figure 9.2 examines the association between GVC participation and the sophistication of a country's export bundle as one measure of its level of technology. The GVC participation index is taken from the OECD-WTO Trade in Value-Added Database; it summarizes the percentage of a country's gross exports that are accounted for by intermediates used in other countries' exports as well as imported intermediates used in the country's own exports. It therefore captures the extent of the backward and forward linkages that lie at the core of the GVC business model. Export sophistication is measured using EXPY (Hausmann, Hwang and Rodrik, 2007), which captures the average income level associated with a country's actual export bundle.

The line of best fit in figure 9.2 is upward sloping, which indicates a positive association between GVC participation and export sophistication. This result is consistent with a global view in which GVC participation can be associated with production upgrading and technology enhancement. It is important to stress, however, that figure 9.2 is just an association, and cannot be read as implying causation. It is possible that countries with more sophisticated export bundles tend to be more involved in GVCs for other reasons, and it tells us nothing about their movement along the value chain. Nonetheless, an initial review of the macro-data shows that there is certainly a possibility that GVCs can promote technology upgrading in countries that participate in them.

## Figure 9.2. GVC participation versus export sophistication, 2009

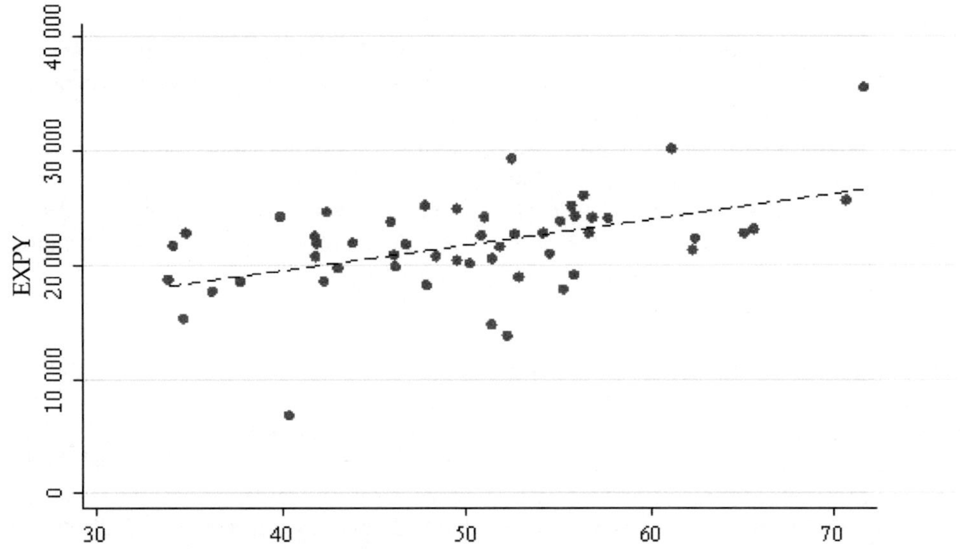


*Sources:* United Nations Comtrade; World Development Indicators; OECD-WTO Trade in Value Added Database; author's calculations.
*Note:* Indicators are defined in the main text.

Against this backdrop, this chapter examines the scope for technology transfer within the GVC production model, focusing on empirically verified mechanisms, and the institutional and economic preconditions that need to be in place in the recipient economy to encourage this process. At this point, it is important to note that technology is interpreted broadly to include the process by which inputs of all kinds – factors of production and intermediate goods as well as organizational and management methods – are combined to produce a final output. Subsequently, a broad view of the term "technology transfer" is also taken, more akin to the literature on technology diffusion that encompasses a variety of different mechanisms (figure 9.1) and is not limited to transaction based relationships.

The chapter proceeds as follows. Section A discusses the direct and indirect channels through which GVCs can support technology diffusion, focusing on investment, licensing and import channels. Section B evaluates those mechanisms in a relevant context by discussing developing economies' capacity to absorb technology, a crucial mediating factor in the relationship between GVC participation and technology. Finally, section C presents the conclusion and discusses policy implications.

# A GLOBAL VALUE CHAINS AND TECHNOLOGY TRANSFER: DIRECT AND INDIRECT CHANNELS

What basis is there to believe that technology transfer can take place within a GVC production model? Those who are skeptical of GVCs see them as static structures, in which each firm or economy is locked into a particular position and cannot move up into higher value-added activities, because that would mean displacing others who are better established and may have had the opportunity to erect barriers to entry.

However, the business reality appears to be quite different in many cases. GVCs are about maximizing profit all the way along the chain.[3] The distribution of profits and the ability of some actors to earn higher margins than others are serious issues that need further research, but the static view of GVCs does not fit with commercial reality. The essence of GVCs is to be competitive and therefore dynamic. Each value chain is constantly looking for new commercial opportunities, both in terms of new markets to serve, and new technologies or methods of production to increase the competitiveness of the chain as a whole.

It is these dynamics that give rise to the rationale for what can be termed explicit (direct) technology transfer, whereby an upwards GVC partner or lead firm (assumed to be located in a developed economy, or North) makes a conscious decision to transfer technology to a firm upstream in the supply chain (frequently presumed to be in a developing economy, or South). The business case for such a transfer is that it can help a developing economy's firm produce more efficiently, and this in turn has benefits for the lead firm that may source its inputs from the upstream firm.

Technology transfer in this case, although not free from risk from the transferor's point of view, is a win-win scenario – the developing economy's firm, and perhaps also its competitors and suppliers, win from a technology upgrade and enhanced productivity, and the lead firm benefits from a more efficient value chain that improves its own competitive position globally. Of course, technology transfers of this type represent a relationship-specific investment, and so will only be undertaken in certain circumstances – in particular, the domestic institutional setting of the recipient firm needs to be strong, especially in the area of contract enforcement and rule of law. More details on this below, in relation to the ability of developing countries to benefit from technology transfer.

In addition to explicit transfers like this, there is also the possibility for technology to diffuse indirectly through GVCs. In essence, the circulation of capital and intermediate goods, and the knowledge that they embody, creates opportunities for technology upgrading, quite apart from the narrow case of an explicit technology transfer. As will be seen, access to imported intermediates in particular can be a spur to domestic productivity upgrading and innovation. This section discusses the main mechanisms – both explicit and implicit – by which GVCs can support technology upgrading in developing countries (figure 9.1; see also Glachant, 2013).

### 1. Foreign direct investment

One common way in which GVC participation can bring technology transfer and upgrading is foreign direct investment (FDI). When a firm receives FDI, it develops a close relationship with the investor, typically a larger firm, and maybe even a lead firm in a GVC. Technology transfer through FDI relies on the investor having access to globally competitive technologies that it can make available to a developing country partner.

One advantage of FDI for the investing company is greater security that the technology in question – which may be proprietary – will not leave its corporate group. Other arrangements, such as licensing (see below), pose greater risks of technology leakage, which can be advantageous for other producers in the industry, but not for the source of the technology. Direct investment is thus a way of limiting the risk of leakage while maintaining competitive advantage vis-à-vis competitors.

A country's investment climate is therefore an important determinant of a lead firm's willingness to assume those risks. Similarly, restrictions on FDI such as a maximum ownership level, or restrictions on legal form such as joint venture requirements, can increase the risk profile of an investment, and will make the lead firm more likely to hang back. Essentially, uncertainty of all types is a major factor that discourages any investment, and technology specific investments in GVCs are no exception to this rule.

Empirical evidence bears out the contention that FDI can be a vector of direct technology transfer at the firm level. Figure 9.3 uses World Bank Enterprise Survey data on firms in developing economies to analyse the labour productivity (value-added per worker) differential between firms that are majority foreign-owned and those that are majority domestically-owned. The kernel density – analogous to a smoothed histogram – is shifted to the right in the case of foreign-owned firms, which indicates that they tend to have a higher level of labour productivity than domestically-owned firms. A simple descriptive regression confirms that after controlling for country, time, and sector specific factors, foreign-owned firms are, on average, 82% more productive than domestically-owned firms. This result is consistent with foreign-owned firms having access to superior technology than do domestic firms. This basic empirical evidence therefore supports the contention that direct investment in a firm, including by a GVC partner or lead firm, can induce technology transfer to it, and lead to productivity upgrading. Such a process is largely confirmed in the empirical literature, and for example Arnold and Javorcik (2009) found evidence of increased labour productivity due to capital investment as well as organizational and management restructuring following acquisition by a foreign affiliate in a sample of Indonesian firms.

## Figure 9.3. Productivity differential between domestic and foreign-owned firms

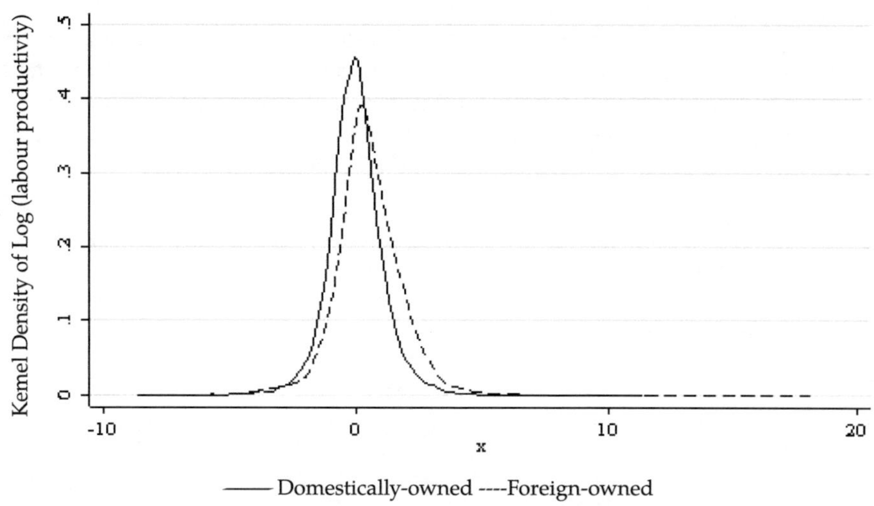


*Sources:* World Bank Enterprise Surveys; author's calculations.
*Note:* Foreign ownership is defined as a 50% share or greater. Labour productivity is demeaned by country-sector-year.

The discussion so far has focused on the direct effects of FDI, i.e. on the firm that receives the investment. However, there is also good reason to believe that FDI generates spillovers for other firms – there is always some leakage of technology or people, so although the primary technology shock from FDI accrues to the firm receiving the investment, some of the benefit is also felt by other firms. This indirect mechanism means that FDI is beneficial not just to a single firm that receives an investment, but also to other firms that remain in domestic hands. It is an indirect way in which FDI can act as a vector of technology transfer, including within the context of GVCs. For a detailed discussion of the ways in which such spillovers can occur in the developing country context, see Farole, Staritz and Winkler (2014), reproduced in summary in figure 9.4.

## Figure 9.4. Conceptual framework for understanding FDI spillovers in developing countries

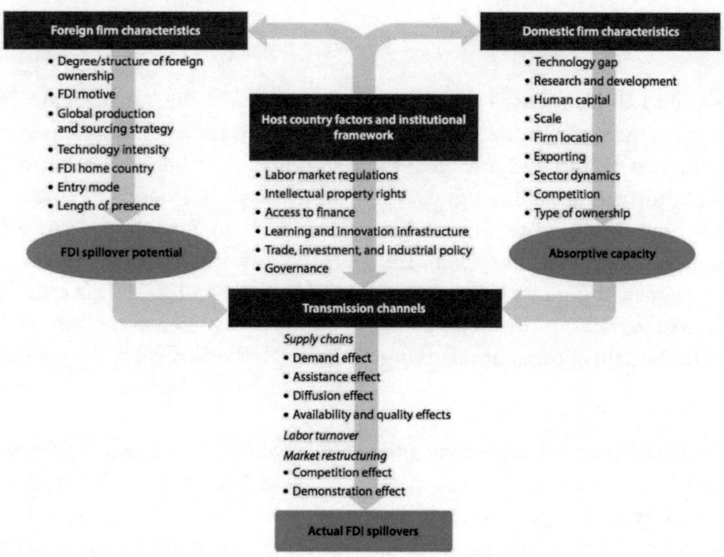


*Source:* Farole, Staritz and Winkler (2014).

CHAPTER 9

Figure 9.5 shows that the data again bear out the existence of this type of mechanism. The figure shows the productivity differential between firms in cities without any foreign-owned firms and those in cities with at least one foreign-owned firm – closest to the case of horizontal spillovers in the literature. The curve in the latter case is shifted to the right, which is consistent with the existence of technology spillovers outside the firm from FDI. A descriptive regression confirms this result; after controlling for country, sector and year specific factors as well as firm-level foreign ownership, there is a statistically significant relationship between the level of foreign investment in a city and firm productivity. Specifically, a one percentage point increase in the proportion of foreign-owned firms is associated with a productivity increase of around 0.8%. Again, this mechanism highlights that FDI can be a vector for technology transfer, both directly and indirectly. To the extent that GVC participation promotes FDI, it too can therefore be seen as a way in which technology can be upgraded by making use of foreign advances, albeit of a much smaller magnitude.

**Figure 9.5. Productivity differential between firms in cities with FDI and those without FDI**

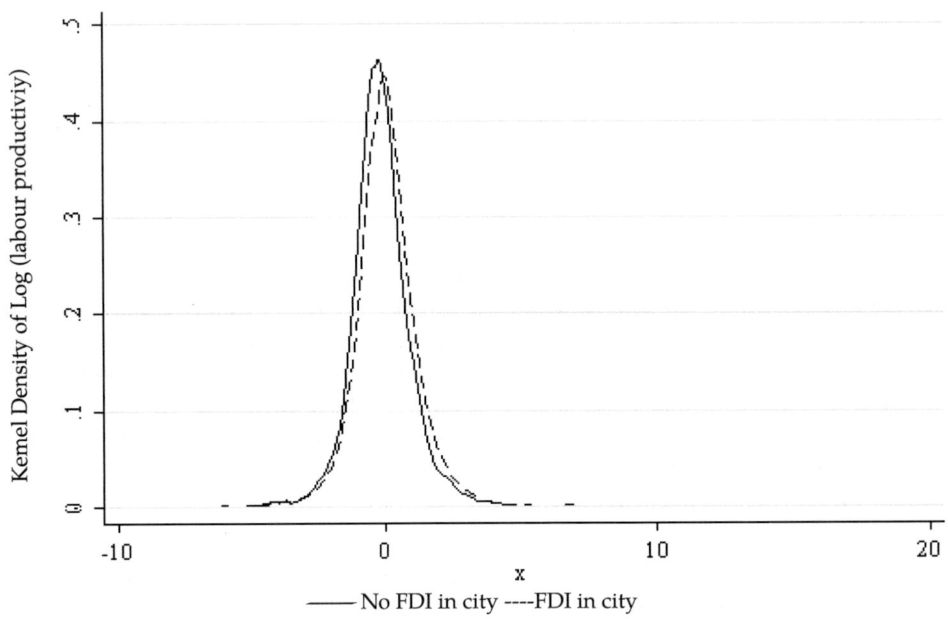


*Sources:* World Bank Enterprise Surveys; author's calculations.
*Note:* Foreign ownership is defined as a 50% share or greater at the firm level. Labour productivity is demeaned by country-sector-year.

The empirical evidence presented above focuses primarily on horizontal spillovers to firms in the same sector. However, in large part, the empirical evidence on horizontal spillovers in the context of developing countries actually suggests a negative effect due to foreign competition capturing market share away from domestic producers (see, for example, Aitken and Harrison 1999). In fact, the general empirical evidence is stronger in relation to vertical spillovers to firms that have a supply linkage with the firm owning or receiving the technology.

Vertical spillovers occur in two directions, backwards and forwards, but it is through backwards spillovers that technology transfer is more likely to happen. Backwards spillovers occur if there is a significant technology upgrading effect for suppliers when one of their clients receives foreign investment. The mechanism is that the recipient firm's demand pattern changes, perhaps focusing more on high standard merchandise required by its foreign partner, and so the supplier needs to upgrade production to meet that demand. In a meta-review of thousands of estimates, Havranek and Irsova (2011) concluded that the data support the view that a 10% increase in foreign presence is associated with a 9% increase in the productivity of local suppliers through the vertical spillover mechanism. This effect clearly has economic and development significance.

Vertical spillovers are of particular importance in the GVC context because of the prevalence of vertical (supply) relationships in those networks. The data suggest that there is scope for developing countries to support technology upgrading on a broad basis by facilitating foreign investment in downstream GVC activities. The spillover effect will then lead to productivity increases in suppliers, under appropriate circumstances, which can boost the country's level of technology more broadly. This type of mechanism can form the basis of an effective strategy for moving up value chains. Of course, it requires a certain amount of industrial depth, in the sense that there need to be upstream industries to benefit from the spillover effect. Other necessary conditions to benefit from technology transfer are discussed in the next section.

### Box 9.1. Technology transfer through GVCs in Thailand

Saliola and Zanfei (2007) used data on more than 1,000 Thai firms to analyse the dynamics of technology transfer in the context of GVCs in that country. They found that a greater presence of foreign subsidiaries in a sector is conducive to the type of value chain governance that is associated with suppliers' involvement in technology, and research and development activities. Their evidence can be interpreted as supporting the FDI spillover mechanism discussed here.

Interestingly, the authors also examined the case in which foreign firms adapted their technology and processes to Thai circumstances. That arrangement demonstrates a strong level of specific involvement in the value chain, and it appears to be consistent with significant technology transfers through the chain.

They also examined the case of imported intermediates (discussed below). They found that in cases where firms relied more heavily on domestic intermediates, it was more likely that the value chain was governed in a way that was not consistent with extensive technology transfer. Their results therefore also support the imported intermediates channel discussed here.

*Source:* Saliola and Zanfei (2007).

**2. Technology licensing**

Another way in which GVCs can facilitate technology transfer is through the licensing of technology by a foreign firm to domestic producers. In this case, the lead firm or technology supplier does not take an equity position in the firm receiving the technology, but instead allows it to use the technology in return for payment of a fixed sum. Clearly, licensing is risky from the technology supplier's point of view, because the possibility of leakage is higher; however, equity investment also carries risks, and in countries with strong rule of law and contract enforcement institutions, licensing can be an effective solution to enable technology upgrading while maintaining an arm's length relationship for other purposes.

Licensing foreign technology can be an effective way of facilitating technology transfer in relation to a specific technique or production method. Unlike FDI, it typically does not involve upgrading of the receiving firm's organizational technology, but it is limited to the use of particular machinery or production processes. Technology licensing has considerable scope to support productivity upgrading, but FDI is likely to be a stronger means by which involvement with a foreign technology supplier has technology enhancing effects, due to its capacity for direct and indirect gains.

Figure 9.6 shows that firm-level data from developing economies provides evidence that foreign technology licensing can be an effective way of increasing productivity. The kernel density estimate for firms that license technology lies to the right of the curve for firms that do not license technology. This pattern is consistent with a higher level of productivity in firms that license foreign technology. A descriptive regression supports this result; firms that license foreign technology are, on average, 48% more productive than firms that do not license foreign technology after controlling for country, sector and time specific factors. As expected, the productivity-enhancing effect of technology licensing is smaller than that of FDI, but it is still highly significant.

**Figure 9.6. Productivity differential between firms that only use domestic technology and those that license foreign technology**

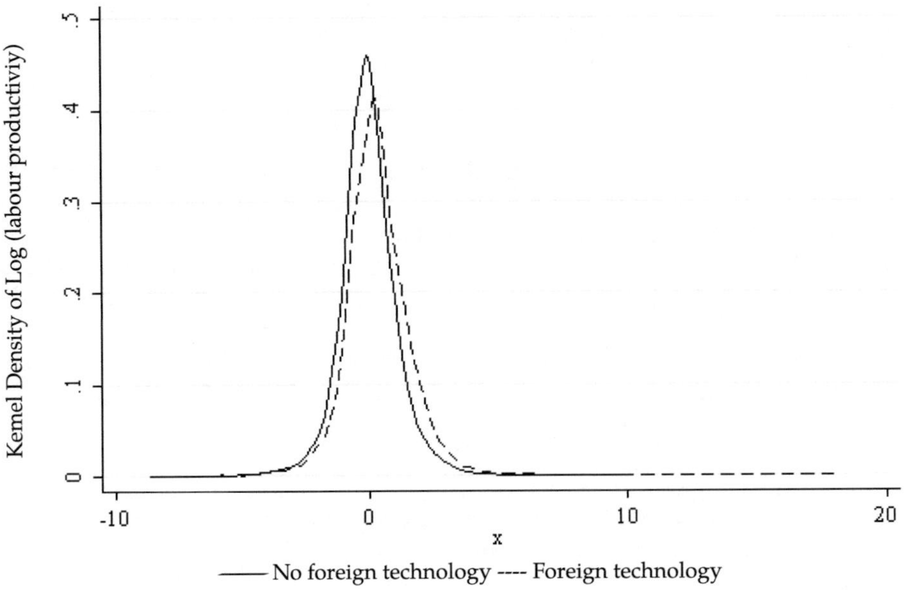


*Sources:* World Bank Enterprise Surveys; author's calculations.
*Note:* Use of foreign inputs is defined as any share greater than zero. Labour productivity is demeaned by country-sector-year.

**3. Imported capital goods**

In addition to relationship-based transactions such as FDI and licensing, it is also possible to gain access to technology within a GVC through transactions in the marketplace. One example is importing appropriate capital goods, such as machinery and equipment. Capital goods will often embody modern technology; therefore, for a developing economy importing capital goods from more advanced countries this implies a direct technology transfer. However, there is also scope for a range of indirect effects.

First, imported capital goods can generate spillovers, as workers learn how to use them, and can take that knowledge with them to other firms that can then acquire the same technology. A related issue is the ability to reverse engineer capital goods; if purchased outright, outside the scope of a licensing agreement, firms can use their own engineering skills to deconstruct and understand the technology they have purchased. That knowledge can be put to work in the development of their own products, and may even support the production of similar capital goods domestically. In addition, once capital goods are imported into an economy, they can circulate subsequently to other firms if the importing firm engages in further technology upgrading that makes the previous technology obsolete. This route raises the potential for additional technology spillovers from the import of capital goods in the developing country context as they are spread beyond the original importing firm.

Empirical evidence on imported capital goods is scarcer than for the other mechanisms examined in this chapter. In part, that is due to the difficulty of classifying goods by end-use based on standard trade categories. Nonetheless, some compelling evidence is available on the importance of capital goods as drivers of technology diffusion and productivity upgrading around the world. Eaton and Kortum (2001), for example, estimated that 25% of cross-country differences in productivity were due to variation in the relative price of equipment, about half of which were attributable to trade barriers affecting the capital goods sector. These estimates make clear that the circulation of capital goods is a potentially important means for developing countries to engage in technology upgrading.

## Box 9.2. Technology upgrading in China's photovoltaic cell industry

China has become a leader in the global photovoltaic cell industry. Despite barely deploying the technology at home in 2008, it accounted for more than 35% of world production in 2009. A total of 98% of that production was exported. Although there are sensitive issues of trade policy involved in the development of this industry, the focus here is on the technological component, without evaluating the competing policy claims surrounding the development of this industry, and its international competitive position.

Production of photovoltaic cells can be conceived of as using value chain methodologies (e.g. Sims, Gallagher and Zhang, 2013). Production requires the completion of a number of steps, and specialization in each area is spread across countries. China is relatively specialized in downstream production stages, while developed economies such as the United States, Germany, and Japan account for the bulk of production upstream.

The downstream segments in which China specializes have relatively low technological barriers to entry, and are correspondingly low in value-added relative to other segments. Although investment costs can be high, activities such as module assembly are labour-intensive – an area in which China has a strong comparative advantage.

Technology transfer has played a crucial role in the development of China's photovoltaic cell industry. Perhaps the most crucial vector was acquisition of foreign capital goods – production equipment that can produce standardized, high-quality products efficiently and reliably. In downstream sectors where Chinese firms have become competitive, there is a global market for turnkey production systems, so it was possible for Chinese entrepreneurs to effectively import their production processes from a competitive global market. Complementary to the acquisition of equipment is the acquisition of skills by workers – the knowledge needed to work with and maintain the equipment, which also comes from the equipment suppliers on a market basis.

FDI has also been an important vector of technology upgrading in China's photovoltaic cell sector. In 2009, China had attracted about one third of global FDI inflows in the sector. Interestingly, the first entrants into the market were indigenous Chinese firms. However, the influx of FDI has been associated with increased technology transfer. By contrast, licensing has played almost no role in the industry.

This case study demonstrates the various ways in which value chain participation can be compatible with technology transfer through different means. It has proved particularly effective in this case, and has allowed China to play a major role in the photovoltaic cell market. However, despite this success, it is important to highlight that the next stage of the industry's development – indigenous technology creation and movement into upstream sectors and higher value-added activities – poses numerous issues for Governments and businesses alike. It will be important to ensure that that transition takes place through the leveraging of market forces and comparative advantage, and not through artificial or distortionary policy interventions.

*Source:* De la Tour, Glachant and Meniere (2011).

### 4. Imported intermediates

Access to world markets for intermediate goods gives firms the ability to use high-quality inputs that may not be available domestically. Imported intermediates can be a source for technology upgrading because they facilitate the production of new and enhanced products and provide a boost to firm-level productivity. A relevant example of this proposition in practice was examined by Goldberg and others (2010), who found that when India liberalized its tariff regime, manufacturing firms were able to access a greater range of intermediate goods at lower overall prices, which in turn made them more productive. Evidence of a similar process is also found by Amiti and Konings (2007) in the context of Indonesia.

This chapter's empirical evidence also shows that imported intermediates can boost the productivity of the importing firm, such a producer importing inputs within a GVC. Figure 9.7 shows that firms using some imported intermediates are generally more productive than firms that use only domestically sourced varieties. As in previous figures, the curve for the former is shifted right relative to the latter, which is indicative of higher levels of productivity, as Goldberg and others (2010) found in the case of India. A descriptive regression confirms this result – firms that import at least some intermediates are, on average, 38% more productive than firms that use only domestic intermediates, after controlling for country, sector, and time specific factors.

**Figure 9.7. Productivity differential between firms that only use domestic inputs and those that use imported inputs**

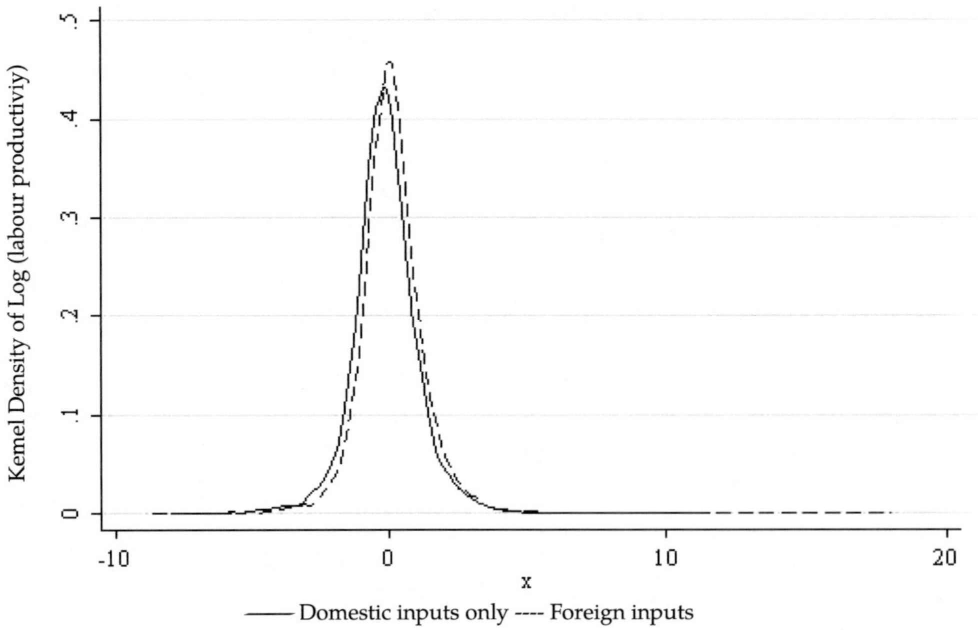


*Sources:* World Bank Enterprise Surveys; author's calculations.
*Note:* Use of foreign inputs is defined as any share greater than zero. Labour productivity is demeaned by country-sector-year.

The discussion above assumed that firms would simply include imported intermediates in their production process, which leads to productivity gains. However, it is also possible to upgrade technology by reverse engineering imported goods and either by learning how to manufacture them domestically, or putting the embodied technology to use in the production of other products. There is, therefore, considerable scope for access to imported intermediate goods to act as a spur to domestic innovation, in addition to static technology upgrading.

### 5. Demand effects

A final indirect way in which GVCs can promote technology upgrading is through consumer demand effects. When producers serve the domestic market of a developing country, demand may often coalesce around low-quality, low-cost items that adhere to local standards, but which are not globally competitive. GVCs, by definition, are interested in global and regional markets. They produce goods that appeal to a wide range of consumers, and tend to emphasize quality and uniformity through the use of product standards, which are often internationally harmonized and recognized. The growing literature on product quality and export patterns establishes this aspect empirically; for example, Manova and Zhang (2009) and Bastos and Silva (2010) found that firms in China and Portugal, respectively, exported higher quality goods to more developed destinations. Another compelling piece of evidence is provided by Atkin and others (2014), in a large, randomized controlled experiment granting export licenses to small Egyptian carpet producers. The authors maintained records of all the interactions between foreign customers in rich countries and local producers, and found that the local producers improved the subsequent quality of the carpets along various different metrics following complaints from foreign costumers, thus highlighting a feedback mechanism between buyers and sellers.

Demand from GVC lead firms can therefore be an incentive for developing firms to endogenously upgrade their production technology, which indirectly supports technology diffusion. This mechanism is consistent with the empirical evidence referred to in the previous sections, related to the fact that firms which are internationalized, including through GVCs, tend to be more productive. This is because unmeasured quality will manifest itself as a higher markup, which will artificially increase the calculated productivity since productivity is calculated as the residual between output and input values.

Demand effects from integration into GVCs can also occur as a result of having access to a larger market, which creates opportunities for reaping economies of scale. Van Biesebroeck (2005) and De Loecker (2007), in the case of Sub-Saharan Africa and Slovenia, respectively, attributed increases in productivity following entry into export markets to such a mechanism. Thus access to larger foreign markets, where payment is more reliable than in the relatively small and inefficient domestic markets, can lead to greater opportunities to scale up operations and achieve a more consistent inflow of profits. For many developing country firms facing large fixed costs that are barring them from entering international markets, integration into GVCs can provide important opportunities to take advantage of established networks and reliable costumers.

# B THE DEVELOPMENT CONTEXT

Clearly, firms and workers in developing economies can only benefit from new technology diffusing through GVCs if the circumstances at home and within the firm are right. An economy's absorptive capacity is going to be a crucial mediating factor in shaping these factors, which will determine the scope of the set of value chain relationships that are established as well as the extent to which technology upgrading can take place within this set of relationships. For example, in the case of FDI, the domestic environment must provide incentives for foreign firms to first engage in meaningful relationships with domestic agents and then in deepening those domestic linkages. For example, an economy with a relatively skilled labour force will be a more attractive destination for FDI with scope that extends beyond merely seeking cheap labour, while a skilled workforce is most likely to increase transfers of technology through channels such as the training of domestic workers, the transfer of complementary high-tech capital etc. This will come, in a large part, from a combination of factors that encompass both policy and business environments; however, there will also be a role for other more contextual factors such as geographic location and closeness to major markets, factor endowment and comparative advantage, political and social considerations etc. A detailed analysis of all of these factors is beyond the scope of this paper.[4] Instead, the focus here is on a small number of broad policy areas that are of particular importance to the creation of an environment that is conducive to taking advantage of technology transfers and which facilitates such transactions to the mutual benefit of the transferor and receiver. Figure 9.8 shows the basic mechanism at work, where the absorptive capacity encourages the establishment of the channels of technology transfer, and then the firms' absorptive capacity determines the extent to which they benefit from these flows of technology. Although it is not obvious here, it will be seen that there is a strong interrelationship between the absorptive capacity of an economy as a whole and that of the firms concerned.

**Figure 9.8. From technology diffusion to national upgrading – the role of absorptive capacity**

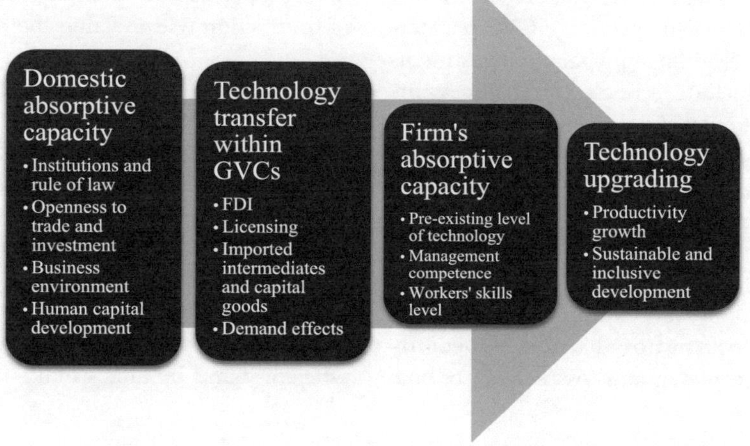


CHAPTER 9

There are four broad policy areas that are essential both to the initial establishment of the channels for technology transfer and to maximizing the magnitude and likelihood of technology diffusion.

First, and perhaps most importantly is institutional capacity, including governance, the rule of law and contract enforcement, as well as respect for intellectual property rights. All types of technology transfer within GVCs rely on some form of legal relationship between the source and the recipient. The relationship can be one of FDI, a licensing arrangement or simply a contract to supply a particular intermediate or capital good; the ability to enforce its terms is a crucial determinant of the willingness of a technology source to engage in this relationship. The importance of institutional development as a determinant of economic growth is widely accepted (e.g. Acemoglu, Johnson and Robinson, 2001); however, this is one area in which institutional development plays a particularly important role. Just as value chains depend on contract enforceability for their ability to operate on a day-to-day basis, so too does technology transfer within those structures depend on the rule of law and the level of development of governmental institutions. Some evidence for such a process comes from the discussion of intellectual property rights. Javorcik (2004) found that weaker protection of intellectual property rights encouraged international investors to undertake investments in distribution and sales rather than production or R&D. In this example, the strength of the institutional environment makes it safer for foreign firms to engage in investments that capture higher value-added, and in turn these investments are more likely to result in significant technology transfer to domestic actors. Focusing on institutional development should therefore be a priority for policymakers who are keen to promote technology transfer within GVCs.

Second is openness to FDI, which is one of the most important and beneficial vectors for technology transfer within GVCs. Many countries have liberalized their foreign investment regimes to some extent during recent years but restrictions remain; these are sometimes sector specific, particularly in services. Appropriate relaxation of foreign investment rules – which includes restrictions on foreign ownership and legal form – can encourage GVC partners and lead firms to make relationship-specific investments with local firms that can include technology transfer. Again, it is important to understand technology broadly – not just as the machines that produce a particular product, but the organizational techniques used to blend inputs of different types together so as to produce an output in a reliable, cost-effective, high-quality way.

Third, developing economies need to maintain an open stance in relation to international trade, especially intermediate inputs and capital goods. Availability of both classes of goods has the capacity to boost domestic technology, and movements of both take place within the scope of GVCs, although the emphasis is primarily on inputs. A liberal trade policy stance, particularly in these sectors, facilitates movements of goods that bring technology embedded in them. If economies make it more expensive for their firms to import such products by maintaining tariff and non-tariff barriers to trade, they implicitly hold back the rate of technological advance that can take place. There is extensive empirical evidence that lower trade costs are associated with firm- and sector-level productivity growth (e.g. Pavcnik, 2002) through a variety of mechanisms including the ones discussed here.

The fourth and final, country-level area overlaps with the issue of absorptive capacity from a more micro perspective – the development of human capital. For technology transfer to be fully effective, the new machines or techniques need to be understood and internalized, as well as potentially adaptable to domestic conditions, both by workers and by local engineers. Human capital is therefore a crucial mediating factor in the relationship between GVC participation and effective technology transfer. If a skilled workforce is available, it also becomes attractive for a GVC partner or lead firm to engage in technology transfer; therefore, causality runs both ways, as human capital is valuable for developing absorptive capacity as well as for attracting FDI in the first place.

Development of human capital is an important prerequisite for moving up in value chains, and leads to a strong policy emphasis on education and training at appropriate levels given an economy's economic development status. In poorer developing countries, the emphasis should to be on basic (primary and secondary) education, with attention then turning to post-secondary education (tertiary and professional) in an organic way. Continuous development of human capital is one way in which policymakers can create a national environment that attracts foreign technology and is conducive to technology transfer. Moreover, well-developed human capital is complementary to improved physical and organization technology, as it makes it possible for them to work optimally in the context of production within value chains.

Firms themselves also need to be able to absorb the new technology that becomes available to them. Some factors that determine this ability include the pre-existing level of technology, including management competence. Clearly, a firm can only move so far in terms of taking up new technology, and the scope of its upgrading is determined at least in part by its existing technology, including its organization and use of resources. In addition, businesses need to be competently managed so as to use resources efficiently and be able to take full advantage of the new technology – that means that they also need appropriate management systems for the specific purpose of tracking the use of new technology and its relationship to business outcomes on the ground. Another factor that is relevant is a firm's pre-existing engagement in activities such as research and development, which have a strong technological component. Of course, the skill level of a company's workers is also an important factor, due to the strong complementarity between physical technology and human capital.

Factors affecting a firm's absorptive capacity are highly correlated with the determinants of a country's absorptive capacity. It implies that policies to strengthen the host country's domestic absorptive capacity can also influence the firms' absorptive capacity. Therefore, the willingness and credibility of a Government to undertake deep and meaningful reform is likely to go a long way in stimulating trade and investment flows and the technology such flows carry along with them.

## C POLICY IMPLICATIONS AND CONCLUSION

This chapter examines the ways in which technology transfer can take place within GVCs. A number of vectors are identified, ranging from inward FDI, imported intermediates and capital goods, to demand effects. The empirical evidence strongly suggests that, under appropriate circumstances, GVC participation can be compatible with the workings of economic forces that support technology upgrading in developing countries.

However, technological progress and movement into higher value-added activities are not an automatic process that occurs regardless of whatever else is happening in the broader economy and social structure. Developing economies need to put in place the right policy and institutional environment to favour technology transfer, and to exert an influence on the type of transfer that takes place. Together, such interventions can be considered to be a type of industrial policy – a position that aims to support industrial development and upgrading – but the emphasis of such policies in the current environment must be on non-discriminatory measures that reinforce, not go against, basic economic processes. There is no role for Governments to "pick winners" as a means of trying to encourage moving up in value chains, as such policies have repeatedly been found wanting, particularly in environments of weak governance. Such a policy stance is therefore often referred to as a "soft" industrial policy.

Indeed, perhaps the most crucial intervention to support technology transfer is building up domestic governance institutions, particularly the rule of law and contract enforcement. Without these institutions in place, foreign businesses will be reluctant to transfer technology through arrangements such as FDI and licensing. In any case, boosting performance in this broad area is a priority for many economies, as it is well-known to be associated with economic growth and development potential over the medium term. Fostering technology transfer, particularly through FDI and licensing, is nevertheless a primary reason why this is an area that deserves priority on a policy level.

Openness to international trade and investment flows is also a crucial policy priority for fostering technology transfer through FDI as well as imports of intermediates and capital goods. Appropriately, liberal trade and investment policy settings – backed by stability and certainty in their administration – can encourage foreign counterparts to engage in mutually beneficial technology-based transactions with firms of developing economies. The movement of goods and capital is a crucial vector by which technology is transferred, including within GVCs, and the ability to move up in a GVC to higher-value-added activities depends on this factor.

It is important to stress the value of openness in order to counteract the view that industrial policy considerations would operate in favor of protection of "new" value chain activities that represent the potential for higher value added retention. Infant industry arguments, although theoretically plausible under certain circumstances, have proved in practice to be difficult to administer effectively – it is hard to make infants "grow up" and become globally competitive. Instead, the approach suggested in this chapter is in line with an incentive neutral trade and investment policy that allows goods and capital – including those with embodied technology – to flow freely across borders and be put to their optimal use.

A final factor to which developing countries need to pay special attention – all the more so as we move into the era of sustainable and inclusive growth – is the development of human capital. Foreign technology can only be put to use if workers and engineers are available who can understand how to operate, maintain and adapt the technology that is at their disposition.[5] Developing countries need to redouble their efforts to develop their human capital stocks in appropriate ways, depending on their level of per capita income. Physical technology and human capital are strong complements, so it is important to move forward on both fronts simultaneously. Companies operating in GVCs frequently cite an educated workforce as a strong factor in their location decisions, so Governments of developing economies need to be responsive to that fact.

## ENDNOTES

[1] This chapter was prepared by Ben Shepherd, Principal of Developing Trade Consultants. The author is grateful to Olivier Cattaneo and Deborah Winkler for helpful exchanges as well as to Luca Parisotto for additional work on the chapter.

[2] See Brach and Kappel (2009) for a general discussion of the issues in a development context.

[3] Presumably profit maximization could be subject to meeting socially responsible business criteria.

[4] Taglioni and Winkler (2015) provide a more complete review.

[5] Technology transfer could be in a form of inter-firm provision of training (i.e. training among local and non-local firms connected by domestic and international productions networks). See, for example, Kimura, Machikita and Ueki (2015).

## REFERENCES


Acemoglu, Daren, Simon Johnson and James Robinson (2001). The colonial origins of comparative development: an empirical investigation. *American Economic Review*, vol. 91, No. 5, pp. 1369-1401.

Aitken, Brian J., and Ann E. Harrison (1999). Do domestic firms benefit from direct foreign investment? Evidence from Venezuela. *American Economic Review,* vol. 89, No. 3, pp. 605-618.

Amiti, Mary, and Jozef Konings (2007). Trade liberalization, intermediate inputs, and productivity: evidence from Indonesia. *American Economic Review,* vol. 97, No. 5, pp. 1611-1638.

Arnold, Jens M., and Beata S. Javorcik (2009). Gifted kids or pushy parents? Foreign direct investment and plant productivity in Indonesia. *Journal of International Economics,* vol. 79, No. 1, pp. 42-53.

Atkin, David, Amit Khandelwal and Adam Osman (2014). Exporting and firm performance: evidence from a randomized trial. NBER Working Paper No. 20690. Cambridge, M.A.: National Bureau of Economic Research.

Aw, Bee Yan, Sukkyun Chung and Mark J. Roberts (2000). Productivity and turnover in the export market: micro-level evidence from the Republic of Korea and Taiwan (China). *World Bank Economic Review,* vol. 14, No. 1, pp. 65-90.

Bastos, Paulo, and Joana Silva (2010). The quality of a firm's exports: where you export to matters. *Journal of International Economics*, vol. 82, No. 2, pp. 99-111.

Brach, Juliane, and Robert Kappel (2009). Global value chains, technology transfer, and local firm upgrading in non-OECD countries. GIGA Working Paper No. 110. Hamburg: German Institute of Global and Area Studies.

De la Tour, Arnaud, Matthieu Glachant and Yann Meniere (2011). Innovation and international technology transfer: the case of the Chinese photovoltaic industry. *Energy Policy*, vol. 39, No. 2, pp. 761-770.

De Loecker, Jan (2007). Do exports generate higher productivity? Evidence from Slovenia. *Journal of International Economics,* vol. 73, No. 1, pp. 69-98.

Eaton, Jonathan, and Samuel Kortum (2001). Trade in capital goods. *European Economic Review,* vol. 45, No. 7, pp. 1195-1235.

Evenett, Simon, Mia Mikic and Ravi Ratnayake, eds. (2011). *Trade-led Growth: A Sound Strategy for Asia.* Bangkok: ESCAP. Sales No. E.11.II.F.4. Available from www.unescap.org/sites/default/files/tipub2618.pdf

Farole, Thomas, Cornelia Staritz and Deborah Winkler (2014). Conceptual Framework. In T. Farole and D. Winkler, eds., *Making Foreign Direct Investment Work for Sub-Saharan Africa: Local Spillovers and Competitiveness in Global Value Chains.* Washington, D.C.: World Bank.

Glachant, Matthieu, and others (2013). Greening global value chains: innovation and the international diffusion of technologies and knowledge. Policy Research Working Paper No. 6467. Washington, D.C.: World Bank.

Goldberg, Pinelopi, and others (2010). Imported intermediate inputs and domestic product growth: evidence for India. *Quarterly Journal of Economics,* vol. 125, No. 4, pp. 1727-1767.

Haddad, Mona, and Ben Shepherd, eds. (2011). *Managing Openness: Trade and Outward Oriented Growth after the Crisis.* Washington, D.C.: World Bank.

Hausmann, Ricardo, Jason Hwang and Dani Rodrik (2007). What you export matters. *Journal of Economic Growth,* vol. 12, No. 1, pp. 1-25.

Havranek, Tomas, and Zuzana Irsova (2011). Estimating vertical spillovers from FDI: why results vary and what the true effect is. *Journal of International Economics*, vol. 85, pp. 234-244.

Javorcik, Beata Smarzynska (2004). The composition of foreign direct investment and protection of intellectual property rights: evidence from transition economies. *European Economic Review*, vol. 48, No.1, pp. 39-62.

Kimura, Fukunari, Tomohiro Machikita and Yasushi Ueki (2015). Technology transfer in ASEAN countries: some evidence from buyer-provided training network data. ERIA Discussion Paper Series No. 2015-40. Jakarta: Economic Research Institute for ASEAN and East Asia.

Manova, Kalina, and Zhiwei Zhang (2009). Export prices across firms and destinations. NBER Working Paper No. 15342. Cambridge, M.A.: National Bureau of Economic Research.

Pavcnik, Nina (2002). Trade liberalization, exit, and productivity improvement: evidence from Chilean plants. *Review of Economic Studies*, vol. 69, No. 1, pp. 245-276.

Saliola, Federica, and Antonello Zanfei (2007). Multinational firms, global value chains, and the organization of technology transfer. WP-EMS No. 2007/10. Urbino, Italy: University of Urbino Carlo Bo, Department of Economics, Society and Politics.

Gallagher, Kelly Sims, and Fang Zhang (2013). Climate change and development case study: innovation and technology transfer across global value chains: evidence from China's PV industry. Medford, M.A.: Tufts University.

Taglioni, Daria, and Deborah Winkler (2015). *Making Global Value Chains Work for Development*. Washington, D.C.: World Bank.

Van Biesebroeck, Johannes (2005). Exporting raises productivity in Sub-Saharan African manufacturing firms. *Journal of International Economics*, vol. 67, No. 2, pp. 373-391.

# 10 POLICIES FOR SUPPORTING PARTICIPATION IN VALUE CHAINS

The changing dynamics in the global economy call for a renewed effort to enhance the prospects of trade-led growth. Looking ahead, in order to mitigate the consequences of considerable uncertainty as the global economy undergoes a series of adjustments, a more aggressive and holistic strategy is needed to regain at least the pre-crisis momentum in the region. This report finds plenty of untapped potential for the expansion of trade and investment growth through further production fragmentation and connectivity to value chains, both regional and global.

The proliferation of value chains in the past two decades is a reflection of the rapid changes that have occurred in business models as well as international trade and foreign direct investment (FDI). Trade patterns have been reshaped by fast growth of trade in intermediates. FDI followed a dynamic process of production fragmentation as global firms moved into sub-contracting, off-shoring and outsourcing as ways of increasing productivity and competitiveness. Global value chains (GVCs) have reinforced a long-standing notion that trade and investment are just an extension of the production process in which domestic and international barriers and obstacles matter significantly with regard to competitiveness. Together with production fragmentation, the related areas of technical innovations in transport, communications, production and consumption, and innovative management practices diffused rapidly across the world, especially in Asia where new job opportunities have lifted many out of poverty and helped reinforce progress towards closing the income gap between developed and developing countries. A surge in purchasing power in the new middle class of developing countries has created new opportunities for South-South trade and investment. On the other hand, a rising challenge is that not all countries have been able to take advatages of the benefits of production fragmentation. As this report shows, many low-income developing countries in Asia and the Pacific have remained either isolated from GVC expansion or locked into their traditional role of commodity or low value-added exporters, with little in the way of new manufacturing opportunities.

GVCs are, of course, not the panacea for these challenges facing low-income economies and, in particular, they are not immune to the malaise of the global economy; on the contrary, in certain cases, trade that is linked to GVCs could be harmed faster and/or to a greater extent as global demand and supply become adversely affected. Some of these factors will be cyclical (as was noted in the immediate aftermath of the 2008-2009 contraction), but some factors are also related to ongoing structural changes and end up permanently changing segments of, or even entire value chains. Furthermore, policies for increasing participation in GVCs should not replace a sound economic development strategy; it must be understood that promoting participation in GVCs, while in itself a comprehensive policy mix, is just a complementary part of a broader economic diversification strategy.

Nevertheless, as highlighted in this report, the Asia-Pacific economies need to upgrade their policies in order to adjust to the "new normal" of slower trade and investment growth, and adjusting GVCs processes. These include both the policies and measures that developing countries can adopt to support direct entry into – or indirect linkages to – GVCs as well as ensure that participation in GVCs contributes beneficially to sustainable development. Measures related to facilitation and access to efficiently provided services and resources, including skills and data, are necessary to (a) the promotion of upgrading within GVCs and (b) allowing a move away from exclusive focus on "low-skilled, low-costs" to higher-value production. These measures will also serve well in achieving a general goal of more equitably shared benefits from participation in global economy.

While one model does not fit all, research by ESCAP has shown that there are a large number of areas where policies tend to converge for countries of certain similar characteristics. The empirical research that was undertaken in preparing this report with regard to GVC-merchandise trade grouped countries by their income status in high, upper-middle, lower-middle and low-income economies and covered GVC-related final and intermediate exports of five sectors: apparel and footwear; automobiles; electronics; agricultural primary; and processed agricultural products. The scope of research has influenced the research findings and thus should be taken into account when reviewing the policy recommendations.

The similar empirical method was taken when exploring the linkages of services in industrial exports and GVCs, and the role of FDI and technology. The recommendations presented are grouped under the objective that is to be achieved, rather than by the group of countries observed in the analysis. However, there is a close association between the income levels of countries and their stage of participation in GVCs. The figure 10.1 summarizes the main policy proiority areas based on empirical analyses undertaken by ESCAP as well as on evidence drawn from other studies, aimed at: (a) securing entry to GVCs; (b) expanding participation in GVCs; and (c) upgrading within GVCs and the creation of new GVCs. However, it must be stressed that these recommendations constitute just the main policy options. Furthermore, they are presented here in a generalized form while in any specific case of policy advice and design these recommendations will have to be tailored to fit the existing circumstances and meet more explicit objectives.

**Figure 10.1. Key policy priority areas for supporting participation in value chains**

**Securing entry to GVCs**

- Hard infrastructure: connectivity , energy and logistics
- Domestic regulatory reforms
- Trade and investment liberalization and trade facilitation

**Expanding participation in GVCs**

- Competitive environment
- Open services sector backed by strong and enforcable regulation (including financial services)
- Preferential trade agreements to support regional integration
- Soft infrastructure: education and training to increase absorptive capacity of firms and workers,ICT development

**Upgrading within GVCs and creating new GVCs**

- Building innovative, human and firm capital
- Governance and intellectual property protection
- Harmonization of rules and standards with international norms
- Openness to FDI and imported technology

# A SECURING ENTRY

As many smaller and low-income regional economies are not yet fully integrated into GVCs, the key question for policymakers is how to create an enabling environment for local firms to gain entry into existing networks. In this regard, it has been found that:

(a) Infrastructure is the main element needed to secure entry to GVCs. The focus at the entry stage should be on a country's "basic needs" for connectivity (e.g., roads, rails and ports), energy supply and logistic systems;

(b) Trade cost reduction is essential to enabling a country to participate more effectively in GVCs, particularly where geographical disadvantages have an impact on producers' competitiveness. Trade-cost reduction policies include liberalization of trade in goods as well as services and investment, with the removal or reduction of direct and indirect barriers. While both trade and investment liberalization are necessary, trade facilitation is the most effective way of dealing with trade costs at the border; and

(c) Domestic regulatory reforms to ensure transparency and consistency are necessary for dealing with trade costs occurring behind-the-border.

## B EXPANDING PARTICIPATION

Once entry is secured, the next stage is the development of policy priorities with a focus on enhancing competitiveness in order to expand GVC participation. This could be done through additionally shaving costs arising from existing barriers in accessing markets or by increasing productivity and efficiency of supply. Once a country is significantly integrated into a GVC, Governments should pay attention to the broader policy environment. Domestic policy and regulatory reforms to facilitate trade and business operations help to maintain attractiveness for FDI inflow as well as preserve competitive advantages; the process of servicification is of particular importance. The main policy areas are:

(a) While liberalizing trade in goods is a starting point for creating new trade opportunities, the value chains of industrial goods also require efficient services. Improvements in the performance of the service sector, including through liberalizing services trade, is a priority. This will enhance the competitiveness of manufacturing firms and facilitate their participation in global production networks. Many regional economies maintain highly restrictive access to their local services markets, which in turn could hamper efforts to promote industrial goods exports;

(b) To encourage development spillovers from GVCs to the rest of the economy, a balanced and sequenced approach to sourcing of intermediate services (and goods) is desirable. The general direction of service trade policy should therefore focus on (i) creating competitive market conditions, and (ii) developing a well-functioning domestic service sector that meets good practice regulatory standards;

(c) The need for measures to vary from sector to sector. For example, ensuring access to the grid or network for new entrants in the telecommunications or electricity sectors should help in creating equal and equitable opportunities, and should result in pro-competitive efficiency gains;

(d) Openness of financial services with a good practice regulatory framework. This could enhance competition and stability in the financial sector and contribute to macro stability;

(e) It is important to have a comprehensive set of policies in place in order to encourage spillovers and technological diffusion from foreign to domestic providers. This may include, for example, public investment in upgrading and improving accessibility to backbone infrastructure such as ICT, railways, ports, health and education;

(f) The provision of education and training (e.g., in IT, languages and professional skills) as well as greater domestic and international labour mobility. Among other things, this will enable domestic firms as well as individuals to take advantage of service-export opportunities; and

(g) Regional economic integration agreements. Such agreements could be a catalyst in enhancing GVC participation by developing Asia-Pacific countries, provided such agreements are deep in commitments, and broad in scope and coverage. However, bilateral and regional trade agreements will have little effect without the necessary trade regimes – in particular, trade facilitation first being in place. Furthermore, there is a need for rationalizing and consolidating existing preferential trade agreements, as their effectiveness may face adverse impacts through the "noodle bowl" phenomenon.

## C UPGRADING

Development benefits from GVCs will be achieved through the process of upgrading within GVC participation, such as capturing a larger share of domestic value-added in exports or the performance of more elaborate tasks within the value chain, and moving away from "low-value, low-costs" segments of the chain. As already elaborated in this report, this is more easily achieved by harnessing benefits from transferred technology through FDI or alternative access to foreign technology such as licensing or direct importation.

Developing economy firms and workers can only benefit from new technology through GVC participation if the domestic policy environment is appropriate. Smooth transitions from labour-intensive to skills-intensive segments of GVCs need enabling policies to facilitate the adjustment process through well-designed labour market and social reforms as well as investment in education and skills. This requires several attention to several poliey areas, including:

(a) Building institutional capacity – including governance, the rule of law and contract enforcement – and respecting intellectual property rights for securing the benefits of technology transfers. All types of technology transfer within GVCs rely on some type of legal relationship between the source and the recipient;

(b) Openness to FDI. This is one of the most vital and beneficial vectors for technology transfer within GVCs. In many countries excessive restrictions remain, particularly in services. Appropriate reform of foreign investment rules –including limits on foreign ownership and legal forms – can encourage GVC partners and lead foreign firms to strengthen relationships with local firms, including through technology transfers;

(c) Maintaining an open stance by developing countries in relation to international trade, particularly in the case of intermediate inputs and capital goods. A liberal trade policy stance facilitates movements of goods that bring technology embedded in them;

(d) Development of human capital to improve the capacity of firms to absorb technology transfer. For technology transfer to be fully effective, new machines and/or techniques need to be clearly understood and internalized as well as potentially adapted to domestic conditions, both by workers and by local engineers.

Together the above policies can help countries to take advantage of the opportunities offered by GVCs. Of course, in all economies, the sequence of policy reforms will be determined by the initial conditions of a country.

There is also a need to manage the risks from greater interdependencies that come with economic integration. Likewise, the social and environmental aspects of GVC participation need careful attention. Enabling GVC development will increasingly require more international cooperation and coordination among Governments. The need to integrate regulation and domestic rules and regulation with international standards is particularly strong in Asia and the Pacific, as burdens created by those rules and regulations can be amplified across GVCs and result in damage to region-wide competitiveness.

## D LOOKING FORWARD

Because GVCs have dominated globalization in the past two decades, they have also commanded high attention in policy dialogues and among research topics. The progress made in understanding the phenomenon and its complexity as well as the measurement of its size and impacts can only be compared to the spread of GVCs themselves. Yet there are many open areas requiring further research by academia, think tanks, business associations and knowledge communities such as ARTNeT. The ESCAP secretariat will remain engaged with other partners in the efforts to strengthen work in this area.

There is a clear understanding that operators behind trade, investment and GVCs are to be found at the micro level – they comprise enterprises and clusters that are frequently associated with a city, while the Governments (including at below national levels) function as enablers. A further study in this area, with a focus on low-income countries, must go even deeper into exploring how firms operate and interact with the local, national and global economies, their processes of adaptability to changes and their preparation for the future. The annex to this chapter provides brief description of a survey of enterprises undertaken by ESCAP to find the main factors influencing their decision on participating in international trade and GVCs.

More efforts are needed to collect hard data on the behaviour of firms, which appears to be the main problem at present when analysing GVCs. Conventional trade statistics, which are still focused on the nineteenth century "Made in a country" concept, do not offer much ground for analysis of GVCs, which reflect a "Made in the world" approach to trade. There is now a consensus that collecting proper statistical data needs to involve value-added production as well as value-added trade data not only at a national level. This could be achieved by more comprehensive and regular data collection from the private sector. Many countries, both in the Asia-Pacific region and globally, lack capacity and resources to undertake such data collection and production. Yet without proper measurements, it will not be possible to fully understand the nature and scope of interactions among firms, locally, regionally and globally, and it will be more difficult to prepare the necessary environment for policy changes required for future development. Thus, there is a critical need for specific capacity-building actions on the part of those countries.

Taking into account the nature and dynamism of GVCs, and their reflection of local realities – as discussed in this report – there is little doubt that they will continue to shape the processes of production, trade, investment and innovation. As such, GVCs are a key factor in designing a governance structure for sustainable development. The ESCAP secretariat offers a key platform for the business community, researchers and policymakers at all levels of government to interact and work together towards delivering on the promise of ending poverty, transforming lives and protecting our planet.

# Annex

## Factors influencing the easiness of GVC-related exports: Evidence from the ESCAP Survey on International Trade and GVCs

The augmented gravity model of trade estimated in chapter 7 of this report supports the claim that, at the country level, some policy variables influence the ability of developing Asia and the Pacific to integrate into GVCs. Specifically, evidence is found that tariff liberalization, RTAs, improvements in logistic and a solid legal system are associated with increments in GVC-related trade. Conversely, non-tariff measures (NTMs) are found to hinder international trade.

Are firms aware of the importance of these factors? The ESCAP Survey of International Trade and GVCs provides the opportunity to investigate the level of awareness among single companies. The survey, which targeted almost exclusively those businesses based in the Asia-Pacific region, consisted of 34 questions divided into the following five sections: (a) perceptions of the relevance of international trade; (b) perceptions of trade barriers; (c) perceptions of business barriers in developing countries; (d) an overview of the surveyed company; and (e)contact details and feedback on the survey. The complete responses totalled 206. Among other questions, firms were asked to assess the importance of a number of factors influencing their activities in international trade, particularly those linked to GVC-related trade. Notably, some of the respondents regarded the relevance of tariffs, custom delays, non-tariff barriers, transport and logistics, protection of propriety rights, the existence of preferential market access schemes, the existence of free trade agreements and the level of transparency in rules and regulations, to be important. The figures 1 and 2 show aggregate results, on a scale ranging from 1 (not important at all) to 6 (extremely important), the average response for each of the elements examined here was between 4 (moderately important), and 5 (very important) for all the elements here considered except for Transparency in rules and regulations (domestic) which had an average response of just above 5. Thus, on average, the firms surveyed recognized the importance of the very same factors that the augmented gravity model of trade finds as having a sizeable impact on GVC-related trade.

Other variables can have an impact on the ability of a firm to export its products, including its integration in production networks and GVCs. Of particular importance, in a setting of heterogeneous firms and economies of scale, is the size of the firms as often only the larger companies are able to directly enter foreign markets. Frequently, only the more productive firms are, in fact, able to overcome (a) the fixed costs, such as tariffs, and (b) variable costs, such as transportation expenses, which originate from operating outside the domestic economy.

The ESCAP survey, inter alia, allows verification of whether such a relationship exists for those firms that responded to the survey. In fact, the survey divided companies into four categories, according to their size: (a) less than 10 employees; (b) 10-49 employees; (c) 50-250 employees; and (d) more than 250 employees. Companies were asked how easy it was for them to export, on a scale ranging from 1 (extremely difficult) to 6 (extremely easy). The findings of the regression analysis reveal that, for the samples analysed, there is a positive and significant correlation between the size of a firm and easiness of exporting, in accord with the model elaborated by Melitz, indicating that larger firms could have better chances of integration into GVCs.

In conclusion, the findings of the ESCAP Survey of International Trade and GVCs (available from www.unescap.org) suggests that policymakers in the Asia-Pacific region can create a supportive environment for companies, when trying to implement reforms aimed at the enhanced integration of domestic firms into GVCs, by intervening in such areas as logistics, preferential trade agreements, tariffs and regulatory systems.

*A representative model is developed in Marc J. Melitz, 2003, "The impact of trade on intra-industry reallocations and aggregate industry productivity", in Econometrica, 71, pp. 1695-1725.

**Annex figure 1. Importance of selected factors influencing international trade: Average answers from the report on the ESCAP Survey on International Trade and GVCs**

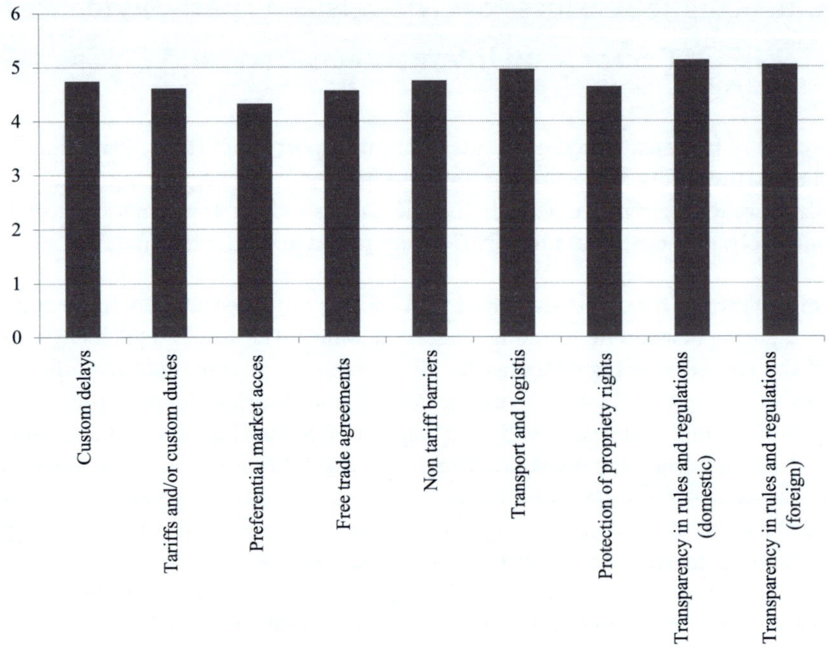


*Source:* Compiled from the ESCAP Survey on International Trade and GVCs, available at www.unescap.org/publications/asia-pacific-trade-investment-report.

*Notes:* The number of firms that cited the following factors were: customs delays, 167; preferential market access, 167; non-tariff barriers, 167; protection of propriety rights, 169; tariffs and/or custom duties, 168; free trade agreements, 168; transport and logistics, 168; transparency in rules and regulations (domestic), 167; transparency in rules and regulations (foreign), 170.

**Annex figure 2. Importance of selected factors influencing international trade depending on firm size: Average answers from the report on the ESCAP Survey on International Trade and GVCs**

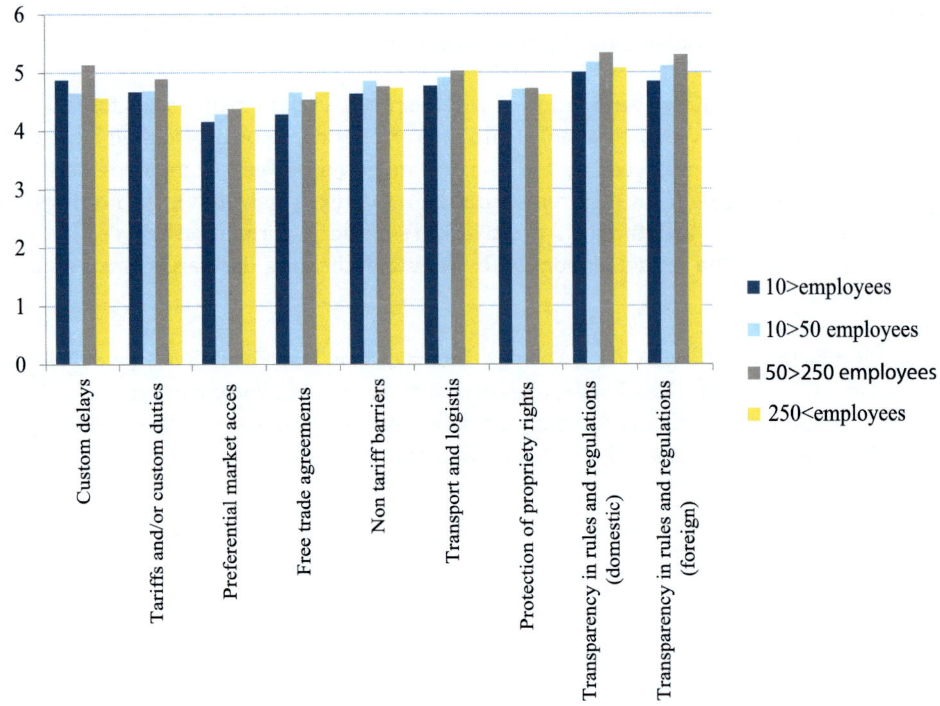


*Source:* Compiled from the ESCAP Survey on International Trade and GVCs, available at www.unescap.org/publications/asia-pacific-trade-investment-report.

*Note:* Number of responding firms by size: 10>employees, 30; 10>50 employees, 33; 50>250 employees, 28; >250 employees, 68.

# READERSHIP SURVEY

## Asia-Pacific Trade and Investment Report 2015

The Trade and Investment Division of ESCAP is undertaking an evaluation of the above publication with a view to improving its quality and usefulness. We would appreciate it if you could complete this questionnaire and return it to us, at the address printed below.

### QUESTIONNAIRE

| | *Rating for quality and usefulness (please circle)* | *Excellent* | *Very good* | *Good* | *Poor* |
|---|---|---|---|---|---|
| 1. | How useful is this publication for your work? | | | | |
| | • Provision of information | 4 | 3 | 2 | 1 |
| | • Clarification of issues | 4 | 3 | 2 | 1 |
| | • Findings | 4 | 3 | 2 | 1 |
| | • Policy suggestions | 4 | 3 | 2 | 1 |
| | • Overall usefulness | 4 | 3 | 2 | 1 |
| 2. | Please indicate your assessment of the quality of | | | | |
| | • Presentation/format | 4 | 3 | 2 | 1 |
| | • Readability | 4 | 3 | 2 | 1 |
| | • Coverage of subject matter | 4 | 3 | 2 | 1 |
| | • Timeliness of information | 4 | 3 | 2 | 1 |
| | • Overall quality | 4 | 3 | 2 | 1 |

3. Suggestions for improvement of the publication:

..........................................................................................................................................

..........................................................................................................................................

..........................................................................................................................................

..........................................................................................................................................

4. Your background information, please:

Name: ..........................................................................................................................

Title/position: ..............................................................................................................

Institution: ...................................................................................................................

Office address: .............................................................................................................

Tel:..................................................... Fax:..................................................................

Email: ...........................................................................................................................

**Please return this questionnaire to:**

Director
Trade and Investment Division
ESCAP
United Nations Building
Rajadamnern Nok Avenue
Bangkok 10200
THAILAND
Fax: (66 2) 288 1027, 288 3066
E-mail: escap-tid@un.org

Thank you for your cooperation.